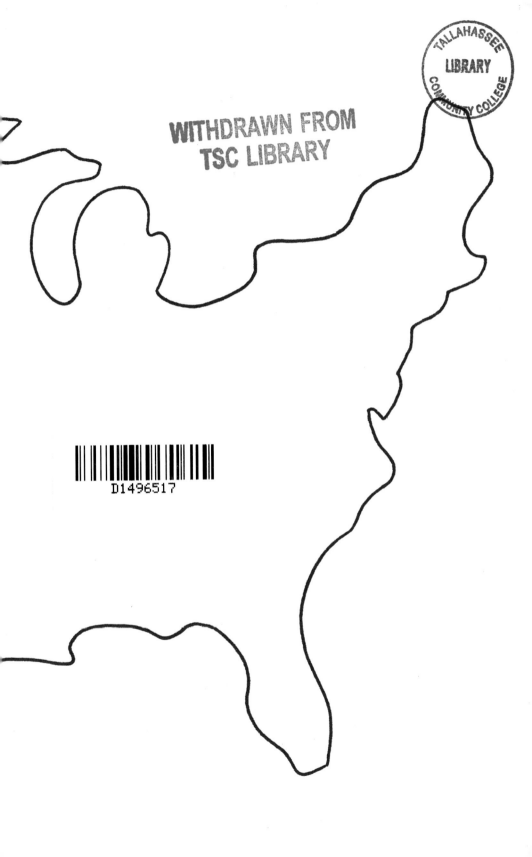

AMERICAN TOURISM

AMERICAN TOURISM
CONSTRUCTING A NATIONAL TRADITION

Edited by
J. Mark Souther and Nicholas Dagen Bloom

Center for American Places
at Columbia College Chicago

Center for American Places
at Columbia College Chicago
600 South Michigan Avenue
Chicago, Illinois 60605-1996, U.S.A.

Distributed by the University of Chicago Press
www.press.chicago.edu
20 19 18 17 16 15 14 13 12   1 2 3 4 5

Library of Congress Cataloging-in-Publication Data <TK>

ISBN: 978-1-935195-23-8

Acknowledgments
The editors would like to thank the contributors, who revised and adapted their essays multiple times. We also thank George F. Thompson and Brandy Savarese at the Center for American Places at Columbia College Chicago, who have patiently guided the project's creation. Permission has been granted for photographs and we thank many institutions and individuals for their generosity. We would also like to thank our families and respective institutions for their ongoing support.

CONTENTS

INTRODUCTION

Leo Tolstoy's insight that "happy families are all alike; every unhappy family is unhappy in its own way," applies equally to tourist destinations. Tourism is a tremendous industry, and by some accounts America's largest, but only a few sites, cities, and regions, such as Walt Disney World, Las Vegas, and the Adirondacks, regularly attract the volume of visitor spending necessary to sustain and grow local economies. Civic leaders, particularly in areas undergoing economic decline, scratch their heads in frustration and wonder why their attractions, seemingly as beautiful and interesting as those frequented by the golden hordes, draw fewer visitors. Local promoters spruce up Main Streets with brick sidewalks and Gay Nineties lamps, slap plaques on historic homes, set out racks of full-color brochures, and subsidize amusements, but the economic impact of tourists rarely becomes the promised panacea.[1]

Successful tourist placemaking at first appears to be simply a matter of appealing to mainstream tastes for novelty and consumption. Creating destinations, in this naïve view, could not possibly be difficult because tourism as an experience is so often superficial. Many promoters have found out the hard way that what often looks easy is in practice quite difficult. Academic critics of tourism until recently encouraged this misconception by overemphasizing the analysis of the most popular sites as tourist bubbles or simulacra that only exploited locals and lacked a deep, organic connection to societies.[2]

In recent years, a growing body of scholarship in such fields as history, sociology, anthropology, and geography has revealed the actual social and cultural complexity underlying tourism past and present.[3] The essays in *American Tourism*, reflecting some of the best new work in historical tourism studies, reveal the complicated history of visionary plans, trial and error, and long-term contests over issues of power, race, ethnicity, and taste at many of America's leading destinations. Researchers in social-science fields have described cycles of tourist place development but find it difficult, using their methods of analysis, to describe change and account for the impact of choices over decades. Our essays, however, draw back the curtain on some of America's most successful tourist destinations to reveal the long-term historical backstage of tourism placemaking, what William Douglass and Paulina Raento term the *tradition of invention*.[4]

American Tourism reveals the remarkable stories and strategies of tourist site development, but it is not a "how-to" manual on tourist site creation. Savvy tourism promoters could learn from the stories here, but our goal is to use the backstory of tourism development at many of our nation's leading sites to explore major themes in American society and culture. Not only is a growing proportion of American leisure time and financial resources devoted to tourist pursuits, leading to economic transformations of towns, cities, and regions, but the culture created in tourist destinations, and the social experience of tourism, also reflects and influences cultural production and social patterns both inside and outside of tourist zones.[5]

Despite differences in scale, climate, and theme, successful tourist destinations like those featured here share in a sense of place that is cultivated and contested over decades. The cumulative impact of these factors over time can significantly alter the texture and content of attractions. Great tourist sites share in national patterns and are powerful in large measure because they have modernized to keep pace with American society. The editors purposely selected sites from the many thousands that exist that are both iconic and innovative. Four major principles of tourism development are in operation at our varied sites over the past two centuries:

1. All of the destinations benefited from powerful leaders who envisioned both ordinary and extraordinary places as major stops on the tourist circuit. At heart, they understood both recreational tastes and what visitors want to believe about the place, themselves, and their nation.

2. Early visionaries established the initial business and institutional model to sustain the enterprise. Successive leaders then reshaped the business model of the oldest places in an attempt to keep pace with America's growing consumer economy, including major shifts in taste, transportation, and mass communication.

3. Innovative developers of the tourist sites examined in this volume, and those that followed them, continuously expanded and redesigned sites using aspects of the built environment (architecture, landscaping, signage, historic codes, and so on) in dramatic and comprehensive fashion to enhance the visitor experience and promote consumption of culture and objects. These places, often self-contained enclaves, look very different from average American surroundings. Over time, these differences became even more pronounced.

4. Founders and their successors generated cultural content and performance for sites in order to create a more powerful visitor experience. The messages in these performances have been regularly updated in content and form to meet contemporary expectations and values. This cultural ambition, in the service of tourist experience (and presumably a profit), has yielded more vibrant, if also more superficial and manipulative, cultural landscapes than those found in everyday American suburbs or cities.[6]

The finding that factors such as leadership, choices, design, and historical context influence placemaking is unique neither to our collection nor to the U.S. tourist sites it examines, but it is useful to see how these patterns repeat themselves at multiple destinations. *American Tourism* provides a middle range of analysis that includes sufficient detail of issues at many sites to gain grounded, critical forms of comparison. Concerns about racial and ethnic representation, for instance, have come to the fore at sites such as Colonial Williamsburg and San Francisco's Chinatown as American society has grappled more openly with its difficult past. Market forces and shifting popular tastes forced reconstruction of experiences, souvenirs, and landscapes at destinations as seemingly different as Disneyland and Beale Street. American historical narratives have been developed and reshaped at such iconic yet geographically distant locations as Independence Hall and El Camino Real. Comparative study provides the opportunity to consider tourism as an integral part of America's political, social, and cultural development.[7]

LEADERSHIP

Without the iterative processes of envisioning, designing, funding, building, and promoting, the most popular American destinations as we know them would not exist. The iconic sites of American tourism sprang from the cultural work of a wide range of actors—railroad executives, writers and artists, wealthy philanthropists, big and small businessmen, churchmen, newspapermen, city planners, preservationists, and municipal officials. But they share common threads in terms of visionary leadership.[8] Many sites, as historian Hal Rothman has argued, began as brainstorms in the minds of men and women who lived hundreds or thousands of miles away or underwent dramatic changes when such people moved to a location and sought to place their imprint on it. At destinations such as Las Vegas and Aspen, these so-called neonatives brought the vision and often the capital to translate their idea into action. They exerted tremendous control over future development of their adopted places.[9] Yet in other locations, like Gatlinburg and New Glarus, development diverged from the neonative model, owing to work by both neonatives and locally based individuals, and not just in the early moments of creating or re-creating places for tourist consumption.[10]

Why were so many American tourist destinations the products of elites? The privileged classes in northern cities and southern plantations could afford the expense in both time and money that were part and parcel of nineteenth-century travel. Many American tourist sites reflect the selfish pursuits of bluebloods, particularly in the nineteenth and early twentieth centuries. Inspired by artistic or literary depictions, elites established retreats for leisurely sociability, invigorating recreation, or restorative respite wherever they found sublime nature, particularly near springs or the seashore. Taking advantage of steamships, canals, and railroads, which pulled remote places into the cultural orbit of coastal cities, they created an American Grand Tour that included stops at Newport on the East Coast; Saratoga Springs, the Catskills, and Adirondacks in upstate New York; and Niagara Falls in the eastern Great Lakes, and many crafted commodious springs retreats built around the popular pastime of "taking the waters."[11] Their interest in having remote places to allow retreat from their workaday existence, coupled with their tendency to frown upon American cities as inferior counterparts to the refined metropolises of England or Europe, dictated a strong preference for rural destinations for most of the nineteenth century.[12]

The creation of Glacier National Park in Montana is illustrative. Louis Warren Hill, chairman of Great Northern Railway, mirrored the inclinations of many elites of his generation to romanticize the American landscape as a place to escape the torrent of societal changes that attended the country's industrialization and urbanization. Envisioning an "American Alps," Hill, as historian Marguerite S. Shaffer has argued, hoped Glacier might "be a rustic refuge where elites like himself could regenerate themselves."[13]

Many elites also felt the need to put their stamp on the places they "discovered." While spending much of their energy in the pursuit of industrial or commercial profit, no few of them channeled money toward cultural work, especially in the early twentieth century. Some grew nostalgic in the early twentieth century for a seemingly simpler past they never knew and tended to locate its essence in places that they considered sufficiently distant from the cultural norms on the East Coast.

Chicago-, New York-, and Paris-educated artist Eanger Irving Couse, for example, became enamored with the Indians of the American Southwest because he viewed their culture as being less Americanized than that of any other people in the United States. He became a founding member of the Taos Society of Artists in northern New Mexico in 1912.[14] Such interest in Native American folkways and handicrafts moved cultural stewards from the East to colonize Santa Fe, New Mexico in the early twentieth century. Others attempted to devise a usable past close to home. Elites in Charleston, South Carolina, many of them women, sought to maintain their vision of their city's character by conserving and packaging colonial homes and African-American spirituals both as a hobby and as a way to control the future development of their hometown. Their efforts mirrored, and in some cases shaped, the actions of prominent whites elsewhere that feared losing their privileged social position.[15] Similar desires for social position and ability to shape public memory motivated white promoters to exploit San Francisco's Chinatown in ways that cast the ethnic enclave as picturesque foil for Anglo modernity and racial superiority.

Wealthy Americans enjoyed access to the instruments that enabled them to articulate and spread their cultural influence in very public ways. They published books on their sites, spun romantic yarns in novels, and placed their restoration and preservation work in the nation's most influential magazines and newspapers. In many instances, they did more than just feature a place, casting their visions of place as the primary frame for further tourism development. Challenges have emerged to these dominant visions, by either competing elites or realities beyond their control, but it is no exaggeration to say that founders and promoters of successful places, including Walt Disney, Walter Paepcke (Aspen), James Rouse (Faneuil Hall), Carl Ray and W. M. Davidson (Silver Springs), and many others, exerted enormous force on placemaking. Our essays affirm the analysis of cultural historians Richard Fox and Jackson Lears, who believe "it is impossible to understand the cultures of ordinary Americans without appreciating the ways those cultures are influenced and delimited by the ideas, plans, and needs of the powerful."[16]

The Business of Tourism

Beyond their interest in leisure and culture for themselves, influential Americans ventured into tourism because they saw opportunities for personal profit and broader economic development. Whether as investors in railroad lines to emerging resorts or as hotel operators, they understood the lucrative potential of tourism. For many originators of tourist attractions, the profit motive intertwined with higher aspirations such as spiritual uplift or preserving and exhibiting distinctive culture. Sites from Martha's Vineyard to Ocean Grove to Chautauqua to Branson bundled religion and recreation for travelers seeking deeper meaning in leisure.[17] Many other promoters, such as Alan Schafer at South of the Border in South Carolina and the Hustead family at the South Dakota-pharmacy-turned-tourist-trap Wall Drug, were only interested in selling experiences and using those experiences to sell tangible products.

At various moments in history, tourism promised the opportunity to profit *and* redirect sagging local economies. Business leaders in declining seaports in early nineteenth-century New England coastal towns saw in tourism a viable future, initiating a now familiar pattern. In the twentieth century, the loss of mining, agricultural, or manufacturing mainstays prompted similar moves toward tourism-based economies either in the early years of the century, during the Great Depression, or amid postwar deindustrialization. The loss of mining inspired a turn toward tourism in Reno, Tombstone, and other western communities. The Great Depression motivated tourism as a supplement to the dairying industry in Wisconsin's Little Switzerland, and postindustrial waterfronts framed re-imagined tourist spaces from Fisherman's Wharf and Cannery Row on the West Coast to Baltimore's Harborplace and New York's South Street Seaport.[18]

Not only the affluent founded tourist attractions; to be sure, visionary individuals of less elevated social status also played a part. Some stumbled upon tourism as an economic boon and dreamed of ways to take advantage. Pioneer Vermont settler Abel Crawford and his family carved out their homestead in the White Mountains in 1790, intending to sell land and open up trade, but within a decade they became guides, innkeepers, road builders, and promoters to capitalize on a growing stream of adventurous and well-heeled travelers that sought to discover northern New England's scenic landscape for themselves.[19] One example in this collection, Wall Drug, is suggestive of this entrée into the tourist trade. The Great Depression prompted the Hustead family to entice tourists to their small-town drugstore with the promise of free ice water. As was true in so many American destinations, economic imperatives intersected with savvy entrepreneurship.

Like individuals, national companies and corporations played key roles in American tourism development. Indeed, one hallmark of American tourism has been the driving force of private enterprise, in contrast with the greater role of the state in many other countries.[20] Steamship and railroad companies provided access to attractions, but they also created or packaged them to generate traveler interest. Companies such as the Great Northern, Northern Pacific, and Santa Fe railroads and their subsidiaries developed tourist accommodations that put a number of prominent scenic wonders—Glacier, Yellowstone, and Grand Canyon National Parks among them—on the tourist map.[21] In other cases, as with the construction of Grand Hotel on Mackinac Island in the 1880s, regional transportation companies built distinctive accommodations whose influence set the tone for entire resorts. By the twentieth century, a wide range of firms exploited the tourist trade. Anheuser-Busch operated theme parks to showcase their breweries. Media companies not only exploited American destinations such as Silver Springs and Tombstone for their cinematic potential but also created some. Most notably, the Walt Disney Company fashioned Disneyland and, later, other theme parks to promote its brand of film and television entertainment. Hollywood itself developed into a tourist destination in part because film producers as early as the 1910s encouraged tourists to watch their productions, tour their stage sets, and meet actors. More recently, the Rouse Company in Boston, Baltimore, and many other cities derived enormous profits in the 1970s and 1980s from the "festival marketplace" concept that promised both urban variety and a cocoon of mall-style safety in renovated urban centers.

Many tourist destinations, especially resort hotels and resort communities, resulted from the aggregation of capital vested in companies and corporations invented solely for the purpose of financing tourism development. Beyond railroads, which by the time of transcontinental routes had begun to delve into lodging, concessions, and land development to profit from the traveling public, dedicated tourism companies appeared as early as the nineteenth century and proliferated in the twentieth. Such resort syndicates, usually drawing upon the wealth of outside developers, built San Diego's signature Hotel del Coronado, the Cloister on Georgia's Sea Island, and numerous other noted hostelries.[22]

A hallmark of post–World War II resort development was the conscious work of specially constituted companies to fashion master-planned resort communities. Two such examples in this collection—the eponymously named Aspen Company and Naples Company—took preexisting towns in Colorado and Florida in the mid-1940s and attempted to impose particular design concepts to heighten their cachet. Other resort companies carefully folded beach resorts like Hilton Head, Kiawah, and Amelia Islands into natural surroundings on pristine Atlantic Coast barrier islands.

Private enterprise provided the engine that drove many sites, but many of America's historic places emerged as tourist attractions as a result of preservation-minded Americans who created nonprofit organizations to safeguard and extend their successes. While many organizations, notably Charleston's Society for the Preservation of Old Dwellings, Old Salem Inc. in North Carolina, the Historic Savannah Foundation, and, in this volume, New Orleans's Vieux Carré Commission, formed expressly to salvage the built fabric of older cities from demolition and modernization, invariably they embraced heritage tourism as a must for advancing their primary goal. Likewise, entities like the Old Santa Fe Association, Colonial Williamsburg

Foundation, and Tombstone Restoration Commission—organized to turn back the clock by destroying or overhauling modern structures to create the appearance of some specified past time—also, directly or indirectly, advanced the tourist trade that drew wide attention to their labors.

Across the twentieth century, concerned citizens also formed nonprofit organizations to galvanize support for preserving notable buildings and, in many cases, cemented commitments from various levels of government to protect, maintain, and promote them. While some, such as the Friends of the Market in Seattle, reflected the widening scope of what was deemed worthy of preservation, others like the Independence Hall Association were more concerned with creating a setting consonant with a long-recognized site of national significance.

Tourism-oriented institution building extended to the use of public agencies, or the formation of new ones, to facilitate the growth of tourism. Through the work of nonprofit groups' advocacy, communities enacted legislation to regulate the built environment, a critical step in making heritage tourism possible. The Old and Historic Charleston District, created in 1931, set the example of a regulatory board that New Orleans, Santa Fe, and other cities also adopted. According to Marguerite S. Shaffer, the National Park Service (NPS), established during the Woodrow Wilson administration, "transformed the national parks from a collection of independent scenic wonders managed by various private railroad corporations into a system of nationalized tourist attractions."[23] As growing environmental awareness prompted a realization that tourism had adverse effects at some attractions, the NPS and state-level bodies such as the Adirondack Park Agency directed resources toward balancing nature and public use.

Finally, as tourism became a recognized and legitimate industry in the twentieth century, local governments moved beyond traditional roles such as providing city services during public celebrations, parades, or other events and began to play generative roles in American tourism. Particularly in the latter half of the century, as the nation shifted from an emphasis on production to consumption and as suburbanization and deindustrialization set in, so-called messiah mayors turned to tourism as one way of reversing urban decay.[24] City governments in Baltimore, New Orleans, St. Louis, and other American cities created special agencies or partnered with private companies to erect monuments, parks, plazas, aquariums, convention centers, and a host of other attractions to make their downtown areas attractive to outsiders. In the 1970s, Boston Mayor Kevin White turned to developer James Rouse and architect Benjamin Thompson, who saw in the derelict Quincy Market an opportunity to create a vibrant urban experience in the heart of the city. Across the continent in Seattle, local officials had to be persuaded by preservationists not to demolish Pike Place Market to build a modern mixed-use complex. Mayors Rudolph Giuliani in New York and Richard Daley in Chicago pushed tourist-oriented reorientations of their cities in the 1990s.[25]

THE TOURIST LANDSCAPE

The essays in this collection highlight destinations, like Disneyland, that were cut from whole cloth as well as those, like San Antonio's River Walk, renovated from preexisting places. Both types of sites required, in spite of their different origins and textures, the conscious intent to design with tourists in mind. Tourism is a physical experience and as such demands a keen sensitivity to place. The built environment is the place where the cultural and social messages are coded and communicated through architecture, sound, signage, and props of a limitless variety. The architecture of tourism has been frequently derided, except in the rare case, as at Walt Disney World, when famous architects contribute signature buildings, but the reality is that successful tourism promoters devote careful attention to the built environment to attract and retain a strong tourist business.[26]

Creative adaptation of buildings within the site is a key element of tourist landscapes. Almost any building type has been converted into a destination through strategic signage and renovation: markets, factories, shops, barns and stables, homes, theaters, bridges, and churches. The nineteenth-century tourism circuit may have included hotels, churches, natural wonders, and a few homes of famous individuals, but over the course of the twentieth century, cultural brokers extended the range of visitor tastes to include everyday landscapes such as Lowell's textile mills, Boston's Quincy Market, and Monterey's Cannery Row. "Nostalgia," argues David Lowenthal, "today engulfs the whole past."[27] Visitors now accept almost any building type as appropriate for a tourist experience. Even a strip mall, given enough anticipatory hype and some façade treatment, as at Wall Drug or South of the Border, can succeed as a tourist draw.

The increasing standardization of building types in suburbs and cities has done much to increase interest in the variety of types from both
the past and fantasy; the promise of escape from a mass-produced world
is a key attraction in almost any kind of tourist destination and has led
to extremes. Visionary promoters have added follies, including Sleeping
Beauty's Castle or the Wall Drug Dinosaur, that would be considered unacceptable in an average landscape.

The architectural motif applied to these diverse building types boils
down to two major, often overlapping, strategies: historic preservation
and eclecticism. Architectural inheritance might seem the easiest way to
develop tourist infrastructure, but the preservation of historic buildings
and districts represented, in places like the French Quarter, Faneuil Hall
Marketplace, and Colonial Williamsburg, a long battle for the recognition
of value in the past in a forward-looking American culture. For most of
American history, buildings simply grew old and outdated; thousands of
buildings, including classics like New York's Pennsylvania Station, were
demolished in the name of progress.

Dramatic shifts in urban land values, architectural trends, and func-
tional needs during the nineteenth and early twentieth century led to
this destruction. In the nineteenth century, increasing land values at the
center pushed out low-density buildings and even entire early American
districts. In the twentieth century, declining land values and the automobile led to urban renewal schemes to clear so-called blighted structures
to open up space for modern office buildings, malls, parking, and highways. That any historic structures survived in many American cities and
towns as a result of these two processes is remarkable and was the result
of an emerging environmental and historic preservation movement in the
twentieth century. Jane Jacobs is the most famous of the citizen leaders
who slowed urban renewal, but across the United States articulate, politically savvy individuals halted the bulldozers just in time to save some
great neighborhoods and buildings.[28]

The preservation of some buildings, moreover, represented only a small
step in the creation of historic tourist zones. Promoters then had to make
difficult decisions about the era to which buildings would be preserved,
appropriate uses of historic buildings, renovation standards, and the extent of historic districts. Visitors to Williamsburg, Virginia, for instance,
have no idea how much of the town was obliterated and rebuilt to create

the "pristine" historic zone they see today. The founders demolished 720 buildings that had the misfortune of being erected after the agreed-upon 1790 cut-off date. The most iconic building on the site, the Governor's Palace, is almost entirely a replica reconstructed between 1930 and 1935 from historical images and documents. Because of such wholesale rebuilding, one of America's most prominent architectural historians, Leland Roth, calls Colonial Williamsburg, "not so much a restoration as a thematic rebuilding." Williamsburg is an extreme example of what can happen in historic preservation, and a legacy of the centralized control established over the whole site, but elements of the strategy have been applied at historic sites and districts across the nation.[29]

Preservation standards in various places have been and continue to be debated by responsible commissions and agencies, particularly as historic districts became popular with tourists. Commercial signs, pedestrian zones, enhanced lighting, security systems, souvenir stores and stands, condominium and hotel conversion, external speaker systems, and other modern tourist interventions have brought modernity and its symbols into the hearts of historic districts. The French Quarter and Los Angeles's Olvera Street, for example, remain contested spaces where groups struggle over visions of place: "Authenticity defined as the accurate presentation of the past through conservation of its relict features has little relevance to the definition of the historic city."[30] The result of those struggles may appear static to the visitor, but long-term examination, as in our essays, reveals dramatic shifts in standards.

Eclectic landscapes, such as Mediterraneanized towns from Naples, Florida, to Venice, California, Swissified New Glarus, Wisconsin, or Sinofied Chinatowns, grow out of a distinct American vernacular tradition. A long history of borrowing foreign architectural styles in the nineteenth and twentieth century interspersed Greek temples, Gothic churches, Moorish synagogues, Tudor castles, and Georgian townhouses in cities and suburbs. In the nineteenth century, in particular, architectural diversity aligned with the Romantic desire to communicate emotional and institutional messages through allusions to particular historical periods. Thus prisons and armories often looked like castles, government buildings imitated Greek and Roman precedents, and world's expositions featured gondola-plied canals lined with classical façades.

Eclecticism for its own sake took on a force of its own and conveyed by the twentieth century, in planned suburbs, for instance, a picturesque, anti-urban preference. The interwar period included a flourishing trade in comfortable suburban "period" houses in Georgian, Tudor, Spanish Colonial, and other styles. The eclectic waned somewhat in the thrall of mid-century Modernism, but survived in suburban mass-produced Cape Cods and Southern-style Tara plantation houses wedged into tiny suburban lots. Recently, eclecticism has come roaring back at quaint, historicist New Urbanist villages such as Seaside and Kentlands. Americans may have often expressed skepticism about foreign cultures and the value of history, but adapting and altering styles from abroad and the past to suit local programmatic and emotional needs is as American as apple pie.[31]

What distinguishes tourist sites from run-of-the-mill eclecticism is the attempt, at Santa Fe, Naples, or New Glarus, to extend one or two dominant eclectic visions over a district. To create picturesque, communally consonant landscapes in a free-market context society with limited planning controls is a difficult task, especially amid existing variety, but where it has been achieved, through comprehensive, ground-up planning or long-term renovation, such landscapes have become destination-worthy curiosities. The key to creating these unified districts has been, in most cases, the establishment of centralized control or at least dominance by leading individuals who share an aesthetic vision.[32]

A few elite visitors have decried the superficiality of these places, or lack of connection to the surrounding landscape, but most tourists delight in the staginess and drama. Even an aging eclectic landscape, like that found at Santa Fe or Miami Beach, can become the object of preservation when eclectic visions are recognized as historic in themselves: "cultural products developed for tourists may over time attain 'emergent authenticity' and be accepted as 'authentic' by both tourists and cultural producers alike."[33]

Within these carefully constructed and regulated tourist sites, pathways for movement have become carefully considered elements of the built environment, particularly in sites that must handle thousands of people a day. In the nineteenth century, people were whisked by train through the countryside to resort terminals. Finding sufficient space for the automobile at twentieth-century tourism destinations, without ruining the place, became a great challenge and necessitated large parking fields, trams, and other means of managing transitions from the road to the sidewalk or trail at the most popular sites.[34]

Walt Disney was one of the first promoters to grasp the necessity of a seamless transition from car to pedestrianism with his little blue-and-white trams, but other promoters have dealt with this reality in creative ways. Innovative means of transit within tourist sites include horse-drawn carriages, glass-bottomed boats, miniature-train rides, monorails, and aerial tramways. Pathways that extend along water features, as at San Antonio's River Walk or Baltimore's Harborplace, are another way promoters have found to turn couch-potato Americans into walkers.[35] Pedestrianized zones in historic and amusement districts represent a further attempt to alter frames of reference for visitors and at the same time accommodate ever larger crowds.

Finally, tourism promoters have restlessly pursued novel vistas and perspectives of the "main attraction" to avoid visitor ennui. To "do" Niagara Falls by the late nineteenth century, for instance, demanded more than simply beholding the thunderous roar and pale-green mist from afar. Wooden viewing platforms, footbridges, and boats placed tourists closer than ever to the falls. The twentieth century brought ever-higher observation decks offering panoramic views of expositions, cities, parks, battlefields, and natural wonders. More daring glass-floored viewing platforms have been added in recent years at the Grand Canyon and the former Sears Tower in Chicago.

CULTURAL CONTENT

Architectural diversity is complemented at tourist sites with a great range of cultural content. Tourist attractions are distinct cultural phenomena, attempting to meet visitor cultural expectations on a daily basis over a comparatively large physical area. A wealthy world city like New York delivers culture from low to high at all times of day, but other places have had to construct cultural activities, what Daniel Boorstin termed *pseudo-events*, to turn what might be otherwise isolated and dull spots into kaleidoscopes of activity. The challenge for all tourist-site operators is to create a consistently powerful experience day in and day out that encourages repeat visits and word-of-mouth promotion.[36]

The cultural experience for most of our sites is initiated even before arrival. Arnold Genthe's photographs carefully constructed San Francisco's

Chinatown as utterly exotic and mysterious—a place that demanded to be seen. The writings of James Fenimore Cooper spurred tourists to Cooperstown, and more recent novels have generated influxes of visitors to Savannah, Georgia, and Madison County, Iowa. Many sites, by dint of their age and fame, carry with them a set of archetypal experiences and iconic structures. Tourists expect gunfights at Tombstone and romantic carriage rides on Mackinac Island. They expect blues in Memphis, jazz in New Orleans, and country music in Austin, Branson, and Nashville. Travel journalism, brochures, television shows, and films frequently provide cultural and social "frames" for visitors that condition a surprising amount of the tourist experience. Carefully conceived pamphlets, videos, and websites create expectations not simply about place and landscapes but also about cultural experiences and messages on site. The physical place and cultural content must provide a congruent experience for visitors primed by this extensive travel literature.[37]

Tour guides have traditionally been the simplest way of brokering and shaping the tourist experience; the tradition of guided tours stretches back into the centuries. Human guides, however, place a barrier to direct experience of a place that is not appreciated by all tourists. Guides can be of varying quality and as a labor force can be difficult to control and cultivate at an adequate level, especially in more isolated locales. Finally, Americans distrust authority and have become accustomed to finding their own way through supermarkets, malls, and superhighways; we even check out our own groceries these days. Our sites increasingly avoid overreliance on tour guides.

Entrepreneurs at leading sites over the course of the twentieth century developed growing sophistication in the staging of cultural and social rituals. The early and middle decades of the century saw the use of dramatic presentations to suggest how visitors should contextualize the places they went. Civic pageantry, such as San Francisco's Portolá Festival or Tombstone's Helldorado, as well as outdoor dramas like Branson's *Shepherd of the Hills*, St. Augustine's *Cross and Sword*, or New Glarus's *Wilhelm Tell*, contributed to the sense of place that promoters packaged for tourists.[38] The rise of living-history settings at Colonial Williamsburg and elsewhere in the early twentieth century set a new standard for cultural presentation that influenced Old Sturbridge Village, Old Salem, Plimoth Plantation, and many other heritage sites. Costumed interpreters represented a sea change in social and cultural presentation; living history has been remarkably well accepted by supposedly cynical and jaded Americans. Costumed characters can now be found in a tremendous variety of roles both historical and fantasy at sites as different as Tombstone and Disneyland.[39] The liminal space that tourist sites occupy allows for a suspension of disbelief rarely tolerated in more traditional domestic and occupational settings.

Costumes are also common at tourist destinations that celebrate ethnic heritage. Staging of ethnic customs had some nineteenth-century precedents in world's expositions, settlement houses, and ethnic festivals and parades, but extended to become an everyday fabric of presentation in places such as Chinatown, Olvera Street, and New Glarus. In early Chinatown tours, for instance, guides staged illusions of opium dens in a honeycombed subterranean realm beneath San Francisco's streets. Ethnicity in these narratives tends to be romanticized and histories of conflict or tension minimized to enhance the pleasure of the tourist experience, although members of exploited groups sometimes devised ways of seizing control of the presentation of their distinctive cultures.[40]

Like panoramic paintings and cycloramas of times past, films, video kiosks, Audio-Animatronics, and other forms of electronic spectacle have been added in recent decades as a means of replicating a strong cultural experience for constant crowds. Promoters have found it necessary to modernize presentations of all kinds in order to keep pace with new technologies and changing attitudes about ethnicity, race, and performance.

THE LEGACY OF TOURISM

The history of tourism as illustrated at our individual sites reveals a great deal about how Americans think about culture, power, and ethnicity, and how they construct places and experiences over time. Yet tourism's influence extends beyond a destination's borders. Even limiting such analysis to the sites included in our collection yields significant evidence of impact. First, tourist sites, viewed as an industry, have transformed the economies and related social relationships of numerous towns, cities, and regions. Our essays consider the mixed effects of secondary tourism business on the life of tourist places, including gentrification of housing, environmental stress, the creation of a secure "tourist bubble," and growing social conflict as the result of inequality in the tourism service industry.

The local economic and social impact of tourism on towns, cities, and regions has been well documented not only in our essays but also in the vast literature of tourism studies. The secondary aspects of tourism—transportation, lodging, restaurants, shopping, and nightlife—have played generative roles, without which no amount of vision could have produced a successful destination. On the most elemental level, the national network of railroads, highways, airports, filling stations, motels, and restaurants standardized and rationalized the tourist experience. Amenities like shopping and nightlife emerged to fill the gaps between sightseeing.[41] Such services and amenities, however, have often either supplanted or at least gained equal status with the primary attraction. In Atlantic City, casinos trumped the Boardwalk that had itself trumped the beach. Las Vegas is the classic example of the economic benefits of overspill from tourism. For a time, Las Vegas was America's fastest growing city as the casinos generated the rising fortune of a growing middle class.[42]

At many successful tourist sites, stores, hotels, and restaurants do more than simply exploit a destination's power to generate profit. They also build on local tourist themes and augment the experience of place. Cooperstown's delightful main street full of baseball memorabilia, and Colonial Williamsburg's carefully designed gift shops frame and augment the messages and aesthetic of the destination. Elsewhere, uncontrolled secondary development of strip malls, fast-food establishments, and motels, as on Disneyland's periphery, undermines the fantasy cultivated at the main attraction. Tourism promoters labor to attract visitors, but they can often be overwhelmed by their own success. Granted, these are troubles many towns dream of, but for those in the middle of mass tourism the problems can seem insoluble and the stakes high.

Residents, business owners, and tourism entrepreneurs compete to impose rules and regulations as the scale of commerce influences both the resident and tourist experience. Efforts to balance tourists' and locals' enjoyment of attractions, notably in urban districts like New Orleans's French Quarter, necessitated ordinances to regulate peddlers, street performers, timeshare condos, walking tours, and other markers of tourist spaces.[43] Safeguarding visitors from real or perceived risk has also been a longtime preoccupation of tourism operators. Just as turn-of-the-century Coney Island amusement parks added fences, gates, and admission booths to dissuade entry by those who might be viewed as undesirable, at mid-century, Atlantic City's Boardwalk and Florida's Silver Springs enforced Jim Crow and Disneyland situated itself out of reach of anyone without a car and a full wallet.[44] Tourism has amplified growing inequality because of centralized ownership and thus profits. In addition, the tradition of low-wage, seasonal work in many destinations (particularly in the South and West) has offered few chances for social mobility, displaced lower-income residents, and driven housing costs beyond the reach of tourism workers. Tourism has thus contributed both to America's general prosperity and growing inequality.[45]

Tourism has both produced deleterious environmental effects and charted the difficult road to environmental protection. Some tourist sites, such as the Grand Canyon, coexist uneasily with sites of industry, power generation, or other uses of the natural environment. Frequent battles flare between partisans of "wilderness" and those demanding urbanization, second homes, and active recreation. Overheated development has frequently led to a so-called tragedy of commons that undermines scenic beauty and local ecosystems, particularly along fragile shorelines. Atlantic City is a classic example of a deteriorated, urbanized barrier island, and a ribbon of urbanization now dominates large stretches of the East Coast. In the best case, however, forms of regulation have been able to preserve the scenic character or experiences that attracted people to the site in the first place. Improvements in technology, such as wastewater treatment, and legal frameworks, such as environmental and historic preservation, have had positive effects in preserving landscapes (be they "natural" or cultural) in locations as varied as the Adirondacks and Hilton Head. Where successful, American destinations have set a high international standard in environmental control, prompting water treatment and land preservation in tourist zones from Mexico to Thailand.[46]

The national economic impact of tourism can be read in the widespread imitation of styles of management perfected in tourist sites. This style of management, discussed frequently in tourism-studies scholarship, has encouraged a high-octane consumer orientation that moves remarkable amounts of merchandise in destination spots. Highly regulated urban selling environments, for instance, Disneyland, Faneuil Hall Marketplace, or Times Square, have generated imitators in cities and suburbs that reproduce the visual style and tight regulation. The new suburban Main Street "lifestyle centers," for instance, can be tracked in form and management to Disney's iconic main street. The style of "tourism urbanization" on view at Las Vegas or Miami Beach, urban tourism destinations that rose from scratch, is thought to have had tremendous influence on emerging destinations both here and abroad. Resorts like Hilton Head have also generated hundreds of resort imitators on coastlines once considered too remote for anything but fishing.

Tourist sites have been successful in spreading ideas about consumption and taste: tourism is a force in national cultural development. Our essayists are circumspect in assigning and tracking national influence, but these sites, when viewed collectively, have been key elements—along with mass media, shopping malls, and credit cards—in the creation of America's modern consumer economy. Tourist sites are instructive about the good life in both obvious and subtle ways. Such places develop visitor cultural capital, and desires, in areas such as architecture, history, music, food, sports, and material culture; desires that can only partly be fulfilled at the site itself. The taste for new music, design, trinkets, and food inspired by tourist sites such as Disneyland, the French Quarter, and Williamsburg have overflowed into the culture at large.

This history of wider cultural influence reaches back into the nineteenth century. The development of the Grand Canyon and the Adirondacks as sightseeing destinations for urban residents played a major role in the environmental and national parks movements. Consuming natural vistas became a legitimate aspect of leisure time and remains a central touchstone of American life. The Chautauqua community pioneered the mixing of self-improvement and leisure time that is not only alive in that little town but also in Elderhostels and summer college experiences here and abroad.[47]

In the twentieth century, our tourist sites continued to influence cultural affairs. The popularity of Chinese food and furnishings, to say nothing of opiates, got much of its currency from tourists' exposure to Chinatowns like those in San Francisco and New York. Williamsburg's renovation did much to inspire a passion for American history and Americana. American cultural passion for jazz and the blues can be linked to performance in the French Quarter, particularly Preservation Hall, and on Beale Street. These iconic nightlife districts, which have also promoted the libidinal side of the American South, have provided a continuous boost to the consumption of live and recorded traditional American music. Aspen pioneered the association of skiing and conspicuous consumption that has become ubiquitous at many Western resorts and the Aspen Institute reinvigorated a Chautauquan mix of uplift and recreation. Disney theme parks have an easily recognized impact on popular culture, and thus daily life, through films, toys, and images widely disseminated to children and young adults. It is no exaggeration to argue that Disney is still shaping a significant portion of American childhood. Hollywood's glamorous image continues to kindle dreams of stardom and glamour among the American population. On the less positive side, sites like Disneyland, as well as Chinatown and South of the Border, have encouraged sloppy, negative stereotypes of ethnic minorities.

The architectural influence of tourist sites on national taste in the twentieth century has been well documented. Tourist sites have inspired new buildings and adventurous patronage elsewhere. The Adirondack rustic furniture and lodge aesthetic, for instance, can be found far from the park's boundaries. Williamsburg's renovation contributed to the Colonial Revival movement in housing and furniture in the twentieth century. The notion of a playful exoticism at Spanish-themed environments got a strong start at the San Diego World's Fair of 1915 and would be affirmed at tourist spots such as El Camino Real, Naples, and Miami Beach; Mediterranean styles then spread from tourist zones to influence vernacular architecture far beyond the destinations. Santa Fe's adobe-style dwellings have come to define not only that small city but also major blocks of housing in the Southwest. San Francisco's hybridized Asian-style architecture set the standard for Chinatown redevelopment across the nation: exotic Chinese elements are still introduced into otherwise standard downtowns as a gambit for increasing visitors to forlorn neighborhoods where very few Chinese people actually live or work. The Gateway Arch can be viewed as one of the predecessors, along with the Guggenheim museum, of the dynamic, modernist event architecture that can be seen across the world from Milwaukee to Bilbao to Beijing. High-profile designs that often form a sharp contrast to the surroundings offer the possibility of enlivening otherwise dull districts.[48]

One of the final marks of long-term national cultural success is imitation. Visitors to many of our sites have been so excited that they have created or adapted local institutions in hopes of inspiring greater recognition and thus consumption of their respective locales. Cooperstown's Baseball Hall of Fame, for example, became the model for the hall of fame concept across the country; halls of fame can become ideal tourist draws, as at Cleveland's Rock and Roll Hall of Fame, by dint of regular events and high-profile induction ceremonies. The San Diego Zoo helped popularize the open style that transformed zoos, here and abroad, from a series of dismal cages to a collection of ecological niches of which animals were only one part. Grant Park in Chicago pioneered the culture-oriented waterfront park that has become a key element of reclaiming industrial sites in cities like Baltimore. Romanticized waterfront promenades like San Antonio's River Walk have spawned imitators, including some unlikely ones: Scottsdale, Arizona, for instance, created the Scottsdale Waterfront along the barren Arizona Canal. Sometimes the legacy is so powerful that it travels full circle. Coney Island's electrified amusement parks of the 1900s, with their combination of high technology and fantasy themes, influenced Disneyland in the 1950s; Disneyland in turn offered an attractive model for recasting Times Square in the 1990s.[49]

These convincing examples of tourism's influence on American society and culture, drawn just from the essays in our collection, reveal the danger in allowing tourism studies to remain at the periphery of intellectual life. We hope, however, that our challenging assemblage of critical historical essays will aid the integration of tourism into mainstream discussions of our nation's history by illustrating the cumulative influence of what are often dismissed as superficial, local, idiosyncratic, place-based systems. The essays included in *American Tourism* provide strong evidence not only that the creation of tourist sites is a serious national activity but that consumption of images, material culture, and design in these places continues to shape American places and identity.

J. Mark Souther   Nicholas Dagen Bloom
Cleveland State University   New York Institute of Technology

AMERICAN TOURISM

THE ADIRONDACKS
NEW YORK

Hallie E. Bond

The Adirondack Park, a vast territory of mountain peaks, clear lakes, and rustic towns, remains a world apart from the urbanized East Coast. Tourists and entrepreneurs, who have been building and clambering around this territory for more than two centuries, have left their mark on the trails, camps, and tourist sprawl carved out of the wilderness. Their pioneering efforts have not only preserved and enhanced a distinctive sense of place but also have generated nationally influential ideas about wilderness preservation, outdoor recreation, and design with nature.

On August 9, 1864, the *New York Times* published an editorial that must have entranced its urban readers. "Within an easy day's ride of our great city, as steam teaches us to measure distance," it grandly proclaimed, "is a tract of country fitted to make a Central Park for the World." This "tract of country" was the Adirondacks, a mountainous region known by New Yorkers of the time only as a wilderness populated by a few rustics and adventurous, wealthy sportsmen. The appeal of the editorial lay in its promise of an unspoiled America, free from the "dust, dirt, and dangers" of the rapidly industrializing cities.[1]

Over the next generation, tourists, entrepreneurs, artists, and surveyors crisscrossed the Adirondacks. As the region became better known, it came to mean different things to different people. Some saw a magical place untainted by the pollution, crime, stress, and hurry caused by industrialization. Some lumped together the region's attractions—fresh air, clean water, wild animals, access to nature—under the general concept of "wilderness." Others celebrated an alternative concept of wilderness—a land rich with unharvested natural resources where fortunes could be

Fig. 1. Arthur Fitzwilliam Tait's "A Good Time Coming," painted in 1862, depicts lei-sured antebellum tourists who have set up camp in the Adirondacks. 1963.37.1, Courtesy of Adirondack Museum.

made. These competing ideas shaped how various actors publicized, enhanced, and manipulated the Adirondacks as a tourist destination.

Artists, government surveyors, and hardy tourists and sportsmen built public curiosity (Fig. 1). In 1837, geologist Ebenezer Emmons made a scientific survey of the region (looking chiefly to signs of valuable minerals) that was published and widely read. Accompanying Emmons was artist Charles Cromwell Ingham, whose painting made "on the spot" on Indian Pass was exhibited for the public. In subsequent summers, Hudson River School artists, including Thomas Cole and Asher Durand, visited the region. Their paintings of sublime scenery firmly fixed the Adirondacks in the public eye. Sportsmen praised their Adirondack hunting and fishing adventures in periodicals and books, also noting the healthful benefits of a vacation in the woods. One such visitor, Reverend Joel Tyler Headley, who visited the Adirondacks in 1848 to recover from an "attack on the brain" brought on by his scholarly labors, praised time spent in nature as "better for me than the thronged city, aye, better for soul and body both."[2]

After the Civil War, the steamboat and rail lines brought larger crowds safely, cheaply, and quickly to the mountains. The postwar economic boom in the Northeast produced not only entrepreneurs who created the transportation networks but also a middle class with sufficient leisure time and wealth for summer vacations. William Henry Harrison Murray, like Headley a preacher who loved the Adirondacks, fueled the postwar tourist boom with *Adventures in the Wilderness*, published in 1869. Murray gave complete instructions for a restorative vacation in the North Woods—how to get there, what to take, what to see, and how to find a knowledgeable guide who would row one around the region's interconnecting waterways. Anticipating by a generation the national concern with the health and fitness of American women, Murray declared that "there was nothing in the trip which the most delicate and fragile need fear. . . . None enjoy the experiences more than ladies, and certain it is that none are more benefited by it."[3]

Murray received considerable criticism at the time for having exaggerated the excellence of Adirondack tourist accommodations, but entrepreneurs soon caught up with the demand. Visitors to Lake George, on the edge of the mountains, could choose among a variety of "civilized" hotel accommodations by the 1830s; by 1881, Blue Mountain Lake, in the very center of the Adirondacks and thirty rugged miles from the nearest railroad, was one of the most fashionable highland resorts in the country. Like other famous vacation spots, it had a grand resort hotel with the amenities expected by the sophisticated traveler. The Prospect House, built by New Yorker Frederic Durant, was the first hotel in the world to have an electric light in every room. Not everyone agreed on the suitability of modern amenities in the wilderness. While Durant boasted of the Prospect House's electric lights, steam heat, and billiard tables, some tourists grumbled about the fact that "no one wants to visit the real wilderness and forego the luxury and social pleasures of the hotels."[4] The debate about appropriate tourist accommodations for the "wilderness"—in the Adirondacks and elsewhere—had begun.

New York State politics, and the ceaseless contest between private and public interests, lent a very different texture to the development of the Adirondacks. By the 1880s, the state legislature debated whether and how to regulate land use in the Adirondacks. Initially, the debate centered on concerns that logging was damaging the watersheds. Much of the state's commerce depended on good water supplies for the Erie, Black River, and Champlain canals, and park advocates like surveyor Verplanck Colvin argued that removing the timber from the slopes would disrupt the water supply. The discussions soon shifted to creating a park with land set aside for the public to enjoy for its own sake. In 1885, the state of New York established the Adirondack Forest Preserve including all its land in the Adirondacks and, in 1892, created the Adirondack Park, which included both private and public land. Two years later, state officials enshrined the preservation of public land in Section 7, Article VII, of the New York State Constitution, which stated that "the lands of the State, now owned or hereafter acquired . . . shall be forever kept as wild forest lands."

The legislators who created it encircled the park with a blue line on a map. Within this "Blue Line" were almost three million acres, of which only five hundred thousand belonged to the state. The rest, in parcels big and small, belonged to so-called inholders, private property owners scattered throughout the park. In the park's early years, many environmentalists were optimistic that inholders eventually would be bought out or otherwise moved, just as inhabitants of the land that became New York's Central Park had been cleared. Perhaps this would have happened had the landowners been primarily poor folk, as were most of the Manhattanites displaced for the city park. By 1892, however, large tracts of Adirondack land belonged to wealthy families or logging or mining companies. These owners lived mostly outside the area, owned their land for vacation or profit, and had no interest in ceding it to the government. The Adirondack League Club, an association of individuals who managed their land for timber and game, was the largest, owning 166,000 acres in the southwestern Adirondacks. Other landowners—farmers and shopkeepers—had tiny parcels but just as big a stake in park governance.

The presence of private land and individual landowners in a public park colored the debate over land use and periodically made strange bedfellows of the people involved. When the state instituted game laws in the 1890s, for example, some resident professional hunting guides, concerned about preservation of the resource, banded together with nonresident landowners to support the laws. Their actions put them at odds with those of their neighbors who wished to continue to harvest game for family subsistence on what had traditionally been seen as common land.

Also in 1892, the first railroad line traversed the Adirondack region, opening a large swath of the interior to traffic from both the north and the south. Like railroads across the country, it created a boom in develop-

Fig. 2. This boathouse on Upper Lake St. Regis at Camp Topridge, a great camp built in 1923 by General Foods founder Marjorie Merriweather Post, exemplifies the detailed twig work that marks the Adirondack style. Courtesy of Doug Shick.

ment along its line. No longer was it necessary to ride a stagecoach thirty miles from the railroad station in North Creek to the Prospect House in Blue Mountain Lake. Now, other mountain resorts were within easy reach, many of them built or enlarged specifically to cater to tourists who had to husband their time and money. The trans-Adirondack line was also a boon to vacationers on the other end of the economic spectrum. "Captains of industry" like the line's builder William Seward Webb could now build rustic "great camps" in the heart of the woods and travel to them in comfort.

A distinctive regional aesthetic emerged during this period as money, talent, and ideas flowed into the region. William West Durant, son of Union Pacific developer Thomas Clark Durant and first cousin of the Prospect House founder, is credited with the invention of the widely admired and imitated Adirondack rustic style. An early historian of the Adirondacks captured the impact of Durant's first woodland home design: "Before it was built there was nothing like it; since then, despite infinite variations, there has been nothing essentially different from it."[5] Durant had been educated in England and combined his knowledge of picturesque gardens of Europe with the rustic bridges and structures in Olmsted and Vaux's Central and Prospect Parks to design his Adirondack "great camps": wilderness complexes for the wealthy few that celebrated natural materials. Durant, for instance, instructed his workmen to use birch bark as wallpaper and natural crooks and burls as structural and decorative elements. Outsiders like Durant patronized and influenced the design of camps, but experienced local carpenters and craftsmen from the surrounding countryside deserve the lion's share of credit for the unique and enduring appeal of the elite camps (Fig. 2).

The early twentieth century brought advances in transportation that in time democratized Adirondack tourism. The first automobile to travel into the central mountains ground its way into Blue Mountain Lake in 1906. The driver reported that very few people he met along the way had ever seen a car. Rough roads and steep grades kept out all but the bravest drivers, so it was not until after the First World War that an appreciable number of tourists drove on their mountain vacations. By the mid-1920s, however, both the state government and private entrepreneurs scrambled to accommodate them. The state began improving and blacktopping the roads, and its Conservation Department built trailheads and campsites for motorists with fireplaces, toilets, and tent sites. Hotel owners wedged in cottages and garages on their grounds; motor courts and private campgrounds sprang up in the smaller hamlets.

The state's efforts to accommodate and entertain the motoring public reinvigorated the debate about developing the supposedly "forever wild" lands. Every public campsite destroyed some of that sacred timber and in theory violated the state constitution—depending on the interpretation of a "reasonable amount" clause. The number of trees cut down for campsites paled in comparison with proposals for a highway to the top of Whiteface Mountain (1927) and a bobsled run near Lake Placid (1929). New York State approved the highway and President Franklin Roosevelt proudly inaugurated it in 1935. The highway backers overcame restrictions and objections to human construction on state "wilderness" land by designating it a memorial to veterans. Perhaps a more potent argument was that it provided a way to the top of one of the state's highest peaks for those who were unable to hike. The bobsled run, however, failed to gain approval. The uproar over forest destruction forced the backers to build the sports facility on private lands.

The traveling public in the postwar era was mobile as never before and used that freedom to see new sights and enjoy new activities. Plenty of people still visited the region to commune with nature, but for many others, nature became the backdrop for active, and often more commercial, leisure activities. Santa's Workshop, reputedly the first non-ride-based theme park in the country, opened at the base of the Whiteface Highway in 1949. Designed by artist and toymaker Arto Monaco, who later assisted with Disneyland, it was such a success that cars overwhelmed the parking lot, and people had to hike a mile along the road to pet the reindeer and shake hands with Santa Claus. Other Monaco-designed theme parks followed in the 1950s. Motels, the latest in accommodations for the motoring public, were built in towns and along shorelines, and ice cream stands, movie houses, souvenir shops, cocktail lounges, and restaurants fulfilled the public's demand for light diversion. Lake George, on the edge of the park, became a crowded retail strip that resembled commercialized boardwalks. A few visionaries realized that cultural ambition could thrive even amid the tourist sprawl and, in 1957, founded a museum to highlight local collections of art, boats, and books in Blue Mountain Lake.

The debate over using Adirondack Forest Preserve lands for public convenience surfaced again in the late 1950s with a proposal for a super-highway linking Albany and Montreal. The highway concept in general elicited few complaints, especially in light of its potential role in national defense. The sticking point was the route. The two main choices were a route that ran along Lake Champlain, serving the industrial and agricultural industries of the valley (mostly on private land), or an interior route that traversed the preserve. Skirting the issue of the 300 acres of forest preserve that would be taken, one promotional pamphlet revealed just how much a part of American life the automobile had become: "Does the Northway violate Conservation principles?" it asked. "By no means. The Forest Preserve belongs to all the people of the State, but because of its inaccessibility, few have enjoyed the many wonderful features the Forest Preserve offers. . . . Surely these enjoyments are in keeping with the conservationists' concept of 'wise use' of a valuable natural resource." Fulfilling its promoters' hopes, the highway helped fuel a second-home boom in the eastern mountains and proved instrumental in the success of Lake Placid's bid for the 1980 Winter Olympics.

The tourism industry delighted in growth, but by the late 1960s, the random and rampant development of the Adirondack region for tourism prompted Governor Nelson Rockefeller to appoint a Temporary Study Commission on the Future of the Adirondacks, which led to the creation of "an independent, bipartisan Adirondack Park Agency" to develop long-range land-use plans for all land in the park, public and private. In 1973, the new agency completed its landmark *Adirondack Park Land Use and Development Plan*, which has guided, and limited, development in the park ever since. The plan, reflecting the growing strength of the national environmental movement, made preserving "nature" the foremost public policy goal for the region in spite of the complex actors and interests in the region.

For more than a century, Adirondack interests had modified the "wilderness" to accommodate visitors. Yet environmental pioneer Bob Marshall (who spent boyhood summers in the region and was one of the founders of the Wilderness Society in 1935) and like-minded environmentalists' aim of preserving land for its own sake gained wider currency with many tourists and locals over the course of the century. Wilderness advocates not only influenced government planning and regulations but also established two visitor interpretive centers and a natural history museum to create an educated constituency for preservation. Under this strict interpretation of wilderness, extending and improving snowmobile trails, installing boat launches, and opening lakes to floatplanes now became violations of nature. The Adirondack land-use debate thus took a new twist in the midst of the modern environmental movement.

For many of the Adirondacks' resident population, however, the growing focus on environmental quality seemed to threaten their communities. Historically, mining and logging helped sustain the region's inhabitants, but tight environmental regulations and less regulated global competition made extractive industries less profitable. In hopes of an economic windfall, some of the park's residents have argued that tourist amenities, as well as services taken for granted in other parts of the country like cellphone towers and power-generating wind turbines, should be permitted in the Adirondacks as in the rest of the United States. But tourism and second-home development brought economic pressures of their own that threatened resident quality of life. Outsiders bought up businesses and homes with profits earned elsewhere. Grand developments of "luxury" second homes, made possible in part by a booming financial sector on the East Coast, sprouted on large tracts of land sold to developers by timber companies. Locals in turn, as in most tourist destinations, found it difficult to obtain well-paying, year-round jobs and affordable housing.

For the past half-century, outsiders have looked on the Adirondack region as a place of great natural beauty that has successfully resisted growing urban sprawl. Yet the growing demands for tourism and resource development, the rise of environmentalism, and the complex legal framework that shields the park from overdevelopment have made "wilderness" an evolving and much debated concept in the Adirondacks.

Aspen,

Colorado

E. Duke Richey

Nestled in a high mountain valley near the base of four ski resorts, Aspen, Colorado, has changed from a forgotten mining town into a sophisticated, internationally famous urban outpost. The tourism industry there has far outlived—economically and culturally—the extractive industries on which the town was founded at the end of the nineteenth century. The town boomed as a center for silver mining for, at most, only thirteen years (ca. 1880-1893), but tourists and cultural brokers have since both transformed the town and given birth to a widely imitated style of elite mountain tourism. Cultural and educational tourism—focused chiefly on classical music and studying the humanities in the summertime— and recreational tourism, namely skiing, have shaped the town's identity for more than six decades.[1]

Aspenites refer to the half-century between the repeal of the Sherman Silver Purchase Act in 1893 and the opening of the world's longest chairlift in 1946 as their "quiet" years, but the town set the stage for tourism throughout this period. By the 1910s, cool temperatures brought in visitors—particularly fishermen—from as far away as Texas during the summer months. Some summer residents during the teens and twenties had lived in Aspen in earlier years during the mining boom and had moved to Denver or elsewhere after the bust. These original absentee owners continued to visit and maintain second homes, but their status as former Aspenites garnered few if any critiques. They lived in the same old homes as everyone else. Little tourism happened in winter.

In 1936, one native Aspenite, then living in California, teamed with a New York banker to build a lodge on the outskirts of town. Locals applauded the possibility of downhill skiing as an economic boon. In a move that certainly belies the idea that Aspen was a "quiet" recreational tourist spot before World War II, the town hosted the national championships in 1941, prompting *TIME Magazine* to say that Aspen offered the most exciting skiing in America. The lodge eventually folded, but some of the racers in the competition joined the 10th Mountain Division ski troops during World War II; the proximity of their base (Camp Hale) to Aspen proved fortuitous during and after the war, as the men visited Aspen regularly while on leave. Like GIs elsewhere in the war years who visited new parts of the country and longed to return—and many did return to the Sunbelt and Mountain West—the men of the 10th proved no exception to the rule. After the war, 10th veterans founded seventeen ski areas and directed more than thirty ski schools across the nation. In the immediate postwar years between 1945 and 1950, more than twenty 10th veterans moved to Aspen, bragging of the perfect mix of small-town charm, blue skies, and powdery snow.

The 10th veterans could not have built the ski town of their dreams without the money generated by a non-skier named Walter Paepcke. Without question the original king of absentee landowners in the ski era, Paepcke is universally considered to be the founder of Aspen as a modern resort. President of the Container Corporation of America in Chicago, Paepcke already owned a historic "working" guest ranch on Colorado's Front Range when he decided to buy more than twenty-five properties in Aspen in 1945. What he saw in the town was the potential for a sort of Williamsburg West—an opportunity to, at once, restore a relic Victorian village and to create a small-town mountain getaway for himself and his wealthy urban friends. While he specifically made the comparison to Williamsburg in his own correspondence, Aspen could not have been more different. Moreover, while Paepcke was wealthy, he was no John D. Rockefeller, Jr. At Colonial Williamsburg, actors dressed in period costumes and pretended to live, work, and play for sightseers in a restored colonial town. Money was essentially no object. They went home at the end of the workday. In Aspen, people were actually going to work, live, and play in an updated Victorian town, albeit with modern ski lifts in the background. Unable to buy the town outright (the 1940 census enumerated nearly 800 residents), Paepcke created the Aspen Company, a real estate venture, and the Aspen Skiing Corporation. For Aspen to exist at all, Paepcke needed to market it and sell it from the start.

Fig. 3. In this 1950 publicity shot, promoters emphasized that skiers might zoom straight from the mountain to the pleasures of the heated pool at the Hotel Jerome, or they could just leave on their coats and watch. While Aspen's ski bums often suggest that rich outsiders came to their hideaway and ruined it, elites have been recreating in—and promoting—Aspen from the beginning. Western History Collection, Floyd Haley McCall, X-6209, Courtesy of Denver Public Library.

With the opening of Lift One in late 1946, and with Aspen's hosting of the world ski championships in 1950, young people—mostly eastern and college-educated—flocked to town seeking a year or two of fun (Fig. 3). Some stayed their whole lives. Although they talked of living hand-to-mouth while working little and skiing much, many of the self-proclaimed ski bums were deliberately avoiding grey-flannel expectations back home.

Ironically, corporate friends of Paepcke bought much of Aspen's real estate, ensuring that older men in suits owned many of Aspen's properties, even as younger folks in blue jeans shaped an image of Aspen as a youthful place of escape. After a festival celebrating Goethe in 1949, Paepcke felt inspired to permanently link together Aspen and summer gatherings of intellectuals and businessmen like himself who might benefit from reconnecting to a college-campus atmosphere. In 1950, he founded the Aspen Institute for Humanistic Studies and created a summer music program. While the ski bums would have preferred jazz, Paepcke brought in highbrow classical musicians. From the start of the "ski era" then, Aspen provided different types of escapes, and it meant different things to different people. But, for the most part, everyone got along because they were all largely from similar elite backgrounds. A ski bum in tattered canvas work pants may have seemed very different than a summer music aficionado, but both had likely gone to an Ivy League college.

By the time Paepcke died in 1960, the demographics of skiing had started to change. When national magazines ran stories on Aspen, and as the town appeared in newsreels, fiction, and films, middle-class suburbanites wanted to visit. Discretionary income allowed for new diversions for middle-class Americans seeking leisure opportunities in the postwar era. Growth in Aspen reflected this trend. New ski areas (Highlands and Buttermilk opened in 1958) provided more terrain and hotel bed numbers increased. Between 1959 and 1960 alone, out-of-state skiers to Colorado doubled. After the Squaw Valley Olympics in 1960 became the first Winter Olympics held in the American West, and the first on television, more Americans were drawn to the sport, just as golf—an elite pastime like skiing—and other new spectator sports on television also lured fresh participants in record numbers. Aspen ski bums protested as the ski company, trying to shorten lift lines, raised ticket prices for "locals." Contemporaneously, federal and state laws made it legal to insure mutually owned apartments, known today as condominiums. As these new developments boomed, Aspenites grappled with growth-related change and fought for planning to control developers. They cried that they wanted to remain distinctly different from Colorado's new faux-Bavarian and tasteless condo-filled mega-resort, Vail, which opened in 1962. When the new ski resort at Snowmass opened in 1967 with a base village reminiscent of Vail, many Aspenites said that the small-town life they had found there earlier was nearly ruined. Many of them started to look for homes elsewhere in the region.

Aspen gained great notoriety in the 1970s. In Hunter S. Thompson's unsuccessful "freak power" bid for sheriff in 1970, his platform railed against both unfair drug dealers and greedy outside developers. Other than changing the name of Aspen to "Fat City," which Thompson proposed, it was unclear what a sheriff might do to limit growth. What was clear was that the countercultural generation, embracing a culture of protest, felt comfortable critiquing the ethos that allowed inclusion for the tasteless rich at Aspen in the first place. While resident John Denver's homilies to crunchy-granola Aspen in song and on television specials tempered the bad boy/girl image of someone like Thompson, the lyrics of his 1973 hit song, "Rocky Mountain High," still questioned "why they try to tear the mountains down to bring in a couple more / More people, more scars upon the land." More important, in the early 1970s, as older buildings gave way to condominiums and other new structures, some Aspen residents pushed for stricter planning and zoning regulations and for government-subsidized employee housing. In 1972, locals created the Historic Preservation Commission (HPC) under the auspices of the city government's planning department. Under the HPC, whose stated goal is "to preserve character defining features of a significant property," Aspenites created two historic districts in town. Today, the commission must approve changes to structural and exterior features (including lights, windows, and doors, but not paint color) on historic buildings. In 1974, Aspenites created a housing program for local employees. By the late 1990s, a city/county program owned and managed more than 2,500 units and provided rent subsidies for a majority of Aspen's full-time working residents.

Hollywood and Aspen tied the knot in 1978 when Twentieth-Century Fox, its coffers fat with profits from *Star Wars*, bought the ski company. That same year, a local newspaper columnist—and former campaign worker for Thompson—used the term *Aspenization* to explain the culture of excess there (including excessive devotion to fitness) that she saw Aspen exporting to America more broadly. In 1985, Chicago's Crown family bought the ski company, continuing the legacy of outside ownership and control of Aspen's most important business. As Aspen's airport filled with private jets in the 1980s, the joke became that the billionaires were replacing the millionaires. While there was some truth to this, total skier num-

Fig. 4. Cooper Avenue Mall, one of Aspen's three pedestrian malls, was born of the same impulse that led cities and towns across the United States to close streets to vehicular traffic in the 1960s-80s. The steady flow of tourists enabled Aspen's pedestrian streets to endure after most malls closed elsewhere. Courtesy of Shihmei Barger.

bers in the early 1990s grew larger than ever. In the same decade, Aspen locals (again, a blurry line with so many part-timers), claiming a link to a simpler past, clashed again with what they labeled as greedy outsiders. Votes to ban the sale of fur and to stop a Trump hotel and a Ritz-Carlton made national headlines chiefly because many Aspenites thought all three were too ostentatious. Trump lost, but fur and the Ritz (now known as the St. Regis) won. Since that time, Aspen's downtown, in spots, has become a sort of Rocky Mountain version of Fifth Avenue, with high-fashion boutiques and swanky restaurants side by side with small-town shops and services. Thanks to the incompleteness of the chain-store intrusion, however, Aspen's three pedestrian malls—one of them with its own brook framed by a flowery center strip separating two brick promenades—achieve the kind of Main Street experience that suburban lifestyle centers and festival marketplaces struggle to concoct (Fig. 4).

Today, the Aspen Institute and the Aspen Music Festival and School thrive in summer; and Aspen is also known for a comedy festival, a writer's festival, Jazz Aspen Snowmass, and the Food and Wine Classic. More than any other resort town in the American West, Paepcke's original vision for Aspen as a place of relaxation and reflection for rich people continues. Yet, there are few, if any, "food bums" or "writing bums" or "cello bums" in Aspen. It is still mostly a skier's town—expressed most clearly in Buttermilk's annual hosting of the Winter X Games—even though the ski bums and snowboarders live increasingly in employee housing or in the more affordable communities down valley of Aspen proper.

ATLANTIC CITY,
New Jersey

Bryant Simon

A man wouldn't be a good American," Teddy Roosevelt proclaimed before World War I, "if he did not know of Atlantic City."[1] The Bull Moose president recognized that Atlantic City thrived because it reflected the American mainstream. Like all mass resorts, Atlantic City, during both its good days and bad, mirrored the dreams and fears of the American middle class. Turning these hopes and anxieties into bricks and mortar, fast rides, and sparkling dining rooms became the job of the city's tourism entrepreneurs.

Atlantic City started out with private dreams of wealth. Throughout the nineteenth century, beach resorts like Cape May and Newport quietly grew catering to the well-heeled and affluent. Looking to capitalize on the emerging tourist trade, in 1854, a pair of Philadelphia developers, Jonathan Pitney and Richard Osborne, pulled out a map and drew a straight line between the city and shore. They landed fifty-five miles away on the spot that became Atlantic City. When they actually got there, they found only a handful of families and a dense thicket of briars and bushes. Within a few years, the land was cleared. Soon there was a hotel and a few houses. But the most important building in those days was the railroad station. The railroad was the city's first lifeline and it would make it a different kind of place than Cape May or Newport. Operating on the industrial model of economies of relative scale, Atlantic City railway operators (and land speculators) kept ticket prices for the trip from the city to the shore low enough, though higher than a trip to Coney Island cost, for accountants, shopkeepers, carpenters, and plumbers to afford the journey. From the start, then, Atlantic City catered not to the rich or working class, but to the vast middle. In many ways, it would become the nation's first great middle-class resort. What city leaders did, then, was create a place of conspicuous consumption for those—and there were many in nineteenth- and twentieth-century America—who wanted to emulate the rich.

Cape May and Newport started out as health resorts, so that is how Atlantic City first positioned itself. "Take a sea voyage," urged an advertisement that early developers placed in a Philadelphia newspaper. A group of doctors boasted that Atlantic City possessed "three of the greatest health giving elements known to science—sunshine, ozone, and recreation." Eager to gaze at the sea and take a break from noxious urban fumes, Philadelphians boarded the trains to the coast in droves.[2]

More tourists meant more business, but also more annoying sand in the seats of hotel lobbies and train cars from Philadelphia. In 1870, Jacob Keim, the owner of a beachfront hotel, and Alexander Boardman, a railroad conductor, suggested to city leaders laying wood planks over the sand for people to walk on. With funds from municipal authorities, they oversaw construction of the first boardwalk. Eight feet wide and a mile long, it was an instant hit. When a storm washed it away, city leaders built a second, third, and then fourth wooden walkway to replace the first. Pounded by winds and waves, none of these lasted. Finally, on the fifth try, in 1896, engineers using steel and concrete reinforcements constructed a more permanent structure. Wider than a two-lane highway, the new five-mile strip emerged as the city's signature attraction, its Fifth Avenue, its Champs-Élysées. The Chamber of Commerce promoted the promenade as "the eighth wonder of world," the only Boardwalk anywhere that deserved to be spelled with a capital B.[3]

The Boardwalk transformed Atlantic City from health resort to urban showplace, a fantasy of a sophisticated urban life of wealth and leisure. From 1920 to 1960—the heyday in many ways of the showy downtown of the American city—Atlantic City became the "Queen of Resorts" and the "Nation's Playground." More visitors than the combined populations of New York City and Philadelphia visited Atlantic City each year. They came to see and be seen. They dressed in their best clothes and indulged their desires—desires nurtured by a growing culture of consumption that taught people to express themselves through buying. Like the Boardwalk itself, everything in Atlantic City was overly ornate and embellished. Women wore mink stoles and men carried jeweled walking sticks. On midsum-

Fig. 5. Well-dressed tourists stroll or enjoy rolling chair rides on the Boardwalk on July 4, 1936. In the background is the Traymore Hotel. Opened in 1915, the Traymore enjoyed its status as the "Taj Mahal of Atlantic City" for several decades but declined as well-heeled vacationers forsook Atlantic City for newer resorts to the south. Courtesy of R. C. Maxwell Company Collection, ROAD digital No. XXX-3198, Hartman Center, Duke University.

mer nights, the throng got so thick that it resembled a subway platform at rush hour. As the crowds grew, the city expanded vertically and horizontally. Amusement piers with fast rides and cavernous showrooms jetted out into the ocean as far as the eye could see. Steel Pier seemed, to one *TIME Magazine* reporter, to begin "on the New Jersey shoreline . . . [and] end somewhere near the coast of Spain.[4] Visitors to this fun place, run for much of the second half of the twentieth century by the former acrobat and Lebanese immigrant George Hamid and his family, could watch the famed diving horses or boxing cats or listen to Duke Ellington or Louis Prima. Towering over the Boardwalk and its long row of pricy jewelry stores and sparkling movie houses rose a string of massive hotels topped with Moorish domes and cathedral-like peaks (Fig. 5). Behind the hotels were smoky nightclubs and dark wood-paneled restaurants that had the look and feel of a Frank Sinatra song. (Not surprisingly, the singer regularly appeared in town.) Farther back, where ride attendants and candy-makers lived and shopped, the city resembled East Baltimore or North Philadelphia with streets lined with tidy row houses that crossed at right angles. At just about every corner there was a grocery store or a tavern. By 1950, almost eighty thousand people lived year-round in compact, urban feeling Atlantic City.

As the twentieth century unfolded, Atlantic City grew even more iconic, perhaps even more American than even Teddy Roosevelt had recognized. It was where the Miss America Pageant and saltwater taffy were invented; where the Ferris wheel was first introduced and perhaps the very first convention center in the country was built; where Jerry Lewis and Dean Martin first got together and where Frank Sinatra and Sammy Davis, Jr., honed their acts before heading to the newer desert palaces of Las Vegas. Atlantic City was where the century's most vibrant labor organization, the Congress of Industrial Organizations, was formed and where feminists announced their arrival on the national scene, burning—or maybe not—bras in front of groups of onlookers on the Boardwalk in stout fifty-five-gallon drums. And it is from Atlantic City's streets named after states and oceans that the immensely popular board game Monopoly took its property names.

Yet for all of its firsts, when it came to the persistent and ongoing American dilemma of race, Atlantic City operated like virtually every other American place, North, South, East, or West. "It was a Jim Crow town to be sure," said a Georgia-born, African-American, lifelong resident. As in Birmingham and Philadelphia, segregation ruled Atlantic City. Well into the 1950s, ballots were marked "W" for white, and "C" for colored. Pier owners and city police kept African-Americans off the Boardwalk, especially during busy times, and away from most of the beaches. Hotel owners did what they could to bar people of color from their restaurants, lobbies, and rooms. Theater owners confined African-Americans to the crammed "crow's nest" above the balconies. Everyone from real-estate agents to city officials, it seemed, made sure that black families lived in a single, redlined, underserviced neighborhood and that their children attended segregated schools. Local stores wouldn't let African-Americans try on clothes or hire them for sales or other decent-paying jobs. In a testament to just how bad things were in the South, lousy seasonal work washing dishes, cleaning rooms, and scrubbing toilets nonetheless still attracted thousands of African-Americans from Maryland and North Carolina to Atlantic City to work and live. By 1920, blacks represented a third of the city's population, the highest percentage of any New Jersey city. This would be true throughout much of the century.

Race played another role in Atlantic City. Very few American places in the twentieth century were integrated, even marginally. The white middle class demanded separation at home and on vacation. But Atlantic City's commercial leaders did more than just divide blacks from whites. They staged affordable, yet still conspicuous, dramas of racial superiority and class ascendance, which together helped turn their town into one of the nation's most popular destinations.

Atlantic City's rolling chairs were the main staging ground for the principal racial and class fantasy for sale in the city. During its heyday, four thousand rickshaw-like, two-passenger buggies plied the Boardwalk every day. A prostitute featured in a novel set in Atlantic City explained the importance of these vehicles: "One of my clients used to say that the key to this city was not the beach or the Boardwalk, but in the rolling chairs. You could ride on a rolling chair and dream that you were the kind of person who deserved the rich life."[5] What she omitted from her sharp analysis, however, was the centrality of race to the city and these attractions. Rolling-chair passengers were always well-dressed whites and the pushers were always black. Once a couple climbed aboard one of these "temples of contentment," they caught what the son of a Baltimore paint-store clerk called "wicker affluence." "Rolling along on flower cushions, feet up on the little metal rest . . . viewing the world without lifting a muscle," this middle-class teen sensed the welling up of an "ineffable superiority." For this one "bewitching" moment, he stood on top of the world.[6] On the rolling chair, he was transformed into a rich man, a real American; rich enough to afford to pay someone else to push him down the Boardwalk. Atlantic City's ability to easily and relatively affordably reproduce this moment of social mobility and racial dominance was why the nation's white middle class, especially aspiring ethnics, went to the Boardwalk in droves in the middle of the twentieth century.

By 1970, the rolling chairs were gone and so were the crowds, "a million going this way, and a million going that way" (Fig. 6). Air travel had made getting to newer resorts cheaper and easier. Television, backyard

Fig. 6. Steel Pier, shown here in the 1970s, once played host to hordes of visitors and the nation's most popular entertainers, everyone from Duke Ellington to Gene Krupa to Ricky Nelson. When this picture was shot, its best days, like the city itself, were well behind the amusement pier. Courtesy of Alfred M. Heston Collection, Atlantic City Free Public Library.

swimming pools, and air conditioning, meanwhile, kept others at home in newly constructed suburbs. But even more important, by this time, South Jersey civil rights activists, aspired by protest in Birmingham and marches in Washington, had successfully desegregated Atlantic City, making the Boardwalk, beaches, movie houses, piers, and hotels open to anyone.

Philadelphia Bulletin columnist Bruce Boyle's grandmother lived in Atlantic City in the 1960s. Her experience turned out to be quite typical. When her neighborhood became, in Boyle's words, "blacker and poorer," she fled to Florida. Boyle knew that tourists fled for the same reasons and that Atlantic City was doomed by dual streams of white flight—one coming from residents and the other from tourists. "It was many years ago," Boyle wrote in 1981, "when technology and racism began to kill this place." Air travel, he explained, "made it possible to get to nice warm beaches in exotic places." Television commercials, at the same time, pictured blue water, and as Boyle noted, the ad men were "careful to show only white people on these exotic beaches." Yet white Philadelphians knew all about Atlantic City. "Atlantic City," these onetime visitors said to themselves, "had black people, thousands of them." Even worse, Boyle reported, whites thought that Atlantic City blacks "were getting cranky, too." Some white customers, he wrote, felt that sullen rolling-chair drivers deliberately took them "over some bumps that could have been avoided."[7]

Atlantic City's problem, as Boyle sensed, was that it could no longer exclude people. Once that happened, Atlantic City slid into decline, as did downtowns from Detroit to Newark and urban amusement parks from Pittsburgh to Los Angeles. Each year, from the mid-1960s onward, another ornate Atlantic City movie house closed; demolition experts blew up another Jazz-Age hotel; another fancy Boardwalk store turned into a hot dog stand; and, another seafood restaurant went bankrupt. The legionnaires and teachers who had attended meetings at the colossal convention hall in the past gathered instead in Miami Beach, Disneyland, and Las Vegas. African-Americans, at the same time, started to come to town, sporting fancy clothes—as whites had done before them—to show off on the Boardwalk that they too had made it in America. But local bankers and business leaders didn't try to build on black tourism. Some, in fact, tried to keep African-Americans away. At one point, the city council considered a statute, responding to the urging of Steel Pier owner George Hamid, Jr., that would have barred excursion buses, which typically brought African-Americans to town from the city. When this didn't happen, and when African-Americans kept coming, hotel owners stopped investing in their properties, and homeowners started dumping their houses. This led to a sharp drop in real estate prices and fewer employment opportunities, triggering a vicious cycle of decline in Atlantic City that mirrored the fate of Camden, Cleveland, Philadelphia, and many of the nation's other former industrial powerhouses.

Throughout the 1960s and 1970s, the urban crisis deepened in Atlantic City, as white tourists and residents continued to flee the city. Commentators compared the ailing resort to bombed-out Dresden and war-torn Beirut. This was, then, no longer the kind of place middle-class families went to show off or even enjoy a few days of vacation, that is, unless they had no other place to go. City leaders tried to revive the town before it was too late. They talked about expanding the convention center and building new amusement parks and maybe an aquarium. One desperate local man suggested turning the city dump into a ski hill. But the owners of most Atlantic City hotels and stores couldn't take their eyes off the sparkling neon lights of Las Vegas, then the only legal place in the United States to play the slots, blackjack, or craps. Boosters promised that casinos would revive the moldering city by bringing the crowds back to the Boardwalk.

When the statewide gambling referendum passed in 1976, locals danced in the streets. They thought yesterday was just around the corner. They imagined the city once again packed with well-dressed visitors and the money these people left behind trickling down—if not rushing—into the pockets of landowners and the cash boxes of local businesspeople. Politicians fueled the fervor, describing the casinos as a "unique tool of urban renewal."[8]

Not all the promises were lies. On May 26, 1978, Resorts International Casino opened its doors to a throng of eager gamblers. During its first seven months in operation, the new casino earned a whopping $134 million. Since then, Resorts and the other casinos have taken in more than $55 billion in earnings. Together, the casinos employ more than fifty thousand people and pay 68 percent of the city's total tax revenues. Investment in the city over the last quarter century, moreover, has exceeded the total private investment over the same period in the state's four other largest cities combined. As a result of the casino boom, Atlantic City has become one of the most popular resorts in America—only Las Vegas attracts more visitors each year.[9]

All these people and all this money, however, have not saved Atlantic City. Actually the city as a city, as a place to live and work, shop and play, has suffered a cruel fate. Ten years after Resorts opened its doors, selling the fantasy of easy money and wealth, Atlantic City lost one-third of its population and one-third of its housing stock. While it once had fifteen movie houses each with lavish lobbies and oversized bathrooms with gold-plated faucets, it didn't, by then, have a single movie theater in operation. Some 400 businesses, including 250 restaurants, closed during the same period. Atlantic Avenue—the city's old Main Street of department stores and fancy stationary shops—turned into a dingy line of pawnshops, greasy spoons, and empty storefronts. Crime rose. So did unemployment along with rates of infant mortality, homelessness, and heroin use. When pollsters asked city residents in 1985 if they would vote for gambling again if given another chance, the majority said no.[10] The next year, *Money* magazine voted Atlantic City the worst place to live in America—worse than Detroit or Gary or Camden or any other place.[11]

Before the onslaught of the New Recession of 2008 and the advent of what seems like permanent double-digit unemployment, conditions had improved somewhat in Atlantic City. Population stabilized, higher-end housing units went up in desolate areas, and banks lent millions to help build new hotel towers, shopping piers and malls, and high-end restaurants. Still Atlantic City—home to twelve casinos and host to thirty-five million people each year—still does not have a single movie theater or department store. There isn't even a supermarket. Gambling, in fact, produced a remarkable paradox of private wealth and public poverty. Again the city, just like it did in Teddy Roosevelt's day, reflects its American moment, the neoliberal moment. In the new Atlantic City, the casinos' private wealth remains segregated and out of reach from most of the city's residents, reproducing the same unbalanced, tourist-led development we see all too often these days from Baltimore's Inner Harbor to Macau's newly minted replica of a Las Vegas version of Venice.

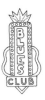

Beale Street
Memphis, Tennessee

Robert Russell

An approximately one-thousand-foot stretch of Beale Street in Memphis, a mere fragment of what was once was once a thriving African-American and immigrant neighborhood, has today become the single most visited tourist attraction in Tennessee. The Jews, Greeks, Italians, and poor and working-class African-Americans are long gone, as are most of the run-down buildings where these people once lived, worked, and shopped. In their place, middle-class blacks and whites share sidewalks and clubs where they consume a sanitized and name-brand simulacrum of what was once known as black America's Main Street.

When W. C. Handy and his band arrived in Memphis in 1909, Beale Street, at the southern end of town, had been a haven for African-American musicians for nearly two generations.[1] The street had not started out that way. In the 1840s, the wealthy speculator and developer Robertson Topp, and others, had platted an area just south of the city of Memphis, which they named South Memphis. Beale Street was the de facto main east-west thoroughfare of this new enterprise and saw some grand mansions—including Topp's own—rise alongside its eastern reaches.[2] After most of the city's white population abandoned the city during the infamous yellow fever epidemics of the 1870s, Robert Church, the South's first black millionaire, began buying property around Beale Street. By the late nineteenth century, African-Americans owned many of the businesses on the street, and several blocks of the western end of the street were home to a dense mix of legitimate businesses as well as a range of enterprises, from the raunchy to the downright illegal. In 1899, Church persuaded the city to build Church's Park, which contained an auditorium that could hold two thousand people and rapidly became the center of black cultural life in Memphis. The auditorium is long gone, but the park still exists, next to the Beale Street Baptist Church. By the early twentieth century, the general wisdom on Beale Street "was that the Jews had the pawn shops and the dry goods stores, the Greeks had the restaurants, the Italians had the entertainment—the theaters, the saloons, the gambling—and the blacks were the customers."[3]

Handy, self-proclaimed "Father of the Blues," had achieved almost instant popularity in the River City with a song written for the 1909 mayoral campaign of Edward "Boss" Crump, who was to rule Memphis politics for the next half century, and who destroyed black Beale Street in 1940. Handy later rewrote the campaign tune, with new words, as his "Memphis Blues." Although Handy left Memphis for New York City in 1917, his association with Beale Street remains permanent, both in his legacy of the blues as an African-American musical form, and in the form of Handy Park, a vest-pocket stretch of sad grass and trees at Third and Beale, much gussied up in recent years with an amphitheater stage. The old Market House was razed in 1931 to make way for the park, which Boss Crump, who still needed the black vote, was persuaded to name after the by-then-famous musician. When the park was dedicated in spring 1931, Handy came to town as the guest of honor, and led a two-mile-long procession of black Memphians, all marching to the beat of his "Beale Street Blues." Ten thousand people attended the dedication.

By the 1930s, Memphis was unofficially known as the murder capital of the world, and Beale Street was the easiest place in the city to get shot or stabbed. Most of the violence, however, was black on black, and upper-class Memphis whites frequently came down to "slum" on Beale Street. The Palace Theater was the best-known venue where whites could hear the likes of Duke Ellington, Count Basie, and Ella Fitzgerald.[4] The city's white political leadership tolerated the street and its very public sin until 1940. In that year, Boss Crump, who had accepted blacks in Memphis as long as they knew their place and stayed in it, finally got fed up with what he felt was an unacceptable level of agitation for social equality. Crump's decision to crack down on "high life" in Memphis hit Beale Street particularly hard, since that was where a good part of the vice was. The street never recovered.

But Beale Street continued to be associated with music. In the early

Fig. 7. Beale Street, ca. 1960. Into the 1960s Beale Street looked much like any other commercial street in a central city and showed little of either its blues roots or the tourist-oriented business of later years. Courtesy of J. Mark Souther.

1950s, a young boy from Mississippi, transplanted to Memphis when his parents came to live in Lauderdale Courts (the public housing project for white people ten blocks or so north of Beale Street) began hanging around the street. He talked his way into the amateur shows at the Palace Theater, where he quickly became a favorite of the audiences, both black and white. Elvis Presley's growing success may well have had something to do with Mayor Edmund Orgill's announced hope in the late 1950s that Beale Street could be turned into an entertainment district along the lines of New Orleans's Bourbon Street (Fig. 7). This marks the genesis of the desire to recreate a manageable and sanitized version of the original Beale Street. By 1964, the Memphis Housing Authority (MHA) had prepared a master plan for the entire Beale Street area that concluded that Beale would have to be destroyed in order to be saved.[5]

The MHA plan envisioned a Beale Street surrounded by new shopping malls rather than the seedy mix of commercial and residential structures, home to a significant number of African-Americans. In order to do this, it was necessary to dismantle the community that surrounded the street. This had become a common enough occurrence in Memphis, where vast swaths of the downtown were cleared away thanks to federal urban renewal dollars. But the money was not forthcoming for this project, and when Martin Luther King, Jr., came to Memphis in 1968 to support the sanitation workers' strike, one of his marches took him down Beale, by now reduced to a shabby street lined by equally shabby buildings.

The assassination of Dr. King on April 4, 1968, caused consternation among the political leaders of Memphis, who feared a general black uprising. A minor riot had already occurred on Beale Street while the city was under martial law because of the sanitation workers' strike. Most particularly, they feared the black area, centered on Beale, which intersected Main Street at the southern end of the business district and appeared to threaten the downtown. Beale Street now had to be destroyed not only to save itself but also to save the center of town. To the city fathers, it now seemed certain that Beale could never become the entertainment center they had dreamed of if it were still in the heart of a black neighborhood. The federal government soon got into the act. In November 1969, the Department of Housing and Urban Development (HUD) set aside $11 million to fund the Beale Street Urban Renewal Program, and in June 1970, another grant for $14 million for renovation of the Beale Street area came through from Washington. The bulldozers were already at work. By the time they were through, all but about 65 of the 625 buildings that had stood on the 113 acres of the renewal area were gone. About fifteen hundred residents were displaced to other parts of the city.[6]

After all this swift destruction, nothing happened. In 1973, the Beale Street Development Corporation (BSDC) was founded by George B. Miller, Jr., to try to save what was left of the street and the district surrounding it. Its mission included the preservation of African-American history and culture, and black contributions to blues music. Miller, though idealistic, had no idea how to run a development corporation, and was soon gone, though the BSDC remains involved with Beale Street. In late 1975 the MHA was ready to let a contract to build a mall that would have put trees, benches, fountains, and cutesy lampposts down the middle of the street, but the National Advisory Council on Historic Preservation put a stop to the plan. Beale Street had been declared a National Historic Landmark in 1966, and the council observed that the proposed mall would turn the street into a suburban shopping center. This, of course, was what the MHA had intended to do, being unable to conceive of any other way to make the street attractive to white people.

Fig. 8. Beale Street looking west. After the 1980s Beale Street became a neon-framed strip that was increasingly reoriented to tourists with blues clubs, gift shops, restaurants and bars. Courtesy of David McDaniel.

It was not until 1980 that renovation work actually began on the street. By that time, a number of the buildings the bulldozers had initially spared, but that had stood abandoned for several years, were so decayed they could not be saved. In 1982, the city of Memphis leased the entire 113-acre Beale Street area to the BSDC, now run by Randle Catron, a veteran of the Civil Rights era and protégé of Ralph Abernathy. Catron, realizing he knew as little about management as Miller had, subleased the street to a management and development firm then called Elkington and Keltner Properties (now known as Performa Entertainment Real Estate Inc.). The two organizations are currently litigating over the ownership of Beale Street, while the city of Memphis makes sporadic and ineffectual claims for *its* ownership of the street. By October 1983, when the first reconstructed section of the street actually opened for business, all that was left of the original Beale were some storefronts between Second and Third, the storefronts across from Handy Park in the next block east, the old and new Daisy Theaters and a couple of other buildings in the next block, and the Beale Street Baptist Church and Solvent Savings Bank Building, still farther east (Fig. 8). Everything else was new, and the new was effectively the work of Elkington and Keltner. Ownership and management was not a problem when Beale Street was struggling. In 1986, sales on the street totaled $2.15 million. In 2006, they topped $32 million.[7]

For nearly twenty years, this new, sanitized version of Beale Street stood cut off from the other fragments of downtown Memphis that had eluded the wrecking ball of urban renewal. It was like a back-lot, movie-set version of what a gritty, dangerous, black-and-blues street "must have been like." Beale was literally separated from the surrounding city by vacant lots and parking areas. As what is for all intents and purposes a privately owned entertainment district, rather than a real part of Memphis, Beale Street continues to capitalize on its long musical tradition, now showcasing such luminaries of the Delta Blues tradition as B. B. King and Earl the Pearl, and though it is harder to find the current versions of Sleepy John Estes or Furry Lewis in the high-priced venues, you can still hear "real" and unknown blues artists on off nights. Unfortunately, you can hear Muzak as well, and the business owners demand that the area be kept "safe and clean."[8]

But time and larger urban changes in Memphis have dealt more kindly than one might have thought with this virtual Beale Street. In 2000, a new baseball field, AutoZone Park, opened as the home of the Memphis minor-league ball club, the Red Birds, three blocks north of Beale Street. Immediately after that, the new venue for Memphis's NBA franchise, the Memphis Grizzlies, was built in the parking lots south of the street. These facilities and substantial new residential developments south of the street have combined to knit the re-created blocks of Beale Street into something like a real urban fabric. The reality is that this is *not* the original fabric, but most of the more than four million visitors a year coming to the street at the beginning of the twenty-first century either do not know or do not care. Beale Street has been Tennessee's single largest tourist attraction for the last decade. People come to visit the Hard Rock Café (fitting, since Beale Street, through Elvis, really did contribute to rock and roll) and other franchise watering holes that line the street. Prostitutes and pawnshops can no longer be found on Beale Street, but T-shirts can.

CHAUTAUQUA,

NEW YORK

Andrew C. Rieser

Chautauqua, which President Theodore Roosevelt once described as "the most American thing in America," occupies an important niche in the history of tourism. Operating for more than a century as an ecumenical cultural retreat, Chautauqua is a 750-acre resort town located in the western corner of New York State, some seventy miles from Buffalo. With its communal atmosphere and conscious historicism, Chautauqua seems aesthetically frozen in time, much like Colonial Williamsburg and the Henry Ford Museum and Greenfield Village (Michigan). But compared with these history theme parks, Chautauqua's is a working landscape, still actively dedicated to the pursuit of something close to its original mission as outlined by its founders in 1874.[1]

The community's careful design, which closely mixes spaces and structures for religion, family, recreation, and culture, has been a key to its success as a destination. At Chautauqua's center is Bestor Plaza, a public square ringed by a library, post office, and various shops, eateries, and inns. Leading away from Bestor Plaza is the Brick Walk, a pedestrian path lined with gingerbread-adorned guest houses run by various Protestant denominations and, more recently, Catholic and Jewish centers (Fig. 11). On or near the Brick Walk can also be found a Second Empire grand hotel (1881) and a handful of impressive performance spaces, including the 4,500-seat Amphitheatre (1893), the Parthenon-like Hall of Philosophy (1874, remodeled 1906), and the ornate, neoclassical Hall of Christ (1909). Surrounding and radiating from this sacred core is a dense street grid packed with mostly Victorian cottages with front porches.

Fig. 11. Chautauqua's Brick Walk traverses the hub of the cultural retreat. Victorian guesthouses such as these line many streets near the Brick Walk. Courtesy of J. Mark Souther.

Chautauqua's cofounder, a Southern-born Methodist minister (later Bishop) named John Heyl Vincent, began his career as a hellfire-and-brimstone preacher on the Methodist circuit in the 1850s. By the early 1870s, Vincent had soured on the Methodist camp-meeting tradition. The spiritual awakenings experienced at the "holiness" revivals, he feared, were too emotional, too superficial. A modernized Sunday school, Vincent reasoned, would root evangelical Protestantism in the more authoritative foundations of biblical learning, scientific literacy, and middle-class propriety. In 1873, Vincent, then living in Chicago, joined forces with Lewis Miller, a wealthy manufacturer of farm implements from Akron, Ohio, to find suitable headquarters for a national training center for Sunday-school teachers. They settled on Fair Point, a cloistered Methodist camp meeting on the shores of Chautauqua Lake (the Miller clan had summered there). The following year, Vincent and Miller forbade impromptu proselytizing and opened Fair Point's doors to both serious students and fun-seeking vacationers—in essence, building on the camp-meeting template while transforming it into a semipublic, ecumenical institute and vacation retreat. It soon abandoned "Fair Point" and adopted the word "Chautauqua" as its own, cleverly hiding its evangelical roots behind an exotic-sounding Indian place name. What followed was an extraordinary cultural experiment, albeit one situated firmly within the context of small-town boosterism that popularized tourist destinations such as Gatlinburg, New Glarus, and Tombstone.

Vincent and Miller embraced leisure as a fact of modern life and made it an occasion for spiritual and social renewal. Modern prosperity had bequeathed the summer vacation, they acknowledged. But the vacation was both a blessing and a curse. Spent properly, leisure time would enable spiritual growth; used unwisely, free time would lead to mental dissipation and moral decline. To discourage temptation and to distinguish Chautauqua from elite watering holes and immigrant theatres, a ban on alcohol was rigidly enforced while a gate kept out intruders. The focus on education also set Chautauqua apart. Vacationers at Chautauqua had ample opportunity for self-improvement. A typical day might include a morning lecture on Shakespeare, an afternoon bike ride, and an evening worship service. While Coney Island offered excitement and release, Chautauqua prescribed uplift and Victorian restraint.

By the 1880s, Chautauqua had evolved into a national cultural movement. Its eight-week summer program combined Bible study with courses in science, history, literature, and the arts, while giving visibility to Social Gospel-minded academics, politicians, preachers, prohibitionists, and reformers. Through correspondence courses, university extension, journals like *The Chautauquan*, and especially reading circles, Chautauqua's influence spread far beyond its campus boundaries. In 1878, Vincent inaugurated the Chautauqua Literary and Scientific Circle (CLSC). Under the leadership of director Kate F. Kimball, 264,000 people—at least three-quarters of them women—had enrolled in the CLSC by century's end. Students completing the four-year reading program received official (if symbolic) diplomas. At a time when few higher education opportunities were open to women, Chautauqua filled a signal role.

Many CLSC women worked to establish independent Chautauqua assemblies in their own communities. Vincent and Miller generally approved of the imitators. However, there were no legal or financial ties between the "mother Chautauqua" and the upstart independent assemblies. By 1900, nearly one hundred towns, mainly in the Midwest, held assemblies on grounds patterned on the original Chautauqua. All had an amphitheater for lectures and services, a hotel or guest house, and streets lined with tents and cottages. Some built classrooms, railroad stations, and administrative buildings. The new assemblies developed close ties with local boosters, streetcar companies, and railroad executives, who saw them as profitable (yet moral) tourist attractions.

For rural towns in the late 1800s, cultural tourism made good economic sense. Faced with falling agricultural prices and a population drain to the big cities, small-town boosters searched frantically for ways to prevent further decay. Tourism—especially the virtuous variety represented by Chautauqua—appealed to many as a source of new investment and permanent settlers. Chautauqua represented a perfect compromise between another church (provident, but unprofitable) and a factory (lucrative but morally dubious). "The newspapers of Austin have talked much of cotton mills," noted one Austin, Texas, journalist in 1893. By contrast, the proposal set forth by a local Chautauqua group, "in its bearing upon the commercial, the moral, the intellectual life of Austin, would be incomparably better than any mill."[2] Competition for assemblies occasionally devolved into bidding wars not unlike those common for contemporary sports franchises. Charges of double-dealing and even lawsuits gave proof to *Forum* magazine's lament that "every town and city is doing its best to stifle its smaller neighbors."[3]

Chautauqua must be viewed as a major tourist phenomenon in the final quarter of the nineteenth century. It did not attract high-society clientele like those that frequented Saratoga, New York, or Newport, Rhode Island. But in sheer numbers, the visitors at assemblies across the country over the course of a summer compared favorably with the total attendance at the big oceanside resorts like Coney Island, New York, or Asbury Park, New Jersey. Daily attendance at individual assemblies varied. As few as five hundred could pass through the gates on a rainy weekend, while crowds of more than five thousand piled in to listen to a speech by William Jennings Bryan. As many as a half-million people visited Chautauqua assemblies annually in the 1880s and 1890s.

Chautauqua made an aesthetic contribution to American tourism as well. Everyone, it seemed, wanted to own a piece of the good life represented by a Chautauqua vacation. Chautauqua's popularity drove up land values in and outside the gate. Tents gave way to summer cottages and eventually permanent, year-round residents. With their curvilinear

Fig. 12. The Hall of Philosophy, an Arts-and-Crafts pavilion along the Brick Walk, is used for public lectures on a wide range of topics during the Chautauqua season. Courtesy of J. Mark Souther.

streets, front porches, and reputations for wholesomeness, these places gave physical form to the sort of differentiated communal life sought by elite visionaries of the suburb. In this way, the assemblies prefigured the tourist destinations associated with post–World War II America, such as Vail, Las Vegas, and Orlando—places that used utopian vacation landscapes as the templates for permanent communities.

In the early 1900s, the Chautauqua movement fell victim to its own success. In 1904, for-profit lyceum organizers introduced a network of mobile chautauquas, or circuits. Using aggressive sales tactics, one-sided contracts, and a carefully orchestrated "tight booking" system, circuit chautauquas brought edifying fare to thousands of communities across the nation. The circuits prefigured a new trend in American tourism. A trip to Chautauqua once meant a long, bumpy train ride from the familiar world of home into an exalted world inside the assembly gates. The assembly did not merely entertain; it ennobled and uplifted. By contrast, the circuit chautauqua asked less of the tourist and repositioned him as a consumer of culture. Circuit events took place not in an idealized vacation landscape, but in a temporary tent in a field outside of town.

Visitors and performers alike came by car and stayed only for the day. The circuit chautauqua was in some ways the automobile age's first cultural destination for day-trippers.

Chautauqua's relevance in national cultural and political life peaked in the Progressive Era. In the 1920s, however, the reform impulses that had shaped Chautauqua's appeal dissipated. By then, the independent assemblies had been nearly decimated by the circuit chautauquas. Competition forced many independent assemblies to hire lecture bureaus to handle their programming, relinquishing the podium to big-city companies and hastening the assemblies' decline. Educational fare gave way to sentimental plays, patriotic rallies, inspirational speakers, and "animal and bird educators" (in other words, pet tricks). Modernist writers like Sinclair Lewis and H. L. Mencken singled out the circuit chautauquas, somewhat unfairly, as symbols of small-minded, bourgeois parochialism. In the mid-1920s, the rise of commercial radio, movies, automobiles, and an expanded consumer culture signaled the end of the circuits' popularity in rural America. The last tent show folded in 1933.

Although the wider Chautauqua movement was over, the original assembly on Chautauqua Lake thrived. The Chautauqua Institution, as it was renamed, expanded steadily until a combination of overbuilding and the Great Depression pushed it to the brink of bankruptcy in 1933. Its survival hung in the balance until a timely gift from John D. Rockefeller returned the institution to sound footing in 1936. No longer a source of much new social or political thought, Chautauqua had discovered a secular principle to sustain it—the need for informed citizenship and vibrant creative arts in modern democracy. Competing perspectives on virtually every major social issue of the twentieth century—from abortion to xenophobia—have at one time or another found their way to the Chautauqua platform. In 1989, the grounds were designated a National Historic Landmark. By the early twenty-first century, a nine-week summer program of lectures and performing arts (including opera, ballet, theatre, and musical acts ranging from Beethoven symphonies to the Beach Boys) attracted as many as eight thousand people a day (Fig. 12).

The Chautauqua Institution's success in the early twenty-first century brought new challenges. Chautauqua cemented its reputation as a singular American tourist destination. Lavish donations resulted in freshly painted new facilities and expanded programs in the performing arts. The institution claimed to generate nearly $100 million in primary or secondary spending in Chautauqua County. However, some feared that skyrocketing housing and ticket prices were remaking the institution into an Aspenized, upper-class gated community, unreachable to many of the middle-class ministers, teachers, and visitors who once shaped Chautauqua's humanistic tradition.

CHINATOWN

SAN FRANCISCO, CALIFORNIA

Raymond W. Rast

Known widely for its colorful pagoda roofs, narrow alleys, herb shops, and dim sum restaurants, Chinatown is a roughly one square-mile district of some 100,000 residents on the northern edge of downtown San Francisco. For more than a century, it has held two key aspects of its identity in tension. On the one hand, Chinatown is a tourist destination—one shaped by the emergence of mass tourism and fueled by the tourism industry's commodification of "authentic" culture. On the other hand, Chinatown has been and remains a community—one defined by its working-class, immigrant population. The vision that defined its appeal as a tourist destination came into focus around the turn of the twentieth century, when Chinatown's merchant elites began to dismantle the built environment of a vice industry that catered to working-class immigrants and to construct, in its place, a sanitized, Sinocized visual landscape and modernized infrastructure that would appeal to middle-class tourists. This shift provided an enduring template for Chinatown's development as a tourist destination. As the Chinatown community itself evolved over the course of the twentieth century, its developers continued to invest in a vision of the neighborhood that had little connection to the realities of its residents' lives.

When the first wave of Chinese immigrants (most of them young men from Guangdong Province) arrived in San Francisco in the 1850s, they entered a booming city that celebrated their presence as an augur of increased trade with China. While most Chinese immigrants made their way to the gold fields of California, many stayed in the city and established businesses and residences. By the early 1860s, several dozen

Chinese-oriented businesses and lodging houses had concentrated around the intersection of Sacramento and Grant, and Chinese-operated laundries and other businesses had begun to spread throughout the city. Facing mounting hostility from white San Franciscans, however, Chinese San Franciscans turned inward. Doing so, they built a distinct community that served the economic, social, and recreational needs of young men living on meager incomes far from home. Cigar and textile factories, laundries, merchandise stores, and restaurants provided an economic foundation for the community, but Chinatown also drew strength from its Chinese-language newspapers, temples, mission houses, and social organizations—including huiguans (whose members took pride in their shared districts of origin) and tongs (whose members profited from illegal business interests). Among nonresidents, Chinatown was best known for its Chinese-oriented places of recreation: theaters, gambling halls, opium dens, and brothels. Chinatown became a vibrant community during the 1860s and 1870s. Its population approached twenty thousand, and it claimed a twelve-block area bounded by California, Stockton, Broadway, and Kearny. But Chinatown's economic vitality, its physical growth, and the growing appeal of its opium dens and brothels (among Chinese and white San Franciscans) fueled moral outrage and racist condemnations from many of the city's white residents. For most San Franciscans—and for the small but growing number of wealthy, eastern tourists brought to the city by the new transcontinental railroad—Chinatown was a place to be avoided.

Anti-Chinese sentiment in San Francisco drove support for the Page Act of 1875 (which targeted prostitutes and thus curtailed the immigration of young Chinese women) and the Chinese Exclusion Act of 1882 (which barred immigration of working-class Chinese men), but these measures bore consequences that white San Franciscans did not anticipate. The Exclusion Act in particular emboldened anti-Chinese vigilantes throughout the California countryside, prompting thousands of Chinese immigrants to seek refuge in the city. Thus, while the overall Chinese population in the United States declined during the 1880s, Chinatown's population grew, surpassing thirty thousand by the end of the decade. Ultimately, restrictions on the immigration of Chinese women and this new influx of Chinese men crystallized Chinatown's identity in the late nineteenth century as a community numerically dominated by working-class bachelors, all of whom faced diminished prospects of finding wives and starting families. Not surprisingly, Chinatown's gambling halls, opium dens, and brothels flourished, and the tong leaders who controlled the neighborhood's vice industry saw their wealth and power grow. Most Chinese San Franciscans, however, saw their living conditions deteriorate. White San Franciscans blocked further expansion of the neighborhood's boundaries during the 1880s, and Chinatown's residents faced the consequences of overcrowding on a daily basis. They responded, in part, by shaping the neighborhood to fit their evolving needs—subdividing living quarters, attaching balconies to buildings, digging out basements and underground passageways, building out back lots, and turning alleyways into commercial corridors, all of which increased residential and commercial capacity but strained the neighborhood's antiquated sanitation systems.

This densely populated neighborhood in the heart of the city, with its "teeming" streets, "tumble-down" buildings, "crooked" alleyways, and "subterranean" dens (as travel writers, guidebook authors, and sensation-minded journalists working for William Randolph Hearst's *San Francisco Examiner* described them), continued to appall and embarrass most San Franciscans during the closing decades of the nineteenth century. Yet these decades also marked the historical moment during which tourism took hold across the American West and, indeed, nationwide. In San Francisco, the emergence of mass tourism began to turn Chinatown into a destination. The economic benefits that San Francisco's economy—and Chinatown's merchant elites in particular—derived from this development ensured that tourism's hold on Chinatown would remain strong well after this moment passed.

San Francisco's artists and writers were the first to cultivate touristic interest in Chinatown. Exploring the neighborhood during the 1880s and 1890s, artist Theodore Wores, photographer Arnold Genthe, writer Frank Norris, and other self-proclaimed "bohemians" celebrated Chinatown as a "picturesque" place filled with aesthetically pleasing varieties of form, texture, and color (Fig. 13). But local bohemians ventured into Chinatown not only to see a distinct place; they also went to experience what they perceived as the "authentic" culture of a distinct community. Wealthy, eastern tourists followed their lead, allowing the tourism industry to establish its first foothold in the vibrant yet marginalized

Fig. 13. "Chinatown Gamblers (by Night)," by Arnold Genthe, Chinatown's most noted photographer, depicts the ordinary Chinese immigrant men who comprised the vast majority of Chinatown's population during the pre-1906 era. It also depicts a typical alleyway-turned-commercial corridor. Genthe's photographs appeared after the earthquake and fire of 1906 destroyed the "old" Chinatown and became immensely popular because they documented what was "lost." FN-02325. Courtesy of California Historical Society.

neighborhood. Touring Chinatown by day to gaze upon its picturesque features, adventurous tourists would return at night, hoping to penetrate behind façades, beneath surfaces, and even beyond social divides. Almost overnight, professional tour guides emerged to exploit this new interest. Invariably, they offered what they thought eastern tourists really wanted: brief visits to the neighborhood's temples, theaters, and restaurants, and then extended tours through underground networks of gambling halls and opium dens—the extent of which was greatly exaggerated. Many guides took advantage of Chinatown's steep hills, leading tourists downhill through the connected basements of adjoining buildings to create the illusion of descent six or seven stories below ground before returning along the same route. To complete the illusion, tour guides paid Chinese men to stage scenes of opium smoking, gambling, and knife fighting.

Chinatown's merchants had long resented the racist depictions of Chinese culture that pervaded popular literature, and they despised white guides and their working-class Chinese accomplices for perpetuating such images in their own neighborhood. As proud members of Chinatown's huiguans, most merchants also envied the growing wealth and power of Chinatown's tongs. At the turn of the century, these merchants thus set out to undermine the tongs, improve Chinatown's image, and ultimately capture control of Chinatown's burgeoning tourism industry. Welcoming support from public officials (including Chinese consul general Ho Yow), they launched two projects. They began to "clean up" Chinatown by curbing vice operations, improving infrastructure, and fighting epidemic disease. At the same time, they began to redirect touristic attention away from the neighborhood's network of gambling halls and opium dens and toward the aspects of Chinatown that *they* considered (or at least could sell as) culturally "authentic," including architectural elements, theatrical productions, imported curios, and gourmet cuisine. The reconstruction of Chinatown after the earthquake and fire of 1906 advanced both projects. Fulfilling the vision of Chinatown business owner Look Tin Eli and other merchant elites, the new Chinatown of the 1910s and 1920s featured what mass tourism conditioned an incoming wave of middle-class tourists to want and expect: a modernized infrastructure and a Sinocized façade. Two buildings constructed at the intersection of California and Grant offered a microcosm of this combination (Fig. 14). The buildings themselves were four-story, steel-framed commercial structures that might be found in any modern city, yet the buildings were distinguished by Sinocized additions to the exterior such as pagoda-like towers, upward-curving eaves, and bright color schemes popularly associated with "authentic" Chinese buildings. The fact that these and other buildings incorporated architectural elements specific to Beijing (but largely unknown in Guangdong Province, where most Chinatown residents came from) reflected merchants' growing inclination to think of Chinatown as a tourist destination more than a community. For many merchants, Chinatown was a spectacle to be shaped *for* the eyes of tourists rather than a neighborhood to be shaped *by* the lived experiences of its residents.

In the short run, efforts to "clean up" Chinatown improved living conditions in the neighborhood and satisfied middle-class tourists' demands for safety and comfort. Moreover, efforts to focus attention on Chinatown's façade reduced tourists' long-tolerated intrusiveness. During the 1930s, however, merchants' success in capturing control of the tourism industry began to reveal a long-term cost. Chinatown had changed in fundamental ways by the 1930s. The intended impact of the Chinese Exclusion Act finally hit Chinatown around the turn of the

Fig. 14. "San Francisco's famous Chinatown, the largest outside of China itself," ca. 1925. This photograph depicts the tourist's Chinatown as it had emerged by the late 1920s. The photograph captures the best-known "look" of Chinatown, including the two buildings at California and Grant (with their pagoda-like towers and upward-curving eaves) as well as one of the many street lamps installed in 1925. FN-31754. Courtesy of California Historical Society.

century, and Chinatown's population dropped below ten thousand during the 1910s. But mortality and the out-migration of Chinese men (and a new influx of Chinese women during the 1920s) allowed gender ratios to balance, the proportion of families to grow, and the population to climb. As a new generation of American-born Chinese San Franciscans came of age during the 1930s and 1940s, many Chinatown residents sought to further modernize and, indeed, "Americanize" Chinatown. Yet merchant elites blocked their efforts, forcing compromises evident, for example, in a public housing project that garnered more attention because of its Sinocized façade than its insufficient capacity. First proposed in 1939 and finally completed in 1951, the Ping Yuen housing complex featured yellow roof tiles, a dragon motif on the exterior, and an entrance modeled after the Paliou Gate at the Yellow Monastery in Beijing. But more than 500 low-income families applied for only 232 available units, and, in a telling oversight, none of the units were set aside for the aging bachelors displaced by construction of the project itself.

During the second half of the twentieth century, this pattern only repeated; Chinatown's merchants continued to control the tourism industry, and the Chinatown they crafted for tourists' consumption was almost entirely divorced from the lives of the neighborhood's residents. Charlie Low's Forbidden City offered a prime example. The interior of the famous nightclub was lavishly decorated with colorful tapestries, urns, and hanging lanterns, but the nightly floor show, featuring an "all-Chinese" cast performing American show tunes, was the key attraction. Performed without pretense of assimilation, the floor show crystallized a sense of "Chinese" identity for tourists, and it anchored that identity in Chinatown. To help complete the charade, Low required many performers to change their names; thus Tony Costa (a dancer of Chinese, Filipino, Portuguese, and Spanish descent), for example, became Tony Wing.

While business at the Forbidden City boomed during the 1950s and into the 1960s, Chinatown was becoming an immigrant community once again. Assimilationist second- and third-generation Chinese San Franciscans left Chinatown for suburban neighborhoods around the Bay Area, but immigrants fleeing poverty and political turmoil in China and Southeast Asia poured in, pushing the population of a physically expanded Chinatown toward fifty thousand during the 1960s. Not surprisingly, older merchants and new investors (arriving from Hong Kong and elsewhere) encouraged tourists to look past the conditions that shaped most of these new residents' lives during the 1970s and 1980s—substandard housing, skyrocketing rents, sweatshop working conditions, poor public health, inadequate schools, gang violence, and chronic poverty.

For their own part, Chinatown's residents faced a daunting task as the twentieth century came to a close: sustaining a sense of community among longtime residents and diverse newcomers who lived in a neighborhood shaped by tourism but otherwise neglected by the city that surrounded it. Stirred by ethnic pride, young Chinese Americans from throughout the Bay Area tried to help; they wanted Chinatown recognized as more than the "mystical land of Buddhas, jade, silk, carved ivory, herbs, and bazaars" that guidebooks continued to tout, and they demanded a renewed effort to modernize the neighborhood.[1] Yet the Loma Prieta earthquake of 1989 and the terrorist attacks of 2001 awakened Chinatown's newest advocates to a long-standing reality. In both cases, sharp declines in tourist revenues cut deeply into Chinatown's economy. Thus even as Chinatown's residents and supporters celebrated Chinatown as a distinct, dynamic, and enduring community, they realized that the community's economic vitality depended upon those who thought of Chinatown as little more than a tourist destination—when they thought of it at all.

Colonial Williamsburg

Williamsburg, Virginia

Anders Greenspan

Since its conception in the 1920s, Colonial Williamsburg has served as an American cultural landmark, emphasizing ideals that its founders saw as integral to the American experience. Episcopal rector W. A. R. Goodwin and philanthropist John D. Rockefeller, Jr., the men who created Colonial Williamsburg, both wished to use the restored capital of Virginia as a site to demonstrate the ideals of democracy, individualism, and representative government—values they believed would sustain Americans through challenges of depression and war. Only in the 1970s did Colonial Williamsburg become a social-history museum dedicated to presenting the lives of the wide variety of people who lived in the eighteenth-century town, placing greater emphasis on the lives of African-Americans, women, and working people. Williamsburg became the capital of Virginia in 1698 and remained so until 1780, when the state government decamped inland to Richmond during the Revolutionary War. Thereafter, and especially after the Civil War, Williamsburg's colonial heart languished as a modern town slowly grew around it, and by the early twentieth century, the few remaining vestiges of the colonial era had fallen into disrepair. The present incarnation of Colonial Williamsburg began in the mid-1920s, when Goodwin, rector of Bruton Parish Church in Williamsburg, sought outside funding for his plan to restore the now dilapidated twentieth-century town to its glorious eighteenth-century form. This would, of course, require substantial economic backing, which Goodwin found in Rockefeller, heir to the Standard Oil fortune, who saw Williamsburg's potential as a place to re-create his vision of the eighteenth century and its importance in the establishment of American values. After much consideration and having viewed architectural plans for Colonial Williamsburg, Rockefeller agreed to fund the restoration and reconstruction project. Ultimately, he and his sons would donate $70 million to Colonial Williamsburg. In so doing, they funded the first modern historical restoration in the United States, which has led to a wide variety of preservation, restoration, and reconstruction efforts across the country.

The restoration itself focused on 301 acres in the middle of Williamsburg, the area where the onetime colonial capital had stood. The project was less a restoration than an exercise in clearance and re-creation. More than 80 buildings survived from the colonial period, but 720 structures built after the colonial period were deemed detractions from the colonial townscape that Goodwin envisioned. A few townspeople questioned plans to invite outside interests to direct the incorporation of public space and make the town into a museum, with one likening it to "a butterfly pinned to a card in a glass cabinet," but Goodwin's project gained approval. The Colonial Williamsburg Foundation, funded generously by Rockefeller, directed the demolition of post-1780s structures and the painstaking re-creation of the landmark Governor's Palace and Capitol, as well as shops, taverns, stables, and other buildings amid fields, sweeping lawns, formal gardens, and open-air markets (Fig. 15). Originally a much-sanitized version of a colonial town, Colonial Williamsburg later added sheep to graze its fields and other accoutrements that made for more realistic "living history" in the so-called Historic Area.

In the early years of Colonial Williamsburg, most visitors were either from the area or wealthier people who had ventured down from the Northeast, anxious to see what one of the nation's wealthiest families had created. To facilitate visitation, Colonial Williamsburg constructed the Williamsburg Inn in 1937 as a luxury hotel for the town's wealthier clientele. The Williamsburg Lodge, completed in 1939, added more affordable accommodations. Although the Depression and World War II stalled visitor growth, a large number of Americans followed the progress of the restoration through a variety of popular magazines such as *House and Garden*. Visiting the restoration might have been a financial impossibility for many Americans during its first decades, but they were able to copy the style of wallpapers and paints popularized by Colonial

Fig. 15. Duke of Gloucester Street, once an ordinary street, was re-imagined in the 1920s as a colonial streetscape flanked by reconstructed colonial houses and buildings. The Colonial Williamsburg Foundation later reserved the street for pedestrian use, adding to its efforts to achieve a more believable colonial atmosphere. Courtesy of J. Mark Souther.

Williamsburg, as well as emulate the type of gardens that were created for the restored town.

The most important phase of Colonial Williamsburg's development as a tourist destination began shortly after World War II. Many veterans, especially those who had visited the restoration from nearby military bases as a treat of the Rockefellers, returned to the city with families in tow. In the process, they established the role of the middle-class visitor in a site that had previously been the vacation spot of the well-to-do. Colonial Williamsburg had to change its way of doing business as it became a mass marketer of the eighteenth-century experience to millions of Americans. The foundation added Williamsburg Woodlands and the Governor's Inn in the 1950s to handle the soaring number of middle-class guests. In addition to these facilities, entrepreneurs opened a large number of hotels in the town of Williamsburg to handle the dramatic increase in tourist numbers. The construction of the Information Center (later called the Visitor Center) was another important ingredient in promoting this change. The restoration also forbade visitors' cars from being parked on the streets of the Historic Area. This meant the restoration needed to incorporate a bus service that would drop the visitors off in the Historic Area when they started their visit and one that would return them to the Visitor Center.

When visitors arrived at Williamsburg they encountered a selective version of the past preferred by the Rockefellers. Until the late 1970s, the restoration promoted a positive, nationalistic vision of the American past that smoothed over troublesome colonial issues including slavery, class conflict, and relations with Native Americans. As a result, the point of Colonial Williamsburg was more indoctrination into what it meant to be "American" than an education in historical complexity—a point that was clearly promoted in the restoration's introductory film, *Williamsburg—The Story of a Patriot*. The film portrayed the events in Williamsburg leading up to the start of the Revolution through the eyes of a fictional character, John Fry. The strong nationalistic message in the film positioned historical tourism as a civic education tool in the fight against communism. Colonial Williamsburg served as a popular stop on the itineraries of visiting foreign dignitaries, such as Britain's Queen Elizabeth and Crown Prince Akihito of Japan. *The Story of a Patriot* has been showing in the Visitor Center since it opened in 1957 and is anachronistic at best.

By the time of the nation's bicentennial in 1976, Colonial Williamsburg's presentation of the past seemed outdated. Visitors were now more skeptical of such patriotic and whitewashed treatments of the past, and many wrote to Colonial Williamsburg to complain about the unrealistic historical portrait on view. Increasingly aware of the Civil Rights, women's, and American Indian movements (among others), many of those who went to Williamsburg wanted to know more about the role of African-Americans, women, Native Americans, working-class whites, and others in the eighteenth century. This shift in visitors' interests moved Colonial Williamsburg in the direction of a presentation based more solidly on a growing body of information that social historians were producing during the 1970s. With a $400,000 grant from AT&T and the hiring of colonial-era social historian Cary Carson to guide the implementation of the new program, Colonial Williamsburg changed the focus. Carson created a program called "Becoming Americans," which would focus on the social and political ways in which Americans in eighteenth-century Williamsburg moved toward their independence from Britain, while also highlighting the roles of previously underrepresented groups.

This new program entailed grafting social history onto the base of the restoration's presentation of political history. A program about women's lives, called "According to the Ladies," presented the first views of women's history at Colonial Williamsburg. Further changes included the reconstruction of slave cabins at the Carter's Grove property to assist in the restoration's interpretation of rural slavery. The foundation also added presentations involving trades such as brick making and printing to broaden the interpretation of those people who worked as laborers in the eighteenth century. These new programs seemed to increase interest in the restoration; by the mid- to late 1980s, Colonial Williamsburg attendance was steadily increasing, peaking at 1.1 million visitors in 1985.

By the mid-1990s, the venture into social history had transformed the restoration, but many critics still felt that Colonial Williamsburg relied too much on its traditional political origins and had not fully embraced the move toward social history. In an attempt to answer its critics and broaden its portrayal of African-American life during the eighteenth century, the restoration re-created a slave auction, which although historically accurate, stirred controversy. Ultimately, the Colonial Williamsburg Foundation retreated from such dramatic portrayals of slavery, fearing that its family-friendly reputation might be damaged by promoting topics that, while historically correct, could also be emotionally traumatic for some visitors, especially children. The goal of presenting history in a way that can be viewed and accepted by a large audience inevitably places strains on Colonial Williamsburg. The foundation has thus designated certain programs as being child friendly, while warning that others involve a considerable amount of adult content.

In this manner, Colonial Williamsburg has continued grafting social history onto political history into the early twenty-first century. Yet after the events of September 11, 2001, growing fear of travel coupled with the foundation's failure (or choice, given its need to maintain a sanitized version of history to appeal to the broadest audience) to develop any major new programs caused a decline in visitation and revenues. Administrators made dramatic personnel cuts in order to avoid running a deficit. In so doing, the restoration unwittingly created a ghost town, with few interpreters and little chance for visitors to interact with those who could help them better understand the past. A resulting air of malaise hung over

Fig. 16. A costumed interpreter narrates a tour outside the reconstructed Capitol, which is a focal point for Colonial Williamsburg's "Revolutionary City," a living-history experience that seeks to transport tourists back to the 1770s. Courtesy of J. Mark Souther.

the restoration, creating an uninviting environment for visitors who, once they resumed traveling, sought out destinations that appeared to have more to offer than Colonial Williamsburg.

Starting in 2005, Colonial Williamsburg's administrators drew up plans once again to reshape the presentation of the past. Since the site was considered to be "colonial," the traditional emphasis had been on presenting the town's history up to 1774. Yet under a new program called the "Revolutionary City," the foundation is now introducing the American Revolution into its presentation of Williamsburg's past (Fig. 16). This new presentation incorporates vignettes of street theater that place historical interpreters and visitors together around some of the major sites of Colonial Williamsburg. This program, which debuted in spring 2006, is a lively way to broaden the interpretive scope of the restoration and to place the emphasis on the variety of people who lived in Williamsburg in the eighteenth century, not simply its famous white men.

In order to maximize visitation, Colonial Williamsburg also markets itself as a luxury resort. The Golf Club and the Spa, along with the Regency Dining Room at the Inn, cater to wealthy patrons. The foundation also offers facilities for business meetings and families, but this desire to promote an air of exclusivity dates back to the Rockefellers. As a result of the relatively high-ticket prices and charges for rooms and food, there is no doubt that Colonial Williamsburg excludes those on a strict budget, as a weekend vacation for a family of four can cost easily upward of $500.

In addition to these programs, Colonial Williamsburg has altered its presentation of rural slavery, which got a rocky start at Carter's Grove. The foundation invested millions of dollars in the Carter's Grove property, including the building of an archeological museum, but attendance was poor and the property was sold. As a replacement, Colonial Williamsburg constructed a new site to demonstrate life on a mid-level plantation. Named Great Hopes, this smaller plantation is being constructed along the footpath from the Visitor Center to the Historic Area. Great Hopes's owners would have worked alongside their slaves, as opposed to Carter's Grove, where there was a dramatic difference in position between the plantation owners and their slaves. Great Hopes brings to light the close contact that existed between master and slave on smaller plantations.

Colonial Williamsburg has succeeded over the past eighty-five years because of its adaptability to changes in American society and tourism. This ability to reinvent itself for changing tastes and historical trends has kept the site in the public eye and on the tourist map. The different managers of the site today have reached an accommodation with its mass audience that combines historical education, commercialism, and a heavy dose of nostalgia.

Cooperstown,
New York

William S. Walker

Cooperstown, New York, is best known as the home of the National Baseball Hall of Fame. Founded in 1939, the hall is one of the country's most popular museums, attracting approximately three hundred thousand visitors each year. As a shrine to baseball and a symbol of physical achievement, Cooperstown holds a privileged spot in the minds of baseball players, fans, and sports reporters. As an actual upstate New York village and a tourist destination, Cooperstown both uses this image to its advantage and struggles with the limitations such a perception creates. While its identity as a baseball town grew over the course of the twentieth century, older identities were subsumed. Although it has remained a resort community for upper- and middle-class vacationers, it is no longer the rural village at the heart of a thriving farming region. The "lovely village" on the shores of "pristine" Otsego Lake is still there for those who care to look, but many if not most of Cooperstown's visitors look no further than the hall of fame, Doubleday Field, and the souvenir shops on Main Street before leaving town.[1]

Cooperstown's residents have witnessed three distinct eras that mirror larger trends in the history of tourism. In the nineteenth and early twentieth centuries, it was a summer resort community that had the added attraction of having played a key role in the novels of James Fenimore Cooper. In the mid-twentieth century, it became a destination for touring motorists who went to visit its new cultural institutions: the hall of fame and the New York State Historical Association. Finally, in the late twentieth and early twenty-first centuries, it transformed into a baseball bonanza, where visitors could attend fantasy camps, purchase all manner of memorabilia, and worship their athletic idols. Rare among upstate New York communities, Cooperstown has survived more than a century and a half as a popular destination. While other tourist locales, such as the Catskills and Saratoga, have faded considerably from their heyday in the nineteenth century, Cooperstown has continued to attract a large number of visitors each year. Such sustained popularity is attributable to the foresight, boosterism, and patronage of two families: the Coopers and the Clarks.

James Fenimore Cooper's bestselling novels *The Pioneers* (1823) and *The Deerslayer* (1841) first brought Cooperstown to the American popular consciousness. In these works, Cooper fictionalized locations and events from the early history of the village, which his father William Cooper had founded in 1786. A land speculator with grand ambitions, William had ventured from New Jersey to upstate New York shortly after the American Revolution in order to secure claim to former Iroquois lands. Exploiting the disruptions the Revolution caused in Native and non-Native populations, he was able to bring a large number of settlers into central New York within a few years and, as a result, amassed a large fortune. Envisioning the village as a market center for surrounding farms, William Cooper laid out Cooperstown at the foot of Otsego Lake, a ten-mile-long glacial lake that is the starting point of the Susquehanna River.[2]

Struggling with the complexities of his father's legacy, James Fenimore Cooper fashioned a fictionalized version of Cooperstown, which he called Templeton. This imagined locale became exceedingly popular among American readers in the nineteenth century and spurred a desire among some to visit the real Templeton. Cooper understood the symbiotic relationship between tourism and the romantic tales he crafted. Indeed, he deliberately chose settings that would have been familiar to visitors to the Hudson Valley and other regions of New York in the nineteenth century in order to enhance the allure and authenticity of his work.[3] Early tourism literature about the village made explicit mention of the connection between Cooper's novels and Cooperstown, and visitors looked for parallels between fictional settings and real-life locations.[4] (Even today, one can see a roadside marker for "Natty Bumppo" on the east side of the lake.)

In his novels, Cooper touted the many extraordinary natural qualities of what is now the Leatherstocking Region of New York State—named after the hero of the series of Cooper's books collectively titled *The*

Leatherstocking Tales. Cooper lived in Cooperstown for a number of years and foresaw its potential as a leisure destination. In 1838, he wrote that "were an effort made, even now, by the erection of proper lodging houses, the establishment of reading rooms and libraries, and the embellishment of a few of the favorable spots, in the way of public promenades and walks, it strikes us that it would be quite easy to bring the place into request, as one of resort for the inhabitants of the large towns during the warm months."[5] As the nineteenth century progressed, this idea of Cooperstown as a resort village came to fruition. In the last three decades of the nineteenth century, Cooperstown and Otsego Lake became popular summer destinations for upper- and middle-class vacationers. Similar to other locales throughout the Northeast, Cooperstown benefited from the emergence of vacationing as a common activity for Americans in the late nineteenth century.[6] Improvements in transportation facilitated this process. After 1870, the combination of railroad and stagecoach lines and steamship routes allowed for relatively easy and inexpensive access to Otsego Lake and its surrounding towns. Seeking a healthful retreat from the increasingly crowded and hectic life of the city, visitors to Cooperstown in this period enjoyed picnics, dances, boat rides, croquet parties, and camping.[7]

From its heyday as a resort destination, Cooperstown might have easily declined, as did so many other upstate New York vacation towns, if not for the patronage of a single family, the Clarks, whose history in the village dates to the mid-nineteenth century, but whose influence was felt most keenly in the twentieth century. In 1854, Edward Clark purchased land in Cooperstown, his wife's hometown, and erected a stone mansion called Fernleigh. Clark had accumulated his wealth as the business partner of Isaac M. Singer, the inventor of the Singer sewing machine and, as a result, was well positioned to bequeath a large fortune to his heirs. Freed from the pressures of earning a living, Clark's descendants were able to focus their energies on philanthropic and creative pursuits.[8]

Edward's grandsons, Edward Severin Clark and Stephen C. Clark, Sr., did more than anyone else to build lasting institutions in Cooperstown and establish a basis for continued tourism in the village. In the early to mid-twentieth century, they oversaw construction of a cultural infrastructure that ensured the village's sustained popularity as a tourist locale. As the automobile came to dominate the touring landscape, this cultural infrastructure, along with the physical infrastructure of state highways, brought families to Cooperstown eager to find entertainment and enrichment through "authentic" encounters with the American past, both real and imagined.⁹

Inspired by the purchase of a baseball that according to local legend had belonged to Abner Doubleday, whom sporting goods magnate Albert G. Spalding had erroneously identified as the inventor of baseball in 1908, Stephen Clark led an effort in the mid-1930s to construct a baseball museum in Cooperstown. Opening on June 12, 1939, during what at the time was thought to be the centennial of baseball's creation, the National Baseball Hall of Fame honored baseball's great players and managers and preserved objects associated with them. Inductees included among others Connie Mack, Cy Young, Walter Johnson, Honus Wagner, Grover Alexander, Christy Mathewson, and Babe Ruth. Along with Doubleday Field, a baseball stadium erected as a Works Progress Administration project during the Great Depression, the hall of fame stood (and continues to stand) on Main Street in the heart of the village. Starting as a two-room museum, the hall has been expanded multiple times from the 1950s to the present, and the Clark family continues to play an integral role in the museum with Jane Forbes Clark serving as its chairman (Fig. 17).¹⁰

Many of the museum's displays constitute secular shrines to beloved teams and outstanding players, such as Mickey Mantle and Roberto Clemente. Red Sox fans can worship, for example, at the foot of Curt Shilling's bloody sock from the 2004 World Series while Yankees fans can take comfort in ogling Hideki Matsui's bat. Other exhibits, however, offer a more historical and contextualized perspective on America's pastime. An exhibit on the Negro Leagues discusses the triumphs and struggles of black ballplayers before and after the integration of the major leagues, and an exhibit on the life and career of Hank Aaron displays the hate mail he received as he pursued and eclipsed Babe Ruth's home-run record. Other sections of the museum present the early history of the game in the nineteenth century, the story of the women's professional league made famous by the film *A League of Their Own*, and Latino participation in baseball both in the United States and abroad. Moreover, for the acolytes of Sabermetrics, the museum contains an entire room of baseball statistics. Finally, at the heart of the museum is the great hall containing plaques memorializing the 295 elected members of the hall of fame.¹¹

In addition to the hall, another of Stephen Clark's successful cultural projects involved the New York State Historical Association (NYSHA).

Fig. 17. Tourists view the Baseball Hall of Fame's main attraction—its great hall, with its memorial plaques. Courtesy of Andrew Wirtanen.

Founded in 1899, NYSHA was originally located in Ticonderoga but came to Cooperstown at Clark's invitation in 1939. Today, the association operates two museums in Cooperstown (Fenimore Art Museum and The Farmers' Museum), maintains a research library, curates large object and photograph collections, and operates history education programs throughout the state. The Fenimore Art Museum, which was founded in the mid-1940s, benefited from the art connoisseurship of Stephen Clark who assembled masterpieces for its collections from artists such as William Sidney Mount, Thomas Cole, and Gilbert Stuart, and helped the institution become a leading displayer of American folk art. Founded in 1942, The Farmers' Museum was one of the country's first living-history museums (Fig. 18). Located on farmland donated by Stephen Clark, the museum includes historic structures from across upstate New York, which it uses to interpret rural life in the nineteenth century. Inspired by the outdoor museums of Europe, the museum's progenitors, perhaps the most important of whom was folklorist Louis C. Jones, envisioned a site in which nineteenth-century handcrafts, farming techniques, and folk culture might be preserved and displayed. In order to complement the museum's work, in 1964, Jones and other museum staff developed one of

Fig. 18. Carriage ride at the Farmers' Museum in Cooperstown. The Farmers' Museum
is an open-air museum that re-creates upstate New York rural life in the 1840s through a
working farmstead and village. Courtesy of Anne White.

the first training programs for museum professionals, the Cooperstown
Graduate Program. Together, NYSHA's various pursuits bring New York
State history and culture to thousands of schoolchildren and adult visitors
each year.[12]

In the late twentieth century, Cooperstown's popularity as baseball's
mecca dramatically expanded. Heightened public interest in the sport
and its history and memorabilia drew thousands to the village each
year, while unprecedented wealth accumulation among certain classes
of Americans enabled the expenditure of large sums of money on
baseball-related activities. Today, people continue to flood Cooperstown
each season to visit the hall of fame, participate in a game at Doubleday
Field, and shop at the souvenir stores. Visitation typically peaks during
induction weekend—especially when popular players, such as Cal Ripken,
Jr., and Tony Gwynn, are inducted. The popularity of the hall has led to
the expansion of baseball-related businesses not only in the immediate
vicinity of the village but also several miles outside of town. Since 1996,
the Cooperstown Dreams Park, a for-profit organization and not affiliated
with the hall of fame, has brought youth baseball teams to the area just
outside of the village to compete in weeklong tournaments.[13] With
parents and other family members in tow, players in cleats and Dreams

Park uniforms fill village streets and sidewalks from June to August, enthusiastically and sometimes brashly displaying their love for the game. According to longtime residents, this most recent phase of tourism has been disruptive to the lifestyles of year-round inhabitants. The dramatic expansion of souvenir shops on Main Street, for example, has reduced the number of other types of businesses that cater to the needs of residents. In addition, the large influx of summertime visitors can make it difficult for year-round residents who do not own a home to find long-term rentals.[14]

Although Cooperstown's primary identity derives from baseball, the sport is only one component—albeit a major one—of a web of institutions that make up the cultural life of an unusual village. In addition to the hall of fame, tourists can visit NYSHA's museums, follow Natty Bumppo's (fictional) footsteps, take in an opera at the Glimmerglass Opera Company, and sample Belgian ales at the Ommegang Brewery. Cooperstown in the twenty-first century is a place where highbrow and middlebrow cultural pursuits exist in relative harmony. Cooperstown has survived as a tourist destination for almost two centuries in part because of its natural beauty, but more importantly, because of the cultural entrepreneurship of the Coopers, Clarks, and others who have built businesses and institutions in and around the village. Embracing, and only occasionally examining critically, the romantic myths of the American past, whether regarding the settling of the frontier, the pastoral origins of baseball, or the handcrafts of nineteenth-century rural towns, Cooperstown's residents have made their village an attractive destination for people seeking an escape from the stresses of modern society.

Disneyland

Anaheim, California

J. Philip Gruen

It was a bold experiment. Amid orange groves in southern California's rural Anaheim in Orange County, an enormous theme park called Disneyland began to take shape in 1954. With its odd juxtaposition of a nineteenth-century main street, rockets, submarines, medieval castle, lakes, islands, steamboats, jungle cruise, haunted mansion, and miniature western mining settlement, there was little guarantee the 140-acre park—some twenty-six miles from downtown Los Angeles—would draw the visitors its heavy television marketing counted on for success. Yet approximately twenty thousand tourists poured forth when the gates officially swung open on July 17, 1955, and by 1958, Disneyland had already entertained more than ten million visitors.[1] Walter Elias Disney's park instantly transformed the physical landscape of Anaheim, southern California, and to a certain degree, the United States and the world.

In Disney's imagination, the transformation was intended to be cultural as well as physical. As tourists entered Disneyland, they abandoned a disconnected contemporary landscape of automobiles and sprawl and entered an ordered environment whose carefully wrought planning and design suggested new possibilities for community amid the cacophony of contemporary life. However fantastical, what was later dubbed the "happiest place on earth" was not purely an exercise in fantasy—it was a model environment that Disney hoped would reform the vagaries of the outside world. Disney intended his mass tourist experiment to inspire civilized behavior that would gradually transform American life and culture for the better.

Disney's dissatisfaction with the contemporary environment and his desire to change it developed slowly, and at a scale considerably smaller than what he eventually developed in Anaheim. Raised in the Midwestern cities of Chicago and Kansas City and on a farm in Marceline, Missouri, in the early twentieth century, Disney dabbled in a variety of jobs until his animation skill and entrepreneurial talent generated a permanent move to Los Angeles in 1923. He eventually opened Walt Disney Studios in Burbank, California, in 1937, having amassed a fortune producing animated movies whose popularity tapped into human desires to upend the natural order of things: particularly the wildly popular anthropomorphic talking mouse named Mickey—a creation of cartoonist Ub Iwerks. Tourists wished to visit the Burbank studios to see where Mickey and other Disney characters were created.

Yet the animation process did not provide much of a visitor spectacle, and Disney found the real world beyond the studios even less engaging. For the general American public—and kids in particular—Disney considered the available entertainment options dull, disorderly, and scattered. Merry-go-rounds, he thought, were repetitive and lackluster—their settings dirty, uninspiring, and run by "tough-looking people."[2] He did appreciate amusement parks for their mass appeal (indeed, by the late nineteenth century, amusement parks and pleasure piers in America attracted huge crowds, and popular zones of entertainment, or "midways," appeared in nearly every major world's fair), but he expressed distaste for their seemingly unregulated behavior.[3]

So, in the vicinity of his Burbank studios, Disney envisioned a comfortable, park-like setting where his animated figures could be brought to life—without the unpredictable happenings of the everyday world. Early renderings for a place called Disneylandia depict his vision: a miniature railroad, pathways, waterways, stagecoaches, and a series of civic buildings in a bucolic nineteenth-century landscape. Disney also began arrangements for a Kiddieland adjacent to the studios, where he hoped to instruct children about American heritage through historical reenactment. Meanwhile, he constructed a 1/8-scale railroad in the Burbank studios' machine shop for the garden of his nearby home in Holmby Hills.[4]

These plans suggested little about animated movies but much about Disney's desire to produce ideal, controlled environments that played upon a supposed collective American memory of the past—a past allegedly disappearing in the face of accelerated modernity in the postwar years. Disney himself had produced propaganda-ridden films for the

war effort and, in 1947, testified before the House Un-American Activities Committee against some of his employees for their supposed Com-
munist leanings.[5] One might read Disney's motives for Disneyland as
growing from this larger social and political context—one rife with the
confidence of technological advancement and American abundance but
tempered by Cold War anxieties and fears of the unknown. Although
the values of hard work and community may have become ingrained in
Disney during his early years on the Missouri farm, his desire to create
order from chaos perhaps derived more directly from the contemporary
situation.[6] Disneyland emerges as a physical response to this social and
political condition—an inspirational setting intended to reveal a bright-
er future.

Yet Disney knew that such settings needed more room than the densely
built Los Angeles metropolitan area could provide; that is, if they were to
have any significant impact. In 1952, Disney commissioned the Stanford
Research Institute to help select an appropriate site for his theme park,
and the institute recommended the Anaheim location for its temperate
weather and, at the time, freedom from haze and pollution.[7] The site's
proximity to the new Santa Ana Freeway also made it conveniently accessible to millions of people traveling by automobile from the Los Angeles
or San Diego metropolitan areas. Disney also hired a group of designers—
the so-called imagineers—to compose renderings, plans, and models for
the new development.

The design ideas were not engineered out of thin air. Precedents existed
for themed environments wielding architecture and planning as instruments of social change, and Disney had long understood the power of design on behavior. Disney's father was a construction worker for the 1893
World's Columbian Exposition in Chicago, where Baroque planning and
Beaux-Arts architecture ordered the freewheeling, speculative industrial
metropolis—even if technological advancements were highlighted inside
many of the buildings and the exposition itself was located three miles
south of downtown. By the 1930s, the outward appearance of world's
fairs—such as the 1939 Golden Gate International Exposition on San
Francisco's Treasure Island, which Disney visited—looked more directly
to the future, and they turned increasingly to major corporations for modern pavilions offering an up-to-date aesthetic. In 1950, Disney also visited
Copenhagen's mid-nineteenth-century Tivoli Gardens amusement park,

whose picturesque features in an urban setting suggested the civilizing effects of the natural environment on the human condition.

Yet as a model community suggesting something fundamental about American values, Disneyland descended more directly from the 1920s creation of Colonial Williamsburg. There, John D. Rockefeller, Jr., paid for the restoration and reconstruction of eighteenth-century buildings intended to recall a period when nascent ideas of democracy and representative government stirred among the townsfolk. Meanwhile, hundreds of nineteenth-century buildings were removed from the historic area and the less pleasant realities of eighteenth-century Southern life were selectively edited from the tourist landscape.[8] The restoration of Williamsburg aimed to symbolize the values of the founding fathers, thus educating visitors to become more virtuous citizens. Rockefeller wanted tourists brought back to a specific time and place: late eighteenth-century Williamsburg. For Disney, the specific place to which tourists would be carried mattered less than the transformative experience itself. He removed tourists from the ordinary environment beyond the park's earthen barriers and immersed them in an idyllic dream world that provided a glimpse of what the world *could* be—not just what it was. Indeed, upon entrance, tourists passed underneath a small plaque affixed to a narrow-gauge steam railroad viaduct informing them they had left "today" and entered the world of "yesterday, tomorrow and fantasy."

Still, the tourist entry sequence for Disneyland favored a specific *time*. After strolling past a Victorian-styled city hall, park-goers found themselves along an immaculate late nineteenth-century street with horse-drawn streetcars, gas lamps, and hanging signs advertising shops selling candies and gifts. This was Main Street U.S.A., the inspiration for which Disney apparently derived from his memory of the main street in Marceline, and some of the architectural inspiration for which imagineer Harper Goff based upon the built environment of his own hometown of Fort Collins, Colorado.[9] Yet the street was emblematic of Disney's values, an ideal version of urban America without physical deterioration, trash, automobiles, or the homeless. Buildings were miniaturized and manipulated at a forced perspective, not quite full size but seemingly taller than they actually were—a technique pioneered for stage sets in the movie industry intended to make the built environment appear more comforting and less threatening. The street was pure fantasy; no street in the "real" world was ever this clean, ordered, or miniaturized. But this was just the point.

Fig. 19. The final frontier: In Disneyland's Frontierland, a small, largely unobtrusive "M" to the left of the "Westward Ho!" nonetheless symbolizes the transformation of overland journey difficulties into a marketable commodity. What better way to symbolize the closing of the frontier than an immobile covered wagon selling McDonald's French fries? Courtesy of J. Philip Gruen.

Through design, Disney implored tourists to consider an ideal street; he thought that the world of everyday contemporary life could be informed, if not *re*-formed, through the practice of mass tourism. Along Main Street U.S.A., a romanticized notion of the past would generate the future.

Disney's desire for a better world hinged upon more than a single nostalgic street, however. Although crucial in illustrating Disney's motives, Main Street U.S.A. only comprised the entry (and exit) area of Disneyland. But the overall park had to be perfect in every way. As originally planned, tourists leaving Main Street U.S.A. could choose to visit one of four themed "lands"—Adventureland, Frontierland, Tomorrowland, and Fantasyland, each of which endeavored to further remove tourists from the ordinary. Fantasyland provided an immediate draw; the multi-turreted presence of the Sleeping Beauty Castle, modeled after Neuschwanstein Castle in the Bavarian Alps, terminated the main-street vista and invited tourists to step briefly through a friendly medieval setting with no danger of falling into the moat. The area beyond the castle offered rides with sets similar to those used in Disney's films, such as Peter Pan's Flight and Snow White's Scary Adventures. Adventureland, with its Jungle Cruise, brought

Fig. 20. Past and future collide: A horse-drawn streetcar plods toward Main Street U.S.A. while the elaborate "Astro Orbitor" ride, announcing the Tomorrowland entrance, looms in the background. Disneyland has long reached into other eras, real or imagined, to suggest alternatives for the present day. Courtesy of J. Philip Gruen.

tourists close to robotic hippos, elephants, and spear-wielding "natives" whose movements were controlled by a process Disney calls Audio-Animatronics. Frontierland, with its paddle-wheel steamboat called the *Mark Twain*, a mining town, and Disney staffers dressed in period garb (known as "cast members") attempted to return visitors to settlement conditions in the early American West (Fig. 19). Tomorrowland, meanwhile, imagined futuristic alternatives to traffic-clogging highways with its monorail, submarine voyage, and intergalactic travel rides and exhibits (Fig. 20). Disney also mandated a spotless environment throughout and established a rigorous training system for employees that focused upon courtesy and propriety to keep Disneyland's "guests"—its tourists—perpetually happy.[10]

Yet Disneyland never left "today" behind altogether, even if present-day conditions, by Walt Disney's standards, seemed in constant need of an upgrade. Contemporary, real-world concerns shaped Disneyland's early years: the Rocket to the Moon exhibit in Tomorrowland attempted to inspire American ingenuity and prowess during the 1950s space race; the Autopia ride, with its small cars that tourists steered around a track, desired to make more humane the experience of driving on nearby freeways. Even the Monsanto Chemical Company's House of the Future, opened in 1957, drew broadly upon contemporary architectural ideas with its modular, open plan and floor-to-ceiling windows rising from a reinforced concrete foundation. It also capitalized on existing technologies and materials, combining a microwave, dishwasher, intercom system, and push-button food-storage compartments with prefabricated walls, furniture, floors, ceilings, and cabinets—all of plastic—promoting the company as much as ideas of modern living. "Tomorrow," reported a promotional short advertising the 1,280-square-foot house, "is always built on today."[11] Some twenty million people reportedly walked through the house during its ten-year run.

The present occasionally wreaked havoc on the future. Opening day proved to be a public relations disaster, as temperatures soared above 100 degrees, the park was only three-quarters complete, the water fountains failed to operate, and freshly poured asphalt paving created mobility problems. In 1959, the political difficulties of the Cold War compelled Disneyland officials to deny Soviet Premier Nikita Khrushchev a visit to the Orange County park during his thirteen-day U.S. tour. Disneyland would grow in popularity, but it also became a victim of its own success. Not long after its opening, gas stations, parking lots, fast-food restaurants, and motels took advantage of the tourist traffic and encroached upon the site, hastening the demise of the once-prevalent orange groves for which the county was named. By the early 1960s, from Disney's perspective, the adjacent commercial strip amounted to aesthetic blight. This spurred him to pursue huge acreage in central Florida for an additional theme park—and better control over ancillary development.

Because of its emphasis on control and fantasy, Disneyland has also come to stand for predictability and artificiality. Critics, for example, have cast the terms *Disneyfication*, *Disneyization*, or *Disneyfied* upon anything in the real world for its dissembling character, whitewashing of the past, or repressive practices limiting personal freedoms.[12] When architect Charles Moore called Disneyland, in 1965, the "most important single piece of construction in the West in the past several decades," he applauded Disney's ability to provide an urban model from which sprawling southern California might learn, but cautioned that the most effectively designed spaces for "public" life might not be free—and might not be public at all.[13] Moreover, Disney's version of the past in Frontierland appears increasingly anachronistic, as it justifies the European-American conquest of the American West while simplifying the social and cultural complexities of the frontier.[14] And its exhibits in Adventureland continue to play upon age-old Western stereotypes about the lack of sophistication and barbarism among non-Western peoples and small-scale societies.[15]

Yet tourists have not been deterred. Despite its site limitations, Disneyland has continually expanded and updated its attractions to pique tourist interest. Since its 1955 opening, three additional "lands" have appeared: New Orleans Square in 1966, Bear Country (later Critter Country) in 1972, and in 1993, Mickey's Toontown, whose warped, cartoon-like buildings drew upon the set of the 1988 Disney movie *Who Framed Roger Rabbit?* In 2001, Disney's California Adventure Park (DCA) rose over the existing Disneyland parking lot with roller coasters; hotels and attractions conjuring a romantic image of an earlier California; and five themed lands of its own. Together with the original Disneyland, the overall Disneyland Resort now includes an admission-free "downtown" area with shops and restaurants and the massive Mickey and Friends parking structure for 10,000-plus vehicles. Presumably aided by more than five million people also visiting DCA, Disneyland hosted an unprecedented 14,870,000 visitors in 2007 alone—second only to Walt Disney World's Magic Kingdom as the world's most visited theme park.[16]

The Disneyland experience is still intended to be transformative, even if "today" has never dissolved completely into yesterday, tomorrow, or fantasy. In 2008, the Innoventions Dream Home opened its doors in Tomorrowland—another house of the future, but this time a sprawling five-thousand-square-foot dwelling with touch screens and sensors that automatically adjust each room's features to the entering individual, and sponsorship by electronic giants such as Microsoft, Hewlett-Packard, and Life|ware. Early twenty-first-century inventions are subtly meant to instruct tourists about a brave new world led by technological advancements; only a fin-de-siècle amalgamation of Craftsman and Art Nouveau design reminds visitors that the future still might best be tempered by the past. Yet sustainable materials, alternative power, and progressive ideas for compact, high-density living are nowhere to be found, their presence, perhaps, too redolent of today's concerns and not enough about dreaming a fantasy world where the problems of limited resources and suburban sprawl no longer exist.[17] One might wonder how notions of community would be fostered in a future marked by such excess, but should that vision become problematic, history suggests that the Walt Disney Company will re-design the exhibit. Disneyland, after all, has forever encouraged tourists to imagine a better world, and its success has hinged upon their willingness to oblige.

El Camino Real

California

Phoebe S. K. Young

The twenty-one Franciscan missions that dot the hills of the California coast number among the state's quintessential tourist destinations. Founded between 1769 and 1823, the California missions seem as intrinsic to the landscape as palm trees or freeways. They currently host approximately five million visitors per year, perhaps 750,000 of them schoolchildren on field trips, and for much of the past century were a compulsory stop on every California tour. For the many who have traveled El Camino Real, the mission road, and peeked in the chapel at Carmel, strolled the gardens in San Juan Capistrano, or lingered at the fountain in Santa Barbara, the missions have offered beguiling visions of California's past. They are both physical places, where visitors can explore history, and imaginative ones, which evoke the idea of California—its classic red-tile roofs, romantic Spanish ambience, and sunny good life.[1]

Among the earliest extant structures in the state, California's missions unquestionably represent unique historic sites. But that alone would not ensure crowds of visitors or cultural significance. How and why the missions rose to iconic status is a story of cultural entrepreneurship and audiences eager for regional public memories. In the early twentieth century, a group of Anglo boosters, many of them women, seized on the missions as quaint and exotic places with Spanish flavor. They raised funds to restore the aging buildings to an imagined splendor. Booster goals, however, reached beyond historic preservation; they promoted a past that worked with visions of modernity, including automobile travel and business opportunities. This was a past, they argued, that could pay. The business-booster alliance was a familiar one in California politics, and in this instance it resonated with Progressive-era trends, from good roads to women's initiatives. Mission boosters fashioned resilient links between bygone days and bright futures that proved key to California's cultural identity in the first half of the twentieth century. Even after the heyday of a Camino Real tour passed, mission themes have continued to echo.

The history and physical appearance of the missions did not always match the legend, but boosters saw potential even in crumbling adobe. Whether in the heart of California's largest cities or tucked in remote foothills, mission buildings were built of stone, or more commonly, of whitewashed adobe and terra-cotta tile. Some were simple, unadorned structures, but the more elaborate among them included picturesque belfries, arcaded breezeways, and enclosed patios—Spanish colonial architectural elements that have come to epitomize California's "mission style." Most have been heavily restored, often from near ruined states, with original decorations and furnishings rarely present. Today, the structures exist in varying approximations of original appearance and degrees of physical soundness, and all require constant maintenance.

Ruins or restorations, missions as tourist sites sometimes suggest a more comfortable life than befits their history as eighteenth- and nineteenth-century frontier settlements. From San Diego north to Sonoma, Fray Junípero Serra led members of the Franciscan Order in establishing missions as colonial religious institutions. Their main purposes were converting Indian populations and strengthening Spain's hold on its remote colony. Mission friars aspired to self-sufficient dominion, raising vast herds of cattle and planting millions of acres with grains, olives, and fruit. By 1832, the missions had recorded more than 80,000 baptisms (and more than 60,000 deaths) of Native California people. Missionization brought harsh treatment and devastating disease to native communities. Indian people alternately resisted and adapted to the new regime, finding ways to sustain and express their cultures. Until recently, remnants of this struggle have been difficult to find at the missions. Much Indian artwork has been whitewashed, gravestones name more friars than Indians, and no placard denotes the location of the old whipping post.

During the middle decades of the nineteenth century, the newly independent Mexican government transformed the missions dramatically. Through a program known as secularization, the missions became parish churches and lost most of their worldly goods and powers. Indians were released from mission obligations but given little assistance in the transition to civilian life. By the time California entered the United States in 1850, many of the mission buildings had been sold into private hands, abandoned and left to molder. Except for a few of the best preserved and those still operated by the Church, as in San Francisco and Santa Barbara, many slipped into ruin.

The hundreds of thousands of newcomers drawn to California in the decades following the gold rush generally ignored the decaying missions. With tourists clustered by railroad companies in a few cities and resorts, missions remained an afterthought, oddities in a California advertised largely for its winning climate and economic vigor. If anything, tourists were dissuaded from visiting the missions. A visitor to San Francisco in the 1880s, for example, might have purchased a stereograph card of Mission Dolores only to learn from the caption that the building did include numerous reminders "associated with the early history of California, but would hardly interest you."

The 1884 publication of Helen Hunt Jackson's melodramatic bestselling novel *Ramona*, which set a Cinderella-style romance against an idyllic Spanish Californian backdrop, piqued interest in the mission past. Intended to protest the mistreatment of mission Indians, *Ramona* struck readers more for its lush description of the pastoral good life of the "old Spanish days." Tourists flocked to southern California ranchos and missions mentioned in the novel, hoping to catch a glimpse of a vanishing past. Boosters tested the market potential of Spanish exotica, which promised to add a mysterious European past to the state's modern outlook. *Ramona* touched off a growing impulse among Anglo Californians to appropriate selected elements of Spanish, Mexican, and Indian culture for their own purposes. Anglo fascination with an imagined Spanish-ness lent California a distinctive tourist lure, while at the same time, by consigning all things Spanish to a bygone past, came to endorse an Anglicized regional future. This connection was not lost on the putative objects of this nostalgia, Mexican and Indian people who struggled for political footing in the present.

Charles Fletcher Lummis, foremost impresario of Los Angeles and the Southwest, turned the missions into a local cause célèbre. Easily one of the era's most eccentric public figures, Lummis dedicated all his faculties as an author, journalist, editor, adventurer, collector, photographer, and lecturer to the cause of raising regional consciousness about the pre-Anglo past. Habitually clad in a green corduroy suit, red Navajo-style sash, and battered sombrero, he promoted Spanish and Indian heritage and himself with equal fervor. Lummis repeatedly featured mission history and preservation in the pages of the widely distributed magazines he edited for the Los Angeles Chamber of Commerce. No fan of *Ramona*, Lummis nonetheless preferred the mythic version of mission life to its more contentious histories. His articles extolled the heroism of the Franciscans, the bringing of "civilization" to California and the alluring beauty of the sites themselves. With this vision in mind, Lummis harangued locals on the economic value of the tourist appeal: "the old missions are worth more money than our oil, our oranges, or even our climate!"

Lummis created spectacle but the energetic boosters that succeeded him, led by ambitious newcomer Mrs. Harrie Forbes, put the missions on the modern tourist map. Forbes had been searching for an outlet for her public and business interests; along with other "social housekeeping" pursuits Progressive-era women initiated, historic preservation offered a platform for public expression. In 1906, Forbes seized on the idea to lobby the state to build a singular, paved road linking the missions, to be called El Camino Real. The plan gathered diverse advocates—clubwomen, preservationists, chambers of commerce, and automobile clubs—who shared a vision both romantic and economic. This road would offer a path to the dreamy Spanish past of pious padres and still patios, dashing caballeros and sultry senoritas, a unique historical experience for which visitors would open their pocketbooks.

Mission boosters mapped and marked a route for El Camino Real in hopes of creating the expectation of a road that the state had no choice but to pave. By the 1920s, the mission road had gained specific inclusion in the new state highway system, then being constructed with funds from legislative appropriations. But before its official designation, it had become etched on the cultural map, in large part due to the emblematic road marker designed by Forbes herself: a replica mission bell, hung on a twenty-five-foot-high standard, with directional signs. Between 1906 and 1915, Forbes's Camino Real Association organized the funds and placement of more than four hundred bells along the anticipated six-hundred-mile route from Sonoma to San Diego, offering travelers simultaneous geographical and historical positioning (Fig. 9). Forbes

Fig. 9. Mission Dolores in San Francisco's Mission District is among the twenty-one surviving Franciscan missions connected by El Camino Real. The bell marker in the foreground is one of the more than four hundred placed along the road in the early 1900s. Courtesy of Wally Gobetz.

seized the opportunity to establish a foundry that manufactured both these markers and miniature souvenir versions. With the growing popularity of Southwestern travel and the increase in automobile tourism, by World War I, tourists began to discover the missions en masse. In 1918, California passed its first comprehensive state highway bill, designating El Camino Real as one of two primary highways.

The automobile became the main vehicle through which travelers experienced the missions, the road as much a destination as the buildings themselves. Tourists often wrote of their travels "in the footsteps of the padres," and marveled at the contrast between the friars' sandals and dusty path and their modern machines and gleaming pavement. Even more frequently, tourists loved to pose their car (with or without its passengers) in front of missions, visually highlighting the distance between the crumbling adobe and the sleek auto. Visitors could even buy postcards that replicated the experience for them, offering views of anonymous automobiles in front of various missions.

Tourists put themselves (and their machines) at the center of the Camino Real experience in part because the missions appeared empty of people (Fig. 10). Both the missions and the Indian populations they once housed were imagined to belong to an ancient past. For those who toured the quiet hallways, Native people seemed merely remnants or ghostly presences. Missions gave visitors very few clues about present-day Native communities and eschewed "living history" presentations even in the 1930s and later when other sites in California and across the nation found this approach a popular one. If reenactors helped other sites come alive, missions seemed most evocative when vacant.

Accordingly, San Juan Capistrano gained fame less for its human history than for hosting flocks of birds and fictional bandits. The annual return of migrating cliff swallows, first noted in 1915 and quickly adopted as Capistrano's brand, sparked fascination, popular songs, live radio broadcasts, seasonal fairs, and a predictable increase in tourist traffic into the present day. Capistrano also became the setting for Johnston McCulley's 1919 novella, *The Curse of Capistrano*, made and remade into dozens of Zorro films between the 1920s and the twenty-first century. Missions appeared frequently as the backdrop for golden-age Hollywood films, associating them with a kind of romance and adventure unrelated to either their colonial histories or local Indian populations. Seeing missions as empty of human presence made them both handy vessels for film sets and inviting stages on which tourists might play starring roles. Elements of mission "style" thus became readily available for appropriation in domestic architecture, with red-tile roofs and patios providing an attractive real-life backdrop for modern California lifestyles.

By mid-century, the abstracted mission metaphor was everywhere, whether in architectural quotations or in the names of places and businesses across the state. If some of the tourist mania for Spanish romance waned in the decades following World War II, the status of the missions as California itself had become fixed. In the 1940s, the state school system began to sponsor annual educational visits and mission-focused curricula. Millions of California kids have built a piece of the Camino Real; sugar-cube mission dioramas remain a feature of fourth-grade state history lessons. New foundations and federal grants have appeared to protect their status as California heritage sites. Bell markers still stand along U.S. 101, the current designation for most of El Camino Real.

As places to visit, missions have remained relatively modest, the old-fashioned presentation surprising in light of the large visitation. Without the oversight of a unified tourist-oriented entity—the Catholic

Fig. 10. This cover illustration for an auto club magazine captures many elements of the mission tourist site—sleek modern cars, palm trees, picturesque landscape, quaintly aged adobe, and a placid Indian man leaning against a mission bell guidepost. The scene collapses time into an imagined space of romance, history and the good life which tourists were eager to inhabit. Raymond Winters, *Touring Topics*, August 1925. Courtesy of Automobile Club of Southern California Archives.

Church operates most and a few are maintained by the state as historic landmarks—the sites did not develop a coordinated theme to guide visitors' experience. The displays are uncomplicated, the gift shops unassuming. While missions often have more stuff, such as furniture, material objects, and interpretive panels, than in previous generations, sightseers continue to find stillness a defining feature of their visit.

As places of imagination, missions remain crucibles for the image of California's historical identity. Because of their significance to the state's self-image, missions have become important spaces for some to contest ethnic appropriation and invisibility. That little mention appears of the thousands of Indians buried on mission grounds has led some tribal groups to make claims on the presentation of their history. They have pressed for on-site acknowledgment of their ancestors' contributions to the building, decoration, and productive efforts of the missions and, perhaps most important, of the many Indian deaths there.

Indian activists successfully altered the landscape of remembrance in Sonoma by installing a Mission Indian Memorial in 1999. Etched into slabs of granite are the names of approximately nine hundred Coast Miwok, Pomo, Patwin, and Wappo men, women, and children who died at the mission between 1824 and 1839—their unmarked graves currently covered by parking lots, sidewalks, and gardens. This represents a small percentage of the tens of thousands of Indians who died at the missions, and it remains to be seen whether such actions will prompt major revisions in the public interpretation of the mission past or the tourist experience on El Camino Real. But with its style, deliberately reminiscent of the Vietnam Veterans Memorial in Washington, DC, the memorial reminds mission visitors of the history behind the red-tiled romance.

FANEUIL HALL MARKETPLACE
BOSTON, MASSACHUSETTS

Nicholas Dagen Bloom

Faneuil Hall Marketplace, a handsome collection of renovated market buildings and bustling pedestrian streets in downtown Boston, is the most famous and enduring of the festival marketplaces created by the Rouse Company in the 1970s and 1980s. The festival marketplace concept has lost its luster today, but it was the opening act in the refashioning of many American downtowns as tourist destinations after decades of white flight and bland urban renewal. Americans found themselves entranced by this sanitized, theatrical version of traditional city markets in cities such as Boston, Baltimore, and New York.[1]

Faneuil Hall (built in 1742 and expanded in 1806) is a combination auditorium and market building that adjoins the famous Quincy Market (1826), an impressive Greek Revival structure, clad in granite, with temple fronts on both ends and an open rotunda at the center (Fig. 21). Bracketing Quincy Market are two long warehouses, known as the North and South Buildings. For over one hundred years the district bubbled as Boston's principal retail and wholesale food market. By the 1960s, however, the market area had declined. Mayor Kevin White provided the official view of the area that became the Faneuil Hall complex: "My office in City Hall looked out over a largely vacant and rodent-infested old public marketplace behind historic Faneuil Hall." The Boston Redevelopment Authority had already moved wholesale operations to suburban Quincy in 1964, initiated building renovation, and preserved Quincy Market as a public stall market of traditional food stalls rented for only three dollars a square foot. The twenty-four existing merchants at Quincy Market in 1973, the year the city signed the market over to

Fig. 22. Interior of Quincy Market, showing central rotunda and market hall. While retaining some functions of a working public market, the Marketplace under Rouse evolved in ways calculated to entice tourists back to a downtown that had slipped amid deindustrialization. Courtesy of Karen Marlene Larsen.

the Rouse Company, included those selling meat, pasta, pastries, fruit, seafood, and flowers.[2]

Architect Benjamin Thompson won a contest to redesign the area in the early 1970s. Thompson had established his professional reputation in partnership with orthodox modernist Walter Gropius, but retained a flexible approach to modern design and sensitivity to historical context. He also had hands-on retail experience as creator and manager of the architecturally distinctive interior-design furnishing stores and gourmet restaurants (with his wife, Jane) in the 1960s. He believed, in these projects and those that followed, that it was possible to create an "architecture of 'joy and sensibility' as a norm for modern urban life."[3]

Thompson, after some false starts, successfully proposed to James Rouse that Quincy Market could, with his help, become a gourmet food center offering a mix of the fresh products it had always been known for, in addition to high-end fast food, cafés, and local restaurants. The adjoining market buildings would feature high-quality galleries, as well as dry-goods, craft, antiques, and clothing stores: "Unlike most modern shopping centers with large department stores as financial anchors, our plan sees a major market of small merchants, with a colorful diversity of life and events competing on a day-to-day basis."[4] Thompson imagined Quincy Market duplicating "the chaotic mix of Les Halles, of the Farmer's Market in Los Angeles, of the Piazza Navona on market day"[5] and waxed poetic about "the natural pageantry of crowds and goods, of meat, fish and crops, of things made and things grown all to be smelled, tasted, seen and touched."[6]

Rouse, at first, seemed to be an unlikely choice to redevelop the marketplace, even in a partnership; some of his executives considered the project better suited to philanthropy, and he had trouble assembling the millions required for Thompson's high-minded renovation. Yet Rouse had become known for his big bets on unorthodox projects; he had gained national recognition as a pioneer of enclosed shopping malls, downtown urban renewal, and a vast suburban planned new town (Columbia, Maryland). He also believed that his suburban malls provided visual and pedestrian excitement on a par with downtowns. During this time, he and his staff, for instance, developed the food-court concept derived from food stalls found in traditional city markets. Above all, Rouse hoped to reap rewards from his decades of urban renewal advocacy. He realized that American downtowns, after decades of redevelopment, were ripe for new venues; urban renewal had created "new access roads, better parking, public squares, new or expanded institutions, new office buildings." Surrounding the market in Boston was, in fact, a growing nucleus of white-collar offices with thousands of highly paid employees.

Faneuil Hall represented the opportunity to bring high-quality management and design standards to what appeared to be a rebounding central city. The key would be to replace city ownership with centralized private ownership that could put suburbanites in the mood to stroll, nosh, and shop downtown. As a Rouse document made clear in 1973, the Rouse Company "emphasized that the inclusion of the Quincy Market Building and Streets, the development of the entire marketplace as an integrated whole, was the essence of the proposal." The district and its streets conceptualized in this manner shared a great deal with suburban malls (Fig. 22).[7]

Rouse, using Thompson's vision, connections, and architectural skills, ultimately won the right to develop the market area in 1973, but Roger Webb, a well-connected developer, proposed a competing version of the renovation for "the central Quincy Building, which will retain its traditional character as *Boston's Public Market*. . . . All the local merchants now

Fig. 21. Tourists stroll the cobblestone pedestrian mall beside Faneuil Hall Marketplace. Quincy Market is at right, with the red-brick Faneuil Hall in the distance. Courtesy of Sheri and Randy Propster, Backpacker Magazine's Brand Ambassadors and Get Out More Road Team.

in the Quincy Building will be invited (and helped) to remain. . . . New merchants will be brought in to make this a major *food center* . . . the complete range of fresh foods to serve Boston residents and employees on a daily basis." Webb promised that his company, acting as a nonprofit developer, would better preserve the market flavor. Quincy Market would even remain city property because "it has always been publicly owned. It has always been the scene of a subsidized food market. We feel it is not necessary for the city to give up complete control for 99 years."[8] Had the Webb option prevailed, Faneuil Hall would have followed the Pike Street Market nonprofit trajectory of a slow and steady gentrification, rather than the hypercapitalism introduced by Rouse.

The Webb alternative possessed a fair amount of political support, but Rouse won support from city government, in part, by promising twenty percent of annual profits or minimum annual payments of $600,000 by the third year of operation. Some festival marketplaces such as that in Flint, Michigan, failed entirely, and some like South Street Seaport are faltering today, but the same cannot be said of Faneuil Hall Marketplace.

Rouse explained, when defending the plan, that "it's much more a civic enterprise than the standard commercial shopping center. Ultimately 25 percent of the gross rent collected goes to the city." Boston has reaped enormous financial returns from the renovated marketplace both in direct payments and increased tourism, even if the export of the concept to other cities (and even countries) has been more difficult than replicating shopping malls.[9]

Rouse's plan, as good as it was for the city coffers, envisioned transferring the revenue levels of suburban malls to merchants selling sides of beef, cheese, and bags of fresh parsley at formerly subsidized monthly rents of three dollars per square foot. As Rouse admitted, "The cost (of renovation) can only be justified by high rents from high productivity in sales and high pedestrian traffic."[10] The vendors needed high-volume sales to survive because they would now be responsible for paying a percentage of sales as well as special service and tax charges. The company knew it might have to subsidize older market tenants, but only intended to do so for three years.[11] Rouse nevertheless reminded his managers developing retail to avoid mall habits: "The overwhelming feeling of the shopping goods stores should be small, special shops run by their owners. An occasional Ann Taylor is okay but, as a whole, it must be a marketplace with stores that shoppers don't find elsewhere . . . we cannot let it slip into being a shopping center."[12]

In the contract signed with the Boston Redevelopment Authority in 1973, the Rouse Company committed to preserving the older market stalls: "Quincy Market is a meat/cheese/produce market and the intention is to keep it the same but increase the number of stalls on the lower level." In the North and South Market Buildings the company also promised "a collection of 'one of a kind' shops plus a very large number of restaurants." Thompson, whose designs for the renovation of the market area won universal praise, still believed Quincy Market "will be operated as a food bazaar, with the first floor kept open as a continuous 'indoor street.' [the Colonnade] Along this street, individual retail concessions will offer meat, fish, produce, dairy goods, specialty foods and wines . . . [while] a variety of ready food stalls . . . will create an enormous international buffet served by a central eating area."[13] In the first years, this retail vision appeared to have been largely realized. In order to fill vacant spaces, Rouse even recruited quirky small merchants for pushcarts along the edge of the market buildings. These pushcarts became the forerunner of the upscale pushcarts Rouse, and others, put in shopping malls across the country.

The press and public raved about the reenergized market. *New York Times Magazine,* for instance, praised the "revival" for its "heaped fruit, vegetables, meat, flowers and baskets, a sensuous still life reminiscent of Les Halles."[14] Architecture critic Robert Campbell praised the "chic" contrasts highlighted in Thompson's subtle redesign: "Where Thompson details a joint between old and new, the detail is crude, deliberately so." Sleek exterior glass sheds for cafes and retailing, for instance, contrasted sharply with both the antique granite walls and the new, deliberately anachronistic, cobblestones on the pedestrian streets. Less visible changes, such as modern lighting and air conditioning, further highlighted the contrast between old world and new. Campbell was one of the few critics who grasped that the market's physical design paled in comparison to the management strategy that included a fifty-four-page tenant rule book "governing the size, placement, material and color of just about anything a tenant might wish to provide." Such detailed codes had more in common with suburban planned communities than a chaotic urban market; the rules at Quincy Market successfully established a classy, clean historical tone of mass appeal. Rouse's team also added a superior level of cleaning including daily "garbage pickup . . . and its own street cleaning (brick and cobbles are steam cleaned nightly)," which elevated the market to that experienced at shopping malls. Market tenants, it should be noted, paid for these extra services through the common maintenance charges above their rents.[15] Finally, professional public relations built visitor expectations. Faneuil Hall Marketplace benefited from good timing (the nation's Bicentennial celebration), a well-oiled public-relations team at the Rouse Company, and a location easily accessible to the media elite in New York City.

In spite of assurances and careful management, experience quickly revealed the true character of the market. Rouse as early as 1976 discovered that although the market was a great hit with the "quick lunch customer, to the family on a lark and to the couple out for dinner," because of the many food choices, "somewhat overwhelmed by the opening crowds has been the shopper who wanted to buy the week's meat, fish, cheese or produce" and many stall merchants were "having an uncertain early experience" with all the rubbernecking and higher prices. But Rouse celebrated the tourist market the company had uncovered, and although he admitted, "we have been so determined not to build 'a tourist trap,'" yet "it is a huge potential for us and it is right that we serve it well. . . . We can do here for the marketplace and the tourist what Disney did for the amusement park."[16]

The millions who came to visit, a mix of locals and tourists, made Faneuil Hall Marketplace a great commercial success story, and the city made money, too. The crush of people and the temptations of tourism, coupled with the hard-driving management of the Rouse Company, began to compromise the initial vision. In a speech from 1977, Rouse explained, "Quincy Market averages $300 in sales per square foot—double that of successful regional shopping centers. In its first year Quincy Market, with only 80,000 square feet, attracted about as many people as Disneyland—10 million." These record sales were not evenly distributed. Market stalls were failing, could not cover their rents and common charges, or had in desperation turned to fast-food selling.[17] MIT urbanist Bernard Frieden explains the process: "One day a produce dealer who had too many ripe pineapples on hand decided to sell them by the slice and found he did it much better that way. . . . Within the first few years fast food took over most of the central arcade."[18]

A memo in 1978 to the Rouse Company from Ben and Jane Thompson outlined the disturbing reality: "The success of fast food and singles drinking operations tends to drive out serious shoppers for groceries, fashion, and durable goods." They discovered that successful tenants from other Rouse centers cannibalized the retail mix by driving out individual merchants. The Thompsons suggested that the company reorganize the fresh-food sellers "to reassert the market's identity as a viable, convenient place to shop for groceries of an unusual and quality kind."[19] One of the initial Rouse managers echoed these complaints: "Quincy Market has been transformed to a giant fast food operation with even the meat and produce merchants emphasizing the sale of fast food items. . . . Quincy Market is now hailed as Boston's latest amusement park and tourist trap with the latest food fads to eat and souvenir-type of items to buy."[20]

Rouse, who had an expensive renovation debt to repay, high standards of cleanliness to maintain, an ambitious payment scheme to the city, and demands from investors, ignored the Thompsons and internal criticism. Rouse may have admitted to his managers, for instance, in 1978, that "there is much evidence of creeping mediocrity in other aspects of Faneuil Hall: unattractive kiosks that have sneaked out on the square between Quincy Market and South Market; the gradual spread of fast foods into all the market stalls," but he did nothing to change the market's destiny.[21] The demand for high returns from all merchants made the balance too precarious. Rouse retired in 1980 and new company leadership capitalized on the growing tourist market. An increase in common maintenance charges in 1982 further squeezed early merchants and increased the number of chain stores and restaurants.[22] As late as 1984, Rouse sent a letter to Rouse Company managers with some revealing notes. Rouse approved of "weeding out weak tenants" and made "an interesting note—Crabtree and Evelyn now 4 times larger—doing over 1600/square feet."[23]

The quality architecture and attractive public spaces Thompson created endure at Faneuil Hall Marketplace, as do the street performers and people watching, but the marketplace's offerings in both food and retail strike familiar shopping-mall notes: eighteen million visitors annually mill through brand names, fast food, T-shirts, and knickknacks. Fresh-food market vendors have long ago closed or moved away. The small Haymarket produce and meat-market district still survives nearby, however, indicating that there remains interest in fresh produce in the central city.

Festival marketplaces, in cities such as New York and Baltimore, began with a similar blend of stall market spaces and quirky retail yet became indistinguishable in retail mix from suburban shopping malls. Most tourists are unaware that the festival marketplace as pioneered by Thompson and Rouse has this interesting, countercultural heritage. This critique is more than academic sourness, because the failure to maintain a distinctive environment has, in recent decades, undercut the popularity of many festival marketplaces including Baltimore's Harborplace and New York's South Street Seaport. Additional seafood-to-go offerings, for instance, in Quincy Market's Colonnade stall market now better capitalize on New England's maritime legacy. The festival marketplaces will either be reinvented or become a forgotten, if important, moment in the rediscovery of the American city.

French Quarter
New Orleans, Louisiana

J. Mark Souther

The French Quarter, also known as the Vieux Carré, is an 85-block (320-acre) district that lies along the Mississippi River adjacent to downtown New Orleans. As early as the nineteenth century, local and national journalists and novelists recognized the Vieux Carré as a rare spot where a visitor might forget he was in the United States. In the twentieth century, artists and writers, followed by preservationists, entrepreneurs, and tourism promoters, and ultimately city officials, discovered both aesthetic and monetary value in its narrow streets, ornate iron-lace galleries, and verdant courtyards. The French Quarter we know today is more than just a historic party zone; it is a layered, complex, carefully constructed tourist system that has spawned imitators from coast to coast.[1]

In French and Spanish colonial Louisiana (1718–1803), the future French Quarter comprised the entire capital city. Devastating fires in 1788 and 1794 wiped out most of the district's French colonial architecture, but for more than a century after the Louisiana Purchase, the French Quarter retained a considerable Francophone population of so-called Creoles. Arrayed around a central plaza later christened Jackson Square following Andrew Jackson's victory over British forces in the Battle of New Orleans in 1815, the Quarter continued to prosper as a commercial hub as steamboats and "King Cotton" began to enrich New Orleans in the decades preceding the Civil War. After the war, the French Quarter gradually lost its share of national commerce but attracted large numbers of southern and eastern European immigrants toward the turn of the century.

In 1887, essayist Charles Dudley Warner wrote in *Harper's* that the

French Quarter, with its peddlers, fruit vendors, bordellos, and unpaved streets, was "[e]specially interesting in its picturesque decay."[2] Warner and other writers called tourists' and locals' attention to the cultural wonders of the Vieux Carré, but the neighboring Storyville red-light district was probably a bigger draw to tourists who stepped off Southern Railway passenger trains at the station across Basin Street and proceeded "down the line" of turreted Victorian mansions that serviced a legalized prostitution trade from 1897 to 1917. Through World War I, most New Orleans leaders still believed the French Quarter, like Storyville, detracted from the image of a progressive city and impeded the expansion of downtown across Canal Street, the city's leading retail thoroughfare.

Following sporadic campaigns to preserve threatened buildings such as the Cabildo (where the Louisiana Purchase was signed), in the 1920s, a full-fledged preservationist movement emerged and began to reshape local attitudes toward the Quarter. Urban pioneers, including artists, writers, and cultural guardians, settled in the neighborhood and created the Vieux Carré Commission (VCC) in 1925 as a means of protecting its historic architecture. After receiving its state charter in 1936, the VCC regulated the French Quarter's appearance. The city government, under Mayor Robert Maestri, began making a more concerted effort to promote the Quarter while the Works Progress Administration (WPA) restored the ancient structures around Jackson Square, increasing their tourist appeal. The WPA also published a city guide to New Orleans, employing the literary talent of New Orleans journalist Lyle Saxon, whose prose captured the romance and grit of the Quarter's historic buildings.

Beginning in the 1920s, with the opening of the Jefferson Highway (U.S. 61) and Old Spanish Trail (U.S. 90), the French Quarter enjoyed easy automotive access. Numerous tourist courts and motels sprouted along the approaches to the city, offering more economical alternatives to older downtown and Quarter hotels. Into the 1940s, however, the French Quarter's tourism-oriented footprint was primarily confined to St. Peter, St. Ann, and Chartres Streets around Jackson Square and a few blocks of Royal and Bourbon Streets behind the St. Louis Cathedral. Much of the rest of the district consisted of townhouses and cottages punctuated by corner bars, grocery stores, laundries, and other small businesses, and a mixture of seamen's taverns and rooming houses that served a transient population along Decatur Street and its side streets near the Mississippi River docks (Fig. 23).

Fig. 23. The corner of Bourbon and Iberville Streets, ca. 1948. This building, which housed a po' boy sandwich shop, a bar, a tailor, and a rooming house on its upper floors, reveals a less gussied up French Quarter. While the Quarter had attracted tourists for decades, only in the second half of the century did it transform to accommodate a burgeoning tourist trade. Photo by Charles L. Franck Photographers, 1979.325.200. Courtesy of Historic New Orleans Collection.

World War II played an important role in stimulating the Quarter's transition toward a tourism-dominated district. Thousands of soldiers and laborers flocked to New Orleans in the 1940s, and many discovered in the French Quarter sensory pleasures—Creole restaurants, jazz music, antique emporiums, historical atmosphere, and vibrant nightlife—that would entice them back on postwar vacations. Increasingly, the Quarter's businesses appealed more consciously to tourists, a trend exemplified by two of the neighborhood's longtime attractions. In 1943, Owen Brennan, the Irish-American son of a foundry laborer, purchased the Old Absinthe House on Bourbon Street, reputedly the nation's oldest saloon and a favored haunt of the pirate Jean Lafitte more than a century before, and set up mannequins to depict the secret pact between Lafitte and Jackson to defend against the British in the Battle of New Orleans. Brennan sold trademark "Pirate's Dream" drinks and, three years later, purchased the Vieux Carré Restaurant across the street. Renamed Owen Brennan's French and Creole Restaurant, it quickly became one of the most widely known destinations in the Quarter.[3]

In the postwar years, the Vieux Carré's preservation-minded residents struggled with nightclub operators who hoped to make Bourbon Street a new incarnation of Storyville, whose brothels had closed under U.S. Navy orders in 1917 and whose buildings had been mostly demolished to construct a public housing project in the 1930s. Bourbon Street annually filled with throngs of costumed locals and tourists who gathered to celebrate Mardi Gras, the city's most important and longstanding public spectacle. Colorful floats' riders tossed countless beaded necklaces, doubloons, and other baubles to parade spectators. Dozens of bars and racy burlesque clubs opened beginning in these years and developed a reputation for keeping the Carnival atmosphere in place year-round. In the years after the war, neon-decked Bourbon Street became a lightning rod for public outcry against the vice operations that lurked in its shadier establishments, particularly when bar operators' carefully choreographed robberies of unsuspecting tourists threatened the city's image.

The French Quarter's transformation into a tourist center accelerated after World War II as preservationists slowly succeeded in shaping public consensus that the Quarter was important to the city's future. Although municipal and business leaders did not always see eye-to-eye with preservationists, they finally awakened to the Quarter's commercial possibilities. In one of his last acts as mayor, Maestri removed several blocks from the VCC's purview in 1946, including the entire block surrounding the Monteleone Hotel, the Quarter's largest hostelry. It took preservationists eighteen years to return the parcels to VCC oversight, but only after the Monteleone had completed an aggressive expansion. The hotel's action reflected a surge in tourism that also prompted the construction of new

Fig. 24. Pete Fountain entertains tourists at his French Quarter Inn in the 1970s. New Orleans–born jazz clarinetist Pete Fountain became nationally known in the 1950s on The Lawrence Welk Show. Fountain returned to New Orleans and opened his own club on Bourbon Street in the 1960s, joining a revival of traditional jazz in the French Quarter sparked by Preservation Hall. Photo by Frank Methe. 1978.118(B).03165. Courtesy of Louisiana State Museum.

hotels in the Vieux Carré. Bowing to VCC rules, developers adorned these hotels with brick or stucco facades wrapped with iron balconies to blend with older structures. In the 1960s, several large hotels—notably the Royal Orleans, Bourbon Orleans, and Royal Sonesta—added nearly two thousand rooms to the Quarter, leading preservationists to lobby successfully in 1969 for a municipal moratorium on further hotel construction.

Just as the French Quarter's distinctive iron balconies became a model for permissible new construction under VCC regulations, they also flanked the entrances to a growing number of jazz clubs that sought to connect the local music to the Vieux Carré in tourists' minds (Fig. 24). Into the 1950s, some white tourists encountered jazz in the predominantly African-American "back o' town" neighborhoods beyond the Quarter in the dimly lit recesses of the Dew Drop Inn and other black-owned clubs. However, the invisibility of such venues to most visitors who stayed in the Vieux Carré meant that more tourists probably encountered a narrow repertoire of Dixieland jazz tunes—especially "When the Saints Go Marching In"—that drummed up business for Bourbon Street beer joints and striptease houses. Business-minded local entrepreneurs, some of them Italian Americans (who had once been so numerous that the Vieux Carré got the nickname "Little Palermo"), and culture-minded newcomers alike opened jazz venues in the Quarter after World War II. Sid Davilla's Mardi Gras Lounge and Steve Valenti's Paddock Lounge routinely hired established jazz bands, while several jazz aficionados who made the leap from tourists to transplants created opportunities for tourists to hear jazz in the French Quarter apart from beer and burlesque. Most notable was Preservation Hall, opened in 1961, a product of the efforts of Milwaukee-born art dealer and French Quarter real-estate investor Larry Borenstein and Philadelphia jazz enthusiasts Alan and Sandra Jaffe. Preservation Hall, which promised "No Drinks—No Girls—No Gimmicks—Just Real Music," was so convincingly authentic behind its weathered-stucco St. Peter Street storefront that many tourists erroneously believed it was the birthplace of jazz.[4]

Perhaps the greatest struggle for the future of the Vieux Carré ensued when a Robert Moses freeway plan threatened to drape a forty-foot-tall concrete ribbon along a stretch of the Mississippi where citizens had lobbied local port officials to remove underused sheds atop the wharves, whose presence had for decades obscured the historic connection between city and river. Although the leading press, business community, and public officials applauded a freeway system touted as a balm for choked downtown streets, a determined citizen revolt drew upon the French Quarter's national renown to rally opposition, ultimately dooming the highway in 1969. Central in the debate were the voices of New Orleanians who argued that the Quarter's mostly nineteenth-century cityscape was important for economic as well as aesthetic reasons. The years that followed demonstrated the success of tourism in fixing public attention on the need to safeguard the Vieux Carré.

Previous mayoral administrations had fostered the expansion of tourism as an important part of New Orleans's economy, but no previous mayor matched Moon Landrieu's policies in the 1970s to enhance tourist interest in the French Quarter. In earlier years, New Orleans mirrored other cities in emphasizing that the Quarter, like San Francisco's Chinatown or Los Angeles's Olvera Street, was a relict space surrounded by a thoroughly modern metropolis. Mayor Landrieu shepherded a number of projects to make the Quarter more appealing to a mostly white, middle-class, suburban clientele. At a time when public and private urban-renewal initiatives sought to create secure, reassuring, modernized urban landscapes that often ignored the past, Landrieu hoped the Vieux Carré might impress visitors with its exotic feel while comforting them with a degree of familiarity.

During Landrieu's tenure, the city closed three streets bordering Jackson Square in 1970, fashioning a flagstone-paved outdoor arcade filled with artists, musicians, peddlers, and entertainers reminiscent of Venice's Piazza San Marco. It also built a tourist path atop the Mississippi River levee and dubbed it the Moonwalk, a creative take on the mayor's name. Landrieu championed the part-time closure of Bourbon and Royal Streets to vehicular traffic to form pedestrian malls in the early 1970s. Perhaps the most important tourist-centered change was the renovation of the city's old French Market from a working public market into a "festival marketplace" filled with shops and eateries aimed at visitors. Reopening in 1975, the market included fountains, benches, and an adjacent riverfront observation platform and tourist information center. Landrieu's policies contributed to noticeable increases in tourism in the Quarter, which presented new challenges. The mayor ordered Mardi Gras parades rerouted around the Vieux Carré as crowds exceeded safe limits, and his administration approved tighter controls on street performers in response to citizen complaints that tourism was making the Quarter unlivable for residents.

The mayor's interest in the Quarter mirrored his dedication to courting private investment in the central city. Following the moratorium on new

French Quarter hotels, Landrieu brokered a deal between a local developer and Marriott to bring a forty-two-story hotel to Canal Street in 1972, ushering in a period of high-rise development on the Quarter's fringe. Landrieu also oversaw the construction of the 70,000-seat Louisiana Superdome, a land-swap deal to make way for a Hilton hotel along the riverfront, the early preparations for a world's fair and its riverfront "residuals," and the early phases of Canal Place, an office, retail, and hotel complex.

The mid-1980s proved a turning point in the French Quarter's development. The hosting of the 1984 Louisiana World Exposition just outside the district and the ensuing collapse of the region's oil industry accelerated local commitment to promoting tourism for economic survival. The world's fair quickened the pace of transforming the Quarter to entice more tourists by bringing a massive streetscape overhaul, the creation of a French Quarter Festival, and a Ghirardelli Square–influenced conversion of Jax Brewery. Just blocks away, the fair's United States Pavilion became the core of the Ernest N. Morial Convention Center, while the Louisiana Pavilion saw new life as the Riverwalk festival marketplace. The exposition also stimulated a construction boom that added thousands of new hotel rooms just outside the Vieux Carré and excited new interest in the riverfront, leading to construction of the Aquarium of the Americas and Woldenberg Park and creating a mile-long corridor of tourist-centered activity serviced by a new streetcar line that connected the convention center with the Quarter.

The crush of increasing numbers of tourists in and after the city's late-1980s oil bust alarmed observers who feared the Quarter's lapse into a "Creole Disneyland," pushing them to demand ongoing efforts by the municipal government to balance the competing interests of preservation and profit. In the second half of the century, the French Quarter simply became unaffordable for most residents, plummeting from about eleven thousand residents in 1940 to about four thousand in 2000 and, in a city with a two-thirds black population, African-Americans dwindled to only 3 percent of the French Quarter's people and existed in the Quarter mainly as musicians and hospitality workers. Tourism had played a key role in preserving the French Quarter's historic buildings—thus giving New Orleans a well-defined showcase for its cultural distinctiveness—but had transformed a socially diverse neighborhood into a place packed with daiquiri stands, trinket shops, and carriage tours. Tourists who had once marveled at the incessant parade of eccentric New Orleanians through the Quarter's streets ultimately had to entertain each other in a district of hotels, beds-and-breakfast, and timeshare condominiums.

The place that New Orleanians and visiting tourists crafted not only gave the Crescent City an internationally recognized symbol and stage for its distinctive culture but it also influenced countless other tourist attractions in the twentieth century. Robert Hugman, an architect who lived in New Orleans in the 1920s, drew the initial plans for San Antonio's River Walk in 1929 with an eye toward emulating the Quarter's distinctive sense of place. After World War II, the Quarter provided a template for other cities' attempts over the next few decades to cash in on a burgeoning tourism industry—St. Louis's Gaslight Square, Memphis's Beale Street, Tampa's Ybor City, Underground Atlanta, and San Diego's Gaslamp Quarter. On a smaller scale, it also inspired Vieux Carré–style hotels and motels ranging from Disney's Port Orleans Resort in Florida to the Holiday Inn–French Quarter outside Toledo, Ohio.

In the wake of Hurricane Katrina in 2005, the French Quarter has been central to New Orleans's aspirations for rebirth with nearly one-third of the city's pre-Katrina population having never returned.[5] The storm furthered a trend in which tourists expected more historically accurate and varied attractions, a trend visible in the appearance of museums and visitor centers operated by the Historic New Orleans Collection and the National Park Service, as well as Le Monde Creole walking tours (which focus on Afro-Creole and African-American history). Although local tour companies offer bus tours of the Lower Ninth Ward and other flood-ravaged areas of the city, whose modest shotgun houses and cottages sheltered many of the workers who kept the tourism industry operating, the Quarter continues to occupy a special place in the national imagination. If many tourists are now willing to peer behind the mask of an image carefully crafted by writers, artists, filmmakers, and tourism promoters over more than a century, the power of the French Quarter to serve as a visible symbol of stereotypical New Orleans imagery remains. Nearly a half century after Walt Disney added New Orleans Square, a scaled-down, cutesy replica of the Quarter to his California theme park, Disney's 2009 animated film *The Princess and the Frog* placed the studio's first African-American heroine amid all the familiar stereotypes associated with New Orleans's most storied attraction.

Gateway Arch
St. Louis, Missouri

Andrew Hurley

Rising majestically from the western bank of the Mississippi River, the 630-foot-tall Gateway Arch attracts 2.5 million visitors from around the world annually and ranks as St. Louis, Missouri's premier tourist attraction. International tourism, however, was far from the minds of the civic leaders, planners, and politicians who initially proposed a radical makeover for the city's "front door." As originally conceived, central harbor reconstruction advanced more parochial ambitions: urban beautification, stabilization of downtown property values, and commemoration of the spot where French fur traders laid out the original town in 1764. A sequence of urban traumas precipitated by the Great Depression and postwar suburbanization intensified efforts to leverage the site's historical value—first as a national monument to western pioneers and later as a destination for retail consumption. As mass tourism increasingly governed the waterfront's transformation, the city struggled to reconcile the aggressive pursuit of outside dollars with a broader array of local revitalization goals. Consequently, the Gateway Arch stands as an ambivalent symbol of civic progress.

During the latter half of the nineteenth century, a steady decline in steamboat activity and corresponding migration of the central business district away from the Mississippi River dragged the St. Louis waterfront toward obsolescence. Investment dwindled, property values plummeted, and structures fell into disrepair. Once the hub of the city's social and economic life, the central harbor became a civic embarrassment. More worrisome was the anticipated effect on the adjacent downtown; popular wisdom identified the waterfront as the source of an infectious urban blight that undermined the stability of neighboring districts. Thus as early as 1907, city planners, backed by downtown business interests, advocated wholesale clearance of the waterfront.[1] Although the central harbor boasted historical significance as the site of the city's founding, most of the structures associated with the early settlers had perished in the Great Fire of 1849, leaving little deemed worthy of preservation.

The prospect of comprehensive clearance inspired a variety of proposals for waterfront redevelopment during the first third of the twentieth century. While varying widely in detail, nearly all sought to bolster civic pride through historical commemoration and modernize the downtown's transportation infrastructure. Restoring the area's dignity demanded something of beauty and grandeur at the water's edge, usually an imposing public plaza with statues and monuments honoring the town's founding fathers. Until the 1930s, then, the site's historical significance continued to be defined primarily in local terms. Prevailing notions of progress mandated that the renewed waterfront simultaneously improve urban efficiency while providing spiritual uplift. Hence some of the earliest plans incorporated streamlined facilities for handling rail and river cargo. By the 1920s, the automobile revolution was in high gear and the strip of property alongside the Mississippi River invited visions of a limited access expressway to alleviate traffic congestion in the central business district. Several reports highlighted the urgent need for commuter parking facilities.[2]

The Great Depression vaulted job creation to the top of the city's agenda and it was as a means to this end that the idea of a national monument to westward expansion blossomed. With the election of Franklin D. Roosevelt to the presidency and the unfurling of the New Deal, new sources of federal money became available for public employment projects. St. Louis politicians seized this opportunity and vigorously lobbied Congress and the Roosevelt administration for funds that would simultaneously put unemployed St. Louisans to work, achieve the longstanding goal of demolishing riverfront properties, and pay for a rehabilitated central harbor. Securing Washington's approval for a historical commemoration project, however, required a reinterpretation of the site's meaning to emphasize its role in a national story, the westward march of pioneers across the continent in the nineteenth century. On December 21, 1935, President Franklin D. Roosevelt authorized the U.S. Department of Interior

Fig. 25. St. Louis Waterfront District shortly before clearance for the Jefferson National Expansion Memorial, ca. 1939. Subsequent industrial decline to the north of the memorial opened the way for the later creation of Laclede's Landing, a downtown entertainment district much like those that emerged in other cities. Courtesy of National Park Service, Jefferson National Expansion Memorial, St. Louis, Missouri.

to acquire and develop the forty-one blocks of waterfront property for the purposes of creating a national park to memorialize Thomas Jefferson, the Louisiana Purchase, and territorial expansion (Fig. 25).

Establishment of the Jefferson National Expansion Memorial did not entirely jeopardize the city's utilitarian redevelopment goals. Federal officials turned a deaf ear to motorists' parking woes, insisting that the presence of commuter garages would defile the memorial. The city scored a decisive victory, however, when the National Park Service permitted construction of an interregional highway on the western edge of the property. In 1956, the Mark Twain Expressway became one of the first high-speed thoroughfares built under the provisions of that year's Federal Aid Highway Act. After considerable wrangling with federal authorities, the Terminal Railroad Association preserved access to the levee by agreeing to submerge its unsightly tracks beneath the memorial grounds.

From the mid-1930s forward, however, the goal of luring out-of-town visitors increasingly drove site development. City boosters, most notably local attorney Luther Ely Smith, insisted on a signature architectural spectacle to rival the Acropolis, the Statue of Liberty, and the Washington Monument.[3] Smith's steadfast promotion of the Expansion Memorial capped a lifetime of community service that included campaigns to establish municipal playgrounds, eliminate smoke pollution, and professionalize city planning. Through a series of legal challenges and the interruption of World War II, Smith kept the project in the public spotlight and held together a coalition of politicians, downtown property owners, and cultural emissaries with his vision of a "shrine for the entire American continent."[4]

Although Smith and his allies had proposed a national architectural competition for the memorial design as early as 1934, the official call for submissions was not issued until thirteen years later. The award jury, composed of nationally prominent architects, unanimously selected Eero Saarinen's modernistic, stainless-steel arch to represent the triumphal spirit of intrepid pioneers. Inspired by the curved dome of Jefferson Memorial in Washington, DC, the monument both referenced the former president and symbolized St. Louis's historical status as the "Gateway to the West." Triumphal arches had long been a staple of Western monumental architecture, but Saarinen's unusual parabolic shape and gleaming metal surface pointed more to the future than the past. Given the technical complexities involved in building such an unusual structure, Saarinen's arch also excited the public's abiding fascination with modern engineering marvels. Like Paris's Eiffel Tower and New York City's Empire State Building, it would demonstrate the power of an artifact of human construction to rearticulate a critical urban space, and in so doing, redefine a city's image. An underground museum, a twenty-two-acre landscaped park, and the refurbished "Old Courthouse" one block west of the cleared area rounded out the memorial's design. To great local fanfare, the shimmering steel structure in the center of the park was topped out on October 28, 1965, and opened its doors to visitors on July 10, 1967. Over the next ten years, it beckoned 16.25 million people to the reconditioned St. Louis waterfront (Fig. 26).[5]

Still, city leaders grumbled that the tourist potential of the waterfront remained unrealized. A survey conducted in the late 1960s revealed that the average Arch visit lasted no more than one hour, after which sightseers left the area.[6] The finding was disturbing because a declining manufacturing

Fig. 26. The Gateway Arch and landscaped grounds, 1986. Photo by Jack Boucher, Historic American Buildings Survey/Historic American Engineering Record Collection. Courtesy of Library of Congress.

sector had convinced the city to revise its economic growth strategy in favor of cultural tourism. The urban crisis hit St. Louis particularly hard. Between

1962 and 1967, 143 manufacturing businesses abandoned the city, taking eleven thousand jobs with them.[7] Some relocated to industrial parks in outlying counties, while others followed the national migration to Sunbelt states. Middle-class residential flight to the metropolitan periphery further eroded the municipal tax base, pushing the city to the brink of insolvency. For Alfonso Cervantes, mayor of St. Louis from 1965 until 1973, pursuit of the "out-of-town dollar" was a logical tonic for the city's fiscal ills. Although the charismatic mayor had cut his teeth in the rough-and-tumble ward politics of working-class neighborhoods, his "new vision" for St. Louis anticipated a "razzle-dazzle" downtown organized around the "smokeless industry" of tourism. To this end, Cervantes established a special fund to market the city to out-of-towners and launched a major bond drive to finance a downtown convention center.[8] Sorely needed, however, were additional cultural attractions that would entice more visitors and encourage them to linger.

Laclede's Landing, a decaying warehouse district located on most of nine blocks just north of the Gateway Arch grounds, emerged as the prime candidate for a complementary tourist district featuring trendy shops, museums, restaurants, and nightclubs. This time there were no calls for comprehensive clearance. New Orleans's French Quarter and San Francisco's Ghirardelli Square demonstrated the popularity and economic viability of tourist landscapes that exuded historical authenticity through the adaptive reuse of older buildings. An example closer to home was St. Louis's own Gaslight Square, although in this case the lesson was cautionary. Three miles west of downtown, a two-block stretch of renovated buildings enjoyed a brief reputation as a mecca for bohemian nightlife. By the end of the 1960s, however, media coverage of violent crime and the infiltration of burlesque houses tarnished the district's image and kept crowds away. To prevent a repeat disaster on the waterfront, the city endorsed a more tightly controlled commercial environment. Under the auspices of Missouri state law, in 1975, the St. Louis city government granted the Laclede's Landing Redevelopment Corporation, a private investment group, central oversight over all planning and design within the officially blighted district, although individual property holders retained responsibility for financing the rehabilitation of buildings and securing commercial tenants.

From the standpoint of external promotion, Laclede's Landing and the Jefferson National Expansion Memorial achieved their aims, anchoring a strong tourist economy.[9] Yet together they created what Dennis Judd has termed a "tourist bubble"—a sealed-off portion of downtown catering exclusively to affluent conventioneers, out-of-town visitors, and weekend suburban commuters.[10] The isolated character of the waterfront cultural tourism complex provoked considerable local criticism, much of it directed at the six-lane expressway cordoning off the downtown business district from riverfront attractions. Unlike San Antonio's River Walk, where a waterway loops around the heart of a centrally located tourist district, in St. Louis, the riverfront lies on the periphery.[11] Numerous proposals to improve access from the downtown business district by way of bridges and tunnels mark the latest chapter in the city's continuing efforts to align mass tourism with multiple civic goals.

The dramatic metamorphosis of St. Louis's central harbor area exerted an influence far beyond the shores of the Mississippi River. In the decades immediately following World War II, dozens of aging industrial cities followed the example of St. Louis and swept dingy factories and warehouses from the water's edge to create landscapes more appropriate to an economy based on services, consumption, and tourism. Some of the revamped waterfronts featured large parks while others filled with hotels, office towers, and convention centers. Moreover, from the 1970s onward, cities increasingly relied on the formula employed at Laclede's Landing, that is, preserving and rehabilitating historic structures to provide a distinctive ambience for commercial entertainment and leisure.

GATLINBURG AND PIGEON FORGE, TENNESSEE

C. Brenden Martin

Situated in the foothills of the Great Smoky Mountains in Sevier County, Tennessee, Gatlinburg and Pigeon Forge are the most visited resort communities in southern Appalachia. Since the 1950s, these towns have evolved from quiet mountain getaways into bustling meccas that draw eight to ten million visitors each year. Their proximity to Great Smoky Mountains National Park, the most visited national park in the United States, undoubtedly fostered the rise of Gatlinburg and Pigeon Forge as important twentieth-century tourist centers.

Visitors to Pigeon Forge and Gatlinburg will notice some fundamental differences between the two resort communities. Most tourists travel to this area by automobile, usually coming off of I-40, through Sevierville to Pigeon Forge before reaching Gatlinburg. As visitors reach Pigeon Forge, they drive by a bizarre hodgepodge of attractions, gift shops, hotels, and restaurants that line the six-lane U.S. 441 running through town. Some of the attractions include "hillbilly" hoedowns, indoor skydiving, go-cart racing, miniature golf, Dixie Stampede rodeo dinner theater, Elvis museums, and of course Dollywood. The strong advertising fixation on Confederate icons, Elvis, and hillbillies alerts visitors that the local tourist attractions are catering to a blue-collar clientele of mostly Southern visitors. Leaving Pigeon Forge, the highway winds through five miles of forested foothills before leading into Gatlinburg, the largest gateway community to the Great Smoky Mountains. Somewhat less kitschy than Pigeon Forge, Gatlinburg is clearly a more upscale resort community with its coherent architectural motifs and pricier accommodations.

Despite the differences in the types of attractions at and visitors attracted to these two resorts, they both project powerful cultural images of Appalachian folk life combined with wholesome family entertainment. The imagery of mountaineers, however, has not always been the dominant vision at these resorts. The cultural image of these communities has evolved over the last several decades as individual entrepreneurs experimented with attractions completely divorced from a sense of southern Appalachia as a place. Still, the enduring pop-culture icons of mountaineers and hillbillies proved to be powerful attractions to tourists seeking "down-home" entertainment.

Although separated by only a few miles, Pigeon Forge and Gatlinburg developed in distinct ways over the last half-century. Nevertheless, both communities originally were isolated rural settlements that were engulfed by the advent of mass tourism in the twentieth century. The phenomenal growth of tourism in these towns can be traced to the nineteenth century, when Sevier County's foremost resort was Henderson Springs, located on a hill above what was then the rural hamlet of Pigeon Forge. Henderson Springs had a reputation as a health spa as early as the 1830s, but it was not until 1878 that a hotel and cabins were built on-site.[1] Since railroads did not arrive in Sevier County until the early twentieth century, Henderson Springs remained a small resort catering to regional health seekers who came to "take the waters."

The growth of modern tourism in Sevier County came first to Gatlinburg. Originally named White Oak Flats by early settlers, the town was renamed Gatlinburg by Radford Gatlin, an outsider who moved to the community in 1854 and opened a general store and post office. Although controversies later drove Gatlin away, the town retained his name. In 1910, Gatlinburg was still a small agrarian village, but some people found supplemental employment with the Little River Railroad and Lumber Company and Andy Huff's lumber mill at Sugarlands. While these lumber operations gave rise to Gatlinburg's first hotel, Huff's Mountain View Hotel, and nearby Elkmont in the Smoky Mountains, tourism did not yet play a major role in the community's economy.[2]

All of this changed within a relatively short period of time for a number of reasons. First, the women's sorority, Pi Beta Phi, established the Arrowmont Settlement School in Gatlinburg in 1912. Three years later, Arrowmont launched a weaving and basket-making program that set the stage for Gatlinburg's rise as a leading handicrafts center of the southern highlands. When the school opened the Arrowcraft Shop in 1926 to sell students' wares, it became a popular stop for car tourists who were eager to buy "authentic" mountain crafts along the new Highway 71 (later U.S. 441), reflecting a broader cultural trend that emerged not only in Appalachia but also, notably, in the American Southwest.[3]

Another factor that led to rise of modern tourism in the area was the growth of Elkmont, the first resort community close to Gatlinburg. As the Little River Lumber Company moved its logging operations out of the Little River's west fork, it sold much of the property to wealthy Knoxvillians who formed the Appalachian and Wonderland Clubs. Opened in 1912, the Wonderland Hotel at Elkmont employed area residents as servants, tour guides, maids, and cooks. Elkmont helped local residents understand that tourism could also succeed in Gatlinburg, especially when it became apparent that Gatlinburg would be a gateway to what would quickly become one of nation's most popular tourist attractions—the Great Smoky Mountains National Park.[4]

The successful movement to create a national park in the Smokies began in 1923, when Willis P. and Anne M. Davis of Knoxville began discussing the idea with their friends. As frequent visitors to Elkmont, they were upset by the destruction of the area's once-pristine forests and wanted to do something to preserve the landscape for future generations. They were able to enlist the help of several other prominent supporters who understood the commercial possibilities of a major national park in the Smoky Mountains. When enough people supported the cause, the Great Smoky Mountains Conservation Association formed and gained support from politicians, newspaper editors, and business leaders in East Tennessee and Western North Carolina. Through massive fundraising efforts, appropriations from the Tennessee and North Carolina legislatures, and a generous donation from the Laura Spelman Rockefeller Foundation, the park movement eventually succeeded in the early 1930s.[5]

After the establishment of the Great Smoky Mountains National Park in 1934, Gatlinburg grew rapidly. From 1930 to 1940, the town's population grew from 75 to nearly 1,300 residents according to census figures. A TVA Agricultural-Industrial Report of Sevier County reported 93 structures in Gatlinburg in 1934. Yet, a TVA map of the area in 1942 showed 641 structures in the community, indicating rapid tourist development in the area.[6]

As a result of the pattern of roads to and through the park, the residents of Gatlinburg quite suddenly found themselves at the entry to a major national park. Those lucky enough to own land along the highway realized that they were sitting on a gold mine. As a result, most residents of Gatlinburg refused to sell their property and chose to develop the land themselves. For the most part, five indigenous families—the Ogles, Whaleys, Maples, Huffs, and Reagans—led the early development of Gatlinburg. In fact, local families were able to maintain control of the business district even during the post–World War II development boom up through the present.[7]

Despite continued local control, the 1960s through the 1990s brought more outside influences into Gatlinburg. After the first chain motel in Gatlinburg opened its doors in 1962, outside investment grew substantially. Although in 1972 local residents owned 83 percent of the property in Gatlinburg's business district, much of this land was leased to outsiders. In an interview in 1975, former mayor Dick Whaley admitted, "I used to know everybody in town. Now the town is filled with new people who own new businesses—but in most cases the land still belongs to us, the original families."[8] Ownership of most of the land outside of Gatlinburg's main business district, however, fell to outsiders. Nonindigenous developers controlled the large second-home subdivisions on the outskirts of Gatlinburg, such as Sky Harbor and Chalet Village. Thus although local families maintained extraordinary control over the property in the business district, a growing presence of outside developers was threatening local control of Gatlinburg by the 1980s.[9]

The use of traditional rustic lodge architectural style, akin to that found in the Adirondacks and other Appalachian communities, has given sections of Gatlinburg a distinctive appearance. Sawn logs and river stones figure prominently in old and new buildings alike (Fig. 27). Gatlinburg is not, however, a carefully manicured, backward-looking community. The streetscape of U.S. 441, the town's main drag, has given way over the past several decades to the concrete, steel, and plate glass common to suburban malls everywhere. Motels, inns, fast food chains, and souvenir shops have sprouted all along the so-called Gatlinburg strip. Modernity has also been embraced at a monumental scale. Following the lead of 1960s world's fairs in Seattle and San Antonio, Gatlinburg added the Space Needle, a 409-foot-tall observation tower, in 1970. In the 1980s, Gatlinburg's boom even produced a sixteen-story Sheraton hotel, the Park Vista, which accentuated the impact of tourism in the small town.

Fig. 27. The Cliff Dweller's Shop, Gatlinburg, 1949. This Swiss-influenced tourist shop enticed passersby with signs for Smoky Mountain paintings and apple candy. Gatlinburg traded on its association with artisans and craftsmen and their production of mountain arts and crafts. Courtesy of Tennessee State Library and Archives.

By the 1980s, rampant tourism development was spilling over into the neighboring community of Pigeon Forge. From the earliest settlements in the late 1700s to the mid-twentieth century, farming had been the primary occupation of most settlers along the Little Pigeon River. Although Isaac Love built a bloomery forge in Pigeon Forge in 1820, it shut down in the 1860s due to the low iron content of the ore mined nearby and inadequate means of transportation. Consequently, small-scale agriculture remained the community's main livelihood into the mid-twentieth century despite economic and demographic trends that made farming less profitable.

Pigeon Forge grew very slowly at first, but construction of U.S. 441 and the subsequent completion of I-40 made the community much more accessible to a growing number of tourists on their way to Gatlinburg and the Smokies and boosted the community's tourism industry.[10] In the early 1950s, the federal government acquired a three-hundred-foot right-of-way to build the highway. While many farmers initially resented the forced government acquisition of their property, some local property owners sensed the potential profits to be had in land speculation along the highway. Following completion of U.S. 441, a flurry of tourism-related development along the highway ensued in the mid- to late 1950s. As in Gatlinburg, local landowners directed much of this early development.[11] Outside entrepreneurs, however, played a much greater role in developing Pigeon Forge than in Gatlinburg. Since local families shut out virtually all outside investors from Gatlinburg, nonindigenous business people who sought to enter the tourist trade in Sevier County turned to Pigeon Forge, where land was more readily available. Consequently, outside entrepreneurs developed the largest and most popular attractions in Pigeon Forge.

Perhaps the best example is Dollywood. The origins of the park date back to 1961, when Grover and Harold Robbins (who owned tourist attractions in Western North Carolina, including the Tweetsie Railroad) opened Rebel Railroad, a Civil War theme park where visitors could ride a Confederate train that was attacked by Yankees. In the late 1960s, the Robbins brothers sold Rebel Railroad to Cleveland Browns owner Art Modell, who transformed the park into Goldrush Junction, an Old West theme park. Despite the success of Goldrush Junction in generating revenue and employment for the community, the park lost money. As a result, Modell sold the park to Jack and Pete Herschend, who owned Branson, Missouri's first theme park, Silver Dollar City. After purchasing the park for $2 million and spending another $800,000 to convert it into a mountaineer theme park named for its Branson counterpart, visitation quadrupled to 500,000 in three years (Fig. 28). The Herschends brought in native Sevier County resident Dolly Parton as a minority partner in 1985, rechristened the park Dollywood, and used Parton's image to market it. Visitation doubled the year Parton signed and continued to grow steadily thereafter.[12] Today, the 125-acre theme park draws more than 2.2 million visitors each year.

Dollywood's popularity propelled the rapid growth of Pigeon Forge. From 1980 to 1992, the total number of motel rooms in Pigeon Forge jumped from 1,932 to 5,852. During this same period, the community's gross business receipts exploded from $51 million to $379 million due in large part to the development of several outlet malls. The boom of outlet malls may have contributed more than any single factor to the rampant growth of the city in the 1980s and 1990s.[13]

Fig. 28. Dollywood Grist Mill, built in 1982 as part of Silver Dollar City, a predecessor theme park to Dollywood, was the first operating grist mill constructed in Tennessee in more than a century. It makes products for sale to Dollywood patrons. Courtesy of Steve Carr.

Today, tourism dominates the economies of both Gatlinburg and Pigeon Forge, making these communities especially vulnerable to economic downturns. As gasoline prices increased over the first decade of the twenty-first century, for example, tourist visitation to the Smoky Mountains declined by nearly 10 percent. Overdevelopment and the degradation of air and water quality also pose fundamental challenges to these communities. As a result, local and regional officials have become increasingly interested in planning for sustainable tourism growth in the future. Regardless of the environmental problems and kitschy developments, Gatlinburg and Pigeon Forge will likely remain the most popular and most visited tourist destinations in the southern highlands for the foreseeable future.

GRAND CANYON
ARIZONA

Lincoln Bramwell

When Spanish explorer García López de Cárdenas halted at the Grand Canyon's rim in 1540, he did not marvel long at the chasm's beauty. Instead, López de Cárdenas saw a great barrier to his contingent of the Vázquez de Coronado expedition into the American Southwest. For centuries afterward, the Grand Canyon remained an imposing obstruction that kept explorers and settlers at bay. Nearly three centuries passed before intrepid scientist explorers traversed the canyon and began examining its geologic singularity and cultural significance. Although the Colorado River imperceptibly deepened the canyon in the twentieth century, Americans' evolving appreciation of natural landscapes transformed the Grand Canyon's once bare rims into a bustling tourist destination resort.

The first group of Euro-Americans to re-conceptualize the "Great Chasm of the Colorado" included John Wesley Powell and Clarence E. Dutton, who mapped the desert Southwest for the U.S. Geological Survey. When Powell first rafted the Colorado River through the canyon in 1869, he experienced equal parts terror and wonder. He employed other scientists and artists to study and promote the canyon, including Thomas Moran who first painted the canyon in 1873 at Powell's behest. Geologist Clarence Dutton played the critical role in shifting the nation's perception of the canyon. He worked closely with Powell over the years and provided much of the scientific work that underpinned Powell's highly influential *Report on the Lands of the Arid Region of the United States, with a More Detailed Account of the Lands of Utah.* According to historian Stephen J. Pyne, Dutton's own work, *The Tertiary History of the Grand Cañon District,* first brought art and science together in a way that introduced the

Grand Canyon to new audiences nationwide. Dutton's writings acquainted the scientific elite with the canyon's geologic significance while noted ethnographer William Henry Holmes's drawings, colored by Moran, conveyed a panoply of dazzling vistas to the nation's cultural elite. Dutton argued that the canyon, quite unlike America's mountain monuments at Yellowstone and Yosemite, presented a "great innovation in modern ideas of scenery," adding that "its full appreciation is a special culture, requiring time, patience, and long familiarity for its consummation."[1] By the 1890s, the work of these early scientist explorers and artists defined the canyon as grand, transforming it from a barrier to a national symbol of the sublime.

Despite interest in the canyon among the nation's beau monde, a lack of access to America's newly recognized natural gem severely restricted visitation and prevented its conversion into a tourist destination. The canyon remained remote and distant from even the closest rail stop in Williams, Arizona, over sixty miles from the canyon's south rim. Rough stage roads provided the only access to the canyon and once there, a variety of shabby establishments exclusively offered services to travelers. To well-heeled American tourists of the day, the lack of accommodations proved as great an impediment to tourism as the remote location. A solution to both problems materialized when the Atchison, Topeka, and Santa Fe Railway (AT&SF) bought the old rail line through Williams and built a spur line to the south rim. On September 17, 1901, the railroad began regular passenger service to the Grand Canyon from Williams at a fraction of the cost of the stage ride. With the AT&SF came the Fred Harvey Company, a hotelier and dining concession that operated along the company's entire line. The arrival of the AT&SF solved the access and promotion barriers to increasing the flow of tourists to the canyon. With improved access and accommodations, the Grand Canyon entered the next phase of its development as a national icon. Together, the AT&SF and Fred Harvey Company brought the capital and promotional expertise to develop the canyon into a grand tourist destination worthy of its beautiful surroundings while the reduced cost of passage put a visit within reach of upper-middle-class Americans for the first time.

Notwithstanding its growing popularity with the American public, the canyon remained unpatented public land. During the late nineteenth century, dozens of mining claims along with concession and grazing operations stretched from the south rim through the Kaibab Plateau in a tangle of local enterprise. President Theodore Roosevelt, worried about development marring the south rim's beauty after a visit in 1903, declared the Grand Canyon a game reserve in 1906 using new executive powers outlined in the Antiquities Act passed that same year. Because the reserve lay within the Grand Canyon National Forest, later renamed the Kaibab National Forest, the U.S. Forest Service managed the 800,000 acres along the south rim. Re-designated a national monument in 1908, the Grand Canyon remained under Forest Service control until the newly created National Park Service (NPS) accepted management responsibility in 1919. Roosevelt's actions spoke directly to the differing cultural perceptions of the canyon held by him and local enterprises. Roosevelt felt that protecting the canyon was his gift for the ages, preserving "one of the great sights for Americans to see." To locals in Flagstaff and Williams, particularly mining, grazing, and timber interests, the park restricted access to public land and opposition remained fierce. Locals complained that the canyon's reservation overstepped the Antiquities Act's bounds and legal actions against the park reached the Supreme Court, which eventually extinguished local claims. Transferring the canyon from local to federal control reflected the land's heightened cultural value in the eyes of the government and much of the public. Heretofore judged solely in economic terms for its mineral wealth by locals, the canyon had attained national significance that merited the oversight of the federal government's premier land preservation agency.

The Grand Canyon immediately benefited from its status as a national park and from the NPS's regulated management policies. Under its first director, self-made millionaire Stephen Mather, the Park Service aggressively promoted national parks to the American traveler. To attract wealthy tourists, Mather sought consistent, first-rate accommodations in parks. The NPS awarded concession monopolies in all parks to companies capable of providing the level of service Mather desired. This practice favored the Fred Harvey Company, which operated luxury hotels in cities along the AT&SF lines, and Mather supported its effort to dominate the tourist trade at the south rim. The company had earlier built the El Tovar Hotel in 1905, a 250-room resort that became the crown jewel of stops along the AT&SF (Fig. 29). The log-sided El Tovar was billed as a combination of Swiss chalet and Norwegian villa and stood astride the earlier Victorian style and an emerging rustic lodge style deemed

Fig. 29. Postcard view of El Tovar Hotel, ca. 1905. El Tovar and other national park lodges in the early twentieth century used structural materials in their natural state, lending a rustic aesthetic similar to that found in the Adirondacks. Courtesy of J. Mark Souther.

appropriate to complement national park scenery. After signing a long-term concession contract with the Fred Harvey Company, the Park Service built the Grand Canyon Village around the El Tovar in the 1920s. This 3.2-square-mile village, created to service a transient resort town of 5,000 to 30,000 visitors, improved administration facilities and standardized the tourist experience within the 1.2-million-acre park. Grand Canyon Village was also emblematic of early NPS landscape architecture that tried to funnel visitors into centralized control points. Standardization and federal control squeezed nearly all locals from the tourist business and inaugurated the intense promotion of the canyon's built amenities.

Central to this promotion was the changing cultural appreciation of the Grand Canyon and its native population. The Havasupai's presence and the tribe's discovered ruins had prompted Roosevelt to invoke the Antiquities Act in protecting the canyon, yet afterward, authorities consistently pushed Indians to the canyon's physical and cultural periphery. Not only did the canyon accommodate visitors, but housing the staff necessary to operate such a popular destination created a neonative community on the Kaibab Plateau. Beginning at the turn of the twentieth century, the Fred Harvey Company, and later NPS, housed employees near the guest

Fig. 30. Tourists observe a Hopi Indian dance outside the Hopi House in Grand Canyon Village in this ca. 1960 postcard view. Courtesy of J. Mark Souther.

accommodations. Here workers formed their own neighborhood, living
together as a community that went unopposed because it did not displace
a local population. The canyon's native tribe, the Havasupai, occupied
Cataract Canyon, a side canyon south and west of the south rim. There
they farmed and gathered essential materials and game from the Kaibab
Plateau above, constantly moving between canyon floor and plateau.
The Park Service employed many of the Havasupai men as did the Fred
Harvey Company. Both the company and the Park Service mythologized
the native presence in the canyon by building visitor centers and hotels
in a faux-Hopi Indian style designed by Mary Jane Colter that purposely
masked the Havasupai's traditional mud-and-stick structures called
hawas. Colter's Hopi House, Grand Canyon Lodge, and Desert View
Watchtower, along with "traditional" craft demonstrations and sales in the
village created a stylized representation of southwestern Puebloan culture
instead of accurately depicting the true native culture. Thus rather than
forcibly removing the tribe, the Park Service first ignored the Havasupai,
then co-opted them to participate in the misrepresentation of the canyon's
native history (Fig. 30).

The 1920s witnessed the rise of auto tourism both at the Grand
Canyon and across the country. For the first time, in 1926, more visitors

traveled to the canyon in their cars than by train. Rising automobile traffic democratized park visitation, bringing the middle class to the south rim in droves. The Park Service responded to burgeoning tourist numbers with more development, including grocery stores, restaurants, gift shops, a post office, and gas stations all designed to accommodate auto tourists. Nowhere was this more apparent than in Grand Canyon Village, where driveways and parking lots encircled El Tovar, Hopi House, and surrounding public services, leaving a much more visible transportation imprint than the adjacent railroad. In a very real way, nineteenth-century discovery had yielded to twentieth-century comforts. As the number and quality of man-made amenities rose and automobile travel improved, the number of visitors and their physical impact on the canyon accelerated from this point forward.

Along with accelerated visitation, nonnative groups continued to disregard the canyon's native population and compete over the canyon's meaning well into the latter half of the twentieth century. The Bureau of Reclamation's Upper Colorado River Storage Project plan proposed building two dams in the Grand Canyon in the 1960s to help offset the project's monetary costs. Competing cultural ideas about the canyon clashed and groups such as the Sierra Club helped the Park Service mount a defense that became "the conservation movement's coming of age."[2] The Sierra Club led the charge to block the Bureau's plan, citing the recent passage of the 1964 Wilderness Act, and how it mandated protection for the Colorado River. The Sierra Club's lobbying efforts, combined with a savvy public relations campaign, proved successful when Congress authorized an alternative water conservation project that did not include dams in the Grand Canyon. The struggle reshaped Grand Canyon National Park into a symbol of victory and a touchstone for the nascent environmental movement.

The Bureau of Reclamation's plan to dam portions of the Colorado River ended the overt threats to the park's environmental well-being. Since that time, the park's greatest challenge stems from the endless stream of park visitors. As visitor numbers increased, the length of their stays decreased, with most spending only a few hours viewing the canyon walls at one of the south rim's scenic overlooks. Recently, layers of smog have obscured their view. The clouds are the byproduct of increasing vehicle traffic to and from the park, along with emissions from coal-fired power plants that provide electricity to the expanding service community surrounding the park.

When tourism in the Grand Canyon began in the nineteenth century, no one imagined its future impact. Designation of the canyon as a national park and its administration by the NPS reflected the nation's shifting attitude toward the natural world over the last century. While the Park Service worked hard to preserve the canyon's environment, its management also mirrored the nation's insouciance toward preserving the native tribe's cultural integrity. Instead, the Park Service co-opted the Havasupai's past, creating a faux-native cultural presentation for tourists, manifested by Colter's Hopi-inspired architectural designs throughout the south rim. The successful promotion of Grand Canyon National Park and the popularity of the south rim's village have their own attendant consequences. As the park enters the twenty-first century, ever-expanding crowds of people and automobiles descend on the park annually. Today regional population growth and spiraling visitation threaten to significantly degrade the park experience. In response to this critical test, the Park Service avoids limiting park visitation and instead seeks to spread development away from its south rim village before the urban problems of traffic jams, overcrowding, and overdevelopment sour the experience of the Grand Canyon's natural beauty for all visitors.

GRANT PARK
CHICAGO, ILLINOIS

Timothy J. Gilfoyle

Chicago's Grant Park represents the earliest American example of a major urban waterfront devoted to recreation and culture. The park's 319 acres along Lake Michigan are located immediately east of the city's central business district and Michigan Avenue. For most of the twentieth century, Grant Park was Chicago's "front yard,"[1] the site of renowned museums and cultural institutions, celebrations of special events and popular festivals, and visits by international dignitaries. Recreational activities—softball, ice skating, rollerblading, tennis, biking, and jogging—were daily and seasonal events throughout the park.[2] The addition of Millennium Park reinforced the centrality of the site as both a cultural center and tourist destination.

In the aftermath of the World's Columbian Exposition of 1893, Chicago civic leaders consciously sought to create a lakefront devoid of commerce and industry. Grant Park was the centerpiece of that project. In 1895, Peter B. Wight, working on behalf of the Municipal Improvement League and the Illinois Chapter of the American Institute of Architects, presented a plan for a lakefront park with monumental and classical architecture, including a peristyle, an exposition building, the John Crerar Library, and the Field Columbian Museum. Wight argued that Chicago should not replicate the naturalistic Lincoln or Jackson Parks, the city's other two large, lakefront parks. Chicago, insisted Wight, "needs another sort of park." The central, lakefront site presented a unique opportunity to create a civic and cultural center. "Here art should predominate over nature," Wight concluded, "and symmetry take precedence over picturesqueness."[3]

During the ensuing decades, Chicago business leaders and public officials debated precisely how to do this. The most famous rendering appeared with Daniel Burnham and Edward Bennett's *Plan of Chicago*
(1909). Like Wight, Burnham and Bennett envisioned a lakefront park
dominated by cultural institutions and magnificent edifices devoted to the
arts and sciences. The authors spoke on behalf of a civic elite that believed
the combined presence of such structures would generate both aesthetic
and economic rewards, transforming Chicago into a tourist "magnet."[4] In
short time, private and public authorities established a series of museums
and cultural institutions that quickly became Chicago's leading tourist and
educational attractions. Later additions devoted to mass leisure and entertainment in (Soldier Field in 1924 and Millennium Park in 2004) and
near (Navy Pier in 1995) Grant Park reflected the symbiotic relationship
among cultural institutions, municipal officials, business leaders, and private philanthropists motivated by the forces of a tourist economy.

Unlike the master-planned grand public parks in other North American cities—Central Park in New York, Prospect Park in Brooklyn, Golden
Gate Park in San Francisco, and Mount Royal Park in Montreal—Grant
Park evolved incrementally for more than a century. The park never had
one comprehensive plan, nor was it the brainchild of a single architect.
Rather, Grant Park developed in a piecemeal fashion, the combined product of various and sometimes-unrelated architects, landscape designers,
planners, artists, and business leaders.[5] Cooperative alliances among public, private, and philanthropic leaders not only created Grant Park but also
demonstrated the increasing importance of tourism, culture, and recreation in the economic history of American cities.[6]

The Grant Park site was originally water—Lake Michigan.[7] In 1836, the
Board of Canal Commissioners organized a public auction to sell Chicago's first city lots. Worried about the impact of unregulated lakefront
commerce, the commissioners left the land from Randolph Street south to
Park Row (Eleventh Street) and east of Michigan Avenue vacant and un-
divided with the notation on the official map: "Public Ground—A Common to Remain Forever Open, Clear and Free of Any Buildings, or Other
Obstruction Whatever."[8] No other document proved as controversial in
the evolution of Grant Park.

In 1847, the narrow strip of real estate east of Michigan Avenue was
designated "Lake Park." Over the next half century, Chicagoans used both

"Lake Park" and "Lake Front Park" to describe the public space.[9] The park's proximity to Lake Michigan attracted promenading pedestrians and tourists alike, generating comparisons with New York's Battery, Boston's Tremont Street Mall, Philadelphia's Fairmount Park, and Charleston's Battery.[10] In 1901, following a national practice of memorializing Civil War heroes, city officials renamed the park in honor of Ulysses S. Grant.[11]

Fierce winter storms off Lake Michigan, however, threatened periodically to wash the park into the lake. So in 1852, Chicago officials cut a deal. The city council granted a right-of-way to the Illinois Central Railroad to enter the city, but only through Lake Michigan. The railroad company complied by constructing a protective breakwater in the lake parallel to Michigan Avenue. Eventually, the railroad controlled over 100 acres north of Monroe Street, some of which later became part of Grant Park.[12] The barrier not only protected Lake Park and Michigan Avenue but also created an attractive lagoon for recreational boating.[13]

After the Great Fire of 1871, the area between Michigan Avenue and the breakwater became a landfill site for charred rubble. Over the next twenty years, the lagoon was filled in and, for the first time, land east of the railroad trestle was created. Civic leaders effectively ignored the "open, clear and free" provision by erecting "temporary" structures in Lake Park: the 165-foot-high Inter-State Industrial Exposition Building (1873-91), a small railroad freight depot next door (1873), two armories (1881), and the Union baseball grounds (1871, 1878-84) built by Albert G. Spaulding, owner of the Chicago White Stockings and forerunners of the Chicago Cubs.[14]

Michigan Avenue landlord and retail magnate Aaron Montgomery Ward grew intolerant of the park's unsightliness and the city's failure to enforce the ban on buildings. In 1890, he initiated the first of several lawsuits to keep the park free of new structures. Over the next two decades, a series of Illinois Supreme Court decisions—the so-called "Montgomery Ward restrictions"—concluded that all landfill east of Michigan Avenue was subject to the "open, clear and free" limitations adopted by the canal commissioners in 1836.[15]

The World's Columbian Exposition of 1893 stimulated a movement devoted to lakefront beautification. "We believe that an opportunity here exists to produce a park and a water front that will have no equal in the world," proclaimed civic leader Ferdinand W. Peck.[16] Whereas nineteenth- and early twentieth-century landscape architects like Frederick Law Olmsted, Calvert Vaux, and Jens Jensen promoted naturalistic and pastoral designs, Chicago civic leaders envisioned the park as an educational and cultural center. Planners such as Charles Atwood, Normand Patton, Peter Wight, and others proposed magnificent sculptures, classical plazas, and monumental cultural institutions.[17]

Tourism shaped this debate. In 1897, in a speech before the Merchants' Club, architect Daniel Burnham lamented how Americans visited Paris, Vienna, Cairo, and the Riviera at the expense of Chicago. Burnham then challenged the city's business community to generate more tourism and recreation: "Why not establish here physical conditions which will make this the pleasure-town of the country, and thus enable our citizens to avail themselves of the fact?"[18] Chicago's lakefront should not be devoted to industry or commerce like other cities. In particular, Burnham later proclaimed, Grant Park should be "the intellectual center of Chicago" because "art everywhere has been a source of wealth and moral influence."[19]

By then, private cultural institutions were already gravitating to the lakefront along Michigan Avenue. The Fine Arts Building (1883) and the Auditorium (1889) overlooked Lake Park. The World's Congresses Building (1893; later the Art Institute of Chicago) became the first structure to obtain unanimous approval from property owners adjoining the park, a precedent that shaped the later evolution of Grant Park.[20] The construction of the Chicago Public Library (1897) and Orchestra Hall (1904) further encouraged cultural development.[21] This "city beautiful" vision culminated in Daniel Burnham and Edward Bennett's *Plan of Chicago* (1909).[22]

Bennett later led a team of architects in designing Grant Park. These plans reflected earlier classical schemes, while adding French garden and Renaissance features: symmetrical spaces, axial views through the landscape, formal rows of plantings, recessed terraces, and sculptures. Ornamental trees, paths, and hedges further subdivided the *salles* or rooms of the park. In 1919, the railroad tracks were depressed below street level. The privately donated Buckingham Fountain (1927) introduced a monumental centerpiece into Grant Park (Fig. 31).[23] Landfill was added at the southern end of the park, just outside the area designated to remain "open, clear and free of any buildings." This allowed for the construction of Municipal Grant Park Stadium (1924; renamed Soldier Field in 1925), as well as privately operated cultural institutions: the Field Museum of Natural History (1919), the John G. Shedd Aquarium (1929), and the Adler Planetarium (1930). Mayor William Hale Thompson defended this lakefront

Fig. 31. Grant Park in 1929, showing Buckingham Fountain and the Michigan Avenue skyline. The park created a dramatic vantage point that encouraged tourists to behold Chicago's canyon-like wall of modern skyscrapers. The rail yard beyond the Art Institute on the northern edge of the park became the site of Millennium Park. Courtesy of Chicago History Museum.

construction by invoking tourism: "Not only would the stadium give the people of Chicago a great deal of enjoyment, but it would attract thousands of visitors." Chicago, he added, would become a place "for holding world championship contests."[24]

Grant Park's Soldier Field quickly became the prime venue for such tourist and civic attractions. In 1926, the 28th Eucharistic Congress produced the largest crowds in Chicago history: approximately 425,000 people inside and outside the stadium.[25] A year later, the boxing match between Jack Dempsey and Gene Tunney—with the so-called "long count"—attracted between 140,000 and 150,000 observers. The 1937 Prep Bowl between Leo and Austin high schools brought 125,000 spectators to Soldier Field, the largest gathering ever for a Chicago football contest. Religious rallies lured thousands of visiting pilgrims to the city. Protestant and Roman Catholic groups regularly sponsored Easter and other services witnessed by more than 50,000. Approximately 260,000 came to Soldier Field in 1954 to celebrate the feast of the Immaculate Conception. A Billy Graham revival attracted more than 116,000 from at least fifteen states to Soldier Field in 1962, the most worshipers Graham ever drew at a U.S. event.[26]

A band shell (1933–78; renamed Petrillo in 1976) modeled after the Hollywood Bowl proved to be an equally significant attraction. Free Grant Park summer concerts initially drew between 2.1 million and 3.5 million people yearly, more than double the annual number of visitors to the Art Institute or spectators attending Soldier Field events. The concerts' popularity ultimately led to the establishment of the Grant Park Symphony Orchestra in 1944.[27]

The automobile proved to be an unexpected and controversial influence. Portions of north and south Lake Shore Drive opened during the 1930s, introducing more and high-speed motor traffic into Grant Park. By 1946, three Grant Park parking lots accommodated more than one million vehicles annually. The Monroe Street Parking Station (opened in 1921 and completed in 1938), with a capacity of 3,500 cars, remained the largest single-fee parking facility in the United States into the 1950s. The automobile's popularity convinced city officials to build three underground garages after World War II. By the 1980s, the annual number of cars parking in Grant Park topped three million.[28]

More cars, however, did not beget more usage of Grant Park. Increasing motor traffic discouraged pedestrian movement from Michigan Avenue to the lakefront; one report discovered that only 50,000 people annually visited the lakeside area of the park. Grant Park, complained journalist Ruth Moore in 1961, "largely belongs to the automobile."[29]

Others criticized Grant Park as a disorderly and dangerous place. The violence associated with antiwar demonstrations during the Democratic Party Convention in 1968 occurred in front of the Hilton Hotel along the western edge of the park. Two years later, a riot broke out after the rock group Sly and the Family Stone failed to appear for a Grant Park concert; more than 100 were injured and another 150 arrested. In 1973, two women were murdered in the park.[30] Famed urbanist William H. Whyte lamented that the "trouble with Grant Park is not so much what the park has got as what it hasn't got enough of—people."[31]

After 1980, Grant Park proved instrumental in efforts by city officials to discourage middle-class migration to suburbs and encourage downtown economic development. Civic leaders adopted programs to attract more public usage of the park. The largest annual festivals moved to Grant Park and were more heavily advertised: Venetian Night (1958), the Chicago

Fig. 32. Crown Fountain is an interactive video sculpture located along South Michigan Avenue in Millennium Park. Designed in 2004 by Catalan artist Jaume Plensa, Crown Fountain consists of two glass brick pillars that generate LED digital videos and spout streams of water onto a black granite reflecting pool. Courtesy of J. Mark Souther.

Jazz Festival (1978), the Taste of Chicago (1981), the Chicago Blues Festival (1984), the Chicago Gospel Fest (1987), and Lollapalooza (2005). The finish and starting lines of the Chicago Marathon were relocated to Grant Park in 1990 and 1994, respectively.[32]

Mayor Richard M. Daley, in particular, encouraged ever-more residen-
tial, commercial, cultural, and tourist activity in and around Grant Park.
The reconfiguration of Lake Shore Drive (1996) and renovation of Soldier
Field (2002-3) at the southern end of Grant Park created the Museum
Campus around the Field Museum, Shedd Aquarium, and Adler Plan-
etarium.[33] By 1995, the area extending from the Museum Campus to Navy
Pier just north of Grant Park reportedly attracted more than ten million
annual visitors, greater than the Grand Canyon and Yosemite National
Park combined.[34]

Efforts to stimulate tourism and downtown development culminated
in the construction of Millennium Park (Fig. 32). Daley conceived of the
24.5-acre addition to be a collaborative public and private sector project
celebrating the passage of the second millennium and completing the
northwest corner of Grant Park.[35] Private fundraiser John Bryan and public director Ed Uhlir attracted more than 115 private gifts of at least $1
million, totaling in excess of $220 million.[36] This philanthropic wealth en-
abled planners to recruit world-renowned artists to design enhancements
in Millennium Park: a music pavilion, trellis, and bridge by architect Frank
Gehry; a music and dance theater by architect Thomas Beeby; a garden by
Kathryn Gustafson, Piet Oudolf, and Robert Israel; a fountain by Jaume
Plensa; and a sculpture by Anish Kapoor. The park epitomized Daley's
vision of transforming Chicago into a global city with an infrastructure
appropriate for a twenty-first-century economy driven by service-sector
businesses, tourism, and culture. Millennium Park was among the top
three tourist attractions in Chicago shortly after opening in 2004.[37]

In the *Plan of Chicago*, Daniel Burnham and Edward Bennett envisioned Chicago as a tourist haven: "the city should become a magnet,
drawing to us those who wish to enjoy life."[38] During the ensuing century, civic authorities built and maintained Grant Park as a waterfront
devoid of commerce and manufacturing. While some events and projects were subsidized by the municipality, the institutions and spaces that
proved most popular were privately built or philanthropic contributions:
the Union baseball grounds in the nineteenth century; the numerous
museums, public art, and Buckingham Fountain in the twentieth; Millennium Park in the twenty-first century. Grant Park thus exemplified the
symbiotic relationship of cultural tourism, leisure-time consumption, and
economic development organized by municipal officials, business leaders
and private philanthropists. These cooperative alliances not only created
Chicago's major lakefront park but they also embodied a consumerist vision necessary for the emergence of a dynamic tourist economy.

HILTON HEAD ISLAND,
SOUTH CAROLINA

James Tuten

The distinctive tourism feature of Hilton Head Island is not its views of the Atlantic Ocean, but the pioneering way that Sea Pines Company began the development of the island's first resort community. Led by Charles Fraser, Sea Pines reflected a different cultural background, one that sought to use wealth in ways that emphasized restraint, an appreciation for nature, and exclusivity, rather than building the largest home possible on an otherwise idealized suburban tract. That vision succeeded in bringing well-heeled retirees and second-home owners along with attention to the island in the 1960s. Later developers, however, came with different cultural backgrounds and they sought to create mass tourism, which meant constructing condominiums and changing the landscape in far more radical ways. Still, they too understood that they had to make some allowances for the Hilton Head style established by Fraser in the late 1950s. The result has largely been that while the Sea Pines approach proved influential in later coastal tourism for the affluent, the island today has multiple styles of development.

Human expectations for Hilton Head Island, defined as they have been by cultural trends, have resulted in three dramatically different visions of land use being imposed by landowners. The intensively cultivated and spectacularly profitable Sea Island cotton plantations of the eighteenth and nineteenth century had all but disappeared from the landscape by the dawn of the twentieth. During the first half of the twentieth century, the descendants of slaves resided on Hilton Head Island where they practiced subsistence agriculture, even as the land slowly returned to a state resembling the heavily forested barrier island English explorer William Hilton sighted in the seventeenth century. In 1949, a group of Hinesville, Georgia, timber investors, recognizing the value of the island's forest, formed the Hilton Head Company and, over the next several years, bought more than 19,000 acres of an island totaling 25,000 acres. In two years of intense lumber extraction they had cut the accessible and valuable timber to feed the lumber appetite of a rapidly suburbanizing nation.[1]

Timber poor but land rich, the Hilton Head Company started selling beachfront lots in its Folly Field development in the mid-1950s, having successfully lobbied for ferry service for the island's eleven hundred residents (nearly all black). In 1956, access dramatically improved with the opening of the first bridge to the island, increasing the value of lots, and finally yielding the hothouse development that frequently accompanies the arrival of cars. Automotive access was but one part of a revolution that visited Hilton Head in 1956. That same year, twenty-six-year-old Yale Law graduate Charles E. Fraser, a "visionary developer," brought his dream of remaking the island for tourism while avoiding what he saw as the "visual pollution" of nearly all Atlantic Coast seaside construction.[2] He disdained the emergence of high-rise hotels and condominiums on the oceanfront in Florida and the tourist-oriented, architecturally bland strip malls that went with them.

Fraser's father, Joseph B. Fraser, one of the major partners in the Hilton Head Company, backed his son's dream by splitting his tract and putting the southern portion of the island in his son's hands. Charles Fraser formed Sea Pines Company and designated his development Sea Pines Plantation in 1957. Unlike Naples, Florida's influential Port Royal development, where John Glen Sample handpicked homeowners to assure exclusivity, Fraser's Sea Pines relied on his penchant for crafting an exclusive atmosphere through architecture and landscape. Drawing upon his interest in conservation, design, and anticipating some of New Urbanism's rejection of 1950s-style suburbanization, Fraser made innovative use of his law background by placing stringent limits on homeowners with forty pages of restrictions in each deed. The layout of houses and streets, even the architecture of the homes themselves, sought to maximize views of forest, creeks, marsh, and the ocean. Fraser micromanaged the process as the extensive building covenants suggest. Houses had to be painted in natural colors so they blended into the mostly natural landscape in which they were planted.[3]

Fig. 33. Harbour Town at Sea Pines Plantation. Completed in 1970, the ninety-foot-tall striped lighthouse serves as a focal point for a circular marina surrounded by condominiums and is the most recognizable place on what has become a heavily developed resort island. Courtesy of Susan McCann @ Island Photography, Hilton Head Island, SC.

Beginning with Charles Fraser and Sea Pines, Hilton Head enjoyed notoriety for conserving natural beauty and developing a resort community in which architecture, golf courses, and landscaping attempted to blend together and where status could not be displayed through ostentatious homes.[4] Moreover, by building Harbour Town with its iconic short, red-and-white striped lighthouse, semicircular marina, and scenic golf course, Sea Pines attracted the PGA Tour to the island for the Heritage Golf Tournament in 1969 (Fig. 33). A live televised PGA event with many views of Harbour Town effectively marketed the image of the island to America's wealthy.[5] Meanwhile, the Hilton Head Company continued to develop Forest Beach and Folly Field. It carved up much of the rest of the island, developing Port Royal Plantation and Shipyard Plantation and selling land to other developers who built Palmetto Dunes, all of which shared something of the concept pioneered by Fraser (Fig. 34). In the 1970s, however, the original stockholders sold their interests in the Hilton Head Company to a holding company, which pursued rampant development that sometimes veered away from earlier visions. Over the next decade and a half, much of Hilton Head would bounce from one

Fig. 34. A typical Hilton Head beach house, shown here in 1971. With its understated design and generous setbacks from the beach amid a strip of maritime forest, this home typifies the Hilton Head approach to blending development with the natural environment of the barrier island. Courtesy of Arthur Lum.

holding company to another, threatening to undo the resort's alabaster reputation.[6]

Resort development in the South frequently displaced communities of poor whites and blacks. In Hilton Head's case, the island's population switched from an all-black Gullah community to an overwhelmingly white and affluent majority in a generation. Many Hilton Head blacks changed employment from fishing, timbering, and farming to jobs supporting the tourism industry. In keeping with broader trends, these jobs reflected a rather marked division by gender. Men worked in landscaping and construction while women provided cleaning, maid service, and food-service labor. These jobs, like agriculture, were seasonal, paid minimum wage or low wages and offered almost no chance for advancement. As property values soared developers frequently bought out black property owners, and generally few black landowners succeeded in gaining capital to convert their land into tourism-based businesses. Black islanders felt shut out of local decision making and economic development. As a result, they established a local chapter of the National Association for the Advancement of Colored People and engaged in community organizing to speak for black concerns.[7]

Fraser and the like-minded developers of Hilton Head subscribed to a double standard in their arguments. When it came to the gentrification of the island—wealthy retirees and absentee owners supplanting black natives—they claimed that the market prevailed. That is, since they could buy the land or owned the land, they had the right to develop it, even if rising tax values, changing quality of life, and exclusion from their gated plantations affected black islanders. However, Fraser and his ilk turned right around and pleaded conservation or environmental values to be more important than market values when a proposed BASF chemical plant at nearby Victoria Bluff threatened the water quality and scenic vistas of the area. Likewise, the move to incorporate Hilton Head in 1983 stemmed as much from Sea Pines Plantation residents' desire to stop what they viewed as lowbrow commercialization of the island as it did from a desire to enhance public services.[8]

By the 1980s, the Hilton Head style had influenced resort development up and down the Atlantic Coast. Fraser himself designed two other notable Southern coastal resorts, Kiawah Island in South Carolina and Amelia Island Plantation in Florida. Since then Fraser's approach to development has extended to the anti-sprawl movement through his former employees and his consulting efforts, the best-known example of which is the Walt Disney Company's famous planned development, Celebration, Florida.[9]

Hilton Head's overdevelopment threatened to overwhelm its commitment to blending the natural and man-made into a harmonious landscape, but the island's image still appeared worth burnishing. In 2007, fifty years into the tourist paradise era of Hilton Head Island and up to three decades into a period of growing competition with resorts that sought to improve on the Hilton Head model, the Hilton Head–Bluffton Chamber of Commerce underscored the island's long-standing "emphasis on . . . key attributes: Strong ecological ties; luxury resorts and first-rate outdoor activities; and most importantly, its serenity and restorative characteristic." Apparently, many beachgoers to Hilton Head were satisfied with the resort's maintenance of a positive visitor experience. Hilton Head owes its success to the founding principle: the self-conscious maintenance of sufficient naturalistic landscape to give tourists the comforting sense that their leisure unfolds in harmony with their environment.

HOLLYWOOD

LOS ANGELES, CALIFORNIA

Ken Breisch

Horace and Daeida Wilcox founded Hollywood in the early 1880s as a small Christian suburb of Los Angeles. They banned alcohol and offered free plots of land to any congregation willing to raise a church. But within three decades, Hollywood had become synonymous with the American film industry, which was in fact widely dispersed across the Los Angeles region and had very little in common with the vision of its Methodist founders. The arrival during the second decade of the last century of legendary directors, such as Cecile B. DeMille, D. W. Griffith, and Mack Sennett, and their studios, initiated the transformation of the once-conservative community into a symbol of this new entertainment form.[1]

With the financial backing of Jesse Lasky, DeMille established the first permanent movie set in Hollywood in a barn at the corner of Selma and Vine for his film *The Squaw Man* in 1913. Two years later, Griffith, who had begun working in the area somewhat earlier, hired English designer Walter Hall to re-create the legendary Gates of Babylon for his epic film *Intolerance*. This exotic set stood near the intersection of Sunset and Hollywood Boulevards until 1919, when it was dismantled as a fire hazard. And Sennet immortalized the streets of Los Angeles in his Keystone comedies. Within a few short years, the film business had become a major industry in the region, introducing the world to what Kevin Starr has described as "a new southern California genre, the Hollywood movie star."[2] This new form of celebrity included luminaries such as Mary Pickford, Lillian and Dorothy Gish, Norma Talmadge, William S. Hart, Charlie Chaplin, Douglas Fairbanks, and Lionel Barrymore, larger-than-life personalities whose every move—on-screen and off—American audiences began to follow with ever-increasing obsession. Hollywood itself began to emerge as a destination for starstruck motion picture fans from around the globe.

In response to its new audiences, Carl Laemmle, as early as 1916, began charging tourists twenty-five cents for a box lunch and the opportunity to witness film productions and ogle their stars on the back lots of his newly created Universal City Studio, which was located across the Cahuenga Pass, some five miles north of Hollywood. This same year, the Hollywood Bowl opened in a natural open-air amphitheater known as Daisy Dell with a theater production of Julius Caesar, which starred Tyrone Power, Douglas Fairbanks, and May Murray.[3] It joined existing tourist destinations such as the De Longpre gardens at the corner of Hollywood Boulevard and Cahuenga Avenue and the grounds of the Bernheimer mansion (Yama Shira), which were laid out as a miniature Japanese garden in 1914. In 1922, the Hollywood Bowl inaugurated its famous Easter sunrise services and five years later Lloyd Wright, son of the famed architect Frank Lloyd Wright, designed a pyramidal wooden band shell to accommodate the still-popular "Symphonies under the Stars," a structure he rebuilt in steel in 1928, this time in a series of concentric circles that became an iconic feature in Hollywood.

During this same period, the introduction of sound began to shift production from open-air sets into sound stages, isolating filmmaking from an audience that previously had been able to unobtrusively observe the shooting of silent films. Simultaneously celebrities began moving out of Hollywood into the more affluent communities of Beverly Hills and Bel Air, and to entertain themselves in new clubs and restaurants along the Sunset Boulevard "Strip" to the west of Hollywood. Professional tour guides and, after the mid-1930s, star maps began directing sightseers past these new homes and exotic haunts, while Hollywood Boulevard began to transform itself into an industry stand-in, a glamorous location for film premieres and often-rumored star sightings, especially—it was said—at the much-ballyhooed corner of Hollywood and Vine.

This new phase of "Hollywood" and its boulevard was ushered in with the opening of the Egyptian Theatre in 1922. This extravagant showplace was originally conceived by theater impresario, Sid Grauman, as a Spanish Colonial palace, but during construction the discovery of the tomb of Tutankhamen led him and his architects, Meyer and Holler, to redesign

Fig. 35. The pagoda-like Grauman's Chinese Theatre, opened by Sid Grauman for the premiere of Cecil B. DeMille's film *The King of Kings*, joined Grauman's earlier Egyptian Theatre (1922) and added to the eclectic appearance of Hollywood. Courtesy of J. Mark Souther.

it as an exotic Egyptian fantasy. Five years later, Grauman opened his even more fabled Chinese Theatre, with its forecourt exhibiting the hand and footprints of Hollywood celebrities (Fig. 35). The theater became an immediate success, attracting more than a half-million visitors in its first four months. And it continues to draw several million tourists a year, who place their hands in the imprints of the young Shirley Temple, or have themselves photographed with a surrogate Charlie Chaplin, Marilyn Monroe, Darth Vader, or Wookie. Grauman's film palaces were soon joined by other equally exotic settings designed to celebrate klieg-lit premieres and first-run films. These included the El Capitan (Morgan, Walls, and Clements, 1926), Warner (G. Albert Landsburgh, 1926-27) and Pantages (Marcus Priteca, 1930) theaters, which by 1930 positioned Hollywood Boulevard as a formidable rival to downtown Los Angeles's Broadway theater district. The appearance of high-end retail emporia, boutiques, hotels, and restaurants during the 1920s further raised the profile of the district, which was heavily promoted by the Hollywood Chamber of Commerce and other civic and merchant groups, such as the Hollywood Boulevard Association.[4]

During the holiday season, elaborate street decorations and the Santa Claus Lane Parade, which featured floats and bands, and the all-important appearance of Hollywood personalities, drew large crowds of locals and winter vacationers to the area. Hovering over this new hub of shopping and entertainment was the colossal 450-foot-long Hollywoodland sign, which was erected in 1923 to advertise a real-estate venture bankrolled by Harry Chandler, editor and owner of the *Los Angeles Times*. Following its deterioration, the chamber of commerce removed its last four letters in 1945 and reconstructed it in steel to create one of southern California's most iconic images.

In 1924, *Los Angeles Times* columnist, A. L. Woodridge noted that Hollywood had surpassed southern California's older tourist attractions—its beaches, orange groves, and missions—as the must-see destination for visitors. And he quotes one local tour guide as saying that "nothing is looked forward to with so much interest as a peek at the place where the motion-picture stars, themselves, really eat and sleep and move about. And if tourists can catch a glimpse of a film star himself or herself, whichever the case may be, they will have something to talk about for the rest of their lives."[5] By 1926, the American film business had become the fifth-largest industry in the United States, grossing $1.5 billion annually, while producing 90 percent of the world's movies. Its phenomenal success only added to the aura of Hollywood.

While the American tourist economy generally languished during the Great Depression, the film industry continued to flourish, further extending its mystique around the globe. From the dazzling extravaganzas of Busby Berkeley to the magical fantasy of Oz, the spell of Hollywood grew in the minds of moviegoers, and the radiant, if elusive, glitter and myth of Tinsel Town beckoned ever larger as both actual destination and psychological escape. The arrival of radio studios in the 1930s and the television industry after the war helped Hollywood maintain its title as Entertainment Capital of the World, but the depressed economy took its toll on fashionable Hollywood Boulevard businesses, as did competition from a growing number of automobile-oriented shopping centers located outside of the urban cores of Hollywood and downtown Los Angeles.[6]

The onset of World War II ushered in a brief period of prosperity as lonely servicemen and servicewomen—as they did in New York's Times Square or New Orleans's Bourbon Street—streamed onto Hollywood

Boulevard and its side streets in search of diversions from wartime duty. USO facilities and "Hollywood Canteens" offered free meals, clean beds, and live entertainment, and the opportunity to mix with Mary Pickford, Bette Davis, Lana Turner, Marlene Dietrich, and other stars who volunteered at these establishments to support the war effort.

Following the war, however, Hollywood continued its Depression-era decline, even while its boosters persisted in conjuring an almost schizophrenic memory of its past. Tourists arrived to discover an empty shell of the Hollywood dream; shoddy theaters, cheap bars, and sex shops; ever-increasing crime and vice; and very little of the glamour and mystique they had come to experience. To counter this shabby reality, the Hollywood and Vine Development Committee unveiled the first of many subsequent "beautification" plans for Hollywood Boulevard in 1955. This proposed the introduction of "bold treatments for intersections, colored sidewalks, canopies, plantings, cases displaying phases of film activities, harmonious signs, modernistic benches, and miscellaneous improvements, including many-hued receptacles for trash."[7] This largely cosmetic scheme was joined several years later by the newly formed Hollywood Improvement Association's proposal to create a three-mile "Walk of Fame" along the boulevard, with new lighting, and pink and charcoal terrazzo sidewalks inset with brass stars displaying the names entertainment personalities (Fig. 36). Delayed by lawsuits, this more successful attraction was dedicated in 1961.

In the meantime, Disneyland, which opened in Anaheim in Orange County in 1955, and the Universal Studios Tours, which were inaugurated nine years later, began to siphon tourists away from downtown Hollywood. Initiated in 1964, when the studio began to allow sightseeing buses to pass through its back lots, Universal Tours continued to expand with the addition of attractions based upon their most successful films. These were augmented in 1993 with the opening of CityWalk, a two-block shopping mall comprising sanitized simulacra of iconic Hollywood and L.A. structures and images designed by Los Angeles architect, Jon Jerde. These combined Universal attractions now draw some five million visitors a year, more than any other tourist venue in Los Angeles County.

By the late 1960s, Sunset Boulevard began to emerge as the focus of a new nightclub scene that expanded west from Hollywood toward the Strip into what is now West Hollywood. Fueled by films and television—the image of

Fig. 36. Alfred Hitchcock's star. Achieving a similar effect to that of various halls of fame across the nation, Vine Street, dubbed the Hollywood Walk of Fame, features stars set in the sidewalk to commemorate celebrities. The first star was laid in January 1961 and to date, approximately 1,720 names are preserved in bronze to evoke those special memories of the entertainment world. Courtesy of Megan Happ.

Hollywood and Sunset Boulevards became synonymous with an exotic mix of hipsters and hippies, drag queens, religious cults, runaways, and street people. This new youth culture was increasingly blamed by the press and others for a rise in vandalism, panhandling, petty crime, drug use, and prostitution, as well as a continued decline in tourism—even as its denizens themselves became a new attraction, with "Middle-America" now arriving to gawk at Hollywood street life.

In an attempt to counter these activities, the Los Angeles City Planning Commission adopted a new Hollywood Master Plan in 1970. This promoted the replacement of the boulevard's now-ubiquitous T-shirt, souvenir, and porn shops with a commercial mall and high-rise entertainment center. More than three decades in the making, Hollywood and Highland Center, which was privately developed with a generous subsidy from the city by the Canadian-owned TrizecHahn Corporation, opened in 2001. The resulting 387,000-square-foot complex includes the now-rehabilitated Chinese Theatre, a 3,000-car underground garage, a luxury hotel, and the Kodak Theatre, which hosts the Academy Awards in Hollywood for the first time since 1960. The central courtyard of the mall is themed around a monumental, if anemic, replica of the D. W. Griffith's 1915 Babylon stage set.

In 1979, the Hollywood Revitalization Committee, in an effort to preserve something of the earlier Hollywood, sponsored a survey of the downtown, which culminated in 1985 in the designation of the Hollywood Boulevard Commercial and Entertainment National Register District. In 1980, the nonprofit preservation organization, Hollywood Heritage, was founded by local residents to further lobby for the preservation of the area's golden era. Through their efforts, and those of others, such as the Los Angeles Conservancy, many historic structures in Hollywood have been saved and rehabilitated, including the Egyptian, El Capitan, Chinese, and Pantages theaters. A handful of other iconic buildings and institutions have weathered the area's many ups and downs, which included the Northridge Earthquake of 1994 and construction of a new subway line beneath Hollywood Boulevard during the 1990s. Among these are the Bernheimer (Yama Shira) Mansion, Musso & Frank Grill, the Capitol Records Tower (Welton Becket Associates, 1954-56) and the recently reconstructed Hollywood Bowl. In 1983, the barn in which DeMille situated his original studio was relocated to a site across from the Hollywood Bowl, where it houses the Hollywood Heritage Museum. Several major studios survive as well, including Paramount and Columbia Pictures (now Sunset Gower Studios), as well as the Charlie Chaplin Studios, which currently house Henson Productions.

Whether its aura is authentic, invented, or just imagined, Hollywood continues to draw tourists. They visit its now-fabled Walk of Fame, the red carpet of the Academy Awards at the Kodak Theatre, the revived musicals at the El Capitan and Pantages theaters, and premieres and handprints of Shirley Temple and Judy Garland at the Chinese. Or they go to shop and eat at Hollywood and Highland or at one of the boulevard's still plentiful fast-food outlets, souvenir and T-shirt shops. They continue to be drawn to a place that seems as elusive, yet as alluring, as the movies and movie stars that made it famous.

Hollywood is a touchstone of American tourism. When filmmakers first erected stage sets, and then preserved them as destinations, they made a powerful gesture toward the idea of inventing "other directed" tourist places. Like Coney Island, Disneyland, and Las Vegas, Hollywood mastered the art of eclectic imagineering. That the film industry outgrew Hollywood hardly mattered. Long after the silver screen reflected images cast in dozens of other studio cities, Hollywood remained etched in the tourist imagination as the iconic capital of American film and celebrity alike.

INDEPENDENCE HALL
PHILADELPHIA, PENNSYLVANIA

Charlene Mires

Independence Hall, the building in Philadelphia where Americans declared their separation from Great Britain in 1776 and drafted a new U.S. Constitution in 1787, began as a governmental meeting place but evolved gradually into a historic landmark anchoring Independence National Historical Park. Desires to establish control, stability, and security for such a treasured fragment of the nation's founding assured its preservation through the nineteenth and twentieth centuries. By the twenty-first century, surviving in the midst of a changing city, Independence Hall became not only a destination in itself but also the anchor for additional attractions aiming to promote American citizenship and build the region's tourist economy.[1]

Originating as the Pennsylvania State House, Independence Hall was a cultural statement from the start. Constructed beginning in 1732, the building's Georgian architecture made a strong statement of British elite culture at a time when Philadelphia was experiencing an influx of German and Scots-Irish immigration. The structure endured as a working government building until the late nineteenth century. Before and after the momentous meetings of the Second Continental Congress and the Constitutional Convention, it served the needs of Pennsylvania government. After the state capital moved west at the end of the eighteenth century, eventually to Harrisburg, the old State House continued to function as a courthouse and meeting place for city government.

Amid the workings of government, installations to preserve the memory of the nation's founding began to take shape. Soon after the removal of state government, from 1802 to 1827, the old State House featured a museum of art and natural history installed on the second floor by artist Charles Willson Peale, whose goals included developing a national culture and an educated citizenry. Although the displays included portraits of signers of the Declaration of Independence, Peale did not promote the State House as a historical attraction or direct special attention to the first-floor meeting space of the Second Continental Congress and Constitutional Convention.

Philadelphians began to take interest in preserving the old State House as the fiftieth anniversary of the Declaration of Independence approached and stirred interest in the memory of the American Revolution. In 1816, city officials agreed to purchase the building rather than see it demolished as surplus state property. In 1824, Philadelphians chose the first-floor meeting room of the Continental Congress and the Constitutional Convention as a reception hall for the Marquis de Lafayette during his extended tour of the United States. While preparing for the visit, Philadelphians began to refer to this single room as the "Hall of Independence"—a phrase soon condensed to "Independence Hall" and gradually applied to the building as a whole. The Lafayette reception also established a ritual for welcoming important visitors to the city with an exchange of speeches about the building's historic associations, thereby sustaining its reputation as the nation's birthplace.

In contrast to the dense commercial and manufacturing district growing around Independence Hall, Philadelphians increased the building's "historic" space beyond the single room on the first floor. City officials designated State House Square as "Independence Square" in 1825, and in 1828, they insisted that a new steeple for the State House resemble the long-demolished steeple of 1776. The new steeple drew visitors for a bird's-eye view of the growing industrial city. But for nineteenth-century travelers, novelties such as Philadelphia's new Eastern State Penitentiary proved more popular than the Hall of Independence, which remained unmarked as a historic place until the early 1830s, when the city installed a brass plaque calling attention to the Declaration of Independence.

A more elaborate setting for appreciating the nation's founders took shape in 1855, after nativist politicians gained control of Philadelphia government. With their reverence for founding fathers, these officeholders decorated the Hall of Independence with historical portraits, artifacts, and a statue of George Washington (Fig. 37). The

Fig. 37. Beginning in 1855, visitors to Independence Hall drew inspiration from historical portraits, a statue of George Washington, and the Liberty Bell placed on a pedestal decorated with symbols recalling the American Revolution. As a shrine to the nation's founders, the setting reflected the patriotism and anti-immigrant sentiment of nativist politicians who gained control of Philadelphia's city government in 1854. Courtesy of the Library Company of Philadelphia.

room was made over once again in 1876 as the "Declaration Chamber" to display art and objects to commemorate the centennial of the Declaration of Independence. At this juncture, elite Philadelphians who traced their ancestry to the Revolution gained control from the city government and expanded the historic space inside the structure to include the entire first floor. Frank Etting, descendant of a prominent colonial-era family from Philadelphia and Baltimore, supervised the renovation of a former courtroom into what was then called the "National Museum." In a manner similar to the Mount Vernon Ladies Association, which launched the preservation of Mount Vernon during the 1850s, women from prominent Philadelphia families organized a national appeal for artifacts and managed the museum's collections. Although the museum provided Philadelphia with an enhanced historic attraction, the great Centennial Exposition in Fairmount Park proved far more popular as a visitor destination.

Not until the end of the nineteenth century did Independence Hall become fully devoted to preserving the memory of the nation's founding. At a time of high immigration and increasing industrialization, Philadelphians with Revolutionary-era ancestors once again took the lead. The Daughters of the American Revolution, after a prolonged struggle for control with the Sons of the Revolution, supervised a Colonial Revival "restoration" of the second floor to re-create the ambiance of the original banquet room of the eighteenth century. As government moved to a new City Hall during the 1890s, the restoration projects continued inside and out, including replacing exterior piazzas that had been demolished early in the nineteenth century.

These projects reached back to Independence Hall's eighteenth-century appearance and emphasized the building's role on the national stage, obscuring its eventful nineteenth-century history as a result. The renewed colonial ambiance on the second floor, for example, replaced the smoky chambers of the Philadelphia City Council and the local government that journalist Lincoln Steffens famously declared to be "corrupt and contented." Earlier, the same space had been leased to federal courts, where fugitive slave hearings after the Compromise of 1850 created a dramatic contrast to the nation's founding ideals.

By the early twentieth century, the elite Philadelphians who placed such great value on Independence Hall's eighteenth-century history began to view the urban environment around their treasured landmark as a jarring and inappropriate contrast. Motivated also by patriotism stirred by two world wars and the 150th anniversaries of the Declaration of Independence and the Constitution, local citizens lobbied for expanded parks around Independence Hall. Led by Common Pleas Court Judge Edwin O. Lewis, a member of the Sons of the American Revolution, a coalition that became known as the Independence Hall Association sought to create an environment for Independence Hall similar to Colonial Williamsburg. At the end of the Second World War, these Philadelphians won approval for an "Independence Mall" state park extending three blocks north of Independence Hall and for Independence National Historical Park extending three blocks east. Both required extensive demolition of the surrounding commercial and manufacturing district, much of it in decline since the Great Depression. The project was thus an act of urban redevelopment as well as historic preservation. Eighteenth-century buildings and the nineteenth-century Second Bank of the United States were considered historic and preserved; others were considered without significance and demolished.

Fig. 38. Family-oriented tourism of the Cold War era drew increasing numbers of visitors to Independence Hall, which became the anchor of Independence National Historical Park. In 1954, the *Philadelphia Bulletin* created this photograph of the visiting Powell family from Clinton, Missouri, to illustrate a typical tourist family's visit to Philadelphia. Courtesy of the Urban Archives, Temple University, Philadelphia.

The resulting parks and plazas situated Independence Hall as Philadelphia's prime tourist attraction as Cold War–era families sought to instill patriotic values in their children during summer vacations (Fig. 38). The National Park Service (NPS), which embarked on extensive research and restoration during the 1950s and 1960s, struggled with managing large numbers of visitors in such a small building. The pressures of tourism led the NPS to limit access to Independence Hall to guided tours beginning in the early 1970s and to move the popular Liberty Bell to a separate pavilion in 1976. By the early twenty-first century, tours of Independence Hall required timed tickets on most days of the year. After the terrorist attacks of September 11, 2001, barricades around the building and searches of visitors further separated the city from its historic landmark.

The expanded parks also created new spaces for public celebrations and demonstrations. During the 1960s, tourists encountered demonstrators for civil rights and on both sides of the Vietnam War. The NPS tolerated dissent as an exercise of free speech and assembly, even when college students staged an overnight sit-in for civil rights inside Independence Hall. In later years, however, more stringent federal regulations limited public demonstrations to designated areas outside the building.

Over time, the environment around Independence Hall became increasingly devoted to tourism and civic education. In a city suffering from deindustrialization, tourism presented a vital alternative for the local economy. With support from major donors including the Pew Charitable Trusts and the Annenberg Foundation, the three-block Independence Mall of the 1950s, viewed as a failure because of limited use of its expansive plazas, evolved once again in the late twentieth century to become a campus of new attractions: a National Constitution Center museum, a block-long Independence Visitor Center, and the Liberty Bell Center to display Independence Hall's most famous and popular artifact. The Visitor Center, especially, aimed to link the historic district around Independence Hall to other attractions in the Philadelphia region so that visitors would stay longer and contribute more to the region's tourist economy.

New understandings of Independence Hall and its historic associations also began to take shape. In the first decade of the twenty-first century, new scholarship and civic activism pushed the NPS toward acknowledging a more complicated national and local history. Attention focused especially on the site of the long-demolished President's House, situated between the new Visitor Center and Liberty Bell Center, where at least nine enslaved Africans worked during the Washington presidency. Under pressure from local historians and African-Americans, with a new organization called the Avenging the Ancestors Coalition at the forefront, exhibits in the Liberty Bell Center were changed to address slavery as well as freedom, and the NPS introduced "Liberty: The Promise and the Paradox" as one of its interpretive themes. Work commenced for an exhibit on the site of the President's House. For visitors to Independence Hall and the elaborate public space around it, the influence of Cold War patriotism showed signs of giving way to a more complex and multicultural understanding of U.S. history.

Las Vegas,
Nevada

Eugene P. Moehring

Las Vegas is a tourist city re-imagined and rebuilt by generations of entrepreneurs. From a small, rustic Western outpost, Las Vegas grew virtually overnight in the 1940s into a neon-decked casino town that replicated itself in the 1950s several miles southeast in the desert along the so-called Strip. Astute businessmen along the Strip then switched out its postwar resorts in the 1970s and 1980s to erect ever-grander, more fanciful settings for gambling and entertainment. Built on a bedrock of shotgun weddings, easy divorce, wide-open gambling, and glitzy entertainment, Las Vegas has since steered around the shoals of obsolescence, capricious consumer desires, and economic doldrums, by weaving dangerously among attractions that include upscale shopping, family fun, and traditional "sin-city" sleaze.

Unlike New Orleans, Memphis, Reno, and other cities where tourism became a dominant economic force, Las Vegas boasted no substantial downtown when Nevada re-legalized casino gambling in 1931. Even in 1940, the railroad stop that had billed itself as the "Gateway to Hoover Dam" for more than a decade still counted barely eight thousand residents. World War II was the key event that enthroned Las Vegas's tourist industry. Beginning in 1940 with the construction of the Army Gunnery School (today Nellis Air Force Base) northeast of town and the huge Basic Magnesium defense plant to the southeast, soldiers and defense workers nightly thronged the city's fledgling casinos. Joined by their counterparts from southern California and Arizona, they taught Las Vegans that casino gambling would be the town's salvation. Wartime Las Vegas boomed because it exploited America's growing romance with moral relativism. More than Reno, Las Vegas popularized a new maverick subculture that embraced and popularized the smoky backroom and the vice-ridden roadhouse on the edge of town. In less than a decade, Las Vegas became America's "sin city," a green-felt community that blatantly defied traditional values, offering Americans an escape from the social restraints of mainstream culture by legitimizing vice—framing it in the guise of frontier liberty and situating it far from "civilization" on a remote desert in a false-fronted Western town whose police, by law, looked the other way.[1]

Helping direct this process was a small group of local casino owners led by former assayer and dam worker J. Kell Houssels. Joining him was a motley assortment of mob and non-mob operators from other states, who built new clubs and small hotels on or near Fremont Street for the growing horde of gamblers. Mob contract killer Benjamin "Bugsy" Siegel was the most famous member of a long line of eastern mobsters who operated clubs for Meyer Lansky and others. Less well-known figures such as Morris "Moe" Dalitz of Detroit's Purple Gang and Cleveland's Mayfield Road Gang, New York's Gus Greenbaum and Moe Sedway, Minneapolis's "Davie" Berman and "Icepick" Willy Alderman, along with others, ran many of the town's multiplying number of casinos. Managing the rest were a group of non-mob gamblers that included major Texas operator Benny Binion, former cruise-ship dealer Sam Boyd, onetime Los Angeles Police Department vice officer Guy McAfee, and Jackie Gaughan, the son of a California bookmaker. These mob and non-mob casino executives brought valuable expertise to town and worked with city and county leaders for the next few decades to secure a convention center (1959), a modern airport, then commonly called a jetport, (1963), an interstate highway (1971), and other essential prerequisites for building a successful tourist economy.

After 1940, the Strip also contributed to the city's success. While McAfee and others operated a few small clubs in the 1930s on the lonely highway coming up from Los Angeles, no one could have imagined what the future held. No single person or group created the Strip, but Thomas Hull helped launch it. In 1940, the city's chamber of commerce, anxious to attract a hotel chain to Las Vegas, invited Hull for a visit. He had built several "motor hotels" in 1930s California. These were one-story, motel-like structures tied to something more than a small office. Hull already owned three El Rancho hotels in the Golden State, and chamber officials hoped he would build a fourth in their town. To that end, they showed him a number of choice lots along Fremont Street, but Hull shocked them all by purchasing land, not downtown, but south of the city line on the Los Angeles Highway (today's Strip). Hull, a southern Californian, recognized that new technologies liberated him from a downtown location. He appreciated how electricity had freed American commerce and industry from their traditional reliance on steam and city water mains. He also understood how the internal combustion engine, with its emphasis on roads, cars, trucks, and buses, would allow him to build in the suburbs where he could escape city taxes. For almost a century, American gambling had flourished on riverboats and in the parlors of small hotels adjoining a stage or railroad station. But Hull rejected a site on narrow city lots for a thirty-acre tract in the desert suburbs where he had the room to place casino gambling in a resort setting. In one stroke, Hull created a dramatically new paradigm that his successors would follow for almost a half century. The El Rancho Vegas, with its large casino, showroom, shopping arcade, chuckwagon buffet, specialty restaurants, and most important, its parking for four hundred cars—an attractive alternative to downtown's clogged streets—was soon joined by the Frontier, the Flamingo, and the Thunderbird. While casino gambling had flourished abroad for years in places like Monte Carlo and for just a few years in Havana, those venues, while sumptuous, were not roadside locations and did not contain the substantial parking lots and other amenities demanded by middle-class American travelers. Indeed, Hull developed the basic formula that, for the next half century, would make the Strip more popular than its central city.

Over time, Las Vegas became a tale of two cities. While "Glitter Gulch" clung to its frontier pretensions for decades more, the Strip immediately reinvented itself after 1945 by debuting a variety of non-Western motifs (Fig. 39). In the 1950s, the Desert Inn, Sands, Sahara, Tropicana, and others vaulted the Strip ahead of Las Vegas in gaming profits and tourist numbers. In this period, Las Vegas also exploited the growing popularity of liberal divorce and easy marriage. Finally liberated from Depression-era poverty and the duties of war, Americans increasingly participated in a postwar culture that celebrated leisure, consumerism, and self-indulgence. The chaos of the war itself, both on the home front

Fig. 39. Partial view of the Las Vegas Strip looking northeast, ca. 1966. This photo shows the themed motels that once lined the automobile-oriented Strip, including El Morocco and La Concha, with its space-age parabolic concrete lobby. Las Vegas News Bureau, 0333_0058. Courtesy of University of Nevada, Las Vegas Special Collections.

and distant battlefronts, had encouraged adultery, promiscuity, abortion, inebriation, and drug dependency. For many soldiers on the front lines, these behaviors confirmed life in the face of death. And so after the war, the Las Vegas Strip, with its feathered showgirls, racy entertainment, and twenty-four-hour gambling, beckoned to veterans as well as to a growing number of tourists.

The trend continued into the 1960s and 1970s. New resort executives like Jay Sarno and Kirk Kerkorian pioneered much larger and royally sumptuous versions of Hull's model, drawing inspiration from the Miami Beach designs of Morris Lapidus. Sarno, a World War II veteran and Missouri building contractor who, like Hull, first constructed opulent motor hotels such as the Atlanta Cabana in Georgia, and Kerkorian, a California pilot and former boxer, took resort building to new heights. In 1965, Sarno used a loan from Teamster Union's pension funds (earlier, Jimmy Hoffa had helped finance Sarno's Atlanta Cabana project) to build Caesars Palace and later Circus Circus, while Kerkorian sold an airline to finance construction of the 1,500-room International Hotel. In 1970-71, he sold that resort and Siegel's old Flamingo to Hilton to fund his first MGM Grand Hotel (today's Bally's). Caesars Palace, the International, and MGM raised the bar for all resorts that followed. Size and sophistication became the new standard that tourists expected. With its increasingly posh resorts, the Strip, more than downtown, exploited the growing middle classification of America by democratizing elegance for the masses with low-priced, deluxe accommodations, once the sole preserve of the wealthy. But Atlantic City's gaming debut in 1978, coupled with a national recession, slowed the town's momentum. New hotels like the Maxim and Imperial Palace appeared, but they were little more than warmed-over versions of Hull's old formula and lacked the splendor of Caesars Palace and MGM. The architectural mediocrity that followed Nevada's 1967 legalization of corporate gaming, which put resort management largely in the hands of staid corporate executives, clearly reflected a lack of imagination.

Enter Steve Wynn, whose experience managing his father's small-time bingo parlors in the Northeast and his own familiarity with hotel operations in Miami Beach prepared him for a career in Las Vegas. Wynn's dramatic makeover of the old downtown Golden Nugget in the early 1980s impressed lenders willing to invest in a young visionary. In 1989, Wynn opened Las Vegas's first megaresort. The Mirage was an immediate sensation, with its soaring rainforest atrium, its $30 million erupting volcano, the free, up-close view of Siegfried and Roy's white tigers, sharks swimming behind the front desk, and eventually dolphins swimming behind the casino. Wynn quickly followed this showstopper with Treasure Island next door. This resort featured an action-packed pirate battle fought nightly in Caribbean-like waters bordering the expansive front sidewalk. After losing many of its high rollers to Wynn, Caesars Palace responded by tearing up its north parking lot and building the Forum Shops right on the Mirage's property line. Wynn countered by acquiring then imploding the Dunes Hotel, replacing it with Bellagio, whose glimmering Tuscan lake, "Dancing Waters," and regal beauty posed an even greater threat to Caesars' high-end clientele. By the late 1990s, the Mirage Revolution was well underway. Throughout that decade and into the twenty-first century, Wynn inspired a building boom southward down the Strip as resort executives struggled to top one another in a feverish effort to snare customers.

As the nationalization of casino gambling and the advent of Indian and Internet gaming began to erode Las Vegas's sin-city image, creative resort owners like Wynn and the Venetian's Sheldon Adelson, a former trade-show executive, replaced the old Strip with a dynamic successor. Gone were the venerable Sands, the Desert Inn and the other low-slung, Late Moderne–style resorts fitted to America's mid-century car culture by Wayne McAllister and other talented architects. Jon Jerde (Bellagio), Dutchman Rem Koolhaas (Venetian), and a new generation of architects designed a new Las Vegas the Rat Pack would never recognize. After 1989, Strip executives resorted to innovative approaches that converted the Strip from highway to midway and drew thousands of people to its widened sidewalks. By 2005, the new MGM, Excalibur, Treasure Island, Bellagio, Paris, Mandalay Bay, Venetian, Luxor, and Monte Carlo, along with a continuously expanding Caesars Palace, had lured millions of new visitors to Las Vegas.

The Strip itself had become a spectacle—a permanent four-mile-long Mardi Gras. Its resorts were no longer hotel-casinos with a pool, showroom, and a few gourmet rooms; they had become theme parks whose iconic architecture, high-end retail, and special attractions now lured even families and nongamblers inside. Unlike their mid-century predecessors who concentrated on gamblers, modern hotel executives broadened the market to attract all types of visitors. One writer has even suggested that the purpose of Bellagio, Caesars Palace, and the Venetian was to resurrect the European Grand Tour of the sixteenth through nineteenth centuries when elites sent their offspring to view historic lands. The Strip thus served as an "archive of memory" where "the past was destroyed."[2] By designing faux landscapes comprising medieval castles, Egyptian pyramids, Roman ruins, the Arc de Triomphe, Statue of Liberty, Brooklyn Bridge, Eiffel Tower, St. Mark's Square, and the Tuscan world of Lake Como, Wynn, Adelson, and the others built idealized versions of many of Western civilization's historic landmarks. These monuments took the form of resorts whose dramatic architecture and lavish interiors offered visitors an engaging juxtaposition of images compressed into an easily traversable, scripted space enhanced by aristocratic shops, palatial spas, high-tech showrooms, chic nightclubs, celebrity-chef restaurants, thrill rides and, of course, the always-beckoning casino—all shrewdly staged to promote unrestrained consumption. There was nothing else like it; no Indian casino, no riverboat, no other gambling center anywhere in the world, including Fremont Street, could match the excitement this

Fig. 40. The Fremont Street Experience at the Four Queens. The Four Queens, which opened in 1966 in downtown Las Vegas, replaced City Drug pharmacy. Noted for the world's largest slot machine, the hotel played a leading role in turning the old "Glitter Gulch" into a pedestrian mall three decades later. Las Vegas News Bureau, 0333_0082. Courtesy of University of Nevada, Las Vegas Special Collections.

experience offered. To be sure, downtown Las Vegas tried. In 1995, it unveiled the Fremont Street Experience, Jon Jerde's barrel-vaulted light show that nightly transformed the former road into a festival mall and impromptu theater (Fig. 40). But it was not nearly enough to challenge the Strip's surging popularity.

Of course, the development of the Strip and downtown came with social consequences. Unlike Renoites, who after 1970 increasingly complained about traffic, lack of sewage capacity and other problems,[3] Las Vegans had mostly embraced development. But after 1990, the social effects of growth became more obvious. Small 1950s-era apartment complexes of mostly gaming workers behind the Strip's older and newer resorts were bought and leveled to accommodate new parking structures and expansion projects. As early as the 1980s, many white families, enriched by the valley's frantic development, left downtown and older subdivisions near the Strip for newer, affluent, and more distant communities to the west and south in places like Summerlin, Anthem, and Green Valley. They were replaced by growing numbers of black and Latino residents who increasingly filled the renovated apartments and aging cottages encircling downtown. But after 2000, they struggled to survive in a city whose obsession with redevelopment and gentrification threatened their communities. The scene resembled Atlantic City in the late 1970s and early 1980s, when casino development priced the old minority sections adjoining the Boardwalk out of existence. Four decades earlier, Las Vegas county and municipal leaders had colluded to route I-15 through the black Westside to maximize access to major resorts and minimize the effects on white districts. Today, there are new fears that the rising trend toward gentrification will pose even more threats to the social fabric, as clusters of high-rise apartments, timeshares, and condominiums continue to encircle the Strip and threaten downtown areas.

Becoming a world-famous tourist destination also came with other costs. From 1986 to 2005, as Las Vegas reigned as America's fastest-growing metropolitan area, it was also fast becoming a house of cards, dependent upon the continued growth of discretionary income and a real-estate bubble that was bound to burst someday. Beginning in 2007, the collapse began. Tourism and home values fell as America's "Great Recession" began to take its toll. In 2008, three major resort projects abruptly halted construction as credit dried up. With thirty thousand homes in foreclosure and home building at a standstill, one hundred thousand construction workers left town. Even greater numbers of manual laborers, landscapers, and other low-paid service workers left, too. By September 2009, Las Vegas's unemployment rate of 13.4 percent was second only to Detroit's. Once-proud union and nonunion hotel-casino workers who rode the boom for two decades saw their hours slashed and jobs cut. Fringe benefits also disappeared for many. Indeed, Stations Casinos (owners of eleven resorts in the area) halted contributions to employees' 401k plans in 2008 as did other companies. Health insurance and other lost benefits only further depleted workers' savings accounts, as MGM-Mirage, Harrah's, and many smaller companies ruthlessly slashed costs to stay afloat. The ripple effect wreaked similar havoc on workers in the city's nongaming sector as well. Not since the casino economy's infancy in the Depression era had discretionary income dropped to such low levels. But in the 2000s, unlike the Depression of the 1930s, Las Vegas was far more vulnerable to a tourism meltdown. Unlike larger commercial and industrial cities, Las Vegas was too dependent upon high-spending tourists and gamblers;

the area's fifty-year failure to diversify its economy finally exposed its precarious position. The difficulties manifested themselves in yet another promotional bid to re-brand Las Vegas—which had added family-friendly entertainment in the 1990s—as a place where one could freely indulge in behavior that would draw frowns back home: "What Happens in Vegas, Stays in Vegas."

Today, Las Vegas stands at a crossroads. Clearly, tourist numbers and casino profits will normalize with economic recovery, but residents have learned a valuable lesson. Tourism is a double-edged sword that can usurp control of a city's economy and its urban fabric. Only time will tell if Las Vegas can liberate itself from its decades-long dependency on this industry.

Mackinac Island
Michigan

Steve Brisson

Mackinac Island is located in the Straits of Mackinac where Lakes Michigan and Huron meet, between the two Michigan peninsulas. Since the mid-nineteenth century it has functioned as the premier summer resort of the Great Lakes, due to its prime location on a major shipping lane, salubrious climate, and picturesque sightseeing venues. By the late nineteenth century, the heavily forested 2,200-acre island was known as "the Newport of the Inland Seas." Its summer population combined cottage owners, convention attendees, and day-trippers from passenger steamers. Two hallmarks of Victorian-era tourism—grandiose hostelries and contact with nature—were made manifest on the island by century's end, with the island boasting one of the nation's largest summer resort hotels and a national park. The island adapted to accommodate middle- and working-class vacationers by the middle of the twentieth century. While the demographics have shifted in the last half-century, the activities of island summer life have remained constant.

At a crossroads of the Great Lakes, the Straits of Mackinac hosted summer travelers for centuries before tourism, as an American Indian seasonal fishing ground and the main fur-trade depot of the upper Great Lakes. From the 1670s, throughout the French, British, and early American eras, it maintained its position as a center of the fur trade, which finally went into decline in the 1830s. While fishing took over as the main commercial activity, by the late 1840s, signs of the island's tourism future were already beginning to appear. The geographic location that made the area suitable for fur trading proved equally advantageous for summer tourism. At mid-century, the greater northern Michigan region was still isolated and unsettled, but Mackinac remained on a major U.S. shipping lane. Residents and entrepreneurs could thus capitalize on both an established travel conduit and the fame of one of the earliest settled locations in the upper Midwest. Upon a visit in 1846, William Cullen Bryant commented that the island's destiny was as a summer resort as "people already begin to repair to it for health and refreshment from the southern borders of Lake Michigan" for "the world has not many islands so beautiful as Mackinac."[1]

Mackinac promoters touted the advantages of the island to the well-heeled residents of Midwestern cities. Meat packers, railroad kings, and lumber barons were soon making Mackinac their summer home. Hay-fever sufferers, prohibited by distance from the resorts of the East Coast, took advantage of the cool marine environment provided by the Great Lakes. Besides the climate, Mackinac Island provided additional natural amenities. Its bluffs offered stunning vistas of the straits and its interior featured sublime paths and limestone geological wonders. Mackinac's picturesque scenery paired well with a romantic past filled with tales of Indian legends, French explorers, missionaries, and the War of 1812. Picturesque Fort Mackinac overlooked a quaint ramshackle village (Fig. 41). Before the Civil War, the island began its transformation into a tourist center. Abandoned structures from its fur-trade heyday, including Astor's American Fur Company warehouse and a New England Protestant mission, were converted to hotels. Both inns—the John Jacob Astor House and Mission House—capitalized on the former use of each venue in their names. Souvenir shops opened along the village's two principal streets, and wealthy tycoons constructed the first summer cottages on the high bluffs overlooking the village. After the Civil War, the island came into its own as a Gilded Age summer resort. In 1875, the creation of Mackinac National Park, the second in the nation, confirmed and increased the island's prominence. About half the island was included in the park. With no National Park Service in existence, it was placed under the care of the U.S. Army soldiers of Fort Mackinac.[2]

Older established families on the island, including French Canadians, Americans, and Métis (aboriginal Canadians), were active participants in retooling for this new industry. Small business and boarding-house owners, once serving the fur trade, adapted their services for the summer leisure visitor. The children of fur-trade laborers found employment as dock porters and carriage-tour drivers. More recent Irish immigrants, initially

Fig. 41. Tourists resting in the park with Fort Mackinac and the village in the background, ca. 1900. Mackinac State Historic Parks Collection. Courtesy of Mackinac State Historic Parks.

serving as laborers in the fishing industry, also became key participants in the early tourism business community. As tourism expanded, other players appeared on the scene such as managers to operate enterprises backed by railroads and navigation companies and former Fort Mackinac officers and soldiers. Others were entrepreneurs drawn to the island specifically to ply the tourist trade. Examples of these include William H. Gardiner, a Canadian-born photographer who specialized in photographic souvenirs and spent his winters in Daytona, Florida, in the winter tourist market; Henry Murdick of Vermont, a confectioner; and Frank Kriesche, a German immigrant who specialized in glass engraving, including high-end stemware for the cottagers and a variety of cheaper keepsakes for the summer tourist.[3]

Tourism increased in the 1880s, partially driven by the arrival of railroads to the Straits of Mackinac. Ferryboats from the mainland communities of St. Ignace (Upper Peninsula) and Mackinaw City (Lower Peninsula) now shared the harbor with Great Lakes passenger vessels. The decade witnessed a flurry of summer-cottage construction with the development of an eighty-acre private cottage community in 1883. A year later, the prime east and west bluffs within the national park became available for cottage leasing, a practice that has continued through the present day. Some of these cottages stood only a decade before being expanded or completely replaced by larger versions. This transformation was the result of the construction of Grand Hotel in 1887 (Fig. 42).[4] Built by a syndicate formed by the Michigan Central Railroad, Grand Rapids and Indiana Railroad, and Detroit and Cleveland Steamship Navigation Company, the palatial structure, constructed from 1.5 million board feet of Michigan white pine, brought a new level of tourist to the island. A mammoth version of the typical nineteenth-century summer resort hotel, its 660-foot-wide porch would ultimately be claimed as the longest in the world.

The 1890s witnessed two events of lasting impact that represent the reach and power tourism had achieved. In 1895, the army finally closed Fort Mackinac. With the loss of soldiers to care for the national park, it too was threatened with closure. Island businessmen and officials were aware of the importance of the park to the tourist economy, and negotiations in Washington resulted in the park's transfer to the state of Michigan. It was the state's first park, and the first in the nation with that designation. A new agency, the Mackinac Island State Park Commission, was created to administer it.

The other event occurred soon after. In 1898, the island enacted its first automobile ban. This move of the village council, which applied to municipal streets, addressed the concerns of carriage-tour drivers who were seeking to protect their lucrative business. Two years later, the park commission also banned cars from park roads.[5] Although originally having nothing to do with historic charm, by the 1920s, the island had grown famous for its auto ban and "old-fashioned" modes of transportation.

The pattern set during the Victorian era continued into the first two decades of the twentieth century. However, the 1920s saw increasing numbers of middle- and working-class travelers as the autos of Detroit, although banned from the island, made their way north along new highways. The egalitarian atmosphere took some of the shine off the island as an exclusive resort and, with transportation abroad becoming easier, some of the wealthy took up lodging elsewhere. Following declines during the Depression and World War II, this pattern of visitation resumed and increased. The last regular passenger ships ended their runs in the late 1960s,

Fig. 42. Grand Hotel guests on the famous porch, ca. 1900. Mackinac State Historic Parks Collection. Courtesy of Mackinac State Historic Parks.

making summer car trips culminating with a passenger ferry the only way to visit the island. Day-trippers, however, generally engaged in the same activities as the Victorian steam-vessel visitors, including a carriage tour, sightseeing, biking in the park, and souvenir shopping. Beginning in the 1920s, fudge increasingly became the most desirable "souvenir." Mackinac fudge was originally popularized by the Murdick family, longtime island candy makers with a flair for showmanship, who further promoted the confection with displays at Midwestern fairs and festivals in the late 1940s. Detroit candy maker Harry Ryba was so impressed that he became associated with the Murdicks and began making "Famous Mackinac Island Fudge" in his Detroit store in the 1950s, finally opening his own shop on the island in 1960. A born marketer, Ryba took fudge promotion to new heights, including encouraging "fudge wars" among the island makers. By the 1960s, Mackinac Island and fudge were inextricably linked and the term *fudgie* had been coined to describe summer tourists.[6]

The postwar era brought increased day visitors, development pressure, and preservation. Located in a remote region, three hundred miles from

Detroit and four hundred miles from Chicago, this three-by-two-mile island continues to draw 750,000 tourists every summer. The greatest check
on overdevelopment has been the growth of the park to include 83 percent of the island. The historical character of Mackinac Island was pro-
fessionalized beginning in 1958, when the park commission, prodded by
Michigan's governor, G. Mennen Williams, launched a highly successful
revenue-bond-financed preservation and museum operation. This campaign included restoration of Fort Mackinac and other park properties
and the introduction of living-history programs. The island became a designated National Historic Landmark in 1961.[7] New cottage and condominium developments surged from the 1980s onward, particularly on the
island's west end. In recent years, development pressure downtown has
also destroyed a number of historic properties.

At about five hundred year-round residents, the population remains
where it has been since the 1820s. Many of these inhabitants are descendants of original French Canadians, Métis, and mid-nineteenth-century
Irish immigrants. Others are descendants of the later arrivals who came
and stayed: army soldiers, hotel and ferry managers, shop owners, and
Coast Guard servicemen. In one form or another, all are involved in the
tourist trade. Winter is long and bleak, with residents awaiting the January
freeze up of the straits that allows the freedom to cross to the mainland
aboard snowmobiles—a motorized vehicle "exemption" granted to island
residents. Local politics are often characterized by both cooperation and
tension between the city of Mackinac Island and the Mackinac Island
State Park Commission. A semiautonomous state agency, the governor-
appointed seven-member board's main focus is preservation and interpretation of the park and historic sites. However, the commission also has
regulatory authority over the majority of the island's acreage, and manages
most of the island's roads, the main freight dock, and the airport, and
provides land for the municipal water system and the landfill (as well as
leasing land for the summer cottages, a golf course, a portion of Grand
Hotel's golf course, and the Mackinac Island Yacht Club).

The allure of the island remains, as it had before, comfortable contact
with nature via well-maintained trails and carriage rides, and the nostalgia
of a bygone era. Early visitors found the ramshackle village and picturesque fort reminiscent of what they perceived as simpler and more heroic
times. What is nostalgic has changed with the generations. In the nine-

teenth century, the era of the past that was most prevalent was the co-lonial period, with heavy emphasis on Indian legends, French explorers, Jesuit missions, and imperial conflicts. By the early twentieth century, the early American period, particularly the War of 1812 and the era of Astor's American Fur Company, eventually dominated the "bygone era" most heavily promoted. The automobile ban, although unintentional, eventu-ally became nostalgic. By the late twentieth century, the Victorian era was as many generations distant as the earliest days of European settlement had been to the Victorians. This was coupled with the fact that, while many early nineteenth-century structures remained, the majority of the island's infrastructure had been constructed between the 1870s and 1910. Thus the island, and even the park commission, began heavily promoting Mackinac's Victorian period. The Victorian tourists, who had come to see history, were now history themselves.

As a tourist destination, the island is a study in contrasts. Grand Hotel is one of the last great Victorian resorts in the country, and, with dinner-dress restrictions and white-jacketed waiters, carefully projects an image of upper-class exclusiveness. Fort Mackinac, professionally restored, is by volume one of the most visited historic sites in the country. However, combined with the ever-present fudge shops, tacky souvenir ware, and the seemingly contrived lack of automobiles, Mackinac Island is to some perhaps nothing more than a middlebrow tourist trap. But the savvy tour-ist will both embrace and transcend this view and find that Mackinac has always been this, and so much more. It remains a cool summer retreat, blessed with natural beauty and rich in legends, nostalgia, and historical charm. Fudge is all the sweeter when enjoyed atop a bluff overlooking the glistening Great Lakes. "A stroll at Mackinac," Horace Greeley commented in 1847, "is worth a day in any man's life."[8] And so it remains.

Miami Beach,
Florida

Robin F. Bachin and James F. Donnelly

Miami Beach is an island city of 7.1 square miles between Biscayne Bay and the Atlantic Ocean. When developer Carl Fisher opened his first luxury hotel in 1920, it marked the rise of Miami Beach as a premier tourist destination. Calling Miami Beach the "American Riviera," Fisher, along with later developers and architects, created an urban oasis amid the sandy beaches and crystal-clear waters of this subtropical location. Captivating postcards and brochures lured guests with promises of relaxation, leisure, and luxury. And while the construction of playfully decorated hotels promising fantasy, exoticism, and adventure enticed many to visit Miami Beach, "Where Summer Spends the Winter," the combination of cheap land and marketing savvy also encouraged many vacationers to buy property and make Miami Beach a city of year-round residents. The tension between catering to tourists and permanent residents has complicated development in Miami Beach since the city's inception.

It was not always apparent that this landscape might emerge as the "winter playground for the rich" or a "sun-seekers' paradise." Throughout most of the nineteenth century, the barrier beach and swath of mangroves that would come to make up Miami Beach was inhabited intermittently by small groups of Seminole Indians and Bahamian fishermen. Similar landscapes have been preserved on the west coast of Florida at Captiva Island and on the east coast at Cape Canaveral. Interest in developing the land began in the 1870s with the arrival of Henry and Charles Lum, who planned to start a coconut plantation.[1] By 1910, enterprising developers including avocado-plantation owner John Collins, a Quaker from New Jersey, and bankers J. N. and J. E. Lummus were clearing land on the beach to make it habitable and profitable. The developers quickly began improvement projects in 1913 to reshape the "swamp" into habitable beachfront property, dredging six million cubic yards of material out of Biscayne Bay.[2]

The incorporation of Miami Beach in 1915 came about largely as a result of the efforts of John Collins and his son-in-law Thomas Pancoast to build a wooden bridge linking Miami Beach with the mainland, thereby making access to the beach much easier and real-estate development more feasible. What some called "Collins' folly" seemed to Fisher, an automobile man, a timely venture sure to increase land values and lure vacationers and speculators to Miami Beach. He loaned Collins $50,000 to build the bridge so cars could replace ferries as the best means of transportation to the beach. Fisher also loaned the Lummus brothers $150,000 to help them pave streets and improve lots. Both loans were secured in exchange for land, so Fisher came out owning over two hundred acres of what would become prime oceanfront property. The stage was set for the promotion of Miami Beach as a major tourist destination and beach resort.[3]

To be a true resort town, Miami Beach needed luxury hotels. As early as 1915, a *Miami Herald* article predicted that a grand hotel with 250 rooms, featuring baths, tennis courts, and luxurious amenities, would soon be built on the beach. Indeed, Scottish immigrant William J. Brown constructed the Atlantic Beach Hotel, later called Brown's Hotel, in 1915, but it was modest and had only twenty-five rooms. In 1917, Miami Beach had only sixty rooms in all. Demand for hotel rooms outpaced room availability, and Fisher believed that opening a grandiose hotel on Miami Beach would not only expand the tourism trade but also drive up land prices and promote development. Fisher began by creating Lincoln Road, along which he built his own home as well as a golf course, tennis courts, a polo field, and an apartment/hotel building, the Lincoln Apartments and Hotel.[4]

In 1919, Fisher hired the Philadelphia firm of William L. Price and M. Hawley McLanahan to draw up plans for a luxury hotel on Miami Beach. The architects chose the Mediterranean revival style, a style that would set the standard for the grandeur and elegance of Miami Beach development, notably Carl Fisher's Nautilus Hotel in 1924 and developer N. B. T. Roney's Roney Plaza in 1926. Both hotels were designed by noted New York architects Leonard Schultze and S. Fullerton Weaver, whose other projects included the Breakers Hotel in Palm Beach, the Biltmore Hotels in Atlanta, Los Angeles, and Coral Gables, and the Waldorf-Astoria in New York. Their Miami Beach hotels featured domed towers, stucco façades, open terraces and loggias, Japanese tea gardens, and Baroque ornamentation typical of Spanish design. The Roney incorporated a replica of the Giralda bell tower in Seville, Spain (a feature they included in the Coral Gables Biltmore and the Miami News and Metropolis Building).[5]

These elaborate resort hotels catered to an exclusive clientele. Rates at the Flamingo in 1920 started at $15 per day, excluding all but the wealthy. Exclusion took a more blatant form through restrictive covenants. Fisher's Alton Beach Realty Company, for example, forbade the rental or sale of property "to any person or persons other than the Caucasian Race."[6] Despite the fact that black workers, both from the South and from the Bahamas, made up the bulk of the workforce on Miami Beach, they were prevented from using the beach itself. In addition, there were visible signs that much of the Miami Beach—at least in Fisher's section north of 15th Street—was off limits to Jews. Hotel promotional brochures boasted that their clientele was "For Gentiles Only" or "Restricted."[7]

The Great Depression helped make Miami Beach much less exclusive, as developers and designers sought to appeal to a more diverse group of travelers to keep the tourist and real-estate economies afloat. By the early 1930s, for example, they were transforming the southern tip of Miami Beach into a community that within two decades would be largely Jewish. In part, this phenomenon was a result of the much less restrictive practices of the Lummus brothers, whose properties were not "restricted."[8] Russian-Jewish immigrant Irving Miller helped foster this development when he bought large parcels of land and built more modest hotels and apartment buildings. He and other owners hired architects such as Henry Wright, Roy France, Henry Hohouser, and L. Murray Dixon, who employed the symmetrical, streamlined styles of modernist design to build high-density, modestly priced hotels that reflected a machine-age aesthetic and a Depression-era sensibility. They introduced whimsical design motifs such as tropical murals and etched-glass flamingoes, and modern materials like Vitrolite (colored glass) to interior design. This modern design, which would shape the largest district of Art Deco architecture in the world, appealed to visitors of more modest means, a necessity given the financial climate of the 1930s (Fig. 43). In 1936 alone, thirty-four new

Fig. 43. Neron Hotel, shown here in 1978, was among the many Art Deco hotels that
gave Miami Beach part of its distinctive atmosphere as a modern resort in the 1930s.
Courtesy of State Library & Archives of Florida.

hotels opened their doors, including the Astor, the Cavalier, the Edgewa-
ter Beach, and the Tides, all hotels that would feature prominently in the
revitalization of the southern portion of Miami Beach in the 1990s.[9]

During 1940, twenty-seven new hotels opened; twenty more came
online in 1941.[10] In December 1940, rough estimates of tourist activity
were running 15 to 20 percent above the previous season. On December
7, 1941, however, the tourist boom of the late 1930s ended, and with it,
new hotel construction. Miami Beach became a vast training base for the
U.S. Army Air Corps, with more than three hundred Miami Beach hotels, apartment houses, and homes requisitioned for use by the trainees by
summer 1943.

The end of World War II opened new opportunities and created new
challenges. Commercial aviation made Miami Beach accessible even for
a weekend stay, and the widespread use of air-conditioning made it comfortable. Early postwar Art Deco design was succeeded by a glamorous
form of modernism, best exemplified by the Fontainebleau and Eden Roc
of Morris Lapidus (Fig. 44). These hotels, known today as MiMo or Miami
Modern in design, were destinations in themselves with all services and
entertainment available within the hotel property. The tourist industry de-

Fig. 44. Miami Beach, looking south from the Fontainebleau Hotel. Designed by Morris Lapidus and opened in 1954, the Fontainebleau firmly established the Miami Modern style that was so influential in resort hotel design. It was the setting for numerous Hollywood motion pictures, including the James Bond film *Goldfinger*. Courtesy of the Special Collections Division, University of Miami Libraries.

veloped the "package," an all-expenses-included menu of transportation, lodging, meals, and entertainment. This modality first came to Miami Beach in 1947, with the "Delta Dreams" program of Delta Airlines and the Deauville-McFadden Hotel.[11]

The Allied victory challenged the religious and racial discrimination practiced almost everywhere by the American tourism industry before World War II. Through the late 1940s and 1950s, Miami Beach gradually overcame this invidious heritage. City ordinances banned "gentiles only" and "restricted clientele" signs in 1947. In 1950, the University of Iowa football team, with five African American players, stayed at a Miami Beach hotel when they played the University of Miami.[12]

While many Miami Beach residents of the 1920s and 1930s were seasonal employees of the tourist industry, after World War II, a more permanent population made itself apparent, not least through the establishment of various soda-fountain hangouts for its adolescent population.[13] Miami Beach was becoming a year-round bedroom community as well as an international tourist destination. The Miami Beach residential community was also more heavily Jewish than it had been before World War II, attracting older retirees to South Beach and families to Middle Beach.[14]

The postwar tourist and residential boom in Miami Beach will be forever linked in the popular imagination with two world-famous entertainers: Arthur Godfrey and Jackie Gleason. Using radio and, later, television, Godfrey and Gleason brought Miami Beach into millions of American homes from 1953 through 1970. The consistent theme was: "You are cold where you are; we are warm where we are," in the spirit of Carl Fisher's bathing beauty photographs sent to newspapers across the wintry North.

While commercial aviation initially facilitated the postwar boom on Miami Beach, jet flight to Caribbean islands eroded Miami Beach's market share of winter tourism, and changing demographics and tastes hastened the process. In addition, South Beach became increasingly a permanent residence for senior citizens, some of whom had come as winter visitors to Miami Beach in the Art Deco era, others who had migrated from Eastern and Central Europe. In American popular culture, Miami Beach had become a "God's waiting room" punch line for jokes about old people. Local boosters formed a Keep Greater Miami Beach Young Committee. Further complicating the demography of Miami Beach was the arrival of Cuban refugees after 1959, who by 1970, made up 13 percent of the South Beach population.

By 1978, the reputation of Miami Beach among tourists had fallen so low that the Americana Hotel in Bal Harbour just north of Miami Beach began to advertise itself as being "twenty-five miles South of Ft Lauderdale."[15] One plan, prepared in 1976 by the city-created Miami Beach Redevelopment Agency, proposed creating "a new 'luxury' resort including hotel rooms, condominiums, restaurants, and shops situated on newly dredged canals in the area of South Beach south of Sixth Street."[16] The revitalization would involve the displacement of almost seven thousand persons and demolition of most existing structures.[17]

While the Miami Beach Redevlopment Agency proposed this more traditional type of urban renewal, another competing vision for redevelopment was put forth by Barbara Capitman who, together with like-minded activists, founded the Miami Design Preservation League (MDPL) in 1976. Capitman and her close colleague, Leonard Horowitz, were primarily interested in using good design to further their vision of "small-is-beautiful" development. They focused on South Beach, where hundreds of relatively small modernist buildings from the 1920s and 1930s sheltered a largely Jewish working-class community with a culture Capitman described as "a well established pattern of recreation, enjoyment of the amenities of beachfront life, and understanding of the means to health and longevity sought by the rest of the population, and a varied international background of arts and crafts. . . . an untapped resource."[18]

An epic battle was joined between these two competing visions of what would most likely restore Miami Beach as a tourist destination. Waged from 1976 through 1992, the contested process included the recognition of the Art Deco District in the National Register of Historic Places in 1979, the commission by MDPL of a redevelopment and preservation plan, and the eventual recognition and protection of the entire Art Deco District by the city of Miami Beach in 1992 after a municipal election in 1991, which brought the first preservationist to the Miami Beach City Commission. Campaigning, newly elected commissioner Neisen Kasdin had proposed a vision for Miami Beach as a "community of quality residential neighborhoods, a regional hub of cultural and entertainment activities, and an international tourist attraction."[19] Kasdin's 1991 campaign also reached out directly and openly for the first time to the growing Miami Beach population of gay men and lesbians. Known sometimes as the "worker bees" of the preservation movement, openly gay men like Leonard Horowitz made generous contributions of time, effort, and investment to the preservation-led urban renaissance of South Beach.

Kasdin; a group of preservationists led by Michael Kinerk, Nancy Liebman, and Matti Bower; and the "Deco Developers," including Tony Goldman, Saul Gross, Craig Robins, Mel Schlesser and Dennis Scholl, all worked during the 1990s to realize the redevelopment plans commissioned ten years earlier by MDPL: "Deco District Development and Preservation Plan." Writing about that decade, Barron Stofik summed up the revival of South Beach, and with it, the rejuvenation of Miami Beach's tourism, as an "ensemble performance. Each decision, each incident, each person affected the outcome in a meaningful way."[20]

By 2000, Miami Beach was not just "back," renewed in a different guise, but more than ever an international tourist destination. South Beach had become a very diverse haven for people often unwanted in their birthplaces or estranged from their hometowns. Middle Beach and the residential islands had become the winter resort of fabulously wealthy people from around the world. While in 2000 fully 77 percent of the housing units were occupied by permanent residents and only 13 percent by seasonal residents, tourism, hospitality, and entertainment remained Miami Beach's dominant industry.[21]

Like Atlantic City and Las Vegas, the Miami Beach visitor experience today is the result of conscious efforts by civic and business leaders to keep pace with changing public tastes. In contrast to these cities, both of which demolished their older landmark hotels in the relentless pursuit of a new image, Miami Beach balanced contending demands by tourists and year-round residents. Ultimately Miami Beach preserved its iconic hostelries as part of its campaign to renew its appeal, situating itself within a national pattern of resistance to plans that would have smashed the old in favor of the new.

NAPLES,
FLORIDA

Aaron Cowan

Carved from mangroves and cypress swamps, Naples, Florida, stretches twelve miles along the Gulf of Mexico. Often heralded for its natural beauty, Naples's enviable tropical landscape is actually the result of a land-planning tradition begun in the early twentieth century: developers sculpted swampland into thousands of upscale condos, shopping centers, gated communities, and golf courses that surround a maze of drainage canals, lagoons, and ponds. Naples's tourism industry flourished both as a result of developers' manipulation of its beautiful natural setting and because of careful cultivation of what is sometimes called the "Naples image"—a depiction of the community as a relaxed-but-refined refuge for the wealthy, protected from the crass and tacky overdevelopment of other Florida vacation locales. The continuing democratization of leisure in postwar American society has, however, led to cracks in this elite façade, as middle-class Americans found the previously exclusive paradise tantalizingly within reach.

Like many Florida communities, Naples owes its character to the ambitions and desires of outsiders. Naples was established in the 1880s, during the first period of intensive interest and real-estate speculation in Florida, when the promotional press touted the state as the "Italy of America."[1] A cohort of Tallahassee bankers and railroad executives formed the Naples Town Improvement Company in 1886, surveyed and platted the land, and then quickly sold the properties to an investment group of Kentuckians led by Louisville newspaper publisher Walter Haldemann. The Kentucky syndicate, composed of a varied group of investors from Louisville railroad magnates and Kentucky "old money" seeking new investment opportunities, published frequent articles in Haldemann's *Courier-Journal* promoting Naples as an ideal vacation spot.[2]

Naples's relatively remote location on the southern Gulf Coast of Florida meant that it grew slowly during the late nineteenth century. Plans by the Kentucky investors to develop tobacco as a cash crop in the region achieved mild success, but the small town remained primarily a rustic winter getaway for wealthy northerners, who delighted in the area's abundant fishing and deer hunting. Permanent homes were few, and the Naples Hotel, built by Haldemann in 1889, was the only formal lodging for visitors. In reality, the locale's limited accessibility and "untamed" natural environment were its primary assets; hunting and sport fishing became fashionable leisure pursuits in the period, particularly for the wealthy and expanding middle class of the Gilded Age. An 1888 promotional brochure published by Haldemann's press described the "abundance of game" and tarpon fishing available to the aspiring sportsman. Outdoor sporting periodicals and travel sections of northern newspapers featured occasional stories about fishing excursions to the area.[3] The company also trumpeted the supposed healthful effects of the semitropical climate for invalids and sufferers of chronic disease.[4]

Despite these promotional efforts, lack of a railroad connection combined with financial instability following the Panic of 1893 limited further development. Haldemann died in 1902, and in 1914, his heirs sold their holdings to a new Naples Improvement Company.[5] This group, headed by Ohio real-estate executive Edward Crayton, planned new residential developments and added fifty additional rooms to the Naples Hotel in anticipation of the expansion of railroads and new highways into the southern part of the state. As one of Naples's largest landowners, Crayton screened potential property buyers carefully and, as president of the town council from 1923 until his death in 1938, held enormous influence in the town's development.

The 1920s saw a transportation revolution in the state of Florida that transformed both the volume and character of tourists visiting Naples. Road construction in southern Florida was particularly difficult and expensive, but by the 1920s, new technologies, a prosperous economy, and pent-up demand for automobile access led to a more than fourfold increase in the state's roads during the decade.[6] In 1923, Barron Collier, a New York businessman and land developer who had migrated to southwest Florida, provided the capital to catalyze construction of the Tamiami Trail, a long-planned highway to connect Naples with Tampa to the north and Miami to the east across the Everglades. The arrival of railroad transportation in 1927 and the completion of the Tamiami Trail in 1928 opened the village to the millions of tourists crossing the country in newly affordable automobiles.[7] The arrival of these transportation links signaled a new era in Naples's tourism industry. The Naples Improvement Company expanded the Naples Hotel in the 1920s and 1930s to more than 250 rooms and began to advertise in national periodicals.[8] Cincinnati native Allen Joslin opened the Naples Golf Club, the town's first full golf course, in 1932.[9]

Auto tourists brought new business opportunities to Naples, but they also threatened its character as a quiet reserve for the wealthy. Motels, "tourist courts," and trailer camps soon sprouted alongside grander hotels and resorts.[10] In 1946, another group of Ohio investors purchased the Naples Hotel and most of the town's undeveloped land. The group, incorporated as the Naples Company, sought to maintain Naples's upper-crust image while still marketing the region to a broader group of tourists. The company wielded its economic power to campaign for strict zoning restrictions within the city to prevent the haphazard development already visible in other Florida resort communities.[11] The new company also initiated a campaign drive to improve the town's infrastructure. The $300,000 project was funded by predominantly private donations rather than a public bond, keeping taxes low and largely bypassing public debate about project implementation.[12] The new company expanded the Naples Hotel once again, and began year-round service in 1946. By the 1950s, the small community's tourist industry was thriving, and Naples was well established as a well-to-do vacation refuge. A 1956 *Holiday* magazine article assured readers that Naples "caters to people of means and good taste."[13] This new manifestation of outside investors, however, also placed increased emphasis on mid-market vacationers as potential real-estate buyers. Federal support for new home construction—via the Federal Housing Administration and GI Bill—led to a boom in Collier County home development. Realtors and homebuilders targeted vacationers, often offering enticements such as sightseeing tours, free meals, and fishing trips to tourists.[14]

The most successful of these residential developments reflected the "Naples image" of refinement, gentility, and leisure—perhaps none more so than the community of Port Royal. Chicago advertising executive John Glen Sample developed the Port Royal residential community just after World War II. Sample's particular genius was an understanding of the larger trends that were changing Florida's tourist and residential demographic. In the late nineteenth and early twentieth centuries, the difficulty of transportation and scarcity of habitable land preserved most of the state as the winter refuge of a small elite. After World War II, however, highways, dredge-and-fill operations, and the rising incomes of a rapidly expanding middle class had combined to place the Florida vacation, or even the winter home, within reach of the "average" American. The next great market, Sample understood, would be to sell not only a pleasant location but also exclusivity. He personally selected each of the early buyers in the Port Royal development and divided property into large lots with architect-designed housing.[15] Such careful selectivity was, of course, well in line with Naples's earlier precedent of elite management. Sample promoted Port Royal in outlets such as *Vogue, Town and Country*, and the *Wall Street Journal* as the haven for "those who have a fondness for salt water and uncluttered beaches—together with the assurance that these will not ever be invaded by touring multitudes."[16]

The destruction wrought by Hurricane Donna in September 1960 only furthered Naples's development, as the storm demolished older structures, and an influx of insurance money brought new development capital, as well as the further tightening of building-code restrictions.[17] Residential construction grew at a rapid pace, but increasingly, the older vision of a small vacation village carefully managed by a few individual landowners gave way to development fueled by much larger national and multinational corporations. The largest of these, Gulf American Land Corporation, developed the nearby community of Cape Coral outside Fort Myers, as well as the famously failed development of Golden Gate Estates on Naples's suburban periphery. Beginning in 1964, General Development Corporation began developing the environmentally fragile barrier island of Marco Island, just south of Naples, into a popular residential address for celebrities, professional athletes, and corporate executives. Westinghouse Communities, Gulf American Corporation, and numerous other developers flooded the Naples metropolitan area with golf communities, country clubs, and luxury high-rises during the period.[18] Older elite interests, such as the Naples Company and the Collier family, still played a prominent role in the development of Naples—

indeed, Collier Development Corporation's Pine Ridge subdivision was Naples's earliest postwar housing development—but neither they nor any other single player held the level of control over the community's social and cultural development that had been possible in earlier decades.[19]

Tourism development in Naples has not been completely dominated by golf courses and lavish resorts. Beneath the veneer of genteel luxury, some "lowbrow" and family-oriented Florida attractions have drawn visitors to the Naples area. The town's Swamp Buggy Days, dating to 1949, brings thousands of visitors each year to watch races of modified dune buggies mounted on giant tires in the "Mile O' Mud." The swamp buggy—a heavily modified automobile with giant balloon tires—is an artifact of "old Florida," developed in the early years of Naples for game hunters navigating the mangrove swamps that once dominated the area. In 1967, zoo operator Larry Tetzlaff, who operated an animal exhibit inside the Cedar Point theme park in Sandusky, Ohio, visited Naples in his search for a winter home for his animals. Two years later, after the death of Cincinnatian Julius Fleischmann (heir to the Fleischmann Yeast business), who had operated a tropical garden attraction in Naples, Tetzlaff opened Jungle Larry's Caribbean Gardens in 1969, which became a popular family roadside tourist attraction just off the Tamiami Trail; today, the property operates as the Naples Zoo.[20] Everglades National Park, opened in 1947, and Corkscrew Swamp Sanctuary, opened by the National Audubon Society in 1955 to protect seventeen square miles of cypress swamp from logging, also drew large numbers of campers and outdoor enthusiasts.

Still, the overwhelming trend in Naples tourist development in more recent decades has been one of ever-increasing luxury. As in earlier periods, the economic boom was closely linked with transportation development—in this case, the extension of I-75 from Tampa south to Naples, completed in the mid-1980s. The opening of a Ritz-Carlton hotel just north of the city in 1985 sparked a new boom in luxury resort building. At the same time, the city redeveloped its central core, with an eye to drawing tourists and residents past the county's proliferating suburban shopping centers. In the early 1990s, the city hired New Urbanist architecture firm Duany Plater-Zybek to develop a master plan for refurbishing the dated 1950s and 1960s buildings of the city's exclusive Fifth Avenue South shopping district (a six-block corridor in central Naples, terminating at the Gulf of Mexico) (Fig. 45). The avenue was reworked to be more pedestrian friendly, and many older buildings were replaced or updated in a faux-

Fig. 45. Fifth Avenue South shops, 1981. Often compared to Palm Beach's Worth Avenue, Fifth Avenue South offered a mix of shops and services that supported winter residents and vacationers. Photo by Mary Lou Norwood. Courtesy of State Library & Archives of Florida.

Mediterranean style, furthering shoppers' sense of exoticism and luxury (Fig. 46).[21] A concurrent restoration of the historic Naples Pier, completed in 1996, completed the rebranded "Old Naples"—a district of fine older homes, retail boutiques, and upscale restaurants.[22] Such redevelopment and marketing catered to the late twentieth-century tourist's taste for gourmet foods, fine consumer goods, and "historic" ambiance in urban design.

Naples was thus poised to capitalize on the economic trends of the late twentieth century, which saw sharp increases in wealth in the upper tier of American society due to the stock-market booms (and Reagan-era tax breaks) of the 1980s and 1990s. The zoning and property-management policies put into place decades earlier made Naples a safe investment for newly affluent Americans looking to purchase retirement or vacation property. The city of Naples was the nation's fastest-growing metropolitan area in the 1980s, and ranked second behind Las Vegas during the 1990s.[23] In recent decades, the desire for exclusivity in the midst of increasingly crowded land has led to an explosion of gated communities, which emphasize security, privacy, and prestige in their marketing, for both

Fig. 46. Mediterranean-style buildings on the redesigned Fifth Avenue South. In recent years, Fifth Avenue South, like Naples in general, has moved increasingly upscale, with more elaborate architecture to showcase high-end restaurants and shops. Courtesy of Jason Helle.

permanent and seasonal residents.

Economic growth in the area has dovetailed with complementary trends in recent American culture, in which leisure travel and luxury have increasingly been perceived as normal—rather than exceptional— conditions of middle-class American life. This "trading-up" trend fit well with Naples's tourist and real-estate marketing, which emphasized its exclusive character while also offering a variety of travel and housing options at price points affordable to a wider swath of the American middle class.[24] Naples's surrounding natural beauty and the earlier limits on development also positioned it to take advantage of what geographers have recently labeled the "amenity migration" phenomenon, in which middle-class Americans have increasingly moved out of urban metropolitan areas to smaller towns and rural areas that offer more preferable amenities, often after traveling to these locales for vacations. The trend has also contributed to the phenomenal residential growth of resort communities in the Rocky Mountains and across the American West.[25]

Such rapid growth has created new challenges for southwest Florida, and in the 1990s and 2000s, debates about growth, sprawl, and traffic gridlock have dominated Naples and Collier County politics. Barebones sewage, water, and electrical utilities, built to minimum specifications to keep residential taxes low, have proven insufficient for increasingly heavy usage.[26] Demand for housing drove home values rapidly skyward, which further decreased socioeconomic diversity by making home ownership, or even rental, unfeasible for the service workers that fuel Naples's tourist economy. Thus economically segregated from the community, many Naples workers submit to lengthy commutes from outlying areas such as Golden Gate and Immokalee, on the outer periphery closest to the Everglades, or Lee and Charlotte Counties to the north.[27] The traffic congestion created (in part) by these daily worker commutes was instrumental in the state's decision in 2007 to fast-track a construction project widening the thirty-mile stretch of I-75 between Naples and Fort Myers to six lanes. As in many amenity-rich locales, rapid population growth has threatened to destroy the tranquility and natural beauty that first drew visitors and new residents.

The boom in luxury homes, golf courses, and lavish hotels in late twentieth-century Naples led numerous national periodicals to proclaim Naples the "West Coast Palm Beach."[28] However, while Naples is often said to have Florida's greatest number of millionaires per capita, it has been not the ultrarich but an increasingly prestige-minded middle class that has swelled the city's population.[29] While the managers of the "Naples image" sought to preserve the city for a small, carefully screened group of visitors and residents, the appeal of the region, combined with the massive upswing in middle-class tourism in postwar America, has drastically altered that reality. For better or worse, market forces trumped elite management, as those with the means increasingly desired to make their tropical vacation a permanent way of life.

New Glarus,
Wisconsin

Steven Hoelscher

More than one hundred years after historian Frederick Jackson Turner famously declared the demise of immigrant cultures in the "crucible of the frontier," countless communities across the country persist in celebrating their ethnic heritage. From the East Coast to the West Coast, dynamic economic and cultural processes have reconstructed many communities visibly into *recognizably* ethnic places: Frankenmuth, Michigan, and New Ulm, Minnesota, are "Bavarianized" by adding half-timbered buildings to their Main Streets; Solvang, California, stands out along the drive from San Francisco and Los Angeles as a quaint "Danish" town; and Louisiana Cajuns and Texas Germans stage traditional music and food festivals to the delight of tourists seeking something "unique." The striking extent of this conspicuous cultural construction—with its self-conscious and profitable display of ethnic heritage—would surely make the nineteenth-century frontier historian scratch his head.

Among the most well-known, and frequently visited, ethnic tourism spectacles is New Glarus, Wisconsin.[1] Famous throughout the Midwest, and even abroad, as "America's Little Switzerland," the small agricultural community of two thousand inhabitants annually attracts tens of thousands of tourists for its many ethnic festivals, Swiss-themed architecture, European cuisine and local microbrewery, and historical museums. Deeply felt ethnic pride conjoins with unabashed commercialization and an international tourist economy to create a place that more than one European visitor has called "more Swiss than Switzerland."

Well before New Glarus offered visitors picturesque chalets, tasty schnitzel, and melodious yodeling, there were Swiss immigrants trying to eke out a living in southern Wisconsin. Unlike such tourist attractions as Leavenworth, Washington, or Helen, Georgia—ethnic theme towns instantly "Germanized" with no connection to an immigrant past—New Glarus owes its 1845 founding and early years as a successful dairying center to transplanted immigrants from the Swiss cantons of Glarus and Bern. A strikingly insular community throughout the nineteenth and early twentieth centuries, the Swiss of New Glarus began staging elaborate festive celebrations shortly after their arrival in the "new world." Historical tableaus depicting Swiss history and immigration to the United States, singing contests, and shooting matches all reinforced the distinctive ethnic identity of the New Glarus Swiss. Such festive occasions attracted curious visitors, but to their nineteenth- and early-twentieth-century participants, solidifying the boundaries of their ethnic identity was of greater importance than anything remotely connected to tourism.

Such insularity came to an end with the first modern performance of *Wilhelm Tell* in 1938 (Fig. 47). A classic "invented tradition" now in its seventh decade, the dramatic production of Switzerland's national founder's story was the brainchild of a displaced Long Island bank clerk with only remote connections to New Glarus. Edwin Barlow returned to the small town with both a thick wallet earned from a timely inheritance and the experience of nine years living abroad, most notably in Lausanne, Switzerland, where he had first seen an outdoor production of *Tell* in its original setting. These foreign experiences, so utterly in contrast with his common, rural upbringing gave Barlow a demeanor and an outsider status that differentiated him from his former neighbors in New Glarus.

It probably took someone like Barlow, a part of the community by birth but apart from it in life experience, to come up with the idea of staging the lengthy German-language play on a nearby farm—of "replanting the Swiss scene" as he put it. In this sense, Barlow served the role of ethnic cultural broker, identified over a half century ago by sociologist Louis Wirth as someone who helps his fellow ethnics recover, disseminate, and inspire "pride in the group's history and civilization . . . pleading its case before world public opinion." Indeed, Barlow's outsider status was crucial; with no vested economic or political interests in the daily life of the village and appealing to his authority as a knowledgeable "world traveler," he could take risks that no local resident, no matter how well connected, ever could.

A SCENE FROM WILHELM TELL PLAY, GIVEN EVERY YEAR AT NEW GLARUS, WIS.

Fig. 47. Postcard, ca. 1940. "From its founding in 1938 until today, annual performances of *Wilhelm Tell* have played a fundamental role in defining ethnicity for generations of tourists to this most conspicuously ethnic place." Courtesy of Steven Hoelscher.

Equally important, it also took the unwavering commitment of hundreds of volunteers to prepare the outdoor stage, sew the elaborate costumes, bring the dozens of farm animals, and learn the lines of Schiller's famous nationalist drama. Local residents had to buy into the idea and make it their own, and much to the astonishment of more than one detractor, a broad base of community support quickly formed around the play. So successful were those early performances—conducted, after all, in the language of a country with which Americans were then at war— that community leaders strived to make the play an annual event. From its early, rather audacious beginning until today, annual performances of *Wilhelm Tell* have played a fundamental role in defining what it means to be ethnic American in this most conspicuously ethnic place.

That meaning hinges, in no small part, on tourism. In the 1930s, with the area's agriculture and dairy industry suffering the effects of the Great Depression, New Glarus leaders consulted with the University of Wisconsin and the Swiss American Historical Society and concluded that tourism might provide a long-term boon to the community. In 1942, the New Glarus Historical Society formed the Swiss Historical Village Museum—including an original settler's log home, a Swiss bee "haus," a Swiss church, and a country school—that worked in tandem with the Swiss drama to entice tourists. Thus, beginning in the Depression, modern tourism began its long and increasingly important role in the community's economic fortune. Complementing *Tell* and older events such as Volksfest, newer annual and periodic festivals have been added to the events calendar, including Polkafest, Heidi Festival (another dramatic production, based on the beloved children's story by Johanna Spryi), Schwingfest (Swiss wrestling), Oktoberfest, Schuetzenfest (or competitive shooting), Maxwell Street Days, Winterfest, and St. Nicholas Day. The result is a calendar of events aimed at providing year-round attractions whereby cultural displays of ethnic culture, once the heart and soul of the community, have become its economic lifeblood.

At roughly the same time that *Wilhelm Tell* helped to replant the Swiss scene, material transformations to New Glarus's physical appearance began to take shape. Beginning in the 1930s, architects and builders, some from Switzerland and some from the United States, began altering the cultural landscape to make it appear more recognizably "Swiss." They added exquisitely detailed chalets to the residential landscape and attached overhanging balconies with potted geraniums to downtown buildings to add a Swiss atmosphere. Hotels, restaurants, and banks hired Swiss-trained architects to re-create the *gemütlichkeit* of the old country. A Swiss veneer gradually enveloped much of New Glarus, and today all sorts of symbols—street signs renamed after villages in Canton (or federal state) of Glarus, colorful shields from each of the twenty-six different Swiss cantons, and seventeen fiberglass cows made in Zürich and painted by local residents—provide unsubtle visual cues about the town's ethnic heritage (Fig. 48). Together, this landscape ensemble regularly earns New Glarus the title of "Wisconsin's most picturesque [or distinctive] town."

With this increasing "Swissification" comes a price. For some local residents, turning their town into a sort of "Swiss Disneyland," as New Glarus native and National Book Award writer Herbert Kubly put it, implies a degraded ethnic identity. "How Swiss can it be when you have to work so hard at it?" is a common refrain among the town's critics. Moreover, tourists themselves visit New Glarus in large measure because of its apparent "authenticity" and genuineness. Presenting an ethnic spectacle that residents and visitors alike would perceive to be "fake," in fact, would threaten the town at both the community level and cash register.

Fig. 48. The Chalet Landhaus Inn, though based on Swiss building traditions, is thoroughly American in scale and functionality. Together with colorfully painted fiberglass,
1980s-era cow sculpture, the motel was part of local business leaders' efforts to make the
town appear more recognizably Swiss. That the building's owner, its chief woodworker,
and many of its employees are themselves Swiss natives makes the landscape feel, for
many visitors, "more Swiss than Switzerland." Courtesy of Steven Hoelscher.

Such concerns came dramatically to the fore in the 1960s and 1970s, when
interest in white ethnicity became something of a national movement.
New Glarus's role as a dairying center was in sharp decline in the wake
of the 1962 closure of the Pet Milk Company condensing plant, and
tourism stood front and center. If Barlow succeeded during the 1930s
and 1940s in garnering widespread community support for his *Wilhelm
Tell* play, his successor—a Swiss immigrant named Robbie Schneider who
was both a champion yodeler and important local businessman—failed.
After leading the New Glarus Yodel Club for years and rehabilitating the
dilapidated 1853 New Glarus Hotel into a Swiss-style structure, Schneider
sought to rework the entire downtown into a miniature Swiss Village. The
plan, known as Project Edelweiss and modeled after what Schneider saw
in the ethnic tourist village of Solvang, California, called for a coordinated
effort of creating a Swiss landscape beyond the haphazard façades and
piecemeal construction that characterized the town; such a landscape was
to be enforced with strict zoning codes. When the community rejected
this plan and another several years later for a Swiss-themed resort as too
extravagant, Schneider moved to Colorado.

The social crisis Schneider engendered pivoted on the question of authenticity and its relation to the power of culture. For Schneider, purging the landscape of anything perceived as non-Swiss would make it authentic—his vision called for only architects trained in traditional Swiss construction styles. Yet, for many third- and fourth-generation Swiss, who could trace their ancestry back to the nineteenth century, authenticity was premised on ownership. Many felt that control of their Swiss identity was slipping away, and resented a relative newcomer (even if he was from Switzerland) cashing in on *their* town's heritage. Opposition was less to ethnic tourism per se than to its tight control in the hands of one person. One person's expression of authenticity and Swiss-ness, no matter how closely patterned on "the real thing," stood the chance of becoming culturally and economically hegemonic.

The interesting case of New Glarus demonstrates that with the rebirth and rediscovery of ethnic identity through tourism—whether constructed through cultural performances like the *Wilhelm Tell* play or though consciously designed landscapes—place-based identities remain in the hand of powerful social actors who are instrumental in directing their growth. Sometimes those efforts are accepted, sometimes they are rejected, but just because an ethnic identity enters the marketplace does not prove ipso facto its demise. If what passes today for Swiss in New Glarus—cultural displays that more self-consciously evoke heritage and identity—bears little resemblance to Swiss culture in Wisconsin during Frederick Jackson Turners's day, we should not be surprised. As a process of continual invention and change, ethnic identity is never static. Neither are the towns devoted to selling ethnic image.

New York,
New York

Art M. Blake

As a quintessential global city, New York City enjoys an iconic status among American metropolises. Home to more than eight million people, one-third of whom were born abroad, it remains a nerve center for global finance, media, fashion, and art. The notion of a planned, organized tourism industry in New York contrasts sharply with the conventional wisdom that the city's mass tourist appeal stems largely from its rich, complex culture and frenetic, spontaneous character. Visitors still have the feeling, in most of the city, of being casual witnesses to the daily life of a vibrant metropolis. It may be true that tourism is absorbed more easily, and rarely overwhelms, the urbane, metropolitan fabric of New York, yet there have been key moments of coalescence when promoters created destinations from scratch, completely repurposed districts, or organized the view of New York's chaos into a safe, consumable framework.

The roots of tourism in New York reflect the contrasting experiences that visitors to such a large and diverse metropolis still seek and find. New York City, for instance, attracted male business travelers beginning in the mid-nineteenth century who enjoyed a variety of saloons, eateries, and various commercial entertainments selected according to income, leisure time, and taste. Some out-of-town male visitors had pursued the euphemistically named "sporting life" of the city, visiting the city's rougher bars or the brothels below 14th Street in Manhattan. With the emergence of an increasingly organized tourist trade in the 1890s, shaped in part by the efforts of the Merchants Association of New York, the city's accommodations and entertainment for visitors grew and changed to attract middle-class men and women.[1]

New York's theatrical, restaurant, shopping, and nightlife venues enthralled middle-class tourists and provided entertainment and work opportunities for the city's fast-growing resident population. The large department stores, which had anchored the nineteenth-century Sixth Avenue shopping district known as "Ladies Mile," moved into more sumptuous palaces close to Broadway and Fifth Avenue, between 34th and 59th Streets, starting with Macy's in 1902. In the 1880s and 1890s, the city's theaters and restaurants also moved north to Midtown and began to cluster in the Broadway area in the late 1880s and 1890s, creating what came to be known as the "Great White Way"—the nickname for the Times Square–Broadway section of Midtown famous for the lights of its theater marquees and revolutionary illuminated advertising signs and billboards.[2] The Broadway Theater at Broadway and 41st Street (1888), the American Theater at Eighth Avenue and 41st Street (1893), and Oscar Hammerstein's Olympia at Broadway and 44th Street (1895) offered the gaudiness and grandeur that defined the area as a nightlife zone. By 1910, through the work of a handful of theatrical real-estate brokers, investors, and producers, almost all of the city's theaters could be found in the Times Square area. Glamorous restaurants that catered to the theater crowds, such as Rector's, Delmonico's, Maxim's, and Murray's Roman Gardens, opened within walking distance of the hotels, theaters, and subway.

Outside Midtown and Manhattan, tourists and residents in search of modern-day thrills overlapped on Coney Island. Developed as a secluded seaside resort, by the early 1900s, Coney Island housed the world's most famous amusement parks. In 1895, showman and adventurer Paul Boyton opened the Sea Lion Park, an aquatic theme park that borrowed a novel concept from his Water Chutes in Chicago—a fenced amusement park that charged admission. In 1897, George C. Tilyou, raised amid the hubbub of a family-run Coney Island restaurant, opened Steeplechase Park, which featured mechanical horse rides and scaled-down models of the Eiffel Tower, Big Ben, and Chicago's Ferris Wheel. Luna Park (1903), the next iteration in the amusement park business, was the brainchild of Frederic Thompson and Elmer "Skip" Dundy, who moved their famed Pan-American Exposition ride, A Trip to the Moon (with its *Luna* spaceship), to Steeplechase a year earlier. Luna Park's pastiche of fantasy architecture glowed with brilliant electric illumination and entranced millions (Fig. 49). The following year, Tammany Hall–affiliated businessman William H.

Fig. 49. Entrance to Coney Island's Luna Park by night, ca. 1905. Luna Park, popular with a broad range of New Yorkers and visitors alike offered this garish, electrically illuminated entrance to its early twentieth-century patrons. Courtesy of J. Mark Souther.

Reynolds opened Dreamland, another park famed for its electric lighting, zany architecture, and odd exhibits such as a Lilliputian Village and state-of-the-art baby incubators.

Coney Island's groundbreaking mechanical rides, roller coasters, and amusements such as the Blowhole Theater, which used jets of air to lift women's skirts, posed playful challenges to the turn-of-the-twentieth-century public decorum common to all classes. Coney Island, accessible by ferry and later by subway, provided commercial amusement that contrasted with even the liveliest Manhattan dance halls. Here, New Yorkers from a range of social classes, native-born and new immigrants, could cast aside lingering Victorian modes of movement, public speech, and fear of strangers, and begin to interact in ways that would not become commonplace in the city until the 1920s. The contrast between the sights, sounds, and public interactions of daily life as compared to a day-trip to Coney Island would have been especially acute—and perhaps therefore especially delightful—for tourists visiting New York from small towns or rural areas.[3]

The early years of the growth of Manhattan's tourist trade coincided with the period of mass immigration from southern and eastern

Europe, bringing the Italians, and Russian and Polish Jews who would so profoundly shape the city's popular culture, vocabulary, accents, food, art, and music in the twentieth century. Initially, the response of tourism entrepreneurs conformed to the prevailing conservative social reform view of the newcomers as problems that needed fixing—through Americanization, restrictions of further arrivals, and interventions in their healthcare, nutrition, and housing. But by the mid-1920s, with a restrictive immigration law in place, guidebook and travel writers felt free to extol the pleasures of "seeing the world" in New York via its "colorful" immigrant neighborhoods, particularly those of Manhattan's Lower East Side.

Other non-native-born and non-"white" neighborhoods also became tourist sites. The leading examples were Chinatown in Lower Manhattan and Harlem on Manhattan's west side above Central Park. Chinatown had been a curiosity since its growth prior to the Chinese Exclusion Act of 1882. It continued to hold a place on tourist itineraries in the early years of the twentieth century, according to evidence from guidebooks and picture postcards. Sightseeing companies hauled "rubber-neck" wagonloads of tourists through Chinatown at the turn of the twentieth century, usually stopping at "joss houses" and at a supposedly authentic restaurant for a bowl of "chop suey."[4]

Harlem, the city's main African-American neighborhood in the twentieth century, did not become a major site for the self-guided tourist until the 1920s. By the late 1920s, however, white visitors from within and outside New York City filled Harlem nightclubs such as the Cotton Club or the Plantation in which African-Americans could only enter as paid entertainers or as club workers. Middle-class tourism to nonwhite neighborhoods required the safe attractions of restaurants catering to white visitors, shops with easily identifiable ethnic curios, or theaters and clubs designed for nonlocal patrons. By the 1920s, standard tourist itineraries included both Chinatown and Harlem as sites for the visitor looking for easy consumption of exotic populations and cultures.[5]

New York's skyline had also become a tourist icon by the 1920s. The massed skyscrapers, the result of frenetic capitalist competition on Manhattan Island, created sublime, breathtaking views like nowhere else in the world. Skyscrapers may not have been planned as destinations, but they became the symbol of New York's modernity. Many towers, especially those that gave rooftop access to visitors eager for views, had featured prominently in tourist guidebooks since the turn of the century.

With the development of Midtown as a hub of entertainment, retail, and white-collar work, a second and even more impressive collection of skyscrapers sprang up from 34th to 59th Streets, between Sixth Avenue and Lexington. Midtown's possession, for most of the twentieth century, of the tallest buildings in the world, heightened the visual experience. The dramatic, sleek Chrysler Building at Lexington and 55th Street, adorned with monumental references to streamlined Chrysler automobiles, opened in 1930. The most iconic Manhattan skyscraper, the Empire State Building, completed the following year on Fifth Avenue at 34th Street, bested the automobile magnate's tower, and remained the tallest in the world for decades. The onset of the Depression, however, left much of the tower empty and called into question the sanity of its promoters.

Tourism is a luxury and few Americans had the money for tourist travel during the Great Depression; refinement of the New York tourist trade thus awaited better times. In the 1940s, the Second World War brought soldiers and sailors into New York, all eager for good times in a great metropolis, but it was during the postwar years that New York was reborn as a tourist city. Many still traveled by boat or rail to New York, but the city's elite made New York accessible to modern airplanes and automobiles. Planner Robert Moses completed his web of parkways, bridges, and tunnels while the Port Authority of New York and New Jersey offered sophisticated, modernist airports in Queens and Newark. It was easier than ever to get to New York from both the United States and abroad, at least for those intrepid suburbanites (or the few wealthy Europeans) with the nerve and money to confront New York's urbanity.

Nationally, the increasing postwar affordability of cars and gasoline, combined with the development of the interstates and of local highways, made summer road trips popular for family vacations. Some of the more adventurous family tourists came to New York City, but until the city's re-branding as a family-friendly tourist destination in the 1990s, most families only came to New York for an event such as the 1964-65 World's Fair, at which Mom, Dad, and the kids could all share in the fun. In this period, therefore, New York's typical tourist remained the middle-class adult, traveling alone, with a spouse, or in an organized group. Most of these adult tourists found their New York in the theaters, hotels, and clubs of Midtown.

Modern tourists might take in one of the must-see sights such the Statue of Liberty or the Empire State Building, but the majority came to New York to shop at Macy's or Saks, attend a baseball game at Yankee Stadium in the Bronx, or see the hit plays and musicals of the era. Broadway had drawn tourists since the 1890s and by the 1950s, big shows such as *Guys and Dolls* (1950) and *West Side Story* (1957) built on the successes of earlier hits. These musicals, in particular, used the "real" New York as a successful subject matter; enjoyed long runs on Broadway; and built a mass audience for American musical theater, centered nationally in New York City.

From the late 1960s through the 1970s, the national recession, television, and cultural decentralization (in other words, regional theater), hit New York's tourist-oriented businesses hard. Promoters faced an uphill struggle attracting domestic tourists—their bread and butter—who could now attend a decent theatrical production, shop in luxury department stores at the mall, catch a movie, or stay at home and watch television without a junket to Manhattan. Worse, what they saw at the movies or on television might well have confirmed the wisdom of their avoiding America's biggest and seemingly most disordered city. Cinematic images of New York from that period certainly did not recommend the city to average Americans. New York–based movies of the 1970s, including *Midnight Cowboy* and *Taxi Driver*, represented New York as home to violent criminals, deranged sociopaths, pimps, and prostitutes. Neil Simon and Arthur Hiller's 1970 movie *The Out of Towners* presented in comic form the dangers naïve visitors might experience in the city.[6]

The decline in New York's industrial economy, apparent lack of effective governance, and the corporate and white flight of the 1970s convinced many onlookers that New York had entered a state of permanent decline, but through luck and pluck, the city pulled out of its economic tailspin. New York City rebuilt its reputation as "a fine place to visit" through innovative marketing, enhanced attractions, and brightening prospects in the FIRE (finance, insurance, real estate) sector.

In 1977, William S. Doyle, deputy commissioner of the New York State Department of Commerce, instigated what became the "I Love New York" campaign. The advertising agency Wells Rich Greene, given the contract by Doyle's office to re-brand New York, hired legendary graphic designer Milton Glaser to design the "I ❤ NY" logo. This effort defined the determination of New York's business sector and city government not only to win back the city's image in the local and national imagination but also to recapture millions of tourist dollars for the city's merchants.

The "I Love New York" campaign grew from administrative desires, but historic landmarks and districts joined the city's tourist attractions as a result of both municipal regulation and citizen activism. After the demolition of the original Pennsylvania Station, in 1965 the city formed the Landmarks Preservation Commission to preserve specific buildings, and to designate historic districts within the five boroughs of New York City. The commission succeeded in preserving many sites that were ideal for tourism; the efforts of concerned citizens augmented the official efforts. The notion of historic preservation, planning to save the past, was certainly novel in a future-oriented city such as New York. The emerging financial and aesthetic benefits of preserving historic buildings and districts in the city nevertheless appealed to growing elements of New York's elite.

Saving the port area around South Street from demolition for "urban renewal" represented an early success for Manhattan's citizen-preservationists. In 1966, soon after the loss of Penn Station, a citizens group formed the Friends of the South Street Maritime Museum. Thanks to their efforts, the South Street Seaport Museum opened in 1967 and went on to become a world-class maritime museum. In 1980, the museum joined forces with the developer James Rouse, whose company had been responsible for the creation of "festival marketplaces" in Baltimore that same year (the Harborplace development) and at Boston's Faneuil Hall in 1976.[7] After Rouse's intervention, starting in the 1980s, in addition to the old sailing vessels moored in the area and the exhibitions at the museum, South Street Seaport featured various restaurants, bars, and a shopping mall built near a "historic" cobblestone pedestrian space and a rebuilt pier. The unvarnished, smelly Fulton Fish Market, located in the shadow of the upscale, redeveloped South Street Seaport, offered the seaport's restaurateurs quick access to a huge array of fresh fish, and gave visitors a sense that the port area remained vital. The Fulton Fish Market also maintained the riverfront's risqué reputation as a place of illegal deals and strong-arm tactics connected to organized crime. South Street Seaport experienced early success and is still a destination, but it is in limbo today. The waterfront mall failed to inspire much shopping and in 2005, the Fulton Fish Market moved to Hunts Point in the Bronx.[8]

Building on the success of the "I Love New York" campaign and the heritage-attuned remaking of the city's waterfront, was the unlikely transformation over two decades of Times Square into a "family-friendly destination." The undertaking took on a City Hall–directed appearance as early as 1980 during Mayor Ed Koch's administration. He proposed an ambitious plan for a new Times Square that envisioned restoring nine ornate theaters along 42nd Street, including the venerable New Amsterdam Theater. Following the late-1980s dip in the national economy, the grand plan faltered. To the chagrin of many a New Yorker and external critic, the Walt Disney Company arrived in 1993 to take the development helm, wresting significant concessions from a city government eager to harness the potential of Disney's "sparkling image of wholesome Americana." By that time, Rudolph Giuliani, with his focus on crime and "quality-of-life" issues, had become mayor, and he enjoyed a resurgent and rapidly globalizing FIRE sector that injected money and jobs into the city. Giuliani, like his predecessors in office, hoped to rid Times Square of its reputation for sex shops, prostitutes, drug dealers, and other influences that had led *Rolling Stone* magazine in 1981 to dub 42nd Street the "sleaziest block in America."[9]

The cultural politics of Times Square's make-over, and in particular the emphasis on attracting families with children to the area, must be understood within the context of the national "culture wars" of the 1980s and 1990s. This period saw a reinvigorated conservative movement pitted against not only its progressive rivals but also specifically gays and lesbians in the wake of the gay liberation gains of the 1970s. The conservative emphasis on the "family" placed the heterosexual married couple with children at the top of the cultural hierarchy and successfully reshaped much of American politics by the close of the twentieth century, to the extent that a place such as Times Square could not be redeveloped in the name of the safety, pleasure, and profit of all New Yorkers or all Americans but instead only in the name of "the family." Achieving "family-friendly" status was particularly challenging for a city such as New York, let alone the Times Square district, since conservatives over the course of the twentieth century had frequently lambasted the city for the ways its culture and diverse population strayed from American "norms." Although single people, gay and lesbian couples (many with children), and childless heterosexual couples form a large part of the national and international tourist market, the cultural politics of the 1980s and 1990s meant that few places seeking to attract visitors at the close of

Fig. 50. Wrigley's Spearmint neon sign in Times Square, 1930s. Then as now, Times Square's vivid assortment of giant illuminated signs beguiled tourists. The Wrigley's sign, billed at the time as the world's largest, extended one block along the east side of Broadway from 44th to 45th Street. With its 1,084 feet of neon tubing and more than 29,000 lamp receptacles, it reportedly carried enough current to serve a city of ten thousand. Courtesy of J. Mark Souther.

the twentieth century risked promoting themselves as anything other than "family-friendly."[10] The most recent version of this clash has occurred on the West side, in Chelsea and the former "meatpacking" district next to the Hudson River.

The Disney mark on the iconic crossroads of New York City today is unmistakable: dazzling electronic signs of unprecedented size, gleaming hotels, glittering multiplexes, and mammoth corporate superstores (Fig. 50). Yet in other ways, the Disney foray into Times Square reflects the city's ability, by dint of its tremendous scale, to absorb tourism without entirely losing character. More than a Disneyfied, sanitized, or privatized public space, all monikers of what Lynn B. Sagalyn has called "nostalgic angst," Times Square, like New Orleans's French Quarter, retains a grittiness manifest in "the impossible traffic, the inescapable noise, the impenetrable sidewalk congestion, the ubiquitous gum-stained pavement."[11]

The most startling and unprecedented change to New York City's tourist profile came as a result of the attack on New York on September 11, 2001. The destruction of the World Trade Center's "Twin Towers" not only took lives but also wiped out a tourist landmark. Since the towers first opened in 1973, they attracted tourists interested in seeing what constituted, until the completion of the Sears Tower in Chicago in 1974, the world's tallest buildings. Offering unmatched views of Lower Manhattan, the Bay, the Statue of Liberty, and the cityscape, the towers drew tourists into a predominantly business-oriented part of Manhattan. But the towers' destruction, in an odd twist, made the site an even more popular tourist destination. Never held as dear by New Yorkers or by tourists in comparison to other Manhattan skyscrapers such as the Empire State or the Chrysler Building, the manner of their destruction and loss of life combined to put the site firmly on memorial and disaster tourist itineraries. Informal shrines to the fallen now keep the district on the tourist itinerary. Plans for the redeveloped site include permanent destinations such as the memorial waterfalls and assorted cultural centers. It remains unclear how much business activity will ever find its way back to the World Trade Center site. An informal, chaotic event in the life of the city is slowly but surely being transformed into a planned destination.

New York's history as a tourist destination is hard to unravel from its history as one of America's, and the world's, great cities. New York City's development as an internationally important urban center and the conscious efforts of its purveyors of shopping, cultural performances, amusements, and sightseeing nevertheless combined to lay the foundation for an industry that has in recent decades has started to define the metropolis. New York City's official tourism agency reported that, in 2006, the 43.8 million tourists who visited the city spent $24.71 billion, which supported 368,179 New York City jobs and $16 billion in wages. Like other major cities that draw large numbers of tourists, New York City holds a dual identity—as a place of ordinary life and work for millions of residents and as a place of fantasy and play for its millions of annual visitors.[12]

Olvera Street
Los Angeles, California

Lynn C. Kronzek

A brown-brick stretch of nineteenth-century Los Angeles (L.A.), Olvera Street and the adjacent Plaza appear as compressed as today's metropolis is sprawling. Deeper exploration of this district, and the vibrant street life that inhabits it, uncovers a diverse cultural and economic heritage that catapulted an unsophisticated Western town into America's second largest city. By the time Olvera Street opened to tourists in 1930, its landscape reflected a complex, and mostly forgotten, mix of Los Angeles's agricultural, residential, commercial, and industrial past.

Originally named Vine Street, Olvera Street flourished as an early center for the production and distribution of wine, made possible by local viticulture. So pervasive was this early enterprise that the city's first seal, vintage 1850, features a fruit-bearing vine. The street was renamed in 1877 to honor recently deceased Agustin Olvera, a Mexican-born farmer who fought against the Americans in 1850 before becoming a pioneering judge and L.A. county supervisor. The histories of Olvera Street and the nearby Plaza, a circular public space relocated and slightly rebuilt at least three times by 1825, are intertwined.

During the nineteenth century, many leading Californio and early Anglo families vacated the Plaza surroundings for newer parts of town, where their wealth could be better displayed. Light industry expanded in the Plaza area, including the L.A. City Water Company. Immigrant populations—and the small retail businesses that served them—came to occupy the aging, modest, subdivided adobes abandoned by well-heeled former residents. French newcomers grew grapes on the peripheries, as Italians turned Olvera Street into the hub of local wine making. Jewish dry-goods merchants and banking pioneer Isaias Hellman found hospitable quarters to the west of the Plaza. On the north stood Sonoratown, named for a Mexican province and its native sons: immigrant miners less admired than the earlier "Spanish Dons." Negro Alley, subsequently Los Angeles Street, flanked the Plaza's south side. The "negroes" were not of the type ordinarily assumed, however; they represented a dark-skinned mix of Hispanic, Native American, African, and Asian races. With their departure, Negro Alley became the first of the city's three Chinatowns.

Los Angeles grew rapidly in the late nineteenth and early twentieth century, exploding from a little town of only eleven thousand residents in 1880 to a bustling city of 1.2 million in 1930. Tensions escalated between the city's small-town past and an increasingly modernized, urban present made possible by oil derricks, streetcars, automobiles, Hollywood glamour, and comfortable suburbs. As L.A. boomed around it, the Plaza and surrounding district languished or fell to the wrecking ball. Olvera Street remained unpaved and the namesake Olvera House was tragically razed in 1917.

In 1926, a college-educated widow and relative newcomer from San Francisco, Christine Sterling, happened upon Olvera Street. At the same time she arrived in L.A., a referendum had just been passed to construct a new railroad station. Voters selected the Plaza, from among five different options, as the ideal place for the new depot—a choice that would have meant destruction of the historic district. Sterling found conditions in the Plaza area appalling, but she did not share the public's desire for slum clearance. She launched a spirited preservation campaign, girded by the "Mexican Marketplace," or *mercado*, to alert Angelenos to the cultural and historical importance of the Plaza district. Sterling's preservation project received favorable notice, but only gained leverage two years later when the city health department condemned the Avila adobe, a deteriorating 1818 structure that once housed Don Francisco Avila, an early *alcalde*, or mayor, of L.A. Sterling secured admission to the building from the Rimpau family of Orange County, Avila's direct descendants.[1] To its front, facing the street, she affixed a ten-by-twelve-foot sign asking L.A. residents "Shall We Condemn?" and providing numerous reasons why the adobe was a landmark worth preserving.

Support for preservation came from many quarters, notably *Los Angeles Times* publisher and Chamber of Commerce booster Harry

Chandler, who maintained interest in many civic projects—the proposed Union Station among them. Favoring demolition of Chinatown over the Plaza for a number of reasons, corporate leaders saw Sterling's plan as a persuasive way to overturn the 1926 public mandate to clear the Plaza area.[2] Wide press coverage and popular opinion soon amplified her hand-lettered plea, and the city council revoked its condemnation order.

Chandler and associates subsequently added hard currency to their verbal support, forming Plaza de Los Angeles, Inc., a stock-bearing development corporation with Sterling as its managing director. Investors included transportation and real estate mogul General Moses L. Sherman (for whom Sherman Oaks, California, is named) and Henry O'Melveny, founder of one of L.A.'s oldest, most prominent law firms. Through fund-raising events, Sterling expanded and diversified her support base. Police Chief James Davis pledged inmate labor, and local businesses provided the crew with supplies needed to initiate the project. Women's clubs and organizations of all types contributed heartily. The final leap, clearing the two-hundred-foot-long "pedestrian mall" from commercial traffic, pitted Sterling against another formidable woman, property owner Constance Simpson, in several courtroom battles.[3] By the time the final verdict was rendered in Sterling's favor, canvas-covered *puestos* had opened for business on Olvera Street. Alas, saving Olvera and the Plaza meant the destruction of the neighboring Chinatown to make way for the new Union Station. The opening of the station, however, flooded the Plaza area with railroad tourists whose first taste of Los Angeles would be a creatively constructed ethnic spectacle.

The official opening of the market occurred Easter Sunday, 1930. *Puesto* merchants, following Sterling's strict orders, were lavishly decked in sombreros and folk costumes. At the time, very few places existed where American-born residents and tourists could explore diverse, non-Anglo cultures (Fig. 51). Gourmands of today can detect differences between Sonoran and Oaxacan regional cuisines, but even the urbane physicist J. Robert Oppenheimer often led his Cal Tech students to Olvera Street for more generic *comidas* during the 1930s.[4]

Public oversight of the area began during the 1950s and has kept pace with the district's changing needs. Today, El Pueblo de Los Angeles Historical Monument (covering the Plaza district and Olvera Street) is administered by a department within the city of Los Angeles and

Fig. 51. Tourists on Olvera Street, 1949. Courtesy of Department of Special Collections, Charles E. Young Research Library, University of California, Los Angeles.

governed by a publicly appointed commission. A professional curatorial staff maintains the integrity of current properties, supervises further historic and archaeological discoveries, and interprets the sites to diverse visitors. Most of the historic properties on Olvera Street and, indeed, El Pueblo, assume a preservationist perspective, designed for education rather than living. Jumbled together but displaying different ethnic origins and economic themes, its twenty-seven historic buildings are preserved in situ, representing a variety of eras and uses.

In spite of early criticism about authenticity, Olvera Street endures as a vibrant public place and community. Some of today's merchants are the children, grandchildren, and great-grandchildren of those who originally occupied the *puestos*. Concession agreements have encouraged entrepreneurism and a loyalty to place often rare in tourist sites. A block of old buildings—some remaining true to their origins, others designated for more commercial purposes—still flanks a strand of *puestos*, the folk-style market stalls that tempt consumers with affordable Central American souvenirs (Fig. 52). The nearly eighty merchants do not sport folk costumes like they did when the "Mother of Olvera Street" choreographed everyday

Fig. 52. Tourists on Olvera Street sample the wares of the puestos. Courtesy of Susan Liepa.

rhythms. Today, they determine the events to be held there and reserve their frocks for such annual rites as Las Posadas, an indigenous Latin American Christmas celebration; the Easter-time Blessing of the Animals; Founders Day, enacting the march from Mission San Gabriel to El Pueblo de la Reina de Los Angeles; Cinco de Mayo; and others. The notion of the pedestrian mall has endured remarkably in this auto-dependent city; cars and buses are still relegated to outlying parking lots. Despite the fact that Union Station is only a minor tourist hub and that Olvera Street lacks hotel chains or upscale restaurants, approximately two million people visit El Pueblo annually.

Sociologically, El Pueblo is a neighborhood with several distinct vibes, depending on the day of the week and the exact location. Sunday afternoon finds Central and South American immigrants packing the pews for masses at Our Lady Queen of the Angels Church (1822). The oldest house of religion operating in L.A., it is more intimately known as the Old Plaza Church or *La Placita*. Outside, folk shrines offer Spanish-speaking worshippers a more personal perspective, recalling celebrations and icons from back home. Street vendors dispense grilled meats, fresh juices, and *churros* (fried-dough pastries). Burial and life-insurance policies also are available here, a reminder of the issues that always have been most important to immigrants with time for little else than labor—and, perhaps, faith.[5]

In contrast to the Plaza, Olvera Street attracts far greater numbers, though fewer regulars. The State mandates that fourth graders study California history, adding many elementary school classes to the street scene. Local guests are not limited to the younger set, however. Entire families and adults alone intentionally stop at the Hellman/Quon Building (1900), Pico House (1870), Italian Hall (1907-8), the Biscailuz Building (1925-26), and other sites to pay respects to their L.A. ancestors, or simply to learn more about a particular immigrant group experience (perhaps theirs). In fact, El Pueblo's mature role may be in excavating personal narratives from a history that once concealed them. And if Los Angeles today proves the nation's most acceptingly diverse city, the opening act—subsequently staged—happened on Olvera Street.

PIKE PLACE MARKET
SEATTLE, WASHINGTON

Judy Mattivi Morley

Clinging to a hillside on the northwestern edge of downtown Seattle, Pike Place Market, a labyrinth of specialty stores and market sheds, exudes a permanent carnival atmosphere. Elderly men, suburban housewives, burned-out hippies, well-dressed business people, artists, and tourists literally rub shoulders amid the crafts, fresh seafood, and produce. The publicized authenticity of Pike Place Market has made it the city's top tourist attraction, even though the preservationists who saved the market in the 1960s hoped it would remain a funky, local place. The market on first glance indeed still appears to be a local farmer's market, and long-term efforts have been taken to preserve the tone of the traditional market stalls, but Pike Place's economic survival depends today on unique, high-end retail targeting tourists.

The market originally opened in 1907, and grew steadily through the first decades of the twentieth century as additional buildings were constructed (Fig. 53). In addition to stalls selling meat, seafood, cheese, and produce, the market had bakeries, taverns frequented by sailors and laborers, and various locally oriented services such as shoe-repair and hardware stores. The Great Depression was Pike Street's heyday as increased demand for affordable produce drove more consumers to the stalls. The market's decline began during World War II, but the era of postwar suburbanization, which both reduced center city populations and gave rise to strip mall supermarkets, seemed to obviate the need for a central city farmer's market. By 1963, the market had fallen into disrepair.

In 1965, the Seattle City Council approved an urban renewal plan, similar to those across the country, which would have flattened the market in

Fig. 53. The Pike Place Market has always drawn crowds of shoppers and spectators. The Corner Market, at the corner of 1st Avenue and Pike Street, 1912. A. Curtis 23706. Courtesy of University of Washington Libraries, Special Collections.

order to erect a parking garage, hotel, and several high-rise office buildings. The plan became known as "Pike Plaza": an empty symbolic gesture to that which the planners hoped to destroy. In order to gain control of the privately owned market properties, the city had to make a case for blight, condemn the market, and exercise eminent domain. As in so many cities, the discovery of blight was preordained. Structural studies and representatives of the Fire, Health, and Planning Departments all concluded that the market was a rat-infested, congested, dilapidated firetrap. The market's dilapidated condition, however, disguised its hidden, robust economic activity. The market still functioned as a strong magnet for downtown, and cultural activists, like those in other American cities at the time, recognized that the planners failed to understand the enduring value of the market district to the city's fabric.

The most prominent group of market supporters called themselves the Friends of the Market. Inspired by internationally recognized artist Mark Tobey, these Seattle artists, architects, students, and professionals fought hard to save the shabby site. University of Washington architectural professor Victor Steinbrueck emerged as the Friends' leader. His books, *Seattle Cityscape* and *Market Sketchbook*, romanticized the working-class atmosphere of the market, and he feared that demolition, or the addition of affluent tourists should the market be upgraded significantly as part of a larger renewal scheme, would irrevocably change that. The Friends wrote letters to local newspapers, talked to the national media, gave tours, and promoted the historic market to any group that would listen. Their persistence paid off, and they persuaded city council to modify the Pike Plaza design in 1968.

The modified plan kept some of the market's buildings, including rehabilitating the market's main arcade and the famous "Public Market" marquee. Had this been the entire plan, the Friends might have been satisfied. The rest of the design, however, still included upscale residential development and hotels. The Friends feared that the market would wither when cut off from its urban surroundings. They gathered 53,000 signatures protesting the new development, forcing the City Council to hold public hearings to reevaluate the project once again. City experts repeated the case for clearing as much of the market as possible, while Steinbrueck presented statistics on the market's economic health. Despite the signatures and compelling testimony, the Friends of the Market lost, and city council unanimously agreed to implement the modified urban-renewal plan. The Friends did not give up, however. Steinbrueck protested to the mayor, council members, the newspapers, the Department of Housing and Urban Development in Washington, Lady Bird Johnson, and even President Richard Nixon.

The Friends ultimately took their crusade directly to the public, forcing a ballot initiative known as Initiative 1. The initiative's physical planning actually paralleled that proposed by the city council, but aimed through management to prevent what Steinbrueck called the "creeping affluence" of tourism. On November 2, 1971, Initiative 1 passed with almost 57 percent of the vote. The ordinance preserved the *use* of the market and its "meet-the-producer" philosophy, in addition to the buildings, making the market unique among historic districts around the country. The Pike Place Market thus combined a heady mixture of market management, historic preservation, and urban renewal. To reconcile competing interests, the city formed a public corporation to develop the market, called the Pike Place Preservation and Development Authority (PDA).

The complexities involved in the market's rehabilitation forced compromises that created a district with a tone and flavor that departed significantly from that initially envisioned by some advocates. Steinbrueck, for instance, became disillusioned and lamented that "we won the battle, and then we put the enemy in charge of administering the peace."[1] By 1978, Steinbrueck openly criticized the direction of the market's rehabilitation by the PDA. He mocked the number of people in the market who "looked and sounded like they were from California and New York and Montana and Cleveland." Steinbrueck believed that the market had become a visual experience rather than a genuine farmers market. "It is not the Market of 1971, nor of Mark Tobey, nor of mine. It is the Market of the developer, the tourist bureau, and of 1978. Oh, well!"[2]

The very act of preservation transformed the market, despite the high-minded goal of some to keep the market exactly as it was. By the time the market was completely "rehabilitated" in 1983, it was radically different than it had been in 1971. Its transformation mirrored similar renovations of other surviving public markets, including Boston's Quincy Market and New Orleans's French Market, as tourist-oriented services became the market's bread and butter. The city located some social services in the market for working-class residents, and maintained traditional market stalls as best it could, but the primary goal of the PDA was to cater to middle-class consumers, including tourists. According to the PDA's first director, George Rolfe, "It is a curious reversal that the idea of a traditional Market—1930s style, meat and vegetables for low-income people—does not come from low-income people today. It comes from the upper and middle income who want to sample what life was like then."[3]

The redesigned market indeed attracted more tourists, who came to partake in its expanded goods and services, including more craftspeople and restaurant and deli space. Merchants changed their hours to cater to tourists, closing at five in the afternoon on weekdays but opening seven days a week. The new schedule favored visitors who could come during the weekday, while reducing access for working people. Tourism helped most businesses, however. Between 1973 and 1982, traffic in the market more than tripled. By the early 1990s, Pike Place Market had become Seattle's leading tourist attraction.

Despite efforts to maintain a farmer's market, capitalist forces changed the district. Until 1970, for example, nearly all of the businesses in the market served the needs of local residents—produce vendors, optometrists, shoe-repair shops, hardware stores, and dressmakers. By 1980, gift shops, antiques, boutiques, gem stores, and import outlets greatly outnumbered produce vendors. Unlike major festival marketplaces such as Faneuil Hall, however, the management deliberately rejected chain stores; a management decision that has helped adjacent Pike Street avoid the problems that have beset festival marketplaces such as Harborplace or South Street Seaport whose chain store offerings and mall tone became indistinguishable from suburban malls. For all the trappings of a tourist destination, Pike Place still has no chain stores by design, except for the original Starbucks coffee shop, and has been a successful incubator of small businesses that can be shoehorned into the warren of market halls.

The Pike Place Market has also taken a creative approach to the declining produce stalls. Early in the renovation it became clear that there were simply not enough family farms in King County to sell produce in the market. To combat this problem, the PDA supported new farms and subsidized farmers to grow local produce. PDA also offered below-market rents to encourage fresh-food retailing. The PDA's decades' long attempts to maintain traditional grocery market stalls appear heroic, and contrast sharply with festival marketplaces like Boston's Faneuil Hall that charged high rent and maintenance costs; market stalls quickly lost out to fast food and tourist junk in the festival marketplaces. In recent years, the produce stalls at Pike Place have continued to fade, but the market has reinvigorated the produce tradition with an organic farmer's market, featuring regional growers and producers, three days a week on the edge of the main market house.

Like all successful tourist destinations, the market cultivates and promotes key attractions. One cultivated tradition is the showmanship at Pike Place Fish Market, where, to tourists' delight, fishmongers throw salmon and other "flying fish" across the counter to each other. Another must-see attraction is the original Starbucks Coffee, which actually relocated to the market in 1977 following six years in a building a block away (and is itself unlike standard Starbuck stores). For decades, the market, much like New Orleans's Jackson Square, has featured numerous street entertainers. Many tourists, of course, come simply for the people watching in a public, safe space that is comparatively exotic; "This is no sanitized Disneyworld. It is a busy, littered market, kept tolerably clean, but showing all the signs of hard use." Of late, trendy theme restaurants have also become a major draw.[4]

Fig. 54. Front entrance to Pike Place Market showing its iconic clock and "Public Market Center" and "Meet the Producer" signs. Courtesy of Alex Abboud.

In the end, Pike Place Market attracted tourists because it romanticized a preindustrial utopia. The farmer's market, and the nostalgia it invoked, created the image of an agrarian paradise in the middle of the city—a time when life was simpler, people did business on a handshake, and producers and consumers met on a daily basis. In the tradition of Mark Tobey and Victor Steinbrueck, artists sit among the vegetable stands and paint scenes of the market to sell to visitors. Pictures of the neon "Public Market" sign are some of the most memorable of the city, and the Pike Place Market continues to draw hordes of tourists (Fig. 54). Pike Place may not be what its initial founders intended, but it retains the spirit that motivated its preservation in the first place.

River Walk

San Antonio, Texas

Char Miller

The San Antonio River beguiles. Early eighteenth-century Spanish explorers were thrilled by its cool, spring-fed waters. Frederick Law Olmsted was smitten by its sweep, writing in the 1850s: "We irresistibly stop to examine it, and are struck with its beauty. It is of a rich blue and pure as crystal, flowing rapidly but noiselessly over pebbles and between reedy banks. One could lean for hours over the bridge-rail." Its serpentine course mesmerized late nineteenth-century journalist Harriet Spofford: "twisting and turning and doubling on itself, so tortuous that the three miles of the straight line from its head to the market-place it makes only in fourteen miles of caprices and surprises, rapids and eddies and falls and narrow curves, reach after reach of soft green and flickering sunshine." Sharing her enthusiasm are many of the twenty-six million visitors who annually stroll down the contemporary River Walk's three miles of grace- ful, tree-lined paths, making it one of the great pedestrian experiences in the United States.[1]

But beneath the river's glittering surface and captivating charm lies a more disturbing story about tourism's complicated impact on San Antonio, the nation's seventh-largest city. To entice the visiting millions, the commu- nity offers a complex infrastructure, including historic eighteenth-century landmarks such as the Alamo and four other Spanish-era missions; the fabled River Walk; as well as a convention center, theme parks, hotels, res- taurants, and museums. The investment has paid considerable dividends: the hospitality industry employs one in eight workers and has an estimated $11 billion impact. Yet these benefits also come with a substantial cost— the large-scale creation of entry-level-only work for those with minimal education. This has proved an enduring pattern: since the mid-nineteenth century, San Antonio often has been more interested in entertaining its guests than in developing greater economic opportunity, better schools, and more affordable housing for its oft-impoverished citizenry. In San Antonio, as elsewhere, tourism has proved a "Devil's Bargain."[2]

Cowboys and vaqueros were the southern Texas city's first real tourists. As they stopped in town on the way north to Kansas railheads, they plunked down hard cash in its many bordellos, saloons, and gambling emporia that catered to their every whim. This boom went bust in the early 1880s, a consequence of overgrazing, increased transportation costs, and greener grass on the northern plains. Drive-by tourism had left the city susceptible to market vagaries.

Serving as a health resort for those suffering from tuberculosis made it just as vulnerable. But there was good money to be made from their care, so much so that touting the region's benign weather became standard fare. In blunt language, a local brochure asserted that anyone who failed to take advantage of its restorative powers would be sorry: those who died of consumption "unfortunately put off coming to this healthy climate until it [was] too late for them to be benefited."[3]

This breathtaking claim was not as confident as it sounded. An attendant graph of the city's mortality rate—14.95 deaths per 1,000—contained this important caveat: "based on residents only." The defenders of the sick-tourist trade knew the high incidence of death associated with tuberculosis; they knew that because it was communicable it also jeopardized the larger community's well-being. Not until the 1920s were San Antonians convinced that the public-health consequences of tending the victims of "white plague" far outstripped the financial benefits to be wrung from their misery.[4]

Historic tourism seemed a more salubrious prospect, yet it too closed off possibilities for a healthier local job market. In 1877, Thomas W. Pierce, president of the Galveston, Harrisburg and San Antonio Railroad, fearing that the iron horse would trample San Antonio's "ancient quaintness," urged that growth be confined to the town's periphery. Local preservationists, also alarmed that progress might turn the town's celebrated missions into rubble, lobbied the state to purchase the Alamo; they succeeded in 1883. Their civic activism established an ineluctable connection between the denotation of this site as "historic" and its touristic implications: hallowing the ground on which so much blood had been spilled in 1836 created a shrine to which large numbers of pilgrim-patriots would journey. "The tourist comes because he has heard of San Antonio's fame as a picturesque, historically interesting city," the *San Antonio Express* editorialized in 1912. "He brings millions of dollars annually." Preservation could be (and has been) profitable.[5]

Yet asking to whom this history was being sold, and why, reveals how the renovation of the Alamo and the other missions embodied the contemporary social order. By their presence at these locales—and by 1900, the city yearly welcomed one hundred thousand visitors—they sanctified these landmarks, turning them into markers of a revolutionary past that ushered in a civilization framed around Anglo dominance of economics, politics, and culture.

Manifest destiny was also embedded in the integration of the San Antonio River's sensual appeal and meditative character into the bourgeoning tourist economy. As the city exploded in size in the late nineteenth and early twentieth centuries, it swallowed up farmlands that Spanish ditches once irrigated and turned the river into a garbage dump. Its once-bounteous flow was diminished as the city drilled artesian wells to slake the citizenry's growing thirst. By 1911, the San Antonio River had "dwindled to a sluggish current running through neglected banks over a riverbed covered with slime and silt."[6]

Sick of its stench, business owners proposed that the river be piped underground, an argument that gained adherents following a devastating September 1921 flood that killed more than fifty people; engineers drew up plans to dam the river's upstream flow, straighten and widen sections of its middle reach, and then force it into culverts just north of downtown. River reformers, among them the formidable San Antonio Conservation Society, fought against the attempt to disappear the river, countering that beautifying its banks would pay off; a carefree clientele would be lured to its waters, where boatmen "dressed in the garb of Aztec Indians will paddle canoes, filled with tourists."[7]

This lurid fantasy of the river as an entertainment zone intensified the process by which this natural space became artificial. In 1929, the Conservation Society sponsored Robert H. H. Hugman's redesign of the river's Great Bend: as the south-flowing river entered the central core, it broke east, then south, then west, before swinging south once more, creating a

Fig. 55. Robert Hugman's 1938 drawing for the River Walk, prepared for the WPA, suggested an evocative Spanish landscape concept for the center of San Antonio and built upon his original idea for a Spanish-themed commercial development along the river in the 1920s. Courtesy of Institute for Texan Cultures, University of Texas, San Antonio.

mile-long loop and a peninsula-like wedge of land. It was this bend's banks that Hugman planned to beautify. Fascinated by New Orleans's vibrant French Quarter, where he had worked as an architect in the mid-1920s, Hugman concocted a clever scheme that incorporated flood-control features so as to protect the refurbished landscape. The plan included the creation of a bypass channel that would flush floodwaters directly south past the Great Bend, with gates that could be raised to keep rampaging floods out of the refashioned terrain. New limestone pathways would be laid down along and bridges would arch over the river, and the whole would be dotted with stores, hotels, and restaurants.[8]

Dubbed "The Shops of Aragon and Romula," Hugman's project wrapped a mundane commercial enterprise in a patina of Spanish exoticism, a romanticized riverscape in which visitors would frolic and consume. Imagine boating "down the river on a balmy night fanned by a gentle breeze carrying the delightful aroma of honeysuckle and sweet olive," Hugman enthused; "old fashioned street lamps casting fantastic shadows on the surface of the water; strains of soft music in the air; all of this would be the night life of Romula."[9]

Some of Hugman's ideas were strikingly realized in the late 1930s (Fig. 55). The support of Mayor Maury Maverick and an infusion of Works Project Administration dollars produced seventeen thousand linear feet of walkways, fanciful stairs, woven-rope ladders, quaint bridges, and extensive landscaping; adding to the area's allure was the construction of the open-air Arneson River Theater and the restoration of nearby La Villita Historic Arts Village, once site of the city's earliest neighborhood.[10]

What evolved into the modern River Walk (also known as Paseo del Rio) gained a major boost as a result of post–World War II prosperity; greater disposable income and increased access to automotive mobility brought thousands of visitors to Alamo City. Banking on these developments, a coalition of business and civic leaders, along with politicians and urban planners, organized HemisFair'68, a world's fair–like extravaganza; tapping federal, state, and local coffers, they converted a large portion of the central business district and a nearby historic neighborhood into a visitors' playground, and extended the river by constructing a concrete lagoon in front of the new convention center. Proponents argued that the enhanced river would stitch together the disparate elements of this new urban fabric, a prime example was Palacio del Rio, a twenty-one-story Hilton Hotel; among its innovative features were street- and river-level entrances that channeled guests and passersby between restaurants, shops, and convention facilities.

Since then, all riverfront hotels in San Antonio have followed suit, generating the substantial foot traffic that is key to the River Walk's profound economic impact. To expand its value, in May 2008, local boosters and political leaders successfully encouraged voters to support the continuation of a venue sales tax that would underwrite $125 million worth of improvements to the River Walk, extending it north and south from the downtown core. In May 2009, the northern or "museum reach," a 1.3-mile-long greenbelt, opened with great fanfare; it links the downtown with several cultural institutions, among them the San Antonio Museum of Art and the rehabbed Pearl Brewery. By 2013, the southern stretch will connect the city with the four historic missions forming the San Antonio Missions National Historic Park—Concepción, San Jose, San Juan, and Espada.[11]

These expansions will alter the natural river's form and function, if in different ways. The northern segment, for example, comes with a series of locks that integrates it with an already highly engineered system artfully concealing flood-control tunnels, pumps, and water-recycling infrastruc-

Fig. 56. The River Walk's iconic stone bridges span the waterway at numerous points along its course through downtown San Antonio. Courtesy of Jon P. Mulzet.

ture. By contrast, the mission project is being paired with an extensive riparian restoration project that the U. S. Army Corps of Engineers and the San Antonio River Authority will manage, and that is designed to return some of the lower river to its original course, repair damaged wetland, and replant native trees and other vegetation. In either case, the human impress will continue to shape the river's evolving flow and purpose.[12]

It will remain especially apparent along the River Walk: this now-historic pedestrian landscape serves as the communal artery and civic stage, albeit without buff Aztec warriors plying its languid waters (Fig. 56). Each year, its meandering walkways and calm surface become home to innumerable processions and parades, celebratory moments that reflect a diversity of cultural, political, social, and religious values. Even more spontaneous celebrations sweep down the river: whenever the San Antonio Spurs win the NBA championship, the victorious team floats past upward of 300,000 cheering fans.

Yet for all its great cultural significance and despite the billions of dollars it generates annually, the River Walk has not been an unalloyed success. San Antonio long has been one of the poorest large cities in the

United States, a status that is tied to relatively low levels of unemployment. Tourism accounts for this anomaly. Serving its innumerable visitors are more than one hundred thousand workers who earn approximately $2 billion in wages; that makes tourism the city's second largest employer, behind health care. But many of these jobs are part-time and/or seasonal, and this episodic character complicates the hospitality industry's capacity to promote sustained economic opportunity and upward mobility. The first step in breaking this vicious cycle is to question tourism's outsized economic clout, and the debilitating dependency it has produced. Until that occurs, San Antonio will remain in a tourist trap of its own making.

San Diego Zoo
San Diego, California

Kyle Ciani

In the early twentieth century, conflicts over bringing a national exposition to the city unleashed a flurry of actions that resulted in the creation of the "world famous" San Diego Zoo, a hundred-acre urban oasis for more than four thousand animals, many of them near extinction in their native habitats. Launched in 1916, the zoo embraced an emerging trend toward naturalistic animal exhibits that established it as one of the nation's foremost zoological parks. It has developed into a key tourist destination for travelers to southern California, rivaling corporation-owned theme parks like Sea World and Legoland for customer dollars.[1] As noted by scholar Susan G. Davis, in addition to its beaches and harbors, "San Diego's more commercial and constructed attractions also help define the city as a nature-oriented, conservation-conscious outdoor place to be. The San Diego Zoo, Wild Animal Park, and Sea World make up a powerful tourism triumvirate, presenting reconstructed natural environments and conserved animals to the tourist audience."[2]

The zoo holds a prime spot in the city's naturalistic jewel, Balboa Park, which was developed to host San Diego's Panama-California Exposition in 1915–16. That effort transformed the 640 acres of ill-used parkland into an array of citrus orchards, formal and wildflower gardens, and nurseries of exotic ornamental species that meandered around an assortment of Pueblo and Spanish Colonial inspired buildings. Neither the exposition nor the zoo emerged, however, without political manipulation at the local, state, and national level. San Diego had long sparred with larger cities like Los Angeles and San Francisco over state resources and business capital for resource development; in the 1910s, these fights continued as city officials fought with northern competitor San Francisco over federal funding and approval to host an international fair. Internal conflicts arose as well. In 1910, the exposition committee contracted with famed landscape architects John C. Olmsted and Frederick Law Olmsted, Jr., to turn the relatively empty expanse of canyon land into pedestrian-friendly grounds and Bertram Grosvenor Goodhue to design its buildings. The Olmsteds resigned over conflicts regarding design and function, and labor concerns over poor wages generated media-bound protests. Despite these setbacks, the exposition opened to great fanfare on January 1, 1915, and is recognized as the spark that fueled tourism as the commercial energy behind San Diego's urban development.

Exposition director-general D. C. Collier had convinced politicians of San Diego's niche in promoting regional flair, ultimately announcing in a *Sunset Magazine* article that the "most interesting things in the world are its peoples," and that San Diego would exhibit such interest through its exposition theme, "The Progress and Possibility of the Human Race."[3] Exhibits highlighted several indigenous cultures of the Southwest and incorporated animals—domestic and exotic—to achieve a real-life allure. Collier could not have imagined that these same animals would become the core of the world-renowned zoo, but other interested San Diegans did envision such a scenario. Physician and animal enthusiast Harry M. Wegeforth feared for the safety and long-term care of the menagerie of wildlife brought in for the Panama-California Exposition. A surgeon for the exposition and member of its board of directors, Wegeforth recognized the dangers to the animals left nearly abandoned when the exposition ended its two-year run. Wegeforth convinced three other physicians (his brother Paul, Fred Baker, and naval commander J. C. Thompson) and mammal specialist Frank Stephens to join him in advocating to the city to organize a zoo.[4] In 1916, the five men formed the Zoological Society of San Diego and began their venture into housing the odd collection of creatures. Buffalo, deer, and elk displayed as species of the western states needed room to roam, and more exotic and harder-penned animals like lions, leopards, bears, and birds lived their days in rudimentary, small cages.

The group's connections were formidable—for instance, Baker's interest in marine life led to his eventual founding of Scripps Institute of Oceanography—but the idea of a zoo did not immediately win the hearts of city boosters, politicians, and taxpayers. Over several years, Wegeforth politicked with the city council to secure a permanent site in Balboa Park and place the zoo's maintenance in the city budget; in the meantime, the animals lived in cages, which lined Park Boulevard on the park's western boundary. In 1921, the city council agreed to both a budget appropriation and a permanent site. Stories of "Caesar," a female Kodiak bear gnawing her way through her cage and tunneling under her first enclosure, encouraged city philanthropists such as Ellen Browning Scripps to make sizeable donations to the Zoological Society for the purpose of building proper animal grottoes.

The movement toward naturalistic settings for zoo animals dates to the 1890s, when zoo planners began to imagine zoological parks without barred cages. As Jeffrey Hyson argues, turn-of-the-twentieth-century park operators found that the visiting public "stubbornly maintained their own ideas of zoological entertainment." The interwar period saw the introduction of moated, barless animal enclosures by German animal dealer and circus entrepreneur Carl Hagenbeck. These animal grottoes, first adopted in the United States by zoos in Denver and St. Louis, enabled zoo-goers to view animals across moats in tree- and rock-filled panoramas that roughly resembled their natural habitats. Hagenbeck's principles, which also took hold at the Detroit Zoo and Chicago's Brookfield Zoo in the 1920s and 1930s, appeared beginning in 1921 on a far larger scale at the San Diego Zoo, where the mild southern California climate facilitated year-round outdoor exhibits. One zoo official extolled the virtues of abandoning what he called "the old style, iron-barred cage [that] belongs to the circus and traveling menagerie."[5]

Operational funds proved tougher to attract but Wegeforth perfected the art of fundraising by using the media to help him highlight the interesting sights and sounds of the wildlife. By 1925, the *San Diego Union* touted it as the fourth largest zoo in America. Wegeforth guided the zoo until his death in 1941. He had hired Belle Jennings Benchley in 1925 as the zoo's bookkeeper, and within two years, she was promoted to executive secretary (later termed director), the zoo's top staff position. The only woman director of a zoo in the world, Benchley quadrupled the zoo's annual attendance during her twenty-three-year tenure. By 1955, more than 1.3 million visitors enjoyed walking the zoo grounds and seeing the likes of koala bears, kangaroos, gorillas, pythons, peacocks, llamas, and giraffes. Marine life also found a home, as sea lions, otters, and seals

Fig. 57. Scripps Aviary, under construction, ca. 1937. Courtesy of San Diego Historical Society.

regularly performed for packed audiences in Wegeforth Bowl. The zoo became known for interesting exhibit spaces, many designed by architect Louis Gill, who created several of the city's more important institutional spaces. His 1926 design of the hospital and research laboratory fit into the Spanish flavor of the other exposition buildings and won meritorious citations from other architects for its simplicity and well-purposed functionality. His aviary design, dedicated in 1937, proved to be the largest birdcage in the world (Fig. 57).

Marketing and public relations allowed the zoo to expand its educational programs and collections. In the 1930s and 1940s, Hollywood first took an interest in the zoo, regularly using it for location shots of California or distant jungles. That relationship continued throughout the twentieth century as the zoo became almost synonymous with Balboa Park and San Diego. It became a restful haven for weary residents during the Depression and World War II despite the era's rationing of gas and food. In the 1950s, the organization understood the importance of children to a growing consumer market and built a petting zoo (named simply the Children's Zoo) within the main grounds. Zoo membership became the bread and butter of the operating budget, as families paid an annual fee for unlimited entry to the grounds. At its fiftieth anniversary in 1966, the zoo boasted that it maintained the world's largest collection of wild animals that totaled over five thousand specimens, demonstrating an understanding of the importance of superlatives in tapping the tourist market. The organization thanked its members by throwing an extravagant party "hosted" by chimpanzees that brought over twenty-five thousand people to the grounds.

As the San Diego Zoo expanded, it added various mechanical conveyances to give tourists a different perspective of the park. In 1969, it contracted with the Bern, Switzerland-based tramway company Von Roll Ltd. to build Skyfari, an overhead gondola lift that added to its guided bus tours of the zoo grounds. In doing so, the zoo borrowed a technique already common in major American theme parks, notably in the monorails at Disneyland and Busch Gardens in Tampa, Florida. The Busch Gardens monorail, opened in 1966, afforded visitors commanding views of exotic animals, tropical landscapes, and amusement rides.

The zoo's fame derives from its clever use of star power—both human and animal—to attract visitors to the grounds, draw members into its educational mission, and convince donors to fund its research agendas. A painting pachyderm (Carol), talk-show regular (Joan Embery), professional football player (San Diego Chargers placekicker Rolf Bernirscke), and a panda bear couple from China's innermost forests are a few of the more famous celebrities to spotlight the zoo's programs and encourage the general public to become interested in controlled habitat. In the mid-1960s, the Zoological Society turned global and began hosting photo safaris to Africa for those members and philanthropists eager to experience the exotic and willing to pay the high cost of such travel, but the exorbitant price tag for the trips limited them to wealthier patrons.

Families had been the mainstay of the zoo but competition from amusement park newcomers—nearby Disneyland, Knott's Berry Farm, and Marineland—drew the family away to more exciting experiences than petting lambs. In its effort to attract the growing family market, the zoo hit upon the television talk show as a venue for attracting new visitors. In 1970, the organization hired a young San Diego State University student, Joan Embery, to add sparkle to its publicity program by bringing interesting animals to the sets of television talk shows. A combination of girl-next-door personality and charisma made Embery a favorite on NBC's *Tonight Show* with Johnny Carson during the 1970s, setting the stage for animal handlers adopting celebrity status. Embery and the animals she introduced to television audiences became media darlings and generated millions of dollars in free advertising and publicity.

The growth of the environmental movement in the 1970s created the first broad consensus favoring naturalistic zoo design, and the San Diego Zoo was perfectly positioned to reap the benefits of its pioneering involvement in zoo design. As Hyson observes, environmentalists, who often criticized zoos as unnatural and inhumane, "also paradoxically looked to zoological parks (if properly designed) as potential sites of inspiration and education."[6] The San Diego Zoo's reputation for excellence in veterinarian care and training attracted international scholars and scientists to the grounds, making it an important site for research on endangered species. When the Zoological Society opened its 1,800-acre Wild Animal Park in 1972, an expansive habitat north of San Diego in Escondido, the organization solidified its unique captive-breeding program responsible for reintroducing nearly extinct animals to the wild. In 1975, the zoo established the center for Conservation and Research for Endangered Species (CRES), housed on the zoo grounds. The operation, massive in its scope and intent to restore ill-fated habitats across the world, soon developed into the largest zoo-based multidisciplinary research unit in the world. CRES researchers remained largely out of the media spotlight and depended on others to make their work appealing to the average consumer and contributor.

The zoo's international reputation helped in attracting such wildlife conservation "stars" as Jane Goodall and Sir David Attenborough but programs like CRES strained the operational budget and sent the society looking for new sources of revenue. New administrators with backgrounds in amusement parks pushed their commercial sensibility on the organization, and some officials naïvely believed they could raise admission fees, charge for parking, and scale back membership benefits with little attention from their adoring public. Instead, members rebelled at the proposed changes and set off a storm of negative publicity by jamming the phone lines with angry calls and writing emotionally charged letters to the editor. San Diegans, both longtime residents and newcomers, understood the zoo as its own backyard and not a place where they paid high prices for the privilege of enjoying green space in the center of urban sprawl.

The public outcry elicited a lengthy response by the society's executive director Charles Bieler. Appearing in the *San Diego Union-Tribune* on April 18, 1984, Bieler's editorial emphasized, "the price you pay for a day at the San Diego Zoo or the San Diego Wild Animal Park is the price of excellence. Even with a new parking fee and higher membership rates, we sincerely feel a visit here is an educational and recreational value. Our admission prices compare favorably to other entertainment facilities, to sporting events, to theaters and even to moves." Bieler explained the society's nonprofit status and its cooperative agreement with the city of San Diego to operate the Zoo and Wild Animal Park, neither of which came cheap. He also reminded readers that the facilities were "top-drawing cards for the substantial tourism and convention segments of this city's economy." By invoking the dual purposes of education and recreation, Bieler used a time-tested tactic of San Diego boosters, yet members won the fight. The zoo backed down on implementing a parking charge at the zoo; Wild Animal Park visitors, however, would have to pay to park their vehicles. Both the zoo and the park began utilizing the grounds for purposes other than animal conservation as popular musicians and variety acts staged shows with the calls of lion-tailed macaques, lynxes, and sun bears as background.

As its enclosures became dated, zoo architects introduced plans to reorganize the grounds by climate and habitat, loosely borrowing from organizational schemes long used in museums and theme parks, leading to a flurry of major fundraising efforts that captured millions of private foundation dollars and donations from individuals. The zoological society also turned to international ventures. In the late 1980s, it successfully

Fig. 58. Visitors view the zoo's naturalistic polar bear exhibit. Balboa Park's Spanish Baroque-style California Bell Tower, in the distance, remains from the 1914-15 Panama-California Exposition. Courtesy of Alexi Holford.

negotiated with the People's Republic of China to host a giant panda couple for a six-month visit. The visit proved both an economic and public-relations coup as it drew thousands of visitors eager to catch a glimpse of the rare animals. In fact, the zoo profited by $4.4 million and secured an ongoing relationship with Chinese wildlife officials. Part of the revenue came from T-shirts, trinkets, and kid games emblazoned with giant panda images. The zoo gift shops excelled at attracting customers as they offered a diverse array of merchandise from the dollar novelty to expensive fine art crafted in the original habitats of species found at the zoo. Using catchy names—Tiger River, Polar Bear Plunge, Reptile Mesa, Wings of Australasia, Sun Bear and Ituri Forests, and Gorilla Tropics— new habitats came to life in the late twentieth century and led the way for zoos across the country, notably Minnesota Zoo and Miami MetroZoo, to adopt naturalized settings. While botanicals and animals are central to these exhibit spaces, food stands, fine restaurants, and gift shops abound to attract tourist dollars, and businesses love the commercial exposure their advertising dollar affords them in sponsoring such naturalized exhibits.

The San Diego Zoo is far more than a wildlife habitat and holds a revered place in the city's local culture. From a few crude cages to a hundred-acre urban oasis, the zoo developed over the twentieth century into a massive, ever-expanding operation that serves both tourists and serious conservation research. The decision to expand and refine cageless exhibits today provides a picturesque naturalistic setting that appeals to visitors' interest in experiencing wildlife without the barriers that made earlier zoos feel like animal prisons or carnival midways (Fig. 58). The exciting people-moving conveyances and geographically sorted theme areas developed over the decades place San Diego Zoo squarely in the context of other sophisticated tourist attractions, including theme parks. Surrounded by freeways and urban sprawl, the San Diego Zoo remains a refuge for exotic animals and plants alike, as well as those millions who tour its grounds.

SANTA FE,
NEW MEXICO

Jay M. Price

Santa Fe, New Mexico, is a paradox. On the one hand, the city is marketed as a place of art, culture, sophistication, and spirituality rooted
in striking desert landscapes and centuries-old ethnic traditions. On the
other hand, the transplants that have turned this once-isolated town into
a regional and national destination have also developed a complex relationship with a tourism industry that demands commodification of local cultures in the name of commerce. Initially promoted and rebuilt as a
contrast to modern society, Santa Fe has in more recent years become, according to some critics, the victim of its own rampant commercialization.

Santa Fe's story has been dominated by neonatives, outsiders who
arrive and remake a place according to their tastes. In time, they joined
the ranks of "locals" who themselves must adjust to the demands of a
new set of arrivals. In 1610, Don Pedro de Peralta established La Villa
Real de la Santa Fe de San Francisco de Asis (The Royal City of the Holy
Faith of St. Francis of Assisi) on the site of an earlier Puebloan settlement.
Situated among the Native American pueblos along the upper Rio
Grande watershed, Santa Fe's Spanish authorities, clergy, and population
developed links and tensions with these diverse pueblo groups. In 1680,
resentment over European treatment and practices boiled over and the
Puebloan peoples rose up against the Spanish, who fled until Don Diego
de Vargas reclaimed Santa Fe in a *reconquista* (reconquest) in 1692.

The city served as the administrative center for one of the most remote
regions of the Spanish Empire, but it retained many features of a typical
Spanish colonial settlement. The community's heart was its main square,
the plaza. Although El Camino Real, the Royal Road (not to be confused

with the twentieth-century road of the same name that runs through California), connected Santa Fe to Mexico City, the region's isolation encouraged the population to develop local crafts and adapt indigenous practices in everything from building to cooking. The result was a hybrid Pueblo/Spanish tradition that later became one of Santa Fe's most identifiable features.

When Mexico won independence from Spain in 1821, trade with the United States grew via the Santa Fe Trail. During the day, the interchange of goods and ideas took place on the plaza. At night, visitors might take up lodging at a structure off one corner of the plaza known simply as La Fonda, Spanish for "the Inn." The Mexican period lasted less than thirty years and in 1848, Santa Fe, along with New Mexico, was grabbed by the United States. Anglo-American and German-Jewish business families, Hispano elite, and French clergy under Archbishop Jean Lamy sought to transform the city along more Anglo and European lines. Among their efforts was covering what they felt were embarrassingly crude mud huts with ornate woodwork and Greek Revival or Victorian details.

The arrival of the railroad both transformed and marginalized the city. The Atchison, Topeka and Santa Fe Railway, or AT&SF (named for the Santa Fe Trail, not the city itself), bypassed the community when it laid out a route between Albuquerque and Las Vegas, New Mexico. A spur line connected the Santa Fe railroad's main station of Lamy, about sixteen miles away, to the city itself. In town, this spur met up with a branch line from the Denver and Rio Grande Western. Las Vegas and Albuquerque, on the main line, flourished as modern, Victorian cities, leaving Santa Fe as a regional backwater whose main claim was being the territorial (and after 1912, state) capital.

It was the AT&SF, and the affiliated Fred Harvey Company, that helped establish Santa Fe as a tourist destination in the early 1900s. Mirroring the marketing of national parks as suitably American getaways, AT&SF/ Harvey literature promoted the region as exotic and romantic, full of quaint customs, unusual food, and ancient traditions. It was foreign but still in the United States. The Fred Harvey Company popularized what became known as "detours," where travelers could get off the train at Las Vegas, Lamy, or Albuquerque for side trips in northern New Mexico. In Santa Fe, they stayed in the newly constructed, Pueblo Revival replacement of the original La Fonda complex. From there, guided auto tours, sometimes

Fig. 59. La Fonda Hotel during Fiesta, 1941. Located at the terminus of the Santa Fe Trail on the Plaza in Santa Fe, the hotel was constructed in 1922 in the Santa Fe Style on the site where previous hotels had stood since the city's founding. The Fred Harvey Company operated the hotel from 1925 to 1968. "Fiesta, Santa Fe, 1941," Image No. 65912, New Mexico Department of Tourism Photograph Collection. Courtesy of New Mexico State Records Center and Archives.

in company-owned "Harveycars," ventured to Taos, nearby pueblos, and ancient ruins. Throughout, purchasing local arts and crafts became an essential element of the tourist experience.

Meanwhile, archaeologists and anthropologists such as Edgar Lee Hewett, Jesse Nusbaum, and Adolph Bandelier came to study the area's Native American and Spanish cultures. Hewitt helped found the Museum of New Mexico in 1909 and proposed, in 1919, the adaptation of a traditional Hispanic commemoration of de Vargas's *reconquista* into a community-wide fall event known as Fiesta (Fig. 59). Part local celebration and part tourist attraction, Fiesta included Hispanic Catholic ceremonies, but grew to include the showcasing of Native American arts and crafts.

Artists and writers in the early twentieth century also began settling in northern New Mexico, including Santa Fe and Taos. Representing the regionalist movement, these figures celebrated the area's connection to the land and centuries-old Puebloan and Hispanic customs as refreshing alternatives to the industrializing North American society they had fled. The group included individuals such as Georgia O'Keeffe, Carlos Vierra, John Sloan, and Witter Bynner. Among them were several tuberculosis sufferers who stayed at Sunmount Sanitarium to recuperate in the warm dry climate. One was Will Shuster, who came to Santa Fe in 1920. Along with four other young artists, Jozef Bakos, Fremont Ellis, Willard Nash, Walter Mruk, Shuster formed a group known as Los Cinco Pintores (the Five Painters), who held their first exhibition in 1921 at the new Museum of Fine Arts. Shuster was also the force behind what became Fiesta's signature kickoff: setting fire to a giant puppet called Zozobra or Old Man Gloom to symbolize the burning off of the previous year's troubles.

Resigned to the fact that Albuquerque was becoming New Mexico's booming city of commerce and industry, Santa Fe's civic leaders joined, sometimes reluctantly, with this cohort of transplanted intelligentsia to lead a citywide remodeling campaign to remove the nineteenth-century Anglo-American styles and return Santa Fe to an earlier look that they felt was more "authentic." Initially, Spanish-inspired revivals seemed the most appropriate look, best embodied in the bright-pink Scottish Rite Temple modeled after the Alhambra. However, the rounded lines and earth tones of Pueblo Revival became Santa Fe's defining architectural feature. The Palace of the Governors had its Victorian porch removed and replaced with one of plaster and stucco, one of the first structures to represent the so-called Santa Fe Style. Isaac Hamilton Rapp and Henry Trost, based in Colorado, received a number of noteworthy commissions in the early 1900s and helped develop Pueblo Revival as an architectural language. Rapp, for example, designed two of the city's signature structures, both located adjacent to the plaza: the Museum of Fine Arts and La Fonda's current multistory edifice.

One of the style's most passionate devotees was John Gaw Meem, an architect who came to the city in the 1920s. Like Shuster, Meem had been afflicted with tuberculosis and, when considering possible sanitaria, decided to visit Santa Fe upon seeing an advertisement from the Santa Fe Railroad. Once at Sunmount Sanitarium, he met with figures such as Carlos Vierra and came to appreciate local construction practices. His passion for Pueblo Revival resulted in a host of commissions throughout northern New Mexico, including Cristo Rey Church in Santa Fe and much of the campus of the University of New Mexico. Meem, along with Ina Sizer Cassidy and others, went on to found the Old Santa Fe Association in 1926 to help preserve the city's built and cultural heritage.

During the interwar years, Santa Fe became the hub of a distinctive architectural style, artistic worldview, and cultural milieu that was both rooted in enduring Native American and Spanish traditions and strikingly cosmopolitan. New Mexico, in general, and Santa Fe, in particular, eclipsed Texas, with its cowboy- and oilman-based image, as the defining center for the American "Southwest." A number of groups and institutions reinforced Santa Fe's reputation as the Southwest's cultural capital. The New Mexico Highway Department, based in Santa Fe, expanded its newsletter into *New Mexico Magazine*, one of the region's most prominent promotional venues. During the Depression, Ina Sizer Cassidy headed the Works Progress Administration's Federal Writers Project in New Mexico, overseeing a team that produced a state travel guide to the state in 1940 in which Santa Fe figured prominently throughout. Civilian Conservation Corps efforts helped develop Bandelier National Monument in the nearby Jemez Mountains into a travel destination. Pecos Ruins, about thirty miles east of Santa Fe along the Old Santa Fe Trail, became a state monument thanks to the efforts of figures like Edgar Lee Hewitt. Writers Frank Applegate and Mary Austin founded the Spanish Colonial Arts Society to both preserve historic examples of Hispanic arts and crafts and encourage the continued practices of various traditions such as the making of *santos*, religious sculptures once common throughout Latin America. In 1936, Maria Chabot with the New Mexico Association on Indian Affairs launched a series of Indian markets that showcased the work of Native American artists such as potter Maria Martinez. Boston-born Mary Cabot Wheelwright and Navajo Hastiin Klah founded the Wheelwright Museum of the American Indian, erecting a building shaped like a *hogan*, the traditional Navajo dwelling, on the hills that were at the time well outside of town yet close to the John D. Rockefeller-sponsored Laboratory of Anthropology.

World War II left its own mark on Santa Fe. During the war, the city was the main local hub for the Manhattan Project, the secret atomic weapons program in the newly created community of Los Alamos, some thirty-three miles northwest. After the war, the booming defense industry and military bases brought new residents, many of them well educated, to western cities such as Denver, Albuquerque, Dallas, and Phoenix— residents who eagerly spread out across the Southwest on vacation. Even eastern families could visit Santa Fe during summer vacations as their station wagons wound their way through the West's national parks.

Initially, the city's travel industry catered to the well-to-do who could afford the Harvey-sponsored tourist packages or those who were intrepid enough to attempt a long-distance car trip. Some of these travelers came out on Route 66, which went through Santa Fe until 1937. After World War II, middle- and working-class Americans could afford automobiles, had the resources to travel, and could take advantage of improved highways, including U.S. 85, which connected Santa Fe with Albuquerque and Las Vegas. Automobile tourism resulted in, for example, a row of early tourist motels along Cerrillos Road leading out of downtown.

Rather than merely preserving past examples of art and culture, groups and organizations in postwar Santa Fe encouraged the continued adaptation of historic practices to modern settings. The New Mexico Association on Indian Affairs, later the Southwestern Association on Indian Affairs, continued the tradition of regular Native American markets. In 1951, the Spanish Colonial Arts Society held an annual market of Hispanic arts and crafts. Concerned over the growing development of Santa Fe as both a tourist site and state capital, the *New Mexican*, in 1956, called for a city ordinance to protect not only historic properties but also the city's distinctive adobe-based architecture. In response, a group of mainly Anglos, including John Gaw Meem, writer Oliver LaFarge, Ina Sizer Cassidy, and members of the Old Santa Fe Association, drafted guidelines mandating that all new structures in the downtown area had to conform to one of three accepted styles: the sculptural forms of Pueblo Revival, the fusion of Greek Revival and adobe called the "Territorial Style," and the tile roofs of the Spanish Revival. Although there was opposition on the part of some that such practices curtailed free expression, widespread public support encouraged the city to pass the ordinance unanimously in 1957. In general, Pueblo Revival became the preferred style for tourist-related and commercial structures downtown such as the Inn at Loretto, while Territorial looks became standard for government buildings, including the unusual, circular state capitol, known affectionately as "the roundhouse."

Santa Fe's recreational and cultural attractions continued their strong growth in the postwar era. In the late 1950s, John Crosby founded a summer opera festival, resulting in an open-air facility where the audience could watch performances under the stars. In the Sangre de Cristo Mountains above the city, a ski basin attracted a new wave of tourists, many of whom came initially from neighboring Texas. Starting in 1964, the newly created Institute of American Indian Arts oversaw a show of Native American art on the plaza held each year just before Fiesta. Museums such as the Museum of International Folk Arts showcased both high art and local folkways. In 1972, the historic Rancho de los Golondrinas south of town became a living-history museum, not far from the Santa Fe Downs racetrack. Santa Fe had firmly placed culture at the center of its tourist industry.

The 1960s counterculture added their cultural sensibilities to the mix. Many "hippies" and "free spirits" integrated themselves into the existing art scene, developing Canyon Road from a local neighborhood into a string of popular galleries and reinvigorating the nearby mining town of Madrid into a haven of art and free expression. Those in the environmental movement constructed solar houses to capture the area's famous sunlight. Several 1960s and 1970s transplants embraced the philosophical and religious traditions that came to be called the New Age. The city's free-spirited image, as much as its Spanish and Puebloan traditions, had become a cornerstone of its identity. It is no coincidence that as the Baby Boom matured into adulthood in the 1970s, 1980s, and 1990s, Santa Fe had become a major tourist destination, with well over a million annual visitors inundating a city of only sixty thousand permanent residents.

Known as "The City Different," Santa Fe has developed a distinct, sometimes manufactured image that combines a host of seemingly incongruous features. The bronco-riding at the rodeo grounds and the western movie sets of the Eaves Ranch are just a short drive from the sophisticated art scene of Canyon Road and the low-rider car processions in Hispanic neighborhoods. Movie stars and other wealthy newcomers step out from their second homes to patronize local Mexican restaurants alongside nuclear engineers from nearby Los Alamos, Puebloan artists, Tibetan Buddhist refugees, lesbian and gay bed-and-breakfast owners, practitioners of alternative medicine, and Hispanic Catholic working-class families. Cafes offer vegetarian options and fusion cuisine alongside red or green chile sauces ("Red or Green?" is the official New Mexico state question). In recent years, California has replaced Texas as a key source of tourists but regardless of background, visitors still buy the silver and turquoise jewelry from Native American artisans who sit under the portal of the Palace of the Governors.

Fig. 60. Looking east from the Santa Fe Plaza toward the Cathedral Basilica of Saint Francis of Assisi during a street festival. Courtesy of Jay M. Price.

Underneath the carefully cultivated multicultural image, however, questions remain. Gentrification has turned old neighborhoods into upscale enclaves. Design guidelines have resulted in what some consider a unique built landscape and others fear is lookalike conformity. Critics warn that Santa Fe has become too sanitized and chic, tied to a commercialized "Santa Fe Style" of pueblo pots, Kokopelli-themed souvenirs, and howling coyotes (Fig. 60). Community events such as Fiesta, Spanish Market, Indian Market, and the viewing of *luminarias* and *farolitos* downtown during Christmas are geared as much toward visitors and seasonal residents as long-time locals. Centuries-old tensions between Latino, Puebloan, and Anglo simmer just beneath the surface of the "tricultural" heritage that is the official attitude in the tourist literature.

As the twenty-first century dawns, Santa Fe seems poised for the next shift in its history. Beyond the downtown core, and the city's architectural design guidelines, glass-and-metal "green" buildings challenge Pueblo Revival orthodoxy. Recent immigrants from Mexico and beyond are realigning the city's Latino demographics. Pueblo-operated casinos nearby attract a different crowd from those who frequents Canyon Road's galleries. The baby boomers that shaped and patronized Santa Fe since the late 1960s are also starting to age and retire. Tourism will remain Santa Fe's bread and butter, but the style that tourism takes, and the identity of future cultural brokers, remains unknown. If the city's past provides any guide, however, Santa Fe is certain to be remade once again.

Silver Springs

Ocala, Florida

Tom Benson

Silver Springs is a 350-acre nature theme park situated around the head-waters of the Silver River, a tributary of the St. John's River. Best known for its glass-bottom boats that enable riders to peer at multitudes of fish in its crystalline depths, it is the most commercially successful of sever-al Florida springs attractions. Long before The Mouse roared in Central Florida, this "eighth natural wonder of the world" was drawing hundreds of thousands of visitors to the remote outskirts of Ocala, Florida. Gushing more than a half-billion gallons a day of crystal-clear water, Silver Springs drew an average of fifty thousand visitors per year in the 1880s, a mile-stone that even famed Yellowstone had yet to achieve.[1]

Accounts of the journey to Silver Springs, one of the largest freshwater artesian spring formations in the world, fit well into contemporary Americans' perceptions and misconceptions of Florida. America's southern frontier represented to some an American Eden—an exotic, tropical paradise. To others, it represented all that was dark and savage about wilderness. To still others, especially those suffering from respiratory and other constitutional ailments, it offered the hope and promise of Ponce de Leon's fabled Fountain of Youth, a legend that was often invoked in describing Silver Springs.

These visions were fueled by the lyricism and poetry of those who made the overnight journey up the Ocklawaha and Silver Rivers to visit and write about it. Among those who sang the praises of the magnificent spring in the late nineteenth century were Sidney Lanier, Constance Fenimore Woolson, and Harriet Beecher Stowe. Many lesser-known writers also penned rhapsodic accounts of their visits in national publications like *Harper's Weekly* and *Scribner's Magazine*.

Before the Civil War, however, Silver Springs did not exist on the map of American consciousness. The first written account of the spring did not occur until 1825 and, even after the Second Seminole War (1835-42) opened up much of the fertile Florida interior to settlement, access remained limited to rutted roads that were often washed out. Transportation to the interior remained slow, unreliable, and uncomfortable and the fear of Seminole attacks persisted through the Third Seminole War in the late 1850s, despite the fact that the remaining Seminoles had long since been pushed to the southern peninsula. Although there is no written record of Native American activity at the springs prior to European contact, archaeological digs show that the spring area was inhabited more or less continuously for nearly ten thousand years, and some have surmised that the springs themselves were likely held sacred by natives. Two Native American names for the springs have been translated as "wells of light" and "sun-glinting water," respectively.

Continuing struggles with the Seminoles and the notorious roughness of the overland route to the springs kept the area a remote outpost until Vermont-born entrepreneur Hubbard Hart, having since moved to Savannah and Darien, Georgia, and finally to Palatka, Florida, saw the springs' commercial potential in the 1850s. In 1860, Hart cleared the notoriously unnavigable Ocklawaha River and began running steamboats specially designed for the narrow river between Palatka and Silver Springs, but the outbreak of the Civil War the following year put his plans on hold. Finally, after the Civil War, displaced Southerners and speculative Northerners began to "discover" Florida. When they did, Silver Springs and the journey to get there quickly came to define the Florida tourist experience. The enchantment of steamboat rides up the mysterious and forbidding Ocklawaha River to the Silver River was soon enhanced by the transfer at the springhead to glass-bottom boats. Such boats, believed to have been invented at the springs in 1878, allowed visitors to peer down as much as eighty feet through the crystal-clear water emanating from the limestone aquifer (Fig. 61). Like other natural wonders that became tourist attractions, Silver Springs's various features soon earned their own dramatic names such as Devil's Kitchen and Lover's Leap.

However, the golden age of the steamboat journeys to the interior of Florida was short-lived. Henry Flagler and Henry Plant's rail lines opened up the peninsula's coastline at the turn of the twentieth century,

Fig. 61. Tourists gaze at fish in one of Silver Springs's specially designed glass-bottomed boats. Courtesy of State Library & Archives of Florida.

creating virtually overnight such resort meccas as Miami and Palm Beach. Meanwhile, the river journey to Silver Springs, albeit exotic, remained relatively slow and tedious, prohibitive to substantial development. Even if the springs did offer rejuvenation, both the voyage and the accommodations were better suited for younger constitutions. Narrow-gauge rail lines and improved stage paths were introduced toward the end of the century but they were still slow and uncomfortable. More important, they lacked the scenic intrigue of the river voyage, which for many visitors was as enticing as the springs themselves. Meanwhile, the more luxurious rails and accessible resorts along the coast were booming. By the end of World War I, Silver Springs had all but faded from national memory.

In 1924, however, two rival suitors for the land around the springs, W. C. "Carl" Ray and W. M. "Shorty" Davidson of Ocala, joined forces to lease and upgrade the property for a potential resurgence. They agreed to reinvest virtually every dollar of revenue—minus only gasoline and tobacco expenses—back into the business, particularly its marketing campaigns. Among the many physical upgrades was the addition of a series of ancillary attractions, most notably the legendary Ross Allen's Florida Reptile Institute (1929), with its snakes, alligators, and Seminole "Indian Village," whose inhabitants the Pittsburgh-born entrepreneur recruited from the Everglades. Ray and Davidson were somewhat unusual. At a time when mostly outsiders were feeding Florida's speculative real estate frenzy, these local entrepreneurs actually built Silver Springs into something of a community resource, hiring relatives of existing employees and hosting numerous community events.

An initial renaissance at the springs, where annual attendance surprisingly boomed throughout the Depression years, was briefly derailed by the outbreak of World War II, but the postwar boom and the rediscovery of Florida as a vacation destination for the increasingly (auto) mobile middle class brought Silver Springs its second golden age, drawing as many as eight hundred thousand visitors a year by 1949 and an average of more than one million per year in the 1950s. With advancements in air-conditioning and mosquito control, the cheap land of sunny Florida was ripe for development and tourism. In keeping with Jim Crow customs that restricted interracial mixing, in 1949, Silver Springs opened Paradise Park, a separate glass-bottom boat dock on the Silver River to the southeast of the main dock, to keep African-American visitors at a distance from white tourists. Thus Silver Springs mirrored efforts to regulate black access to the most fundamental attraction—water—at resorts like Atlantic City, yet was praised for providing any access at all to African-Americans at a time when many other attractions did not.

The resurgence of Silver Springs was in no small part due to Ray and Davidson's mammoth advertising efforts, from customized promotional gimmicks like "mileage meters" (indicating the distance to Silver Springs) in motels across the East Coast to single-brochure press runs in the millions to massive billboard campaigns that would make the attraction a household word. Hollywood also bolstered Silver Springs's national appeal, filming a series of movies and TV shows at the spring. Props from *Sea Hunt* (1958-61) still sit at the basin's bottom and rhesus monkeys, commonly believed to have descended from escapees from a 1930s *Tarzan* movie, still chatter along the river's banks. (The monkeys actually are remnants of an earlier, ill-planned attraction along the river.) Silver Springs's promoters got an additional boost from the underwater photography of Bruce Mozert, an Ohio-born photographer drawn to the attraction in 1938 in hopes of watching Johnny Weissmuller film one of his *Tarzan* movies there.

Fig. 62. Bruce Mozert took many underwater photos like this one in the 1950s. His scenes of attractive young women engaging in everyday activities in the crystal-clear springs captivated tourists and provided priceless advertising for the attraction in the mid-twentieth century. Courtesy of Bruce Mozert.

Building his own waterproof camera housings, Mozert's iconic images of attractive young women engaging in various ordinary activities in a rather extraordinary place—underwater (playing golf, barbecuing, reading the newspaper, talking on the phone)—dramatized the springs' stunning clarity and appeared in much of the attraction's postwar publicity (Fig. 62).

By 1962, Silver Springs was attracting more than a passing fancy from entertainment giant ABC-Paramount, which had bought Weeki Wachee, another Florida springs attraction famous for its performing "mermaids," three years earlier, and Ray and Davidson sold their interests. Within a year, the media giant began revamping and restructuring Silver Springs's traditional offerings in more of a theme-park style, while another developer opened Six Gun Territory, an adjacent 200-acre Wild West–theme attraction that capitalized upon the peak of American fascination with silver-screen and television Westerns. One of many such Western-themed tourist attractions that opened across the U.S. in the 1960s, Six Gun Territory featured a Main Street flanked by stereotypical Western boomtown "businesses" and regularly scheduled mock gunfights—a direct imitation of similar performances in actual western towns like Tombstone, Arizona. With ABC-Paramount's financial and promotional support, as well as its own well-established brand, Silver Springs survived better than most Florida attractions as the Interstate Highway System bypassed long-traveled blue highways in the 1960s and Walt Disney World re-sculpted the Central Florida landscape in 1971.

Still, the heyday was clearly in the rearview mirror by this time. ABC-Paramount began charging admission to the park as a single, collective attraction, and the neighboring attractions that had symbiotically helped make Silver Springs such a consistent draw in the past began to disappear. In 1984, ABC-Paramount itself sold to another entity, Florida Leisure Attractions, and Six Gun Territory closed, to be replaced by a shopping center. In 1988, the park was sold to Florida Leisure Acquisition Corporation, which in 1993 sold the land to the state of Florida in return for an ongoing lease contract to run the attraction at the springhead. Since then, that contract has changed hands three more times, most recently going to Palace Entertainment, a California-based subsidiary of a Spanish amusement conglomerate.

During this time, the national dawning of environmental consciousness had taken hold in Florida as concerns grew that wholesale development was doing irreparable harm to the environment, pragmatic as well as ecological concerns. Natural Florida had not only intrinsic value but also economic value as a draw for tourists and transplants. Consequently, the state government began purchasing lands and expanding its park system. Today, much of the land around the spring and its river is publicly owned, including the 5,000+-acre Silver River State Park. Those who want to boat up the Silver River to the springhead as Stowe and Lanier did 130 years ago may still set in at the park or at the confluence of the Ocklawaha and Silver Rivers, but they may not land or swim at the springhead.

Efforts by the state to retain the natural beauty of Silver Springs have been encouraging, and a recent study concluded that "the overall structure and function of Silver Springs appears similar to qualitative observations" from the 1950s and 1970s. Nevertheless, the report also found that nitrates and algae in the river have nearly tripled in that time and the once-shimmering springhead bottom is slowly disappearing under encroaching algae and other flora. Experts blame runoff from residential development and fertilization, the same culprit that has threatened many of Florida's springs, rivers, and lakes.

Meanwhile, the attraction itself has been expanded in recent years with myriad exhibits. A fleet of glass-bottom boats—now electric—still glides almost silently over the basin. Attendance figures are not made public, but by all accounts, the park appears to be doing fine as other off-the-beaten-path Florida attractions have gone defunct in the past few decades. One research report estimates annual attendance at nearly 1.1 million. On some days, particularly during the park's annual concert series, the park can be filled to overflowing. Still, recent concerns about the park's upkeep and environmental impact have prodded public officials to consider taking over the site and returning it to a more natural state as a county park.

Today, the blitz-marketing days of nationwide billboards and mileage meters are long gone and the park's scaled-down and toned-down regional marketing campaign promotes Silver Springs as "Nature's Theme Park." In almost ironic contrast, a single ancillary attraction remains outside of the park. Located just across the parking lot from the entrance to the attraction, Wild Waters offers waterslides, wave pools, and flumes— entirely fabricated aquatic entertainment to complement the natural wonder next door.

South of the Border
Dillon, South Carolina

Meeghan Kane

South of the Border is an enduring tourist center and roadside attraction in Dillon County, South Carolina, near the North Carolina state line. Established in 1949, the resort began as a one-room beer stand but eventually became a sprawling 350-acre compound with a variety of services and accommodations, all focused on a theme of Mexican kitsch and featuring mascot Pedro as its host. In the six decades since it was created, South of the Border has been the first stop for many travelers as they enter South Carolina and the last stop for those leaving, but for even more passersby the spectacle of hundreds of beckoning billboards was enough to remember the resort. Never lacking a diversity of amusements, South of the Border offered at one time or another horse racing, fireworks, petting zoos, motel rooms, a golf course, and gambling. Yet the broad and winding course of this attraction always reflected the careful calculations of its founder and promoter Alan Schafer, a successful beer distributor from Little Rock, South Carolina. Roadside attractions reflected the marked gains in mobility, a sustained culture of affluence, and the social tensions of postwar America. For decades, Schafer successfully harnessed the cultural force of tourism that changed the national landscape and shaped national identity in the post–World War II years.[1]

By 1949, Schafer was already one of the largest employers in Dillon County and a controversial figure in local politics when he expanded his distribution operation to include a "beer depot." Among the few Jewish businessmen operating in the South at the time, Schafer claimed that he understood discrimination and therefore encouraged black patronage and employment and led voting drives to register African-Americans in

255

South Carolina. Schafer also challenged another Southern taboo by open-ing the beer depot. When several North Carolina counties banned the sale of alcohol, Schafer took advantage of this new market. Situating his beer depot on U.S. 301, a highway providing a straight route from Wash-ington, DC, to Florida, Schafer also expected to attract a growing number of tourists heading south to Florida from northeastern states. Inspired by the construction materials marked "Schafer project: south of the border," Schafer named the new business "South of the Border." Despite threats from the Ku Klux Klan and local protests that Schafer was undermining dry laws, the Dillon County Sheriff only asked that Schafer sell food in order to obtain a liquor license as mandated by county law. This was the beginning of the sombrero-roofed South of the Border Drive-In that be-came a twenty-four-hour diner within a year with private dining rooms to entice vacationing families on their way to Florida destinations.[2]

South of the Border benefited from the growth of a massive tourism in-dustry in America, fueled by the post–World War II economic boom. On the Atlantic Coast, Florida led the way in promoting tourism and attract-ing vacationers, which in turn spawned thousands of roadside attractions aimed at Florida-bound travelers. Increasingly, Schafer tried to make South of the Border a destination in its own right, and revealed a flair early on for experimentation in advertising and marketing. Initially banking on the allure of the Southern experience, Schafer advertised "Confederate cooking" for "Yankee" customers. But as other businesses like Dixieland and Tobaccoland along U.S. 301 began to rely on kitsch fantasies to tempt tourists from their cars, Schafer decided on a Mexican theme. By 1953, an enormous sombrero sat atop the diner, which became the symbol of South of the Border. A growing market for souvenirs made South of the Border placemats and pencils popular items for tourists collecting memories of their vacations.

To some extent, Schafer attempted to capitalize on the popular, though narrow-minded, Mexican image in popular culture of the era, where Mex-icans sported thick mustaches and sombreros. Schafer soon expanded the theme to include Mexican food and what would become the ubiquitous Pedro, the fictive host of South of the Border (Fig. 63). For some patrons, there was an air of authenticity to Schafer's creation. South of the Border even hosted local schoolchildren whose teachers hoped to immerse their students in Mexican culture. This encouraged Schafer to open the Mexico

Fig. 63. This larger-than-life Pedro statue, one of several at South of the Border, is a favorite place for tourists to pose for photographs. The 165-foot Sombrero Tower, with its
observation deck, rises in the background. Courtesy of Rob Svirskas.

Shop in 1955, which featured trinkets, curios, and souvenirs like sombreros and straw purses. Drug stores, ice-cream parlors, casinos, and race-
tracks followed. Schafer cast a wide net in his advertising strategy, relying
on Pedro to attract tourists to the growing resort with his stereotypical
Mexican dialect scrawled on hundreds of billboards lining U.S. 301.[3]

From the beginning, Schafer planned a strategy of inundating tourists with billboards promoting South of the Border, first on U.S. 301 and
later on I-95. Similar campaigns—hundreds of billboards across the Upper Midwest advertising Wall Drug, and the iconic "See Rock City" signs
painted on barns within several hundred miles of the famed Georgia attraction—had been staples of roadside attractions for decades. Schafer created his own firm, Ace Hi Advertising, to produce the billboards inexpen-
sively and he placed them liberally as far north as Delaware and well into
Florida. Brightly colored and often located only a few miles apart, Schafer's
billboards epitomized the roadside clutter and aggressive advertising that
drove Lady Bird Johnson's campaign for the 1965 Highway Beautification

Act. Many of them highlighted Pedro, who beckoned tourists with his clichéd Mexican dialect scrawled on hundreds of billboards. Comments included, "You never sausage a place—You're always a wiener at Pedro's" and "Eef you follow Pedro's signz, ze treep seem moch shorter." Eventually, South of the Border itself grew so large and distinct that travelers could not help but notice it, particularly with a 100-foot, 77-ton statue of Pedro.[4]

In the early 1960s, plans for a major new interstate, I-95, running from Maine to Florida, threatened the future of southern roadside attractions located along smaller highways. But by the time construction began in the early 1970s, I-95 was slated to run through Dillon County with an interchange at South of the Border. Rumors circulated that Schafer, by then a political, as well as economic force, in Dillon County, had pressured or bribed legislators in order to secure the placement of the interchange. But while state officials launched a political investigation, Schafer began preparing for the new wave of motorists that would now pass by South of the Border. He built hundreds of new billboards, a golf course, and a series of new attractions, including Confederateland. Reinforcing the Mexican kitsch were new additions, such as Pedro's Plantation, a new Pedro sign lit with neon lights, and a petting zoo with burro rides for children (Fig. 64).[5]

For the most part, South of the Border's Mexican theme depended on stereotypical images like thick mustaches and sombreros in order to exploit vacationers' search for an exotic experience. Operating a Mexican-theme attraction in a part of the country that had not yet experienced the immigration of large numbers of Hispanics, Schafer faced neither concerted criticism nor challenges from immigrants seeking to control visitors' experience of their culture, as happened in San Francisco's Chinatown decades earlier. However, his marketing strategy was not without its critics. Some suggested that the Pedro character represented a spectacle of Mexican culture, emphasizing laziness and simplicity. This image, along with the merchandise, replaced cultural distinctiveness with a stereotypical otherness, portraying Mexicans as primitive and quaint. For years, Schafer deflected criticism that he was ethnically insensitive. He insisted that as a Jewish man he had always been sympathetic to social causes and racial equality, and that during the 1950s and 1960s, his was the only motel in Dillon County to offer accommodations to African-Americans. He also employed African-Americans and Mexicans, along with Lumbee Indians from nearby Robeson County, North Carolina. When the Mexican Embassy complained in 1993 about his portrayal of Mexicans, Schafer

Fig. 64. This iconic Pedro sign stands astride the parking lot for a Mexican-themed strip mall. The Mexican theme extends to most other buildings in the tourist complex. Courtesy of Susanna Lee.

indignantly replied that he spent $1.5 million each year on merchandise from Mexico. But a few years later, as he began to replace older billboards, Schafer substituted the much-maligned "Pedro speak" with innocuous phrases like "Shop til you flop" and "A little razzle, a lotta dazzle."[6]

In his political posturing, Schafer also had his critics. While his business dealings expanded beyond South of the Border, throughout the decades the resort was repeatedly at the center of local controversy. As one of the primary employers in Dillon County and a prominent leader in the state and local Democratic Party, Schafer exercised a great deal of political influence. Beyond the rumors surrounding the placement of I-95, Schafer's political enemies insisted that he controlled the sheriff's office and engaged in and promoted illicit activities at South of the Border. In 1981, Schafer political machinations were exposed when he was convicted of voter fraud and sent to a federal prison in Florida for eighteen months.[7]

Not unlike Las Vegas, the success of South of the Border throughout its six decades in operation has rested on its ability to straddle two images, a family establishment and a place of taboos, both of which were aggressively promoted. In 1958, a "Men Only—Ladies Keep Out" section was included in the Mexico Shop. With fireworks, beer, and marriage licenses, Schafer took advantage of lenient Dillon County laws to persuade tourists to stop at South of the Border. The business began by enticing dry-county denizens to cross the border to buy beer and in later years, miles of billboards would promise fireworks that were illegal in other states. Couples from North Carolina had long traveled to Dillon County to marry for its more lenient age limits and lower marriage license fees, and South of the Border offered a reasonably priced honeymoon suite for newlyweds who had rushed to the county courthouse. Further, the ever-present Pedro embodied the roadside kitsch and the self-conscious exoticness of Schafer's resort. Indeed, the South itself became a taboo tourist destination in its own right, particularly in the politically polarized postwar years. But Schafer also created a family atmosphere of fun and kitsch with dozens of stores, restaurants, and amusement rides. When he died in 2001, Schafer was lauded for his marketing genius in making South of the Border a major tourist attraction in an era of heavy competition.[8] Today, South of the Border stands at a crossroads. Buffeted by Schafer's loss, growing competition from newer businesses along I-95, and the state ban on video poker (which had become a staple there), the compound has cut its workforce by more than half and ceased adding new attractions.[9] Though still an icon of American tourism, it must either expand or redefine itself if it is to enjoy continued success.

TOMBSTONE, ARIZONA

Kevin Britz

The American West is almost synonymous with the term *authenticity*. This has been the case with dime novels, Wild West shows, dramas, popular literature, and movies. Authenticity when it comes to the West, is not really about historical accuracy but about a universally agreed set of expectations—cowboy hats and boots, cactus-strewn landscapes, boothills, and false-front buildings. These are powerful images created over generations by all the versions of Western-style entertainments. When Tombstone, Arizona, first turned to tourism in the 1920s it was confronted with two important issues faced by many Western towns in the same situation: should it preserve its buildings and town character and cast itself as an educational shrine? Or should it satisfy tourist expectations of gunslinging cowboys sauntering down dirt streets and eschew its industrial past? Throughout much of its twentieth-century history, this struggle between market forces and preservation has marked the history of Tombstone.[1]

Today, any Western history buff can rattle off the name of famous Old West places—Deadwood, Dodge City, Cheyenne—and of course, Tombstone. Like many of these towns, the Southwestern camp was a boomtown that grew from a few tents in 1879 to as many as ten thousand tents a few years later. During its mining heyday, a visitor to Tombstone would have witnessed large numbers of milling miners on their way to work in one of many silver mines, strutting lawyers, proud clerks showing their wares, and lace-booted engineers. Tombstone was a buzzing industrial town in the southeastern Arizona desert in the 1880s, but one would be hard-pressed to see much of its mining history now. Today, Tombstone—once home of legendary figures like lawmen Wyatt Earp and

Doc Holliday and outlaw Johnny Ringo—is a tourist town that exploits its fame as an "authentic" Wild West town.

Tombstone originally set out on its path to become a major destination attraction in the 1920s, well after its boom had faded. The camp was founded in 1878 by Edward Schieffelin, a prospector who ignored warnings of hostile Apaches, ventured into the Arizona desert, and discovered large silver deposits near the San Pedro River. Schieffelin called it "Tombstone," in reference to naysayers who had warned that was all he was likely to find in the harsh desert landscape. News of the discovery traveled at lightning speed. Within two years, the erstwhile camp boasted an official government, two newspapers, hotels, restaurants, four theaters, two bakeries, schools, telegraph lines, and four churches. At the same time, Tombstone displayed the characteristics of a town that was home to large numbers of drifting male workers: saloons, prostitution, and gambling. It was this aspect of Tombstone that found its way into dime novels and journals, which fixed the town with the wild-and-woolly reputation befitting its name. Civic boosters were horrified by such notoriety, and they consciously downplayed its sordid aspects and promoted its piety, law and order, sturdy architecture, prosperous business climate, and modernity.

Boosters began to see things differently when water flooded the mines in 1887, completely ceasing most major mining operations. By 1900, only 646 souls remained in the once-booming town, eking out a living through small mining, ranching, and government services. Tombstone was briefly reborn between 1901 and 1910 during a vain attempt to dewater the rich ore veins, but the venture failed and the town returned to what appeared its grim fate as a ghost town.

At this point in Tombstone's evolution, the unruly past that once embarrassed promoters took on new meaning. Following World War I, magazine writers and history-minded journalists searched the West for rousing tales to grace their publications. It wasn't long before journalists like Frederick Bechdolt and Walter Noble Burns discovered Tombstone. In 1919, Bechdolt, a freelance writer searching for stories about the Old West, featured Tombstone in a series of articles in the *Saturday Evening Post*, where he focused primarily on the notorious Earp brothers and Doc Holliday of the gunfight-at-OK-Corral fame, Apache leader Cochise, and gunfighter Johnny Ringo. In 1922, he compiled the stories into a book entitled *When the West Was Young*. Five years later, popular historian Burns published *Tombstone: An Iliad of the Southwest*, which also highlighted the Earps. The book unleashed a flood of similar books, articles, and memoirs on the Earps, local outlaws, gunslingers, and Apaches. Tombstone, at least in the literary world, was becoming a shrine to the "Old West."

Fortunately, the roaring twenties brought cheap automobiles and a curiosity about the West created by films, pulps, and literature. As a result of their town's newfound literary fame, residents noticed increased numbers of curious visitors clanking into town in their Model Ts in search of the Wild West town they had read about. Unfortunately, most travelers left disappointed. Those who made the hard journey over dusty and bumpy dirt roads hoping to catch a glimpse of a booming mining camp, instead found Jazz-Age Tombstone a sorry sight. True, the town had maintained many of its famed buildings, such as the Bird Cage Theater and the Crystal Palace, but many others were abandoned, dilapidated, and in danger of collapse. Most embarrassing was the city's old cemetery (one of two city cemeteries in Tombstone). Instead of finding the legendary boothill graveyard depicted by Frederick Bechdolt—a wistful and romantic final resting place of outlaws and gunslingers, where ancient wooden markers leaned from the wind—tourists found broken bottles, rusted pots and pans, and old shoes. The fabled boothill was a trash dump.

Embarrassment over the cemetery's condition spurred the town's chamber of commerce into action to transform Tombstone into a proper Old West mecca befitting tourist expectations. Chamber head Arlington Gardner hoped he could capitalize on Tombstone's fledgling tourism industry by transforming the abandoned graveyard into a major attraction. In 1923, he organized a cleanup of the cemetery, persuaded the town to officially call it "Boothill," and began the slow task of re-marking graves. The refurbished site became Tombstone's first official tourist attraction. It was followed by many more as markers were installed at destinations like the infamous OK Corral, where the Earps had battled the Clantons and McLaurys in 1881. Other buildings, such as the Bird Cage Theater, Schieffelin Hall, and the old Courthouse, were also featured in promotional literature, all of which underscored the town's historic authenticity.

Tombstone's official embracement of the tourism industry was dramatically evident with the introduction of its first civic celebration, Helldorado, in 1929. Helldorado was part of a trend by Western towns such as Deadwood, Cheyenne, Prescott, and Dodge City to commemorate their founding. The events usually followed a familiar formula: a long parade with costumed locals and floats depicting aspects of the town's founding, followed by staged reenactments of historic episodes and a rodeo. In the 1920s, towns experimented with formal pageants but audiences preferred Wild West entertainments rather than gossamer-clad spirits and they were quietly retired.

Helldorado was the brainchild of William Kelly, the enthusiastic young editor and publisher of the *Tombstone Epitaph*, the community's sole surviving newspaper. Kelly's motivations in developing the commemorative event were multifaceted. At one level, he designed it to mark the fiftieth anniversary of the town's founding; at another, it was intended to rally state support to ward off rival town Bisbee's challenge for the county seat. Kelly hoped Helldorado would serve as a massive advertisement of Tombstone's heritage and its rightful place in Western history—*and* attract large numbers of tourists.

Kelly envisioned Helldorado as a Wild West time machine. He wanted to transform the Tombstone of 1929 back to its beginnings of 1879 using existing buildings and costumed locals to create an authentic Old West atmosphere. The task of restoring buildings, however, was a daunting prospect. Borrowing against his newspaper, Kelly embarked on a feverish campaign to repair decrepit buildings, hire Western-style entertainers, and advertise the event. For added authenticity, he arranged a reunion of old Tombstone pioneers such as John Clum, its first mayor, and collected historic relics to furnish refurbished buildings.

After months of frantic preparation, the inaugural Helldorado celebration was held in October 1929. It consisted of a long parade of bewhiskered prospectors, horse-drawn wagons filled with costumed pioneer women and children, groups of mounted cowboys, and Apaches in traditional clothing. Kelly insisted on maintaining the vintage nature of the event so he was chagrined when the Yuma Indian marching band arrived clad in modern uniforms and feathered plains-style warbonnets. The band elicited a number of wry comments from some of the old pioneers.

Following the parade, Helldorado visitors were free to participate in a number of vintage-style amusements held in the streets and buildings. Faux gambling was available in the old Crystal Palace Saloon, vaudeville shows took place in the Bird Cage Theater, and the streets ran red with imaginary blood from reenactments of various gunfights such as the OK

Fig. 65. "Historically accurate" reenacted violent episodes have been a mainstay of Tombstone's historic commemoration since the first Helldorado celebration in 1929. In reality, Tombstone was a generally peaceful town and early promoters did everything possible to distance the town from the unsavory images generated by dime novels. AHS# 46747. Courtesy of Arizona Historical Society.

Corral (Fig. 65). The event was successful enough that it became an annual event (despite a hiatus in the late 1930s and during World War II) and has continued into the present. It failed, however, in keeping the county seat in Tombstone—a blow to the civic pride of the community that helped inspire Walter Cole, Kelly's successor as *Tombstone Epitaph* publisher, to coin its famous tag line: "the town too tough to die."

By the 1950s, continual depiction in movies and on television had launched Tombstone to the height of national fame. Each film or TV program affirmed its place as a shrine to the Old West. Tombstone and its chief character, Wyatt Earp, remained at center stage in successive movies such as *Frontier Marshall* (1934), *Tombstone, the Town Too Tough To Die* (1942), *My Darling Clementine* (1946), and *Gunfight at the OK Corral* (1957). Earp and the city were also depicted in two television series, *Tombstone Territory* (1957-59) and *The Life and Legend of Wyatt Earp* (1955-61). In addition, the town was perpetually referenced in popular literature, comic books, and pulp magazines like *True West* and *Frontier Times*. Tombstone also witnessed a significant change in demographics after World War II. Joining the small local population were health seekers and many former military personnel who were stationed in the area during the war. The new group was fascinated by Tombstone's history, but also brought with them attitudes toward the Old West honed by Hollywood. In many cases, newcomers felt the urge to re-create the Old West as they envisioned it should be.

The more this free advertising brought affluent post-World War II tourists and their much-needed dollars into Tombstone, the more the town needed to fit the image of what visitors expected a Wild West town to be—an image now being drawn from movies and TV (Fig. 66). In 1947, Helldorado was revitalized and a new local group called the Vigilantes made their debut. The Vigilantes not only dressed the part of Old West characters but also reenacted moments of its past for tourists' benefit, most of which were gunfights and other mayhem. In 1954, the Vigilantes split over whether to include women and a new rival group offering equal membership, the Ghosts of Old Tombstone, was born. Over the next decade, the rival groups competed over the honor of authentic reenactment. In the midst of the battle, the chamber of commerce orchestrated a campaign to give the town a more Western appearance, recommending that businesses rename themselves to befit Tombstone's storied past: Wagon Wheel Inn, Boothill Motel, OK Café, Can Can Trailer Court, Wyatt Earp Café, and the Iron Chinaman Laundry. The organization also urged citizens to "dress Western" year-round, recommending the wearing of Stetson hats and cowboy boots.

The most daunting task of Tombstone's transformation into a complete Western tourist attraction remained architectural. Since the late 1930s, a preservation group later called the Tombstone Restoration Commission— composed of a core of old and new residents—struggled to find the wherewithal to preserve the historic integrity of its decaying buildings. Successes were hit and miss. While the group succeeded in preserving some important buildings, others like the original post office and sheriff's office were razed. Despite the overt boosterism, tensions remained within the community over the question of preservation. Many older residents who made up much of the rank and file of the restoration commission advocated preservation for educational purposes. On the other side were

Fig. 66. By the late 1950s, Tombstone fully embraced the romanticized Wild West image that was given increased national attention from films such as *The Gunfight at OK Corral* and the TV programs *Tombstone Territory* and *Wyatt Earp*. Serious preservation efforts after World War II reflected community attempts to provide tourists with an authentic experience befitting expectations borne from Hollywood. AHS# MS 1077 B23 F465_A. Courtesy of Arizona Historical Society.

new motel owners and restaurateurs who strongly advocated capitalizing on the growing tourism industry. Despite the infighting, the restoration commission scored two major successes with the recognition of the town as a National Historic Landmark in 1958 and the designation of its courthouse as a National Historic Landmark in 1962. In spite of these efforts, public monies for preservation only trickled in.

The quest for funding took a strange twist in 1963 when a group of investors from Detroit arrived in Tombstone with grand visions of transforming it into a Western Williamsburg. Many residents were chagrined at the event because they feared the loss of local control and felt their kitschy dioramas and museums already gave Tombstone an aura of authenticity. Calling themselves Historic Tombstone Adventures, the group came with the intention of buying local historic properties in hopes of creating a Western theme park and capitalizing on the national attention Tombstone was receiving from TV shows like *Tombstone Territory* and *Wyatt Earp*. Over the next few years, the eager group purchased all the town's principal historic properties, including the OK Corral; built a motel; and enlisted actor Vincent Price to narrate an electronic diorama called the Tombstone Historama. The high cost of preservation, however, eroded the group's enthusiasm, and by the 1970s, its grandiose dreams had faded.

Tensions between private- and public-minded preservationists abated when both sides agreed to a master preservation plan in 1973 with historic guidelines to restore the town to its 1885 configuration. With the plan, Tombstone now locked itself in a permanent Wild West moment. By 2000, its transformation into a total tourist town was complete. Each year, it keeps its reputation alive as a Western Sodom—a direct reflection of Hollywood's adaption of its history. The annual Helldorado celebration's costumed groups of reenactors roam the streets looking and playing the part of gunfighters or saloon girls; fictional and historic works on its early history abound; films like *Tombstone* (1990) keep the image alive; and the architecture has been arranged to suit the purpose. Today, part of the historic district has been "dirted" over so bullet-riddled reenactors can bite the dust rather than asphalt. Surrounding the dirt street are shops catering to reenactors. Here, tourists can personally relive the fantasy Old West with ten-gallon hats, highly decorated boots, buckskins, dusters, and six-shooters. Those wanting to express their Western individualism further can sport Western-style camouflage gear.

Modern Tombstone epitomizes an extreme example of a community's attempt to market itself as an "authentic" Old West town. In the quest to satisfy commercial needs, it has chosen to emphasize historical Western "flavor" by selecting a specific and narrow slice of what tourists desire and expect, instead of a more accurate depiction of its past. In this case, the town sacrificed its mining and civic building past for the sake of the mythical and marketable Wild West. Tombstone is not alone in this regard. Deadwood, South Dakota, has also completely erased its industrial past.

VENICE

LOS ANGELES, CALIFORNIA

J. Philip Gruen

In the contemporary imagination, Venice, California, a district of Los Angeles along the Pacific Ocean, is synonymous with the Venice Beach boardwalk and its tourists, street performers, outdoor weight-lifting gym, tattoo parlors, basketball courts, murals, vendors, surfers, roller skaters, ethnically diverse population, and radical politics—or at least as radical as typically aloof and laid-back Los Angeles and southern California can get. Tourists worldwide are routinely propelled to its shores to encounter a pedestrian-friendly, offbeat, and vibrant setting in a much larger city too often dismissed for its smog, traffic, and sprawl—a place to encounter local culture in a city whose visitor image has been shaped by the predictable, escape-driven entertainment generated in Hollywood, Disneyland, and Universal Studios.

It was not always this way. Like many American resorts and attractions that emerged in the late nineteenth and early twentieth centuries, Venice did not begin as a tourist destination when it opened on July 4, 1905—at least not exclusively. New Jersey tobacco magnate Abbott Kinney arguably had higher-minded ideas when he purchased unincorporated coastal marshland, just south of his moderately successful pleasure pier, casino, and resort in Ocean Park (today part of Santa Monica). Kinney dreamed of transforming that marsh into the "Venice of America," a genteel resort community intended as much for permanent residents as it was for temporary visitors. He constructed a three-block arcaded business district, residences, canals, bridges, and a large pier with buildings for events, all loosely patterned after the legendary Italian city on the Adriatic.

Kinney had visited the real Venice. A well-traveled American born in 1850 to a politically connected East Coast family, he had studied in Europe in the late 1860s and toured Italy during that time. After working for the U.S. Geological Survey and briefly joining his brother's tobacco company in New York (which eventually earned him a financial windfall), he set out on a worldwide journey that took him to Egypt, India, Sri Lanka, and Australia before he landed in California. Like so many late nineteenth-century California-bound travelers with health ailments (Kinney was asthmatic), he disembarked in San Francisco and promptly headed for the temperate weather and health resorts of southern California. He never left much after that.

As he established himself in the Los Angeles area in the 1880s, Kinney became involved with humanitarian issues, such as an investigation into the loss of indigenous culture in California, and conservation projects, which earned him positions on the State Board of Forestry and the Yosemite Commission. He also founded three public libraries, advocated the planting of drought-resistant eucalyptus trees in southern California, and wrote essays on topics ranging from nervous disorders to aesthetic beauty. There was little question that Kinney's Venice would rise from the Pacific shores as a place of learning and high culture—at least in part. But in turn-of-the-twentieth-century southern California, few models existed as to how such an environment might be shaped, and the Los Angeles area itself was still a "new" place with few pretensions to grandeur on a civic scale. Downtown Los Angeles, with a handful of commercial high-rises whose façades harkened to European tradition, and the original Plaza and Olvera Street, with its romantic connections to earlier Spanish and Mexican settlement, stood approximately fifteen miles inland from the Venice site.

To help plan for a suitable dose of culture, Kinney looked elsewhere. He sent his building superintendent, Frank Dunham, on an East Coast trip that included a visit to the Olmsted Brothers landscape architecture office in Brookline, Massachusetts. Kinney sought to hire a planner who could realize his Venetian, seaside fantasy with an ordered layout that arranged canals, lagoons, and streets in the grand manner—much as the firm's founder, Frederick Law Olmsted, had crafted along the marshy coastline of Lake Michigan for Chicago's 1893 World's Columbian Exposition.[1] For the appropriate high-minded attractions, the original Venice plat also included provisions for a 3,500-seat multipurpose auditorium for musical performances and a chautauqua-style set of lectures on topics of philosophical, religious, political, and scientific import.[2] Meanwhile, the Venetian-inspired stylistic palette for many of the principal buildings, designed by Los Angeles–based architects Norman Marsh and Clarence Russell, offered a stately backdrop for the cultural drama Kinney hoped would play out along the shoreline. Kinney's was a romantic vision, to be sure, but nonetheless aligned with long-standing elite nineteenth-century notions that seemingly uncivilized parts of the world—such as the American West—must turn to "Old World" design and cultural attractions for proper refinement and moral uplift.

But as Venice, California, rose, references to the architecture and culture of Venice, Italy, proved superficial—much like subsequent Venice recreations in America, such as the Venetian Pool in Coral Gables, Florida (1921), the town of Venice, Florida (planned in 1926), and the Venetian Hotel Resort and Casino in Las Vegas, Nevada (1999). Early visitors to Venice, California, could discover classical architectural orders, pointed arches, arcades recalling those of the Piazza San Marco, and a hotel called "St. Mark's" meant to resemble the Doge's Palace, but no building in the California version replicated Venetian examples precisely. The most literal reference arrived in the form of gondolas with singing gondoliers, which Kinney brought in to ply fifteen miles of newly dredged canals, including a seventy-foot-wide "Grand Canal," extending slightly inland from the pier and the business district (Fig. 67). But no visitor was likely to mistake Kinney's development for the real thing.

Historical accuracy was never a major concern, however. Venice, California, was a speculative venture as much as a civilizing one, and architectural references to European prototypes were meant to generate profit along with moral order. Kinney was no utopian dreamer; he maintained a pragmatic, businesslike efficiency that helped support many of his cultivated, catholic interests.[3] His purchase of the undeveloped marshy tract was strategic: although it did not provide the sturdiest land upon which to build, he was aware of plans to extend a streetcar line to the property, thus providing convenient transportation to visitors and potential investors from throughout the region. To spur investment, Kinney constructed a series of rentable, canal-side tents and bungalows and built a miniature railroad to transport investors from his planned business district to the 504 residential lots, more than half of which fronted the canals.

Fig. 67. Gondoliers in Los Angeles? In the early twentieth century, Venice emerged as a setting for high culture: Chautauqua-like lectures along the pier; architecture in the business district loosely suggesting the Venetian Gothic of Italy; and a series of canals replete with gondolas and gondoliers. Visitors in their Sunday finery glide along a canal lined with classic examples of the California bungalow in this early 1900s postcard view. Courtesy of J. Philip Gruen.

On the East Coast trip to the Olmsted Brothers office, Kinney also asked Dunham to investigate the nation's most successful pleasure piers and seaside resorts, including New Jersey's Atlantic City and the theme parks at New York's Coney Island, where fantasy environments and amusements drew the masses to the shoreline at the turn of the twentieth century. The Venice project differed initially from these destinations with its greater emphasis on high culture and development of a residential area and business district beyond the waterfront. But it learned from them as well. High culture alone, Kinney knew, would not sustain Venice. Gentility had to be tempered with informality; the beachside setting begged for somewhat less buttoned-up attractions to keep tourists entertained.[4]

When the final plans for Venice were ready, the loosely Baroque layout with its canals also included provisions for the beachfront and pier area with a casino, bowling alleys, a boardwalk, and hotels, including one in the form of a galleon that doubled as a café. Just six months after opening day, a collection of carnival-like amusements, such as the sensational Streets of Cairo and Darkness & Dawn, arrived from earlier national expositions and were assembled along an inland lagoon.[5] Accompanied by the summer 1906 opening of the Helter Skelter slide and the 1907 introduction of a large bathhouse plunge, attractions such as these found enormous popularity with the visiting public and helped tilt Venice's balance toward amusement and tourism rather than high culture. By 1911, the auditorium, a dance hall, and a pavilion catering to a more genteel clientele on the pier found themselves competing with an aquarium, penny arcade, and "scenic" railway winding through artificial mountains—and losing. When the massive Race Thru the Clouds rollercoaster opened near the lagoon in 1911, Kinney had transformed Venice into something much closer to Coney Island than Chautauqua.

Early Venice achieved success as a mass tourist destination, particularly in the summertime. But the residential district around the canals never quite took off the way Kinney expected, partly because the realities of the natural environment overwhelmed the desire to transform it and the canals became noisome rather than nostalgic. Engineering miscalculations led to silt-filled and polluted canals that occasionally flooded with the ocean's tides, and in 1913, the state declared them health hazards. Although attractions rose again on the piers in Venice and Ocean Park following disastrous fires in 1920 and 1924, respectively, Venice citizens opted for infrastructural and safety improvements over further pier development and voted narrowly for annexation with the city of Los Angeles in 1925. By 1929, city leaders elected to pave over most of the existing canals and turn them into streets more accommodating to automobile traffic.

When wildcatters struck oil in the vicinity of the Venice business district on the eve of the Depression in late 1929, the potential profits during an economic downturn inspired city planners in 1930 to rezone the area and permit drilling. Between 1930 and 1931, hundreds of oil derricks jostled for space from Venice south to Playa Del Rey, and the remaining canals became dumping grounds for residual waste.[6] Enough tourists still visited the beachfront area that the 1939 Federal Writers' Project guide to California described Venice as an "ocean-front pleasure town" with its "flying circus, giant dipper, bamboo slide, and rolling barrels."[7] But it had long since begun to deteriorate. The Venice pier was removed in 1947 and its attractions dismantled or burned; those at Ocean Park lasted into the 1960s, but it too fell into disarray. In 1958, Orson Welles found Venice seedy enough that he chose it as a double for Tijuana in *A Touch of Evil*, and when noted architectural critic and historian Reyner Banham visited the canals in the early 1970s, he described dangerous bridges wrapped in barbed wire spanning a single slimy canal. "Desolation," wrote Banham, "was everywhere."[8]

Yet Banham did not see that the desolation itself provided the seeds for Venice's revival. The pleasure pier and amusements were gone, but remaining were four canals, the boardwalk (Ocean Front Walk), and some original, if altered, Venetian-styled buildings along Windward Avenue and Speedway. In the 1950s and 1960s, declining rents for existing housing stock had begun to attract a certain "beat generation" clientele of artists, musicians, and entertainers, who—as with New York City's Greenwich Village and San Francisco's North Beach—gathered in cafés and whose free-spirited nature and bohemian lifestyle set the tone for the area's rejuvenation as a tourist destination. By the 1970s, along Ocean Front Walk and the beach, an outdoor bazaar had materialized with vendors, impromptu performances, weightlifting, and nude sunbathers. Residents along the nearby canals, threatened with its transformation into an exclusive, private enclave, staged annual "canal festivals" from 1969 to 1975 to protest changes and to advertise the canals as a public resource.[9] Without the realization of any grand redevelopment scheme or cohesive entrepreneurial vision, tourists gradually returned to Venice to participate in, or gawk at, the unplanned, somewhat haphazard social and cultural environment.

But piecemeal "improvements" also facilitated the return of tourists to the area. The widening of the boardwalk and addition of a bicycle lane, for example, encouraged a roller-skating craze in the late 1970s that briefly transformed Venice Beach into a moving festival. In 1980, locals founded the annual Venice Art Walk to raise funds for the Venice Family Clinic (the nation's largest free clinic), draw attention to the artistic and architectural efforts of the local community, and offer tours of artists' studios. Mass tourism had returned to Venice, but the nature of the "attractions" had shifted entirely from the refined aspects of Kinney's original vision. Indeed, tourists now came to Venice specifically to engage a culture that took issue with notions of order, civility, and refinement. This time, tourists did not require staged settings for amusement.

The tourist appeal of Venice's counterculture spurred redevelopment pressure in the community as a whole. The city did eventually flush and restore the canals, setting the stage for new million-dollar homes, only a handful of which suggested anything about Old World Venetian architec-

Fig. 68. In the early twenty-first century, Venice is better known for its free-spirited set-ting along the boardwalk than for its once-genteel past or its beach. Here, visitors stroll past clothing shops, a tobacco store, and a pizza stand. Courtesy of J. Philip Gruen.

ture. The gentrification of Venice in the 1980s and 1990s created the usual tensions between lower-income residents whose lifestyles or cultural tra-ditions had encouraged redevelopment in the first place, and a wealthier demographic that began to remove them—a situation that finds paral-lels in the late twentieth-century transformation of other once-"marginal" communities into tourist attractions, such as Santa Fe, Miami Beach, and New York's Harlem. But despite the occasional call from local officials to rid the boardwalk of "undesirables" and various regulations enacted to limit street vending and performance, Venice has not lost its alternative and free-spirited edge (Fig. 68).

Nor has Venice lost its appeal as a tourist attraction. Waves of recon-struction and time have clouded its original purpose, which was driven by Kinney's entrepreneurial spirit and desire to refine a once-remote corner of the continent. But refinement could only do so much. The longevity of Venice, California, as a tourist attraction has relied as much, if not more, upon that which provides alternatives to high culture as it has generated popularity from its recollections of the Old World.

Wall Drug
Wall, South Dakota

Troy Henderson

Wall Drug is simultaneously one of the most unlikely and famous roadside attractions in the United States. The probability was small that a modest drugstore in a remote South Dakota town, which could always count its population in the hundreds, would turn into a huge tourist shopping and entertainment destination advertised all over the world. A drive through South Dakota on the interstate illuminates a major reason for the store's past and present success: signs, signs, and more signs. Some are clever, others are bold, and a handful of them are even subtle—and they all point to Wall Drug. Wall Drug is a unique monument to roadside tourism in part because it succeeded in capitalizing on billboard saturation to such an extent that it weathered national legislation that encouraged the removal of excessive advertising along the country's highways.

Wall Drug's triumph in attracting masses of tourists is also linked to a collective yearning by Americans for a mythical Western past. In the 1890s, historian Frederick Jackson Turner declared that the Western frontier was gone, and the notion of a past that was somehow lost or disconnected with the changing nation spurred Americans to reflect, imagine, and physically undertake pilgrimages to the American West. Tombstone, Arizona, benefited and continues to profit from this nostalgic impulse, but Tombstone's boosters also had explosive, highly publicized historic events to exploit. The history of Wall, South Dakota, contains no legendary gunfight, cattle drive, or battle to focus public awareness. Wall Drug's allure was manufactured by a family with innovative ideas on how to lure traveling American families and provide them with an attractive vision of the West that they yearned for. Over time, the centralizing feature of Wall

Drug became the shared family experiences of millions of Americans at the place.

Adding to the implausibility of the store's success is that it was founded during the Great Depression. In 1929, Ted Hustead was a newlywed pharmacist desperately looking for a quality job in his trade. After struggling through a series of dead-end jobs, Hustead, along with his wife Dorothy and young son Bill, used the modest inheritance from his father to purchase a small drugstore in Wall in 1931. The original store, which primarily served the needs of the local community, was discreetly nestled between larger buildings on Main Street. The initial hand-painted sign on the exterior of the building was diminutive and did little to encourage motorists to stop at the drugstore, let alone Wall. The Husteads stayed afloat for several years, but the depressed agricultural market, which dominated the local economy, did little to assure the Hustead family that it had invested its inheritance wisely.[1] The clatter of automobiles driving across the gravel roads near Wall was consistent, in frequency from a regular flow of passersby, and in tone because automobile traffic rarely slowed down to pull over and visit Wall.

The Husteads solved their economic woes by creating their own market that catered to motorists. Inspired by roadside Burma Shave advertisements, which were witty billboards that created interest and anticipation in drivers by delivering the geographically spaced-out message phrase by phrase, family lore has it that Dorothy took the initiative and tailor-made similar signs for the Hustead drugstore. On signs that were spaced out just south on the highway through Wall, Dorothy's advertisement read: "Get a Soda / Get a Beer / Turn the Next Corner / Just as Near / To Highway 16 and 14 / Free Ice Water / Wall Drug."[2] The two phrases that struck gold for the Husteads were "Wall Drug" and "Free Ice Water." To fit the letters on the road sign, "Hustead Drug Store" was shortened to "Wall Drug," a name change that proved catchy and economical for the millions of signs and bumper stickers created since that time. "Free ice water" became a lure for thirsty motorists traveling through the parched landscape of South Dakota.

After Dorothy's successful experiment in 1937, more signage advertising Wall Drug arose along the highway. The dissemination of road signs was effective in part because of the monotony of much of the South Dakotan landscape. This was particularly true for motorists traveling west across the state. Wall was auspiciously situated with respect to popular

Fig. 69. Wall Drug in the 1950s. The license plates on the automobiles parked in front of the store reveal the vacationers had come from Wisconsin and Iowa. A hand-carved totem on the front sidewalk greeted the road-weary tourists. Courtesy of Wall Drug.

tourist destinations. Tourists from the Chicago area, intent on visiting the Badlands and the Black Hills, could not help but notice the lavish advertising for Wall Drug, a business that by the 1940s had already doubled in size. An informal *Chicago Tribune* survey estimated that in the immediate postwar years, nearly one in three out-of-state automobiles had Illinois license plates (Fig. 69).[3] Smaller signs and bumper stickers were sold or given to customers, the result of which was essentially free advertising. In a short period of time, Wall's drugstore moved far beyond supplying local pharmaceutical needs. The Hustead family had created a tourist-oriented niche.

For Wall Drug, advertising was the crux of the tourism business, but of almost equal importance was a manufactured worldwide curiosity about the store. As early as World War II, American soldiers familiar with the store's prolific advertising humorously plastered Wall Drug signs in Europe and posed for photographs near them. GIs in Korea and Vietnam continued the trend. Further spurring the international marvel of Wall Drug, Ted Hustead bought advertisements on the London subway and in Paris.[4] Europeans, just like Americans reading bumper stickers or signs in locales far away from Wall, were forced to wonder about the remote drug-store and speculate on its importance, or what Wall Drug even was. Inquisitive letters from various far-flung locations arrived at Wall Drug, and responses from the Hustead family usually included tourism literature for the store and surrounding destinations, as well as a personal invitation to visit the ever-expanding store.

The interstate highway system, for which construction got underway during the Eisenhower administration in the 1950s, helped funnel traffic to Wall Drug. It also facilitated a national dialogue on whether to temper the corresponding and burgeoning billboard industry. Some decried the numerous billboards springing up across the country as nothing more than pollution.[5] The Johnson administration, owing in no small part to Lady Bird's philosophy that beauty can uplift society, passed the Highway Beautification Act in 1965. The legislation sought to preserve the natural beauty of the countryside by restricting billboards. Bill Hustead, who by that time had taken over much of the managerial control of the store from his father, did not share the sentiments of proponents of restricting billboard advertisements. Instead, Bill supported roadside advertising by linking it to business and tourism in rural American communities.[6] Wall certainly fit the bill of small-town Americana, and indeed much of the store's charm is its nostalgic atmosphere clad in Western motif.

Mount Rushmore, the Badlands, and the Black Hills all surround Wall Drug as visual representations of the American West. Wall Drug offers a place for the consumption of the West, whether in the form of Western art, food, clothing, trinkets, or entertainment. The most widespread signs or bumper stickers simply read "Wall Drug" in a classic Western font similar that of old saloon and hotel signs. Advertising alone does not define the success of Wall Drug. Many potential tourist destinations undertook similar mass-advertising campaigns without equal results. Wall Drug's advertising, however, created a niche and fulfilled a desire among American tourists similar to South of the Border's Mexican theme with its ubiquitous sombrero-wearing host "Pedro." Wall Drug's initial offering of "free ice water" in the 1930s had expanded into a defining aspect of the Western tourist experience decades later.

Despite the removal of many of Wall Drug's prized billboards, the store continued to grow thanks to the Husteads' decision in the 1970s to pour money into a major expansion rather than yield to the same fate that marked so many other roadside attractions bypassed by the freeways. In-

Fig. 70. By the 1990s, Wall Drug had expanded considerably from the original store, which can be seen here behind the ever-present totem. Whether traveling on the roadways leading to Wall Drug or at the actual store, visitors are encountered with a barrage of signage, a key feature in the success of the store's growth. Courtesy of Wall Drug.

stead of becoming a relic of the beautification era, Wall Drug went from a stop along the way to a destination to the destination itself. From humble beginnings, the store has expanded into a block-long, 76,000-square-foot mall combining indoor and outdoor shopping and entertainment (Fig. 70). Wall Drug houses numerous shops selling everything from T-shirts to jewelry made from Black Hills gold. An eighty-foot-tall green dinosaur with red light-bulb eyes, constructed in the 1960s next to I-90, greets visitors as they turn off to Wall Drug, where they can shop, eat, relax, picnic, or take in an animated "cowboy orchestra." Many families eager for a shared experience find it at the unlikely tourist trap. Children are entertained in the "Back Yard" by a miniature Mount Rushmore, a bucking bronco, or the six-foot-tall rabbit. Adults, some of whom visited the store themselves in their youth, can enjoy a number of shops where gaudy souvenirs await a new home. Wall Drug's success in intertwining itself with automobile tourism has brought millions of travelers to witness its distinctive American story.

NOTES AND ADDITIONAL SOURCES

INTRODUCTION

1.   See, for instance, Edith Szivas and Michael Rile, "Tourism Employment during Economic Transition," *Annals of Tourism Research* 26, no. 4 (1999): 747–71, on the complicated role of the tourism sector in deindustrialization. See also Allan Williams and Gareth Shaw, *Tourism and Economic Development: Western European Experiences* (London: Belhaven, 1991). A good overview of different disciplinary approaches to tourism studies is provided in Andrew Holden, *Tourism Studies and the Social Sciences* (New York: Routledge, 1995).

2.   On placemaking, see "What is Placemaking?" *Project for Public Spaces*, http://www.pps.org/articles/what_is_placemaking/. On the "tourist bubble," see Dennis R. Judd, "Constructing the Tourist Bubble," in *The Tourist City*, ed. Dennis R. Judd and Susan S. Fainstein (New Haven, CT: Yale University Press, 1999), 35–53. On simulacra, see Umberto Eco, *Travels in Hyperreality*, trans. William Weaver (New York: Harcourt Brace, 1986), 1–58. Eco examines American places such as Disneyland and Walt Disney World and finds them emblematic of artificiality in the American cultural landscape.

3.   For an excellent review of the debates on authenticity see Ning Wang, "Rethinking Authenticity in Tourism Experience," *Annals of Tourism Research* 26, no. 2 (1999): 349–70; Gordon Waitt, "Consuming Heritage: Perceived Historical Authenticity," *Annals of Tourism Research* 27, no. 4 (2000): 835–62. See classics that set the tone on tourism studies such as Louis Turner and John Ash, *The Golden Hordes* (New York: St. Martin's, 1976); Dean MacCannell, *The Tourist* (New York: Schocken, 1976); and Daniel Boorstin, *The Image: A Guide to Pseudo-Events in America* (New York: Vintage, 1961). Recent work of a critical variety, and widely cited, includes Sharon Zukin, *Landscapes of Power: From Detroit to Disneyland* (Berkeley: University of California, 1991); Jean Baudrillard, *The Consumer Society: Myths and Structures* (Thousand Oaks, CA: Sage, 1998); and John Urry, *The Tourist Gaze: Leisure and Travel in Contemporary Societies* (London: Sage, 1990).

4.   A critique of the academic approach to tourism places can be found in texts such as *Cities and Visitors: Regulating People, Markets, and City Space*, ed. Lily Hoffman, Susan Fainstein, and Dennis Judd (Oxford: Blackwell, 2003); William Douglass and Pauliina Raento, "The Tradition of Invention: Conceiving Las Vegas," *Annals of Tourism Research* 31, no. 1 (2004): 7–23; and John Jakle, *The Tourist: Travel in Twentieth-Century America* (Lincoln: University of Nebraska Press, 1985).

5.   See, for instance, G. Richards, *Cultural Tourism in Europe* (Wallingford, UK: CAB International, 1996) for an overview of the culture/tourism relationship.

6.   A succinct overview of the literature and strategies of tourism space development and regulation can be found in Tim Edensor, "Staging Tourism: Tourists as Performers," *Annals of Tourism Research* 27, no. 2 (2000): 322–44.

7.   See, for instance, Michael Pretes, "Tourism and Nationalism," *Annals of Tourism Research* 30, no. 1 (2003): 125–42, on messages encoded in sites such as Wall Drug and Mt. Rushmore.

8.   Recent tourism scholarship disagrees over whether greater emphasis belongs to

elites as producers of tourist demand or to tourists as determinants in how places develop as destinations. An example of the former is Michael Dawson, *Selling British Columbia: Tourism and Consumer Culture, 1890–1970* (Vancouver: University of British Columbia Press, 2004). An example of the latter is Dydia DeLyser, *Ramona Memories: Tourism and the Shaping of Southern California* (Minneapolis: University of Minnesota Press, 2005).

9. Hal K. Rothman, *Devil's Bargains: Tourism in the Twentieth-Century American West* (Lawrence: University Press of Kansas, 1998).

10. Scholars are beginning to question Rothman's neonative thesis and examine the complexities of tourist site development. A notable example is Alicia Barber, *Reno's Big Gamble: Image and Reputation in the Biggest Little City* (Lawrence: University Press of Kansas, 2008).

11. Cindy S. Aron, *Working at Play: A History of Vacations in the United States* (New York: Oxford University Press, 1999); Anne Farrar Hyde, *An American Vision: Far Western Landscape and National Culture, 1820–1920* (New York: New York University Press, 1990); Richard H. Gassan, *The Birth of American Tourism: New York, the Hudson Valley, and American Culture, 1790–1830* (Amherst: University of Massachusetts Press, 2008), 52–69; Jon Sterngass, *First Resorts: Pursuing Pleasure at Saratoga Springs, Newport, and Coney Island* (Baltimore: Johns Hopkins University Press, 2001); John F. Sears, *Sacred Places: American Tourist Attractions in the Nineteenth Century* (New York: Oxford University Press, 1989); and Charlene M. Boyer Lewis, *Ladies and Gentlemen on Display: Planter Society at the Virginia Springs, 1790–1860* (Charlottesville: University of Virginia Press, 2001).

12. Catherine Cocks, *Doing the Town: The Rise of Urban Tourism in the United States, 1850–1915* (Berkeley: University of California Press, 2001). On American travelers' preference for European cities, see especially Harvey Levenstein, *Seductive Journey: American Tourists in France from Jefferson to the Jazz Age* (Chicago: University of Chicago Press, 1998), 85–92.

13. Marguerite S. Shaffer, *See America First: Tourism and National Identity, 1880–1940* (Washington, DC: Smithsonian Institution Press, 2001), 64.

14. Rina Swentzell, "Anglo Artists and the Creation of Pueblo Worlds," in *The Culture of Tourism, the Tourism of Culture: Selling the Past to the Present in the American Southwest,* ed. Hal K. Rothman (Albuquerque: University of New Mexico Press, 2003), 67–68.

15. Stephanie E. Yuhl, *A Golden Haze of Memory: The Making of Historic Charleston* (Chapel Hill: University of North Carolina Press, 2005), 6–9, 11. On the connection between the preservation impulse and tourism, see also Dona Brown, *Inventing New England: Regional Tourism in the Nineteenth Century* (Washington, DC: Smithsonian Institution Press, 1995); Anthony J. Stanonis, *Creating the Big Easy: New Orleans and the Emergence of Modern Tourism, 1918–1945* (Athens: University of Georgia Press, 2006); M. Barron Stofik, *Saving South Beach* (Gainesville: University Press of Florida, 2005); and Robert R. Weyeneth, *Historic Preservation for a Living City: Historic Charleston Foundation, 1947–1997* (Columbia: University of South Carolina Press, 2000).

16. Richard Wightman Fox and T. J. Jackson Lears, "Introduction," *The Culture of Consumption: Critical Essays in American History, 1880–1980*, ed. Fox and Lears (New York: Pantheon, 1983), x–xi.

17. Aron, *Working at Play*; Katherine C. Grier, "Recreation in a Christian America: Ocean Grove and Asbury Park, New Jersey, 1869–1914," in *Hard at Play: Leisure in America, 1840–1940*, ed. Kathryn Grover (Amherst: University of Massachusetts Press; Rochester: Strong Museum, 1992); Troy Messenger, *Holy Leisure: Recreation and Religion in God's*

Square Mile (Minneapolis: University of Minnesota Press, 1999); Andrew C. Rieser, *The Chautauqua Moment: Protestants, Progressives, and the Culture of Modern Liberalism* (New York: Columbia University Press, 2003); and Aaron S. Ketchell, *Holy Hills of the Ozarks: Religion and Tourism in Branson, Missouri* (Baltimore: Johns Hopkins University Press, 2007).

18. On the shift from maritime trade to tourism, see Brown, *Inventing New England*, 106. On early twentieth-century economic transformations, see, for example, Steven D. Hoelscher, *Heritage on Display: The Invention of Ethnic Place in America's Little Switzerland* (Madison: University of Wisconsin Press, 1998); Barber, *Reno's Big Gamble*; and Annie Gilbert Coleman, *Ski Style: Sport and Culture in the Rockies* (Lawrence: University Press of Kansas, 2004). On tourism in the context of postwar deindustrialization, see Cathy Stanton, *The Lowell Experiment: Public History in a Postindustrial City* (Amherst: University of Massachusetts Press, 2006); and Connie Y. Chiang, *Shaping the Shoreline: Fisheries and Tourism on the Monterey Coast* (Seattle: University of Washington Press, 2008).

19. Brown, *Inventing New England*, 43.

20. On the role of the state in foreign tourism development, see especially Dennis Merrill, *Negotiating Paradise: U.S. Tourism and Empire in Twentieth-Century Latin America* (Chapel Hill: University of North Carolina Press, 2009); Dina Berger, *The Development of Mexico's Tourism Industry: Pyramids by Day, Martinis by Night* (New York: Palgrave Macmillan, 2006); and Christopher Endy, *Cold War Holidays: American Tourism in France* (Chapel Hill: University of North Carolina Press, 2004).

21. Shaffer, *See America First*.

22. Burke Ormsby, "The Lady Who Lives by the Sea: The Story of Hotel del Coronado," *Journal of San Diego History* 12, no. 1 (January 1966), https://www.sandiegohistory.org/journal/66january/ladybysea.htm; and "Sea Island Company," *New Georgia Encyclopedia*, http://www.georgiaencyclopedia.org.

23. Shaffer, *See America First*, 94.

24. Jon C. Teaford, *The Rough Road to Renaissance: Urban Revitalization in America, 1940–1985* (Baltimore: Johns Hopkins University Press, 1990). For the global social science perspective, see works such as Colin Hall, *Tourism and Politics: Policy, Power, and Place* (New York: Wiley, 1994) and David Harvey, *The Condition of Postmodernity* (Oxford: Basil Blackwell, 1989).

25. On the remaking of American downtowns, see especially Alison Isenberg, *Downtown America: A History of the Place and the People Who Made It* (Chicago: University of Chicago Press, 2004), chap. 7.

26. For a broad look at the changing design, use, and meanings of landscapes, see J. B. Jackson, *The Necessity for Ruins, and Other Topics* (Amherst: University of Massachusetts Press, 1980). For case studies of the growing sophistication of mediating the tourist experience of place, see Jim Weeks, *Gettysburg: Memory, Market, and an American Shrine* (Princeton, NJ: Princeton University Press, 2003); and *Architourism: Authentic, Exotic, Escapist, Spectacular*, ed. Joan Ockman (Munich: Prestel, 2005).

27. Stanton, *The Lowell Experiment*; Chiang, *Shaping the Shoreline*, 138–52; and David Lowenthal, *The Past is a Foreign Country* (Cambridge: Cambridge University Press, 1985), 44.

28. Jane Jacobs, *The Death and Life of Great American Cities* (New York: Random House, 1961).

29. Leland Roth, *American Architecture: A History* (Boulder, CO: Westview, 2000), 353–55.

30. G. J. Ashworth and J. E. Turnbridge, *The Tourist-Historic City* (London: Belhaven, 1990), 26. See also David Hamer, *History in Urban Places: The Historic Districts of the United States* (Columbus: Ohio State University Press, 1998); J. Mark Souther, *New Orleans on Parade: Tourism and the Transformation of the Crescent City* (Baton Rouge: Louisiana State University Press, 2006), chaps. 2, 6–7; and Robert C. Davis and Garry R. Marvin, *Venice, the Tourist Maze: A Cultural Critique of the World's Most Touristed City* (Berkeley: University of California Press, 2004), 120–26.

31. Roth, *American Architecture*, 339–409. An excellent overview is Dolores Hayden, *Building Suburbia: Green Fields and Urban Growth, 1820–2000* (New York: Vintage, 2004).

32. On architectural theming in tourist-oriented communities, see Coleman, *Ski Style*, 145–66; and Hoelscher, *Heritage on Display*, 181–220. See also Robert Venturi, Steven Izenour, and Denise Scott Brown, *Learning from Las Vegas; The Forgotten Symbolism of Architectural Form* (Cambridge, MA: MIT Press, 1977); *Architecture and Tourism: Perception, Performance and Place*, ed. D. Medina Lasansky (Oxford: Berg, 2004); and Ockman, *Architourism*.

33. Richards, *Cultural Tourism in Europe*, 21.

34. See for example David Louter, *Windshield Wilderness: Cars, Roads, and Nature in Washington's National Parks* (Seattle: University of Washington Press, 2006); Margaret Lynn Brown, *The Wild East: A Biography of the Great Smoky Mountains* (Gainesville: University Press of Florida, 2001).

35. On planners' efforts to accommodate a presumed disinclination to walk long distances, see M. Jeffrey Hardwick, *Mall Maker: Victor Gruen, Architect of an American Dream* (Philadelphia: University of Pennsylvania Press, 2004), 133.

36. See, for instance, on the many dimensions of performance at tourist sites, Tim Edensor, "Staging Tourism: Tourists as Performers," *Annals of Tourism Research* 27, no. 2 (2000): 322–44; Richard Prentice and Vivien Anderson, "Festival as Creative Destination," *Annals of Tourism Research* 30, no. 1 (2003): 7–30; and David Jamison, "Tourism and Ethnicity: The Brotherhood of Coconuts," *Annals of Tourism Research* 26, no. 4 (1999): 944–67.

37. DeLyser, *Ramona Memories*, 173–76; and Carla Almeida Santos, "Framing Portugal: Representational Dynamics," *Annals of Tourism Research* 31, no. 1 (2004): 122–38. See also Andrew McGregor, "Dynamic Texts and Tourist Gaze," *Annals of Tourism Research* 27, no. 1 (2000): 27–50; Cees Gooseens, "Tourism Information and Pleasure Motivation," *Annals of Tourism Research* 27, no. 2 (2000): 301–21; Marion Markwick, "Postcards from Malta," *Annals of Tourism Research* 28, no. 2 (2001): 417–38; Hyounggon Kim and Sarah Richardson, "Motion Picture Impacts on Destination Impacts," *Annals of Tourism Research* 30, no. 1 (2003): 216–37; and Julie Andsager and Jolanta Drzewiecka, "Desirability of Differences in Destinations," *Annals of Tourism Research* 29, no. 2 (2002): 401–21.

38. Michael Kammen, *The Mystic Chords of Memory: The Transformation of Tradition in American Culture* (New York: Vintage, 1993), esp. part 4; David S. Glassberg, *Sense of History: The Place of the Past in American Life* (Amherst: University of Massachusetts Press, 2001), 59–86; and Ketchell, *Holy Hills of the Ozarks*.

39. Scholarly examinations of living history include Warren Leon and Margaret Piatt, "Living-History Museums," *History Museums in the United States: A Critical Assessment*, ed. Warren Leon and Roy Rosenzweig (Urbana: University of Illinois Press, 1989), chap. 3, esp. 64–97; Stephen Eddy Snow, *Performing the Pilgrims: A Study of Ethnohistorical Role-Playing at Plimoth Plantation* (Jackson: University Press of Mississippi, 1993); Richard Handler and Eric Gable, *The New History in an Old Museum: Creating the Past at Colonial Williamsburg*

(Durham, NC: Duke University Press, 1997); Scott Magelssen, *Living History Museums: Undoing History through Performance* (Lanham, MD: Scarecrow Press, 2007); and *Historical Reenactment: From Realism to the Affective Turn*, ed. Iain McCalman and Paul A. Pickering (Houndsmill, UK: Palgrave Macmillan, 2010).

40. On staging ethnicity at world's expositions, see Robert W. Rydell, *All the World's a Fair: Visions of Empire at American International Expositions, 1876–1916* (Chicago: University of Chicago Press, 1987). On settlement workers' fascination with ethnic customs, see especially Mina Carson, *Settlement Folk: Social Thought and the American Settlement Movement, 1885–1930* (Chicago: University of Chicago Press, 1990), 103–6. On ethnic themes in civic celebrations, see especially Susan G. Davis, *Parades and Power: Street Theatre in Nineteenth-Century Philadelphia* (Berkeley: University of California Press, 1988). Many scholars have examined the staging of ethnicity at tourist destinations. See for example Leah Dilworth, *Imagining Indians in the Southwest: Persistent Visions of a Primitive Past* (Washington, DC: Smithsonian Institution Press, 1997); Sarah H. Hill, *Weaving New Worlds: Southeastern Cherokee Women and Their Basketry* (Chapel Hill: University of North Carolina Press, 1997); Patsy West, *The Enduring Seminoles: From Alligator Wrestling to Ecotourism* (Gainesville: University Press of Florida, 1998); *Unpacking Culture: Art and Commodity in Colonial and Postcolonial Worlds*, ed. Ruth B. Phillips and Christopher B. Steiner (Berkeley: University of California Press, 1999); and *Selling the Indian: Commercializing and Appropriating American Indian Cultures*, ed. Carter Jones Meyer and Diana Royer (Tucson: University of Arizona Press, 2001).

41. On highways, see John A. Jakle and Keith A. Sculle, *Motoring: The Highway Experience in America* (Athens: University of Georgia Press, 2008), 105–26; Anne Mitchell Whisnant, *Super-Scenic Motorway: A Blue Ridge Parkway History* (Chapel Hill: University of North Carolina Press, 2006). On airports, see Douglas G. Karsner, "Leaving on a Jet Plane: Commercial Aviation, Airports, and Post-Industrial American Society, 1933–1970" (PhD diss., Temple University, 1993). On the development and impact of lodging, see especially Andrew K. Sandoval-Strausz, *Hotel: An American History* (New Haven, CT: Yale University Press, 2007); Warren Belasco, *Americans on the Road: From Autocamp to Motel, 1910–1945* (Cambridge, MA: MIT Press, 1979); and John A. Jakle, Keith A. Sculle, and Jefferson S. Rogers, *The Motel in America* (Baltimore: Johns Hopkins University Press, 1996). On other rail and roadside services, see Stephen Fried, *Appetite for America: How Visionary Businessman Fred Harvey Built a Railroad Hospitality Empire that Civilized the Wild West* (New York: Bantam Books, 2010); John A. Jakle and Keith A. Sculle, *The Gas Station in America* (Baltimore: Johns Hopkins University Press, 1994); and Andrew Hurley, *Diners, Bowling Alleys, and Trailer Parks: Chasing the American Dream in Postwar Consumer Culture* (New York: Basic Books, 2001). On entertainment venues, see John Hannigan, *Fantasy City: Pleasure and Profit in the Postmodern Metropolis* (London: Routledge, 1998).

42. Bryant Simon, *Boardwalk of Dreams: Atlantic City and the Fate of Urban America* (New York: Oxford University Press, 2004); and Hal Rothman, *Neon Metropolis: How Las Vegas Started the Twenty-First Century* (London: Routledge, 2003).

43. Perhaps the best account of the delicate coexistence of locals and tourists in a city is Barber, *Reno's Big Gamble*.

44. David Nasaw, *Going Out: The Rise and Fall of Public Amusements* (New York: Basic Books, 1993), 254–55.

45. On tourism growth and effects, see Fred P. Bossleman, Craig A. Peterson, and Claire McCarthy, *Managing Tourism Growth: Issue and Applications* (Washington, DC: Island Press,

1999); Hoffman, Fainstein, and Judd, *Cities and Visitors*; David J. Snepenger, Leann Murphy, Ryan O'Connell, and Eric Gregg, "Tourists and Residents Use of a Shopping Space," *Annals of Tourism Research* 30, no. 3 (2003): 567–80, provides a concise overview of the literature and role of shopping in tourism zones. See also Rothman, *Devil's Bargains*; Frank Taylor, *To Hell with Paradise: A History of the Jamaican Tourist Industry* (Pittsburgh: University of Pittsburgh Press, 1993); Merrill, *Negotiating Paradise*, 79–86, 122, 135–36; R. Keith Schwer, "Air Tour Impacts: The Grand Canyon Case," *Annals of Tourism Research* 27, no. 3 (2000): 611–23; Paul Brunt and Paul Courtney, "Host Perceptions of Sociocultural Impacts," *Annals of Tourism Research* 26. no. 3 (1999); 493–515; and Natan Uriely and Arie Reichel, "Working Tourists and Their Attitudes to Hosts," *Annals of Tourism Research* 27, no. 2 (2000): 267–83.

46. Chiang, *Shaping the Shoreline*; Ginger Strand, *Inventing Niagara* (New York: Simon and Schuster, 2008); Margaret Lynn Brown, *The Wild East: A Biography of the Great Smoky Mountains* (Gainesville: University Press of Florida, 2000); and Stanford E. Demars, *The Tourist in Yosemite, 1855–1985* (Salt Lake City: University of Utah Press, 1991). Holden, *Tourism and the Social Sciences*, provides a good overview of environmental impact of tourism from a global perspective.

47. On the history of Elderhostel, see Eugene S. Mills, *The Story of Elderhostel* (Hanover, NH: University Press of New England, 1993).

48. Roth documents the influence of exotic tourist styles in *American Architecture*, 346–50.

49. On Coney Island's influence, see especially Gary S. Cross and John K. Walton, *The Playful Crowd: Pleasure Places in the Twentieth Century* (New York: Columbia University Press, 2005), chap. 5. On the Disney influence on Times Square's revitalization, see Alexander J. Reichl, *Reconstructing Times Square: Politics and Culture in Urban Redevelopment* (Lawrence: University Press of Kansas, 1999), 174–79; and Lynne B. Sagalyn, *Times Square Roulette: Remaking the City Icon* (Cambridge, MA: MIT Press, 2003), 344–45.

Adirondacks

1. "Brant Lake Camp," ca. 1965, n.p., Adirondack Museum Library, Blue Mountain Lake, NY. The brochure discusses the reasons the first boys visited the camp when it was founded in 1917.

2. Joel Tyler Headley, *The Adirondack: or, Life in the Woods*, introduction by Philip G. Terrie (1849; reprint, Harrison, NY: Harbor Hills Books, 1982), 167.

3. William H. H. Murray, *Adventures in the Wilderness*, ed. William K. Verner, introduction and notes by Warder H. Cadbury (1869; reprint, [Syracuse, NY]: Adirondack Museum, 1970), 19.

4. Thomas G. King, "Adirondack Guides," *Recreation* 17 (September 1902): 183.

5. Alfred L. Donaldson, *A History of the Adirondacks*, 2 vols. (New York: The Century Co., 1921), 2:92.

Gilborn, Craig A. *Adirondack Furniture and the Rustic Tradition*. New York: Abrams, 1987.
Jacoby, Karl. *Crimes against Nature: Squatters, Poachers, Thieves, and the Hidden History of American Conservation*. Berkeley: University of California Press, 2001.
Kaiser, Harvey H. *Great Camps of the Adirondacks*. Jaffrey, NH: David R. Godine, Publisher, Inc., 1982.

Schneider, Paul. *The Adirondacks: A History of America's First Wilderness.* New York: Henry Holt and Company, 1997.

Terrie, Philip G. *Contested Terrain: A New History of Nature and People in the Adirondacks.* Blue Mountain Lake, NY: Adirondack Museum; Syracuse: Syracuse University Press, 1997.

Tolles, Bryant Franklin. *Resort Hotels of the Adirondacks: The Architecture of a Summer Paradise, 1850–1950.* Hanover, NH: University Press of New England, 2003.

Aspen

1.   This essay distills and updates my dissertation "Living It Up in Aspen: Postwar America, Ski Town Culture, and the New Western Dream, 1945–1975" (PhD diss., University of Colorado at Boulder, 2006), currently under revision as a book manuscript.

Allen, James Sloan. The Romance of Commerce and Culture: Capitalism, Modernism, and the Chicago-Aspen Crusade for Cultural Reform (1983; reprint, Boulder: University Press of Colorado, 2002).

Clifford, Peggy. *To Aspen and Back: An American Journey* (New York: St. Martin's Press, 1980).

———. "The 'Aspenization' of the Rest of America,'" *Rocky Mountain News,* March 12, 1978, 1.

Coleman, Annie Gilbert. "'A hell of a time all the time': Farmers, Ranchers, and the Roaring Fork Valley during 'the Quiet Years,'" *Montana: Magazine of Western History,* Spring 1997, 32–45.

———. *Ski Style: Sport and Culture in the Rockies* (Lawrence: University Press of Kansas, 2004).

Conover, Ted. *Whiteout: Lost in Aspen* (New York: Random House, 1991).

Ott, Christopher. "Legacy of the Ski Troops," *Denver Business Journal,* April 24, 1998, http://www.bizjournals.com/denver/stories/1998/04/27/story3.html.

Rohrbough, Malcolm J. *Aspen: The History of a Silver-Mining Town, 1879–1893* (New York: Oxford University Press, 1986).

Rothman, Hal K. *Devil's Bargains: Tourism in the Twentieth-Century American West* (Lawrence: University Press of Kansas, 1998).

Wrobel, David M., and Patrick T. Long, eds., *Seeing and Being Seen: Tourism in the American West* (Lawrence: University Press of Kansas, 2001).

Atlantic City

1.   Charles E. Funnell, *By the Beautiful Sea: The Rise and High Times of That Great American Resort, Atlantic City* (New York: Knopf, 1975), inside cover.

2.   Vicki Gold Levi, *Atlantic City: 125 Years of Ocean Madness* (Berkeley: Ten Speed Press, 1992), 8.

3.   Ibid., 17–25; Mark Tyrrell, "The Boardwalk," *Atlantic City Magazine,* June 1992, 94–95; Frank Ward O'Malley, "The Board-Walkers," *Everybody's Magazine,* August 1908, 233–43; Sam Baol, "Eighty Years of 'The Eighth Wonder,'" *New York Times Magazine,* June

25, 1960, 16; and G. Patrick Pawling, "Boardwalk: The People's Park Place," American Legion Magazine, August 1998, 27–28.

    4.   "Bridge to the Old World," Time (June 7, 1961), 53–54.

    5.   Bill Kent, Down by the Sea (New York: St. Martin's, 1993), 130.

    6.   Robert Kotlowitz, The Boardwalk (New York: Knopf, 1977), 185, 186. On the "bewitching" quality, see Vicki Gold Levi, "Rolling Chairs: The Sex Symbol of 1905," Philadelphia Bulletin, January 10, 1981.

    7.   Bruce Boyle, "Of the Inlet Irish: It Was Summertime and the Card Fell Right," and "Technology, Racism, and Rolling Chairs May Revive Us Yet," Philadelphia Bulletin, December 22, 1980, and September 23, 1981.

    8.   For more on the campaigns see George Sternlieb and James W. Hughes, The Atlantic City Gamble (Cambridge, MA: Harvard University, 1983); John Dombrink and William N. Thompson, The Last Resort: Success and Failure in Campaigns for Casinos (Reno and Las Vegas: University of Nevada Press, 1990), chap. 2; and Geoffrey Douglas, "The Selling of Casino Gambling," New Jersey Monthly, January 1977, 21–24.

    9.   For statistics and assessments of gambling in Atlantic City, see Bob Drogin, "For Atlantic City, Casino Jackpot's Still a Long Shot," Los Angeles Times, August 7, 1989; and Mary Jo Patterson, Robin Gaby Fisher, and Christine Baird, "Atlantic City Shell Game," Newark Star-Ledger, May 4, 1997. On the demise of local restaurants, see Victoria Foote, "Casinos' Success is Bad Luck for Other A.C. Spots," Restaurant Exchange News 6 (November 1984), miscellaneous files, Greater Atlantic City Chamber of Commerce; and Robert Goodman, The Luck Business: The Devastating Consequences and Broken Promises of America's Gambling Explosion (New York: The Free Press, 1995), 21–23.

    10.   The polls were reported as part of Bill Moyers Reports, "Big Gamble in Atlantic City," CBS Television, July 28, 1986.

    11.   Paul E. Wiseman, "Money Talks; AC Talks Back," Courier Post, July 26, 1988; and William Manchester, Hype and Glory (New York: Villard Books, 1990), 225–26.

Rothman, Hal. Neon Metropolis: How Las Vegas Started the Twenty-First Century. New York and London: Routledge, 2002.

Simon, Bryant. Boardwalk of Dreams: Atlantic City and the Fate of Urban America. New York: Oxford University Press, 2004.

Sugrue, Thomas. Sweet Land of Liberty: The Forgotten Struggle for Civil Rights in the North. New York: Random House, 2008.

Beale Street

    1.   This essay is partly a distillation of the section on Beale Street first published in Eugene J. Johnson and Robert Russell, Memphis an Architectural Guide (Knoxville: University of Tennessee Press, 1990), 133–47. More recent information on the slow but steady reintegration of the street into downtown Memphis has been gleaned from reports in the Memphis Commercial Appeal and the Memphis Business Journal.

    2.   The tourist-oriented parts of Beale Street run from Main Street on the west to Danny Thomas Boulevard to the east: five blocks. The vast majority of its music venues are concentrated in the three blocks from Second to Fourth streets.

    3.   Margaret McKee and Fred Chisenhall, Beale Black and Blue: Life and Music on Black America's Main Street (Baton Rouge: Louisiana State University Press, 1981), 17.

4. Ibid., 67.

5. The master plan ran to eight hundred pages and was rarely, if ever, read by anyone. The report was accompanied by a short brochure that illustrated all the street's monuments that were *not* associated with black Memphis (Johnson and Russell, *Memphis an Architectural Guide*, 133–34).

6. Ibid., 134.

7. Memphis *Commercial Appeal*, December, 9, 2007.

8. "As a tourist attraction, we need to make the area safe and clean . . . and we are not getting what we paid for" (Charlie Ryan, owner, Club 152 and Blues City Café, quoted in the *Memphis Flyer*, http://www.memphisflyer.com/TheDailyBuzz/archives/2007/11/06/memphis-city-council-to-hear-beale-street-developmentperforma-conflict-tuesday.

Bond, Beverly G. *Beale Street*. Charleston, SC: Arcadia Publishing, 2006.

Raichelson, Richard M. *Beale Street Talks: A Walking Tour down the Home of the Blues*. 2nd ed. Memphis: Arcadia Records, 1999.

CAMINO REAL

1. This essay summarizes and updates portions of my book, *California Vieja: Culture and Memory in a Modern American Place* (Berkeley: University of California Press, 2006) and draws upon the following sources.

DeLyser, Dydia. *Ramona Memories: Tourism and the Shaping of Southern California*. Minneapolis: University of Minnesota Press, 2005.

Deverell, William. *Whitewashed Adobe: The Rise of Los Angeles and the Remaking of Its Mexican Past*. Berkeley: University of California Press, 2004.

Haas, Lisabeth. *Conquests and Historical Identities in California, 1769–1936*. Berkeley: University of California Press, 1995.

Kropp, Phoebe S. *California Vieja: Culture and Memory in a Modern American Place*. Berkeley: University of California Press, 2006.

Kurillo, Max and Erline S. Tuttle. *California's El Camino Real and Its Historic Bells*. San Diego: Sunbelt Publications, 2000.

Sagarena, Roberto Lint. *Arcadia and Aztlán: Religion, Ethnicity, and the Creation of History*. New York: NYU Press, 2010.

Smith, Sherry. *Reimagining Indians: Native Americans through Anglo Eyes, 1880–1940*. New York: Oxford University Press, 2000.

Starr, Kevin. *Inventing the Dream: California through the Progressive Era*. New York: Oxford University Press, 1985.

Thompson, Mark. *American Character: The Curious Life of Charles Fletcher Lummis and the Rediscovery of the Southwest*. New York: Arcade Publishing, 2001.

CHAUTAUQUA

1. This essay draws upon my book, *The Chautauqua Moment: Protestants, Progressives, and the Culture of Modern Liberalism* (New York: Columbia University Press, 2003).

2. "Prospectus of the Colorado Lake Chautauqua Association," 1893, 1–2, Center for

American History, University of Texas at Austin, Austin, Texas.

    3.   Henry J. Fletcher, "The Doom of the Small Town," *The Forum* 19 (March-August 1895): 214–23, esp. 219.

Simpson, Jeffrey. *Chautauqua: An American Utopia.* New York: Harry N. Abrams, Inc., 1999.

Chinatown

    1.   Vincent McHugh, "San Francisco: Little China," *Holiday* 29 (April 1961): 100–103, 210–18, esp. 100.

Chang, Iris. *The Chinese in America: A Narrative History.* New York: Viking, 2003.

Chen, Yong. *Chinese San Francisco, 1850–1943: A Trans-Pacific Community.* Stanford, CA: Stanford University Press, 2000.

Chun, Gloria Heyung. *Of Orphans and Warriors: Inventing Chinese American Culture and Identity.* New Brunswick, NJ: Rutgers University Press, 2000.

Lee, Anthony W. *Picturing Chinatown: Art and Orientalism in San Francisco.* Berkeley: University of California Press, 2001.

Rast, Raymond W. "The Cultural Politics of Tourism in San Francisco's Chinatown, 1882–1917." *Pacific Historical Review* 76 (February 2007): 29–60.

Yip, Christopher. "San Francisco's Chinatown: An Architectural and Urban History." PhD diss., University of California, Berkeley, 1985.

Colonial Williamsburg

    1.   This essay draws from my book, *Creating Colonial Williamsburg: The Restoration of Virginia's Eighteenth-Century Capital,* 2nd ed. (Chapel Hill: University of North Carolina Press, 2009).

Handler, Richard, and Eric Gable. *The New History in an Old Museum: Creating the Past at Colonial Williamsburg.* Durham, NC: Duke University Press, 1997.

Huxtable, Ada Louise. *Unreal America: Architecture and Illusion.* New York: New Press, 1997.

Kopper, Philip. *Colonial Williamsburg.* New York: Harry N. Abrams, 1986.

Cooperstown

    1.   *2006–2007 Visitors' Guide Cooperstown and Vicinity* (Cooperstown, NY: Cooperstown Chamber of Commerce, 2006), 3.

    2.   Alan Taylor, *William Cooper's Town: Power and Persuasion on the Frontier in the Early American Republic* (New York: Vintage, 1996).

    3.   Richard H. Gassan, *The Birth of American Tourism: New York, the Hudson Valley, and American Culture, 1790–1830* (Amherst: University of Massachusetts Press, 2008), 80–83, 106–9.

4. Heidi L. Hill, "The Attractions of Cooperstown and Otsego Lake, 1870–1900" (master's thesis, State University of New York College at Oneonta, 1993), 2.

5. James Fenimore Cooper, *The Chronicles of Cooperstown* (Cooperstown, NY: H. & E. Phinney, 1838), quoted in Louis C. Jones, *Cooperstown* (Cooperstown, NY: New York State Historical Association, 2002), 33.

6. Marguerite Shaffer, *See America First: Tourism and National Identity, 1880–1940* (Washington, DC: Smithsonian Institution Press, 2001), 15.

7. Hill, "Attractions of Cooperstown and Otsego Lake," 3–5.

8. Jones, *Cooperstown*, 47–48.

9. Shaffer, *See America First*, 132–33.

10. Jones, *Cooperstown*, 48–52; Walter R. Littell, *A Visit to Cooperstown* (Cooperstown, NY: Otsego County Historical Society, 1946), 15–18.

11. Observations from author's personal visits to the National Baseball Hall of Fame and Museum, 2008–2010; and National Baseball Hall of Fame and Museum, "Hall of Famers," http://baseballhall.org/hall-famers.

12. Jones, *Cooperstown*, 90–100; and Littell, *A Visit to Cooperstown*, 23–24.

13. Cooperstown Dreams Park, "Cooperstown Dreams Park," http://www.cooperstowndreamspark.com.

14. Observations about changes in Cooperstown in recent decades come from the author's conversations with local residents as well as oral histories conducted by students at the Cooperstown Graduate Program, which are archived at the New York State Historical Association Library, Cooperstown, NY.

Disneyland

1. Gladwin Hill, "Disneyland Reports on Its First Ten Million," *New York Times*, February 2, 1958.

2. Richard Schickel, *The Disney Version: The Life, Times, Art, and Commerce of Walt Disney* (New York: Simon and Schuster, 1968), 310.

3. Neil Harris, "Expository Expositions: Preparing for the Theme Parks," in *Designing Disney's Theme Parks*, ed. Karal Ann Marling (Montreal: Canadian Centre for Architecture, 1997), 19–27; and John M. Findlay, *Magic Lands: Western Cityscapes and American Culture after 1940* (Berkeley: University of California Press, 1992), 66.

4. Karal Ann Marling, "Imagineering the Disney Theme Parks," in Marling, *Designing Disney's Theme Parks*, 38–43.

5. For Disney's testimony, see "The Testimony of Walter E. Disney before the House Committee on Unamerican Activities," October 24, 1947, http://filmtv.eserver.org/disney-huac-testimony.txt.

6. For the dichotomies of order and chaos that shaped Disneyland, see Erika Doss, "Making Imagination Safe in the 1950s: Disneyland's Fantasy Art and Architecture," in Marling, *Designing Disney's Theme Parks*, 180. Regarding Disney's Missouri years, see Schickel, *Disney Version*, 48–49.

7. Schickel, *Disney Version*, 311.

8. On Colonial Williamsburg, see James Marston Fitch, *Historic Preservation: Curatorial Management of the Built World* (Charlottesville: University of Virginia Press, 1990), 89–104; Ada Louise Huxtable, *The Unreal America: Architecture and Illusion* (New York: New Press, 1997), 14–15.

9. Julie V. Iovine, "A Tale of Two Main Streets: The Towns That Inspired Disney Are Searching for a Little Magic of Their Own," *New York Times*, October 15, 1998.

10. Alan Bryman, *Disney and His Worlds* (London: Routledge, 1995), 99–126.

11. "The Monsanto House of the Future," Bay State Film Productions, Inc., accessible via YouTube at http://www.treehugger.com/files/2007/06/it_was_fifty_ye.php.

12. See Richard V. Francaviglia, "Main Street U.S.A.: A Comparison/Contrast of Streetscapes in Disneyland and Walt Disney World," *Journal of Popular Culture* 15 (Summer 1981): 141–56, esp. 146; George Ritzer and Allan Liska, "'McDisneyization' and 'Post-Tourism': Complementary Perspectives on Contemporary Tourism," in *Touring Cultures: Transformations of Travel and Theory*, ed. Chris Rojek and John Urry (London: Routledge, 1997): 96–109; and Michael Sorkin, "See You in Disneyland," in *Variations on a Theme Park: The New American City and the End of Public Space*, ed. Michael Sorkin (New York: Noonday Press, 1992): 216–28.

13. Charles W. Moore. "You Have to Pay for the Public Life," *Perspecta* 9 (1965): 9, 36.

14. Diane Ghirardo, *Architecture after Modernism* (London: Thames and Hudson, 1996), 46.

15. Eric Avila, *Popular Culture in the Age of White Flight: Fear and Fantasy in Suburban Los Angeles* (Berkeley: University of California Press, 2004), 135.

16. Attendance figures from the Themed Entertainment Association/Economic Research Associates' Attraction (TEA/ERA) Attendance Report http://www.connectingindustry.com/downloads/pwteaerasupp.pdf (May 2008). In 2008, Disneyland remained the world's second-most visited theme park, but the overall numbers dropped by nearly 150,000 during an economic recession. For the 2008 TEA/ERA figures, see http://www.themeit.com/TEAERA2008.pdf.

17. David Rakoff, "The Future Knocks Again," *New York Times*, July 10, 2008.

Faneuil Hall Marketplace

1. This essay is a shortened and updated version of a section of chapter 6 of my book, *Merchant of Illusion: James Rouse, America's Salesman of the Businessman's Utopia* (Columbus: Ohio State University Press, 2004).

2. Kevin White, "Faneuil Hall and Quincy Marketplace," in a People for the American Way publication, October 14, 1993, Rouse Papers, Columbia Archives; and Margo Miller, "The Day the Marketplace Opened," *Boston Globe*, August 27, 1976, 1.

3. [Dennis Dewitt], BTA Architects, "Benjamin Thompson, FAIA (1918–2002)," http://www.bta-architects.com/c/BenjaminThompsonFAIA.html.

4. Benjamin Thompson to John Harkness, Board of Directors of Boston Society of Architects, January 9, 1973, Series 1.5, Box 435, folder: FHM; and James Rouse, Speech to the International Council of Shopping Centers, May 3, 1960, 4, both in Rouse Papers, Columbia Archives.

5. Thompson to Harkness, January 9, 1973.

6. Benjamin Thompson and Jane Thompson, "Restoration of Faneuil Hall Marketplace," ca. 1976, Series 1.5, Box 435, folder: FHM, Rouse Papers, Columbia Archives.

7. "Faneuil Hall Marketplace," Rouse Company Internal Document, July 10, 1973, Series 1.5, Box 435, Folder: FHM, Rouse Papers, Columbia Archives.

8. Luix Overbea, "BRA Decision Awaited on Market Project," *Christian Science Monitor*, March 21, 1973.

9. Anthony Yuddis, "Boston Market Plans Show Marked Differences," *Boston Globe*, January 7, 1973, A-49.

10. Webb Plan, Rouse Papers, [ca. 1973], Series 1.5, Box 435, Folder: FHM, Rouse Papers, Columbia Archives; Anthony Yuddis, "Not JUST an Opening," *Boston Globe*, August 22, 1976, 4; and James Rouse, "Are We Losing Our Downtowns by Default?" speech to the Main Street Revitalization Conference, ca. 1977, Rouse Papers Columbia Archives.

11. Roy Williams, Faneuil Hall Marketplace, memorandum, July 10, 1973, Series 1.5, Box 435, Folder: FHM, Rouse Papers, Columbia Archives.

12. James Rouse, "Fanueil Hall Marketplace: Its Special Meaning and Potential for the Rouse Company," memorandum, September 1976, Series 1.5, Box 435, folder FHM, 1976–77, Rouse Papers, Columbia Archives.

13. Intra-Office Memorandum, Rouse Company, August 31, 1973. Series 1.5, Box 435, folder: FHM; "Minutes Design Review," Rouse Company, October 31 1973; and Joseph Tierney, Boston City Council, letter sent by Thompson to Rouse, March 12, 1973, all in Rouse Papers, Columbia Archives.

14. Jane Davison, "Bringing Life to Market," *New York Times Magazine*, October 10, 1976; and Robert Campbell, "Evaluation: Boston's Upper of Urbanity," *AIA Journal*, June 1981, 29.

15. Campbell, "Evaluation: Boston's Upper of Urbanity," 28–29.

16. Rouse, "Faneuil Hall Marketplace: Its Special Meaning and Potential for the Rouse Company."

17. Rouse, "Are We Losing Our Downtowns By Default?"

18. Bernard J. Freiden and Lynne B. Sagalyn, *Downtown, Inc.: How America Rebuilds Cities* (Cambridge, MA: MIT Press, 1991), 175.

19. Frieden and Sagalyn, *Downtown, Inc.*, 175Ibid.; and Benjamin Thompson and Jane Thompson to the Rouse Company, "Guiding the Future of Faneuil Hall Marketplace," December 5, 1978, Series 1.5, Box 435, Folder: FHM, Rouse Papers, Columbia Archives.

20. Carol Todreas to James Rouse, 5 October 5, 1978, Series 1.5, Box 435, folder: FHM—Critiques 1978, Rouse Papers, Columbia Archives.

21. James Rouse to Michael Spear, October 4, 1978, 2, Series 1.5, Box 435, folder: FHM, Columbia University Archives

22. Peter Del Busto, "The Marginalization of Intent: The Transformation of Management in the Rouse Company's Faneuil Hall Marketplace, 1976–1986," Harvard University, http://www.hks.harvard.edu/rappaport/downloads/building_boston/delbusto_downtown.pdf.

23. James Rouse to K. A Gorman, October 17, 1984. Series 4, Box 32, folder: Mail by Month, October 1984, Rouse Papers, Columbia Archives.

Isenberg, Alison. *Downtown America: A History of the Place and the People Who* Made *It* (Chicago: University of Chicago Press, 2005).

Olsen, Joshua. *Better Places, Better Lives: A Biography of James Rouse* (Washington, DC: Urban Land Institute, 2004).

Tangires, Helen. *Public Markets and Civic Culture in Nineteenth-Century America* (Baltimore: Johns Hopkins, University Press 2003).

French Quarter

1.   This essay summarizes and updates portions of my book, *New Orleans on Parade: Tourism and the Transformation of the Crescent City* (Baton Rouge: Louisiana State University Press, 2006).

2.   Charles Dudley Warner, "New Orleans," *Harper's New Monthly Magazine*, January 1887, vertical file "French Quarter," Department of Special Collections, Tulane University, New Orleans, LA.

3.   "Brennan's, A New Orleans Tradition since 1946," http://www.brennansneworleans.com/history.html.

4.   Preservation Hall handbill [1961], vertical file "Bars, Buildings, Etc., Local: Preservation Hall, 1961–1962," Hogan Jazz Archive, Tulane University, New Orleans, LA.

5.   On New Orleans after Hurricane Katrina, see especially, "Through the Eye of Katrina: The Past as Prologue?" *Journal of American History* 94 (December 2007): 693–876; and "In the Wake of Hurricane Katrina: New Paradigms and Social Visions," ed. Clyde Woods, special issue of *American Quarterly* 61, no. 3 (September 2009).

Ellis, Scott S. *Madame Vieux Carré: The French Quarter in the Twentieth Century*. Jackson: University Press of Mississippi, 2009.

Gotham, Kevin Fox. *Authentic New Orleans: Tourism, Culture, and Race in the Big Easy*. New York: New York University Press, 2007.

Long, Alecia. *The Great Southern Babylon: Sex, Race, and Respectability in New Orleans, 1865–1920*. Baton Rouge: Louisiana State University Press, 2004.

Souther, J. Mark. *New Orleans on Parade: Tourism and the Transformation of the Crescent City*. Baton Rouge: Louisiana State University Press, 2006.

Stanonis, Anthony J. *Creating the Big Easy: New Orleans and the Emergence of Modern Tourism, 1918–1945*. Athens: University of Georgia Press, 2006.

Gateway Arch

1.   Civic Improvement League of St. Louis, *A City Plan for St. Louis* (St. Louis, 1907), 59–61.

2.   City Plan Commission of St. Louis, *St. Louis Riverfront*, (St. Louis, 1915); City Plan Commission of St. Louis, *A Plan for the Central Riverfront, Saint Louis, Missouri* (St. Louis, 1928); "River Front Memorial," *St. Louis Globe Democrat*, December 29, 1933; and W. C. Bernard, *A Comprehensive Program for Reclamation of the St. Louis Riverfront to be Effected by the Construction and Operation of a Riverview Freeway* (St. Louis, 1934).

3.   "U.S. to Maintain Memorial, Says Luther Ely Smith," *St. Louis Globe-Democrat*, October 29, 1949. Jefferson National-Expansion Memorial Association, solicitation letter, February 28, 1946, Luther Ely Smith collection, Missouri Historical Society, St. Louis, Missouri.

4.   Comments of Luther Ely Smith, "Meeting of United States Territorial Expansion Memorial Commission," transcript, December 13, 1934, St. Louis, Missouri, 41, Record Unit 104, Box 36, Folder 4, Jefferson National Expansion Memorial Archives, St. Louis, Missouri.

5.   James Neal Primm, *Lion of the Valley: St. Louis, Missouri* (Boulder, CO: Pruett Publishing, 1990), 484.

6. Levee Redevelopment Corporation, "The Laclede's Landing Plan," information packet, 1970, Missouri Historical Society Library Collection, St. Louis, Missouri, 8–10; and Fruco and Associates, *Central Riverfront Study* (St. Louis, 1966).

7. Executive Board, Challenge of the Seventies Plan, *Challenge of the Seventies* (St. Louis: Challenge of the Seventies Plan, 1971), 1–1.

8. A. J. Cervantes, *Mr. Mayor* (Los Angeles: Nash Publishing, 1974), 121–38.

9. Missouri Economic Research and Information Center, Missouri Department of Economic Development, "Missouri Tourism," 2003, 1–9, http://www.missourieconomy. org/pdfs/tourismbrief2003.pdf.

10. Dennis R. Judd, "Constructing the Tourist Bubble," in *The Tourist City*, ed. Dennis R. Judd and Susan S. Fainstein (New Haven, CT: Yale University Press, 1999), 35–53.

11. David Laslo, Claude Louishomme, Donald Phares, Dennis R. Judd, "Building the Infrastructure of Urban Tourism: The Case of St. Louis," *The Infrastructure of Play: Building the Tourist City*, ed. Dennis R. Judd (Armonk, NY: M. E. Sharpe, 2003), 84–85.

Brown, Sharon Alice. "Making a Memorial: Developing the Jefferson National Expansion Memorial National Historic Site, 1933–1980" (PhD diss., St. Louis University, 1983).
Hammerstrom, Kirsten. "The St. Louis Scene: History, Place, and the St. Louis Arch." *Gateway Heritage* 19 (Fall 1998): 20–27.
Kathriner, Danny. "The Rise and Fall of Gaslight Square." *Gateway Heritage* 22 (Fall 2001): 32–43.
Merhoff, Arthur W. "The New Frontier: A Case in Cultural Tourism." *Canadian Review of American Studies* 22 (Fall 1991): 251–52.

Gatlinburg and Pigeon Forge

1. Mary Ruth Chiles, comp., Resorts in the Smoky Mountains Region, 1832 to 1930, typescript files, National Park Service Archives, Sugarlands.

2. W. R. Woolrich et al., Agricultural-Industrial Report-Sevier County, Tennessee, 1934, typescript volume, 89–90, Tennessee Valley Authority Archives, Knoxville (TVA Archives); and Ed Trout, *Gatlinburg: Cinderella City* (Sevierville, TN: Griffin Graphics, 1984), 81–107.

3. "Notes on the History of the Settlement School," November 25, 1953, Special Collections, Arrowmont School, Gatlinburg; and Philis Alvic, *Weavers of the Southern Highlands: The Early Years in Gatlinburg* (Lexington: University Press of Kentucky, 2003), 56–63.

4. Vic Weals, *Last Train to Elkmont: A Look Back at Life on Little River in the Great Smoky Mountains* (Knoxville: Olden Press, 1993), 95–96; and Chiles, comp., Resorts in the Smoky Mountain Region, 1832–1930.

5. See Daniel S. Pierce, *The Great Smokies: From Natural Habitat to National Park* (Knoxville; University Tennessee Press, 2000); and Carlos Campbell, *Birth of a National Park in the Great Smoky Mountains* (Knoxville: University of Tennessee Press, 1960).

6. Woolrich et al., Agricultural-Industrial Report—Sevier County, 1934, 87–90.

7. "Dominant Native Families"; Russell Shaw, *The Gatlinburg Story* (Gatlinburg: Russell Shaw Inc., 1979), 25–26; and Ernie Pyle, "Roving Reporter," *Knoxville New-Sentinel*, October 31, 1940.

8. "Fortress from Change," *Knoxville News-Sentinel*, June 21, 1965; Flo Gullickson,

"Resorts Must Keep Pace, Says Whaley," *Knoxville News-Sentinel,* January 26, 1975; and Jerome Eric Dobson, "The Changing Control of Economic Activity in the Gatlinburg, Tennessee Area, 1930–1975" (PhD diss., University of Tennessee, Knoxville, 1975), 77–85.

    9.   Dobson, "Changing Control of Economic Activity," 80–93; and Venable, "Something's New on the Mountain," *Knoxville News-Sentinel,* February 2, 1978.

    10.   "New Highway Opens Opportunities," *Pigeon Forge Anvil,* September 17, 1968.

    11.   Julia Householder, interview by C. Brenden Martin, Pigeon Forge, TN, November 6, 1992, tape recording in author's possession.

    12.   Pat Arnow, "Tourist Central: Scourge or Salvation?" *Now and Then* 8, (Spring 1991), 6; Lisa Gubernick, "A Curb on the Ego," *Forbes,* September 14, 1992, 418–19; "Family Emphasis Planned, Says New Goldrush Owners," *Knoxville Journal,* April 8, 1976; and "Goldrush Junction Creating Old-Time Atmosphere," *Knoxville Journal,* May 13, 1971.

    13.   Pigeon Forge Department of Tourism, *Statistics for Prospective New Businesses* (Pigeon Forge: Department of Tourism, 1991), 11, 37, 42; and Arnow, "Tourist Central," 8.

Martin, C. Brenden. *Tourism in the Mountain South: A Double-Edged Sword.* Knoxville: University of Tennessee Press, 2007.

Grand Canyon

    1.   Clarence E. Dutton, *Tertiary History of the Grand Cañon District,* U.S. Geological Survey Monograph 2 (Washington, DC: Government Printing Office, 1882), 141–43.

    2.   Marc Reisner, *Cadillac Desert: The American West and Its Disappearing Water* (New York: Viking Penguin Inc., 1986), 285.

Beus, Stanley S., and Michael Morales, eds. *Grand Canyon Geology.* New York: Oxford University Press, 2002.

Fletcher, Colin. *The Man Who Walked through Time.* New York: Vintage Books, 1989.

Pyne, Stephen J. *How the Canyon Became Grand: A Short History.* New York: Penguin, 1999.

Sellares, Richard West. *Preserving Nature in the National Parks: A History.* New Haven, CT: Yale University Press, 1997.

Stegner, Wallace. *Beyond the Hundredth Meridian: John Wesley Powell and the Second Opening of the West.* New York: Penguin, 1992.

Worster, Donald. *A River Running West: The Life of John Wesley Powell.* New York: Oxford University Press, 2001.

Grant Park

    1.   The earliest reference I found to Grant Park as Chicago's "front yard" was a cartoon published in the *Chicago Tribune,* March 25, 1914.

    2.   Julia Sniderman and William W. Tippens, "Grant Park," National Register of Historic Places Registration Form, U.S. Department of the Interior, National Park Service, July 13, 1992, sec. 8, p. 23.

    3.   *Daily Inter Ocean,* August 10, 1895; and *Chicago Tribune,* August 10, 1895. Also see the Chicago Architectural Club Plan of 1896, which was prepared in conjunction with

the Municipal Improvement League: Chicago Architectural Club Plan (1896), in Chicago Architectural Club, *Catalogue of Ninth Annual Exhibition, 1896*, unpaginated.

4. Daniel H. Burnham and Edward Bennett, Plan of Chicago (1909; reprint, Princeton, NJ: Princeton Architectural Press, 1993), 110–12, 124 (magnet).

5. Chicago Park District (hereafter CPD), *Grant Park Design Guidelines* (Chicago: Chicago Park District, Office of Research and Planning, July 1, 1992), 23.

6. On commercial interests promoting tourism in late nineteenth- and early twentieth-century North American cities, see Catherine Cocks, *Doing the Town: The Rise of Urban Tourism in the United States, 1859–1915* (Berkeley: University of California Press, 2001), esp. 106–42; and Michael Dawson, *Selling British Columbia: Tourism and Consumer Culture, 1890–1970* (Vancouver: University of British Columbia Press, 2004). On the founding of cultural institutions in Grant Park, see Helen Lefkowitz Horowitz, *Culture and the City: Cultural Philanthropy in Chicago from 1880s-1917* (Lexington: University Press of Kentucky, 1976).

7. Joshua Hathaway, Jr., "Chicago with the School Section, Wabansia and Kinzie's Addition," 1834, map, Graff Collection #1817 (in color); and J. S. Wright, "Chicago," 1834, map, Graff Collection, #4755, both in Newberry Library, Chicago; and J. S. Wright, "Chicago," 1834, CHS G4104 C4 1834 W8, Chicago History Museum, Chicago (hereafter CHM).

8. Lois Wille, *Forever Open, Clear and Free: The Struggle for Chicago's Lakefront*, 2nd ed. (Chicago: University of Chicago Press, 1991), 22–23; J. Theodore Fink, *Grant Park Tomorrow: Future of Chicago's Front Yard* (Chicago: Open Lands Project, 1979), 11–17; Harold M. Mayer and Richard C. Wade, *Chicago: Growth of a Metropolis* (Chicago: University of Chicago Press, 1969), 14, 26; and Robin F. Bachin, *Building the South Side: Urban Space and Civic Culture in Chicago, 1890–1919* (Chicago: University of Chicago Press, 2004), chap. 4. The official date given in case law for the "open, clear and free" provision or Fort Dearborn addition is June 6, 1837. See *John and Mildred Boaz v. City of Chicago, Chicago Park District, and Plan Commission of the City of Chicago*, Case 99L, Number 3804, April 5, 1999. The 1836 date is based on Wille and .

9. City of Chicago, Special Park Commission (Dwight Heald Perkins), *Report of the Special Park Commission to the City Council of Chicago on the Subject of a Metropolitan Park System* (Chicago: Special Park Commission, 1904), 22–24; City of Chicago, South Park Commissioners, *Annual Report . . . [for 1896]* (Chicago: South Park Commissioners, 1897), 6 (Lake Front Park), 16 (Lake Park); A. T. Andreas, *History of Chicago*, 3 vols. (Chicago: A. T. Andreas, 1886), 3:168 (Lake Park), 3:192 (Lake Front Park). For other examples of "Lake Park," see *Chicago Tribune*, February 5 and March 7, 1871; Currier & Ives, "The City of Chicago," 1892; Theodore R. Davis, "Bird's-Eye View of Chicago as It Was before the Great Fire," 1871, *Harper's Weekly*; Rand, McNally & Co., *Map Showing the Boulevards and Park System and Twelve Miles of Lake Frontage of the City of Chicago* (Chicago, 1886); *Blanchard's Guide Map of Chicago and Suburbs* (Chicago, 1886), all in Newberry Library. For examples of "Lake Front Park" and "Lake Front Grounds," see *Chicago Tribune*, February 12, 1871, and March 24 and April 7, 1878; *Railroad Gazette* 24 (April 22, 1892): 301; *Harper's Weekly*, November 12, 1892, 1091; and *Inland Architect and News Record* 27 (February 1896), 8.

10. Illustration caption, Michigan Avenue (from Park Row), in James W. Sheahan, *Chicago Illustrated* (Chicago: Jevne and Almini, 1866), part 2, in Newberry Library; Frederick Francis Cook, *Bygone Days in Chicago* (Chicago: A. C. McClurg & Co., 1910), 339–40; and Daniel Bluestone, *Constructing Chicago* (New Haven, CT: Yale University Press, 1991), 13–20.

11. South Park Commissioners, Map of Grant Park Showing Areas of Land Made Each Year from 1897 to 1907, Grant Park Folder, Chicago Park District Archives, Chicago; City of Chicago, South Park Commissioners, *Report . . . from March 1, 1909, to February 28, 1910, Inclusive* (Chicago: South Park Commissioners, 1911), 13.

12. Philip J. Maggio, Transportation Research, Confidential Report on the Illinois Central Railroad, September 12, 1961, 10, Folder 2, Box 7; and *Southtown_Economist*, July 26, 29, 1959, Folder 12, Box 60, both in Accession 80–49, Metropolitan Housing and Planning Council Papers, University of Illinois at Chicago (MHPC Papers).

13. Cook, *Bygone Days in Chicago*, 339–40; Craig E. Colton, "Chicago's Waste Lands: Refuse Disposal and Urban Growth, 1840–1900," *Journal of Historical Geography* 20 (1994): 124–42; and Charles H. Mottier, "History of Illinois Central Passenger Stations on the Chicago Lake Front," *Bulletin of the Railway and Locomotive Historical Society* 43 (April 1937): 69–70.

14. The variety of "temporary" structures appears in: *The Inter-State Exposition Souvenir; Containing a Historical Sketch of Chicago; Also a Record of the Great Inter-State Exposition of 1873* (Chicago: Van Arsdale & Massie, 1873), 38; Baltimore and Ohio Railroad Company. *Forty-ninth Annual Report* (Baltimore, MD: Baltimore and Ohio Railroad Co., 1875), 21; Andreas, *History of Chicago*, 3:191, 222; Mottier, "History of Illinois Central Passenger Stations," 73; *Blanchard's Guide Map*, 1886; and Rand, McNally, *Map Showing the Boulevards and Park System . . . of the City of Chicago*, 1886. On the baseball grounds, see Michael Benson, *Ballparks of North America: A Comprehensive Historical Reference to Baseball Grounds, Yards, and Stadiums, 1845 to Present* (Jefferson, NC: McFarland, 1989), 80–83; Michael Gershman, *Diamonds: The Evolution of the Ballpark from Elysian Fields to Camden Yards* (Boston: Houghton Mifflin, 1993), 19–20, 30–31; Philip J. Lowry, *Green Cathedrals: The Ultimate Celebration of All 271 Major League and Negro League Ballparks Past and Present* (Reading, MA: Addison-Wesley, 1992), 42–43; *Chicago Tribune*, April 22, 1883; *Harper's Weekly*, May 12, 1883, 299; Dennis Cremin, "Building Chicago's Front Yard: Grant Park, 1836–1936" (PhD diss., Loyola University Chicago, 1999), 115–20; Map of Chicago Harbor, June 30, 1883, in W. H. H. Benyaurd (Major of Engineers), *Annual Report upon the Improvement of the Harbors of Chicago and Calumet, Lake Michigan, and the Illinois River . . . Being Appendix GG of the Annual Report of the Chief of Engineers for 1883* (Washington, DC: GPO, 1883), after p. 1744; W. H. H. Benyaurd (Major of Engineers), *Annual Report Upon the Improvement of the Harbors of Chicago and Calumet, Lake Michigan and the Illinois River . . . Being Appendix JJ of the Annual Report of the Chief of Engineers for 1885* (Washington, DC: GPO, 1885), after p. 2050; and Illinois Central Map "on Lake Front question," 1885, based on Mr. Ayer's Report, December 13, 1884, Illinois Central Railroad Collection, Newberry Library.

15. Wille, *Forever Open, Clear and Free*, 71–81; Sniderman and Tippens, "Grant Park," 8:27; and Bachin, *Building the South Side*, chap. 4. The "Montgomery Ward cases" are *City of Chicago v. A. Montgomery Ward*, 169 Ill. 392 (1897), referred to as *Ward I*; *E.R. Bliss v. A. Montgomery Ward*, 198 Ill. 104; *A. Montgomery Ward v. Field Museum of Natural History*, 241 Ill. 496 (1909); and *South Park Commissioners v. Ward & Co.*, 248 Ill. 299.

16. *Chicago Tribune*, June 4, 1895.

17. *Chicago Tribune*, December 30, 1894, quoted in Bluestone, *Constructing Chicago*, 187; and Timothy J. Gilfoyle, *Millennium Park: Creating a Chicago Landmark* (Chicago: University of Chicago Press, 2006), 20–27.

18. Daniel Burnham address to the Merchants' Club, April 13, 1897, quoted in

Charles Moore, *Daniel H. Burnham: Architect, Planner of Cities*, 2 vols. (New York, 1921), 2:101–3.

19. Burnham and Bennett, *Plan of Chicago*, 112.

20. Sniderman and Tippens, "Grant Park," 8:27.

21. Mayer and Wade, *Chicago*, 292–94.

22. Bluestone, *Constructing Chicago*, 183, 188, 190–91; and Burnham and Bennett, *Plan of Chicago*.

23. Sniderman and Tippens, "Grant Park," 7:1, 8–9, 8:36; CPD, *Grant Park Design Guidelines* (Chicago: Chicago Park District, Office of Research and Planning, July 1, 1992), 27 (trees), 29.

24. *Chicago Herald and Examiner*, May 2, 1919 (Thompson quotation). The best examination of Soldier Field is Liam T. A. Ford, *Soldier Field: A Stadium and Its City* (Chicago: University of Chicago Press, 2009).

25. Inside Soldier Field were 175,000 seated, 50,000 standing, and 200,000 outside. See Cornelius Francis Donovan, *The Story of the XXVIII Eucharistic Congress* (Chicago: Eucharistic Committee, 1927) 102–4. For other stories documenting 250,000 or more in attendance, see *New York Times*, June 22, 23, 1926. Also in 1926, over 350,000 spectators watched a rodeo over several days. See *Chicago Tribune*, July 5 and August 24, 1925, and August 22, 1926.

26. On the Prep Bowl record crowd, see *Chicago Tribune*, November 28, 1937, and November 27, 1987; http://www.ihsa.org/activity/fb/records/agen.htm. For Protestant services attracting over 50,000, see *Chicago Tribune*, April 17, 1933, April 18, 1938, and April 13, 1941. The Catholic Holy Name Society held "Holy Hours" events that frequently generated more than 100,000 participants. See *Chicago Tribune*, September 15, 1941 (150,000), and September 14, 1942 (120,000). On the Immaculate Conception attendance, see *Chicago Tribune*, September 9, 1954 (200,000); and *New York Times*, September 9, 1954 (260,000). *New York Times* estimated 180,000 inside and 80,000 outside the stadium. The Billy Graham estimate appears in *Chicago Tribune*, June 18, 1962.

27. The first Grant Park concert took place on July 4, 1935. See CPD, *Annual Report for 1978* (Chicago: Chicago Park District, 1989), 5; *Chicago Tribune*, June 11, 1978; Rob Cuscaden, "Grant Park's Bandshell Bombshell," *Chicago Guide*, August 1972 (50,000); and Skidmore, Owings & Merrill and C. F. Murphy Associates, *Lakefront Development Plan: Central Area, Chicago, Illinois* (Chicago, March 3, 1966), 27. For attendance figures, see Gilfoyle, *Millennium Park*, 49. Also see "Summer in Grant Park," *Central Manufacturing District Magazine*, June 1957, 40, copy in CHM; and CPD, *General Information* (Chicago: Chicago Park District, 1947), 10.

28. On the Monroe Street Parking Station and annual parking statistics, see Chicago Association of Commerce and Industry, *Parking Plan for the Central Area of Chicago* (Chicago, December 1949), copy in Folder 33, Box 2, Accession 80–59, MHPC Papers; Chicago Association of Commerce and Industry, *Parking Plan*, 10–11; CPD, *Fourth Annual Report*, 47; CPD, *General Information* (Chicago: Chicago Park District, 1947), 12; CPD, *General Information* (Chicago: Chicago Park District, 1950), 12; CPD, *General Information* (Chicago: Chicago Park District, 1956), 12; and CPD, *General Information* (Chicago: Chicago Park District, 1961), 14–15. On the construction of Grant Park parking facilities, see Chicago Central Area Committee and Chicago Department of Planning [CCAC/CDP], *Downtown Parking*, 4, unattributed clipping, November 28, 1972, Folder 2, Box 14, Accession 80–59, MHPC Papers; Skidmore, Owings & Merrill

and C. F. Murphy Associates, *Lakefront Development Plan*, 28; and CPD, *Annual Report 1978*, 15.

29. Presentation of Grant Park Improvement Program by Harold Moore, May 25, 1960, before Michigan Boulevard Association, p. 7 (50,000); Douglas Schroeder, *The Issue of the Lakefront: An Historical Critical Survey* (Chicago: Chicago Heritage Committee, [1964]), 26; and Ruth Moore, "Moore Park II," typescript, 1961, all in Central Area Chicago Folder, Box 2, Ruth Moore Papers, CHM; CCAC/CDP, *Downtown Parking*, 4; Skidmore, Owings & Merrill and C. F. Murphy Associates, *Lakefront Development Plan*, 28 (opened in 1965); and CPD, *Annual Report 1978*, 15.

30. *Chicago Sun-Times, Chicago Tribune,* July 20, 1978 (Whyte); David Farber, *Chicago '68* (Chicago, 1988), 184, 189, 191; *New York Times,* July 29, 1970; *Chicago Tribune, Chicago Sun-Times,* July 28, 29, 1970; *Chicago American,* May 17, 1964; and *Chicago Sun-Times,* June 24, 1960. Summer band-shell concerts that previously attracted 50,000 people averaged less than 9,500 by 1972. By 1972, the best-attended concerts drew only 25,000 spectators. See *Chicago Sun-Times,* April 3, 1977; and *Chicago Tribune,* August 21, 1977. An approximate total of 350,000 attended 37 concerts in 1972. An estimated 25,000 attended on August1, 7, and 8. See attendance figures for 1972 Grant Park Concerts, Folder 6, Box 28, Accession 80–49, MHPC Papers; and CPD, *[Eighteenth] Annual Report for 1952,* 25. An estimated 634,600 attended the 31 concerts in 1952.

31. *Chicago Sun-Times, Chicago Tribune,* July 20, 1978 (Whyte). For earlier criticisms on the lack of pedestrian traffic in Grant Park, see Harry Weese, "Grant Park, 1963–1968: A Proposition for Settling the Issues of Grant Park," August 5, 1968, 3, copies in Folder 6, Box 28, Accession 80–49, MHPC Papers; Grant Park Bandstand Folder, Box 16, HWC; *Chicago American,* May 17, 1964; and *Chicago Sun-Times,* June 24, 1960.

32. *Chicago Sun-Times,* June 19, 1987 (for Gospel Fest moving to Grant Park); Wikipedia, "Grant Park (Chicago)," http://en.wikipedia.org/wiki/Grant_Park_(Chicago); Wikipedia, "Taste of Chicago," http://en.wikipedia.org/wiki/Taste_of_Chicago; Wikipedia, "Chicago Jazz Festival," http://en.wikipedia.org/wiki/Chicago_Jazz_Festival; Chicago Yachting Association, "Venetian Parade of Boats," http://www.chicagoyachtingassociation. org/events/venetian.html; and Central Elementary School, Grade 3 Virtual Museum Project, "Venetian Night," http://www.wilmette39.org/virtualmuseum/museum05/mirabelli05/ night.html. See also Andrew Suozzo, *The Chicago Marathon* (Urbana: University of Illinois Press, 2006), 30 (Grant Park start); *Chicago Tribune,* October 26, 1990 (first finish in Grant Park); and October 31, 1994 (first start in Grant Park).

33. Costas Spirou and Larry Bennett. *It's Hardly Sportin': Stadiums, Neighborhoods, and the New Chicago* (DeKalb: Northern Illinois University Press, 2003), 159–60.

34. Metropolitan Planning Council, *Urban Development: Fact Sheet No. 1,* May 1997.

35. *Notes: The Newsletter of the Lakefront Millennium Project,* No. 1, July 1998.

36. This figure includes $160 million raised by Millennium Park, Inc., and $63 million raised by the Music and Dance Theater.

37. The enhancements also generated new expenses, which pushed the final price tag to more than $500 million. See *Chicago Tribune,* March 27, 2008 (over $500 million).

38. Burnham and Bennett, *Plan of Chicago,* 124.

Smith, Carl. *The Plan of Chicago: Daniel Burnham and the Remaking of the American City.* Chicago: University of Chicago Press, 2006.

Hilton Head Island

1.   Michael N. Danielson, *Profits and Politics in Paradise: The Development of Hilton Head Island* (Columbia: University of South Carolina Press, 1995), 10–14. Margaret Greer, *The Sands of Time: A History of Hilton Head Island* (Hilton Head: SouthArt, Inc., 1989), 55, 62.

2.   John McPhee, *Encounters with the Archdruid* (New York: Farrar, Straus and Giroux, 1971), 89; Douglas Martin, "Charles E. Fraser, 73 Dies; Developer of Hilton Head," *New York Times*, December 19, 2002, B14.

3.   McPhee, *Encounters*, 91–95; and Danielson, *Profits and Politics*, 32–42.

4.   Danielson, *Profits and Politics*, 115–17.

5.   Ibid., 50–54.

6.   *Hilton Head Island History*, http://www.hiltonheadislandsc.gov/ourisland/history.cfm; Albert Scardino, "A Gust of Bankruptcy and Scandal Rattles Elegant Hilton Head," *New York Times*, March 15, 1987.

7.   June M. Thomas, "The Impact of Corporate Tourism on Gullah Blacks: Notes on Issues of Employment," *Phylon* 41 (1980): 1–11. June M. Thomas, "No Place in the Sun for the Hired Help," *Southern Exposure* 10 (1982), 35–36; Margaret Anne Shannon, "From Tomato Fields to Tourists: Hilton Head Island and Beaufort County, South Carolina, 1950–1983" (master's thesis, University of Tennessee, Knoxville, 1996), 19–31.

8.   Margaret A. Shannon and Stephen W. Taylor, "Astride the Plantation Gates: Tourism, Racial Politics, and the Development of Hilton Head Island," *Southern Journeys: Tourism, History, and Culture in the Modern South*, ed. Richard D. Starnes (Tuscaloosa: University of Alabama Press, 2003), 188–89.

9.   Lyn Riddle, "The Visionary Pioneer of Hilton Head Island, S.C." *New York Times*, May 5, 1996.

Hollywood

1.   Gregory Paul Williams, *The Story of Hollywood: An Illustrated History* (Los Angeles: BL Press LLC, 2005); Carey McWilliams, *Southern California: An Island on the Land* (1946; reprint, Layton, UT: Peregrine Smith, 1990), 330–49; Steven J. Ross, "How Hollywood Became Hollywood: Money, Politics, and Movies," Tom Sitton and William Deverell, eds., *Metropolis in the Making: Los Angeles in the 1920s* (Berkeley: University of California Press, 2001), 255–76; and Kevin Starr, *Inventing the Dream: California through the Progressive Era* (New York: Oxford University Press, 1985), 283–393.

2.   Starr, *Inventing the Dream*, 317.

3.   Catherine Parsons Smith, "Founding the Hollywood Bowl," *American Music* 11 (summer 1993): 206–42.

4.   A. L. Woodridge, "Movie Making Lures Tourists," *Los Angeles Times*, September 7, 1924. B21. For the promotion of Southern California tourism in general, see Susan G. Davis, "Landscapes of Imagination: Tourism in Southern California," *Pacific Historical Review* 68 (May 1999): 173–91; and Clark Davis, "Oasis to Metropolis: Southern California and the Changing Context of American Leisure," *Pacific Historical Review* 61 (May 1992): 357–86.

5. Richard Longstreth, *City Center to Regional Mall: Architecture, the Automobile, and Retailing in Los Angeles, 1920–1950* (Cambridge, MA: MIT Press, 1997), 81–101.
6. Ibid.
7. Los Angeles Times, March 1, 1955, A1.

Williams, Gregory Paul. *The Story of Hollywood: An Illustrated History.* Los Angeles: BL Press LLC, 2005.

INDEPENDENCE HALL

1. This essay draws upon my book, *Independence Hall in American Memory* (Philadelphia: University of Pennsylvania Press, 2002).

Mires, Charlene. "Invisible House, Invisible Slavery: Struggles of Public History at Independence National Historical Park." In *Culture and Belonging in Divided Societies: Contestation and Symbolic Landscapes*, edited by Marc Howard Ross. Philadelphia: University of Pennsylvania Press, 2009.
Nash, Gary. "For Whom Will the Liberty Bell Toll? From Controversy to Cooperation." In *Slavery and Public History: The Tough Stuff of American Memory*, edited by James Oliver Horton and Lois E. Horton. New York: The New Press, 2006.

LAS VEGAS

1. This essay is a distillation of my book, *Resort City in the Sunbelt: Las Vegas, 1930–2000*, 2nd ed. (Reno: University of Nevada Press, 2000).
2. Giovanna Franchi, *Dreaming of Italy: Las Vegas and the Virtual Grand Tour* (Reno: University of Nevada Press, 2005).
3. Alicia Barber, *Reno's Big Gamble: Image and Reputation in the Biggest Little City* (Lawrence: University Press of Kansas, 2008).

Findlay, John M. *People of Chance: Gambling in American Society from Jamestown to Las Vegas.* New York: Oxford University Press, 1986.
Gottdiener, M., Claudia C. Collins, and David Dickens. *Las Vegas: The Social Production of an All-American City.* Malden, MA: Blackwell Publishers, 1999.
Moehring, Eugene P. *Resort City in the Sunbelt: Las Vegas, 1930–2000.* 2nd ed. Reno: University of Nevada Press, 2000.
Rothman, Hal K. *Neon Metropolis: How Las Vegas Started the Twenty-first Century.* London: Routledge, 2002.

MACKINAC ISLAND

1. William Cullen Bryant, *Letters of a Traveler, Or, Notes of Things Seen in Europe and America* (New York: George P. Putnam, 1850).
2. Keith R. Widder, *Mackinac National Park, 1875–1895* (Mackinac Island: Mackinac Island State Park Commission, 1975).

3. Steven C. Brisson, *Mackinac Treasures: The Museum Collections of Mackinac State Historic Parks* (Mackinac Island: Mackinac Island State Park Commission, 2008).

4. Phil Porter, *View from The Veranda: The History and Architecture of the Summer Cottages on Mackinac Island*, 2nd ed. (Mackinac Island: Mackinac Island State Park Commission, 2006).

5. Phil Porter, *Mackinac: An Island Famous in These Regions* (Mackinac Island: Mackinac Island State Park Commission, 1998), 68.

6. Phil Porter, *Fudge, Mackinac's Sweet Souvenir* (Mackinac Island: Mackinac Island State Park Commission, 2001).

7. David A. Armour, *100 Years at Mackinac: A Centennial History of the Mackinac Island State Park Commission* (Mackinac Island: Mackinac Island State Park Commission, 1995).

8. Horace Greeley, "Lake Superior and the North-West," in Samuel Fenton Cary, ed., *The National Temperance Offering* (New York: R. Vandien, 1850), 113.

Aron, Cindy S. *Working at Play: A History of Vacations in the United States*. New York: Oxford University Press, 2001.

Miami Beach

1. Abraham D. Lavender, *Miami Beach in 1920: The Making of a Winter Resort* (Charleston, SC: Arcadia Publishing, 2002), 10–11.

2. Helen Muir, *Miami, U.S.A.* (1953; reprint, Miami: Pickering Press, 1990), 113.

3. Mark S. Foster, *Castles in the Sand: The Life and Times of Carl Graham Fischer* (Gainesville: University Press of Florida, 2000), 44, 55, 75–79; and Polly Redford, *Billion-Dollar Sandbar: A Biography of Miami Beach* (New York: E. P. Dutton and Co., 1970), 54–64.

4. Howard Kleinberg, *Woggles and Cheese Holes: The History of Miami Beach's Hotels* (Miami Beach: Greater Miami and the Beaches Hotel Association, 2005), 10–11.

5. Redford, *Billion-Dollar Sandbar*, 127; and Marianne Lamonaca and Jonathan Mogul, eds., *Grand Hotels of the Jazz Age: The Architecture of Schultze and Weaver* (Princeton, NJ: Princeton Architectural Press, 2005), 125–27, 163–64.

6. From *Dade County, Florida Deed Book*, 112, p. 88, March 19, 1914, quoted in Howard Kleinberg, *Miami Beach: A History* (Miami: Centennial Press, 1994), 52.

7. Redford, *Billion-Dollar Sandbar*, 214; and Deborah Dash Moore, *To the Golden Cities: Pursuing the American Jewish Dream in Miami and L.A.* (Cambridge, MA: Harvard University Press, 1994), 48, 154–55, 167–71. See advertising brochures for Miami Beach hotels that were "Restricted" or "For Gentiles Only" in the Mark F. Boyd Collection, Florida Promotional Materials, no. 37, series 6, Archives and Special Collections, Otto G. Richter Library, University of Miami.

8. Kleinberg, *Miami Beach*, 74–76; Lavender, *Miami Beach in 1920*, 83–84; and Redford, *Billion-Dollar Sandbar*, 211–15.

9. Kleinberg, *Woggles and Cheese Holes*, 35–40; and Jean Francois Lejeune and Allan T. Shulman, *The Making of Miami Beach: The Architecture of Lawrence Murray Dixon, 1933–42* (Miami Beach: Bass Museum of Art, 2000), 52–62.

10. Kleinberg, *Woggles and Cheese Holes*, 51–52.

11. Redford, *Billion-Dollar Sandbar*, 231.

12. Kleinberg, *Woggles and Cheese Holes*, 46.

13. Kleinberg, *Miami Beach*, 155.

14. Ibid., 161.

15. Editorial and editorial reply, WTVJ, Miami, May 16, 1978, 1970s folder, Helen Muir Florida Room, Main Library, Miami-Dade Public Library System.

16. Michael Railey, Linda G. Polansky, and Aristedes J. Millas, *Old Miami Beach: A Case Study in Historic Preservation, July 1976–July 1980* (originally prepared as a report to the Florida State Historic Preservation Office in September 1980, it was published by the Miami Design Preservation League in 1994), 27.

17. Railey, Polansky, and Millas, *Old Miami Beach*, 22

18. MDPL Document from the 1976 Design Forum, cited in ibid., 29.

19. From "General Information about Neisen Kasdin for Use in Telephone Calls," Kasdin campaign documents, Fall 1991, in possession of the one of the authors.

20. M. Barron Stofik, *Saving South Beach* (Gainesville: University Press of South Florida, 2005), xiv.

21. U.S. Census, Table DP-1. Profile of General Demographic Characteristics: 2000, geographic area: Miami Beach City, Florida, http://censtats.census.gov/data/FL/1601245025.pdf.

Naples

1. On the influence of an extensive winter-resort press on Florida's growth, see Larry R. Youngs, "Lifestyle Enclaves: Winter Resorts in the South Atlantic States, 1870–1930" (PhD diss., Georgia State University, 2001), esp. 30–37.

2. The Kentucky group also hoped that the region would be a productive tobacco plantation to bolster Kentucky tobacco companies facing increased competition from both domestic and foreign growers. Ron Jamro and Gerald Lanterman, *The Founding of Naples* (Naples, FL: Friends of the Collier County Museum, 1985), 21–30.

3. See, for example, "Down the Gulf of Mexico," *New York Times*, February 14, 1892, 20; and "In the Land of the Tarpon," *New York Times*, March 5, 1893, 20.

4. The Naples Company, *Naples Florida* (Louisville, KY, 1888), 24–28.

5. Jamro and Lanterman, *Founding*, 53.

6. Charlton W. Tebeau, *A History of Florida* (Coral Gables: University of Miami Press, 1971), 378–80.

7. On autotourism and the national road-building surge, see Warren Belasco, *Americans on the Road: From Autocamp to Motel, 1910–1945* (Cambridge, MA: MIT Press, 1979); Marguerite S. Shaffer, *See America First: Tourism and National Identity, 1880–1940* (Washington, DC: Smithsonian Institution Press, 2001); and John Jakle, *The Tourist: Travel in Twentieth-Century North America* (Omaha: University of Nebraska Press, 1985), esp.101–45.

8. Dr. Earl Baum, a long-time Naples resident, recalled first being drawn to Naples in the 1920s by an advertisement for the Naples Hotel in a *Field and Stream* magazine. Earl Baum, *Early Naples and Collier County* (Naples, FL: Collier County Historical Society, 1973), 13.

9. Virginia Dean, *Naples-on-the-Gulf: An Illustrated History* (Chatsworth, CA: Windsor Publications, 1991), 52.

10. Tourist courts and trailer camps were appearing in Naples as early as the 1930s, and grew rapidly on the town's outskirts along the Tamiami Trail in the postwar period. Lynn Howard Frazer, *Naples* (Charleston, SC: Arcadia Publishing, 2004), 88, 109. A 1936 *New York Times* article also describes Naples and the southwest coast of Florida as an emerging "stronghold of the army of trailer tourists." "By Motor into a Sunny Land," *New York Times*, December 27, 1936, XX1.

11. Frazier, *Naples*, 50–53.

12. Charlton W. Tebeau, *Florida's Last Frontier: The History of Collier County* (Coral Gables: University of Miami Press, 1957), 186.

13. Quoted in Frazier, *Naples*, 8.

14. Lynn Howard Frazer, *Naples: 1940s to 1970s* (Charleston, SC: Arcadia Publishing, 2006), 8.

15. Prudy Taylor Board, *The History of the Port Royal Club: One Man's Vision* (Virginia Beach, VA: Donning Co., 2002), 10–12.

16. Advertisement copy from *Wall Street Journal*, April 15, 1969, 14.

17. John Durant, "A Newer Naples: Construction Wave Changes the Face of Gulf Resort," *New York Times*, December 22, 1963, X31; and Dean, *Naples-on-the-Gulf*, 65.

18. A good discussion of the activity of major developers in the area can be found in Gary Mormino, *Land of Sunshine, Land of Dreams: A Social History of Modern Florida* (Gainesville: University of Florida Press, 2005), 54–59. See also David E. Dodrill, *Selling the Dream: The Gulf American Corporation and the Building of Cape Coral, Florida* (Tuscaloosa: University of Alabama Press, 1993).

19. Naples Daily News, *The Collier Story*, July 1976.

20. *Naples Zoo at Caribbean Gardens History*, http://www.caribbeangardens.com/visitor_info/History.htm.

21. Andres Duany and Elizabeth Plater-Zybek, *Fifth Avenue South, Naples Florida: Master Plan*, vols. 1–2, April 1994.

22. While "Old Naples" is an informal designation, the city of Naples established a National Register historic district in the southern portion of its central core in 1987; the district is only a small portion of the area commonly called "Old Naples."

23. "Naples, Fla Grew Up in the '80s, Report Says," *USA Today*, February 14, 1990; U.S. Census Bureau, Census 2000; and 1990 Census, Population and Housing Unit Counts, United States (1990 CPH-2-1).

24. "Moving Up in South Florida," *New York Times*, November 3, 1996, 9:1. See also Michael J. Silverstein and Neil Fiske, "Luxury for the Masses," *Harvard Business Review* 81, no. 4 (April 2003).

25. For a discussion of amenity migration as a national trend, see Peter B. Nelson, "Geographic Perspective on Amenity Migration across the USA: National, Regional, and Local-Scale Analysis," in *The Amenity Migrants: Seeking and Sustaining Mountains and Their Cultures*, ed. Laurence A. G. Moss (Cambridge, MA: CABI Press, 2006), 55–72.

26. "Growing Problem is Repeated in Collier," *St. Petersburg Times*, April 15, 2001, 1A.

27. "Workers Pushed Out by Posh Prices in Fla.'s 'Bubble City,'" *Washington Post*, August 12, 2006, F34.

28. "On Florida's West Coast, A Would-Be Palm Beach," *New York Times*, March 12, 2004, F1; and "Rich Florida Retreat Has Budget Prices, Too," *Globe and Mail (Canada)*, January 27, 1990.

29. Rachel S. Franklin, "Census Special Reports: Migration of the Young, Single, and College Educated: 1995 to 2000" (Washington, DC: U.S. Census Bureau, 2003) identified the Naples metropolitan area as having the highest growth rate in the country for the "young, single, and college educated" demographic.

New Glarus

1. This essay distills and updates my book, *Heritage on Stage: The Invention of Ethnic Place in America's Little Switzerland* (Madison: University of Wisconsin Press, 1998).

Frenkel, Stephen and Judy Walton. "Bavarian Leavenworth and the Symbolic Economy of a Theme Town." *Geographical Review* 90, no. 4 (October 2000): 559–85.
Schnell, Steven. "Creating Narratives of Place and Identity in 'Little Sweden, U.S.A.'" *Geographical Review* 93, no. 1 (January 2003): 1–29.

New York City

1. On the history of tourism in New York, see Angela M. Blake, *How New York Became American, 1890–1924* (Baltimore: Johns Hopkins University Press, 2006), esp. chap. 2.

2. See the essays on Las Vegas and Bourbon Street in this volume for other examples of the role played by neon and other forms of dramatic street and theatrical lighting to build the reputation of an area as a tourist destination.

3. John F. Kasson, *Amusing the Million: Coney Island at the Turn of the Century* (New York: Hill and Wang, 1978), 3–9. See also Kathy Peiss, *Cheap Amusements: Working Women and Leisure in Turn-of-the-Century New York* (Philadelphia: Temple University Press, 1986), 115–38.

4. See the essay in this volume on San Francisco's Chinatown.

5. See the essays on Chinatown and New Glarus in this volume, which also address issues of ethnic tourism.

6. On New York and the United States more generally in the 1970s, see *American in the Seventies*, ed. Beth Bailey and David Farber (Lawrence: University Press of Kansas, 2004), esp. Peter Braunstein, "Adults Only: The Construction of an Erotic City in New York during the 1970s." On American film in the seventies, see *The Last Great American Picture Show: New Hollywood Cinema in the 1970s*, ed. Thomas Elsaesser, Noel King, and Alexander Horwath (Amsterdam: Amsterdam University Press, 2005); and Robin Wood, *Hollywood from Vietnam to Reagan . . . and Beyond* (New York: Columbia University Press, 2003).

7. See the essay on Faneuil Hall in this volume. For a detailed history of James Rouse see Nicholas Dagen Bloom, *Merchant of Illusion: James Rouse: America's Salesman of the Businessman's Utopia* (Columbus: Ohio State University Press, 2004).

8. For the story of South Street and the fish market, largely in images, see Barbara Mensch, *South Street* (New York: Columbia University Press, 2007).

9. Quoted in Lynne B. Sagalyn, *Times Square Roulette: Remaking the City Icon* (Cambridge, MA: MIT Press, 2001), 7. On changes to Times Square in the 1990s, see also Daniel

Makagon, *Where the Ball Drops: Days and Nights in Times Square* (Minneapolis: University of Minnesota University Press, 2004); Samuel R. Delany, *Times Square Red, Times Square Blue* (New York: New York University Press, 2001); and Alexander J. Reichl, *Reconstructing Times Square: Politics and Culture in Urban Development* (Lawrence: University Press of Kansas, 1999).

10. On the recent ending of the "culture wars," see Frank Rich, "The Culture Warriors Get Laid Off," *New York Times*, March 14, 2009.

11. Sagalyn, *Times Square Roulette*, 443, 453–62.

12. From New York City and Company website, a useful source for current and recent statistics on visitors and income from tourism, http://nycgo.com.

Taylor, William R., ed. *Inventing Times Square: Commerce and Culture at the Crossroads of the World.* New York: Russell Sage Foundation, 1991.

Olvera Street

1. A chronological and abundantly illustrated history of Olvera Street from the pueblo's founding through the present is William D. Estrada, *Los Angeles's Olvera Street* (Charleston, SC: Arcadia Publishing Company, 2006).

2. For a description of the referendum and controversy over the station's location, see Lynn C. Kronzek, *Place of Possibilities: The People and Resources that Created Los Angeles* (Carlsbad, CA: Heritage Media, 1999), 20–21.

3. The tensions between public and private sectors are discussed in considerable detail in "The Market: Olvera Street and Urban Space," chap. 5 of Phoebe S. Kropp, *California Vieja: Culture and Memory in a Modern American Place* (Berkeley: University of California Press, 2006), 207–60.

4. Abraham Pais (with supplemental material by Robert P. Crease), *J. Robert Oppenheimer, A Life* (New York: Oxford University Press, 2006), 22.

5. Excerpted from Kronzek, *Place of Possibilities*, 19.

Pike Place Market

1. Memo to DCD, Victor Steinbrueck Papers, University of Washington Manuscripts, Special Collections, and University Archives, Seattle, WA.

2. Victor Steinbrueck quoted in *Seattle Post-Intelligencer*, August 3, 1978, B3.

3. George Rolfe quoted in *A Decade of Change: A Final Report on the Preservation and Redevelopment of the Pike Place Market* ([Seattle]: City of Seattle, 1983), 24.

4. Bernard J. Freiden and Lynne B. Sagalyn, *Downtown, Inc.: How America Rebuilds Cities* (Cambridge, MA: MIT Press, 1991), 180–81, 183.

Morley, Judy Mattivi. *Historic Preservation and the Imagined West: Albuquerque, Denver, and Seattle.* Lawrence: University Press of Kansas, 2006.

Steinbrueck, Victor. *Market Sketchbook.* Seattle: University of Washington Press, 1968.

———. *Seattle Cityscape.* Seattle: University of Washington Press, 1962.

RIVER WALK

1. Frederick Law Olmsted, *A Journey Through Texas, or, A saddle-trip on the southwestern frontier* (New York: Mason Brothers, 1860), 149; and Harriet Spofford, "San Antonio de Bexar," *Harper's New Monthly Magazine* 55, no. 330 (November 1877): 835.

2. Hal K. Rothman, *Devil's Bargain: Tourism in the Twentieth-Century American West* (Lawrence: University Press of Kansas, 2000).

3. *Beautiful San Antonio: The Commercial and Industrial Center of the Southwest: The Great Health Resort of America* (San Antonio: Business Men's Club of San Antonio, 1905), n.p.

4. Ibid.

5. Lewis F. Fisher, *Saving San Antonio: The Precarious Preservation of a Heritage* (Lubbock: Texas Tech University Press, 1996), 77.

6. *San Antonio Express*, February 5, 1911, 1A; May 18, 1913, 1A.

7. *San Antonio Express*, September 8, 1912, 1.

8. Vernon G. Zunker, *A Dream Come True: Robert Hugman and San Antonio's River Walk* (San Antonio: V. G. Zunker, 1983).

9. Christopher Long, "Paseo del Rio [River Walk]," *Handbook of Texas Online* (http://www.tshaonline.org/handbook/online/articles/hpp01), accessed July 08, 2011. Published by the Texas State Historical Association.

10. Char Miller, *Deep in the Heart of San Antonio: Land and Life in South Texas* (San Antonio: Trinity University Press, 2004), 71–80.

11. For a discussion of the proposed project, see San Antonio River Authority, "San Antonio River Improvement Projects," http://www.sanantonioriver.org.

12. *San Antonio Express*, April 27, 2008.

Black, Sinclair. "San Antonio's Linear Paradise." *AIA Journal* 68 (July 1979): 30–39.
Speck, Lawrence. *Landmarks of Texas Architecture*. Austin: University of Texas Press, 1986.

SAN DIEGO ZOO

1. Sea World opened in 1964 and the 128-acre Legoland California opened in 1999.

2. Susan G. Davis, *Spectacular Nature: Corporate Culture and the Sea World Experience* (Berkeley: University of California Press, 1997), 48.

3. Matthew F. Bokovoy, *The San Diego World's Fairs and Southwestern Memory, 1880–1940* (Albuquerque: University of New Mexico Press, 2005), 49.

4. Marjorie Betts Shaw, "The San Diego Zoological Garden: A Foundation to Build On," *Journal of San Diego History* 24, no. 3 (Summer 1978): 300–310.

5. Jeffrey Hyson, "Jungles of Eden: The Design of American Zoos," in Michel Conan, *Environmentalism in Landscape Architecture* (Washington, DC: Dumbarton Oaks, 2000), 31–33.

6. Ibid., 37–38.

Hanson, Elizabeth Anne. "Nature Civilized: A Cultural History of American Zoos, 1870–1940." PhD diss., University of Pennsylvania, 1996.
Wegeforth, H. M., and N. Morgan. *It Began with a Roar: The Beginning of the World-Famous San Diego Zoo*. Rev. ed. San Diego, CA: Crest Offset Printing Company, 1953.

South of the Border

1.   Laura Koser, "Planned by Pedro: South of the Border," (master's thesis, University of South Carolina, 2004), 1–3; and Durward T. Stokes, *The History of Dillon County* (Columbia: University of South Carolina Press, 1978), 377.

2.   Marguerite S. Shaffer, *See America First: Tourism and National Identity, 1880–1940* (Washington, DC: Smithsonian Institution Press, 2001), 311–20; Stokes, *History of Dillon County*, 376; Koser, "Planned by Pedro," 4–20; Thelma Smyth, "'South of Border' Brings Fame to South Carolina," *Florence (SC) Morning News*, March 17, 1955; and Nicole King, "Behind the Sombrero: Identity and Power at South of the Border, 1949–2001," in *Dixie Emporium: Tourism, Foodways, and Consumer Culture in the American South*, ed. Anthony J. Stanonis (Athens: University of Georgia Press, 2009), 153–54.

3.   Koser, "Planned by Pedro," 18; Rudy Maxa, "South of the Border Down Carolina Way," *Washington Post*, January 7, 1979; "Tourist Council Sets Meeting Near Dillon," *Florence Morning News*, April 16, 1962; and George M. MacNabb, "South Carolina Goes after the Lucrative Tourist Business," *South Carolina Magazine*, October 1952, 10–11, 21.

4.   Stokes, *History of Dillon County*, 277; Tim Hollis, *Dixie before Disney: 100 Years of Roadside Fun* (Jackson: University Press of Mississippi, 1999), 16; Koser, "Planned by Pedro," 27–44 ; Dave Scheiber, "The Accent's on Tacky," *St. Petersburg (FL) Times*, October 5, 1989; G. D. Gearno, "Hasta La Vista, Pedro," *News and Observer (Raleigh, NC)*, October 17, 1997 (quotation); and Roy Furchgott, "You'll Never Get Bored Driving to 'South of the Border,'" *Adweek*, April 11, 1988.

5.   Bob Wierich, "Dillon County Golf Course Plans Aired," *Florence Morning News*, August 9, 1963; "South of the Border Expansion," *Robesonion (Lumberton, NC)*, August 14, 1963; "Dixie Gunboat Being Hauled to New 'Port,'" *Florence Morning News*, August 23, 1961; Tom English, "95–301 Interchange Plan Is Defended by Pearman," *Florence Morning News*, September 30, 1970; "Baskin Promises Probe," *Florence Morning News*, October 31, 1970; and Koser, "Planned by Pedro," 70–71, 82–84.

6.   Koser, "Planned by Pedro," 33, 44; Leah Dilworth, "Tourists and Indians in Fred Harvey's Southwest," in *Seeing and Being Seen: Tourism in the American West*, ed. David M. Wrobel and Patrick T. Long (Lawrence: University Press of Kansas, 2001), 142–64; and Gearno, "Hasta la Vista, Pedro."

7.   Wierich, "Dillon County Golf Course Plans Aired"; "South of the Border Expansion"; "Dixie Gunboat Being Hauled to New 'Port'"; English, "95–301 Interchange Plan Is Defended by Pearman"; "Baskin Promises Probe," *Florence Morning News*, October 31, 1970; and Koser, "Planned by Pedro," 70–71, 82–84.

8.   Koser, "Planned by Pedro," 60–63; and King, "Behind the Sombrero," 163.

9.   "South of the Border Hopes to See Next Boom," *WRAL.com* (Raleigh, Durham, Fayetteville, NC), December 29, 2009, http://www.wral.com/news/local/story/6705686/.

Santa Fe

Bunting, Bainbridge. *John Gaw Meem: Southwestern Architect*. Albuquerque: University of New Mexico Press, 1983.

Dorman, Robert L. *Revolt of the Provinces: The Regionalist Movement in America, 1920–1945*. Chapel Hill: University of North Carolina Press, 1993.

Grimes, Ronald. *Symbol and Conquest: Public Ritual and Drama in Santa Fe, New Mexico*.

Ithaca, NY: Cornell University Press, 1976.

"The History of Santa Fe Indian Market and the Southwestern Association for Indian Arts." *SWAIA – Santa Fe Indian Market*, http://swaia.org/About_SWAIA/History/index.html.

Mather, Christine, and Sharon Woods. *Santa Fe Style*. New York: Rizzoli, 1986.

Rothman, Hal K. *Devil's Bargains: Tourism in the Twentieth Century West*. Lawrence: University Press of Kansas, 1998.

Sheppard, Carl D. *Creator of the Santa Fe Style: Isaac Hamilton Rapp, Architect*. Albuquerque: University of New Mexico Press, 1988.

Tobias, Henry J., and Charles E. Woodhouse. *Santa Fe: A Modern History, 1880–1990*. Albuquerque: University of New Mexico Press, 2001.

Wilson, Chris. *The Myth of Santa Fe: Creating a Modern Regional Tradition*. Albuquerque: University of New Mexico Press, 1997.

Writers' Program of the Works Progress Administration. *The WPA Guide to 1930s New Mexico*. Reprint. Tucson: University of Arizona Press, 1989.

SILVER SPRINGS

1. This essay draws upon my dissertation, "Silver Springs: The Florida Interior in the American Imagination" (PhD diss., University of Florida, 2010).

Ammidown, Margot. "Edens, Underworlds, and Shrines: Florida's Small Tourist Attractions." *Journal of Decorative and Propaganda Arts* 25 (2005): 239–59.

Corse, Carita Doggett. *Shrine of the Water Gods*. Gainesville, FL: Pepper Printing Company, [1935].

Hollis, Tim. *Glass Bottom Boats and Mermaid Tails: Florida's Tourist Springs*. Mechanicsburg, PA: Stackpole Books, 2006.

Martin, Richard. *Eternal Spring; Man's 10,000 Years of History at Florida's Silver Springs*. St. Petersburg, FL: Great Outdoors Pub. Co., 1966.

Monroe, Gary. *Silver Springs: The Underwater Photography of Bruce Mozert*. Gainesville: University Press of Florida, 2008.

Ott, Eloise Robinson, and Louis Hickman Chazal. *Ocali Country, Kingdom of the Sun: A History of Marion County, Florida*. Oklawaha, FL: Marion Publishers, 1966.

TOMBSTONE

1. This essay distills a portion of my dissertation, "Long May Their Legend Survive: Memory and Authenticity in Deadwood, South Dakota; Tombstone, Arizona; and Dodge City, Kansas" (PhD diss., University of Arizona, 1999).

Bailey, Lynn R. *"Too Tough to Die": The Rise, Fall, and Resurrection of a Silver Camp, 1878 to 1990*. Tuscon, AZ: Westernlore Press, 2004.

Burns, Walter Noble. *Tombstone: An Illiad of the Southwest*. New York: Doubleday, Page and Company, 1927.

Clum, John P. "It All Happened in Tombstone." *Arizona Historical Review* 2 (April 1929).

Garrett, Billy, and James Garrison. *Plan for the Creation of a Historic Environment in Tomb-*

stone, Arizona. Tombstone: Tombstone Restoration Commission, 1972.

Wallace, Marian, William Cox, and Andrea Hitzeman. *Tourists in Tombstone: The Nature of Tourism in Tombstone, Papers in Community and Rural Development*, No. 8. Tucson: University of Arizona Cooperative Extension Service, 1980.

VENICE

1.   Jeffrey Stanton, *Venice California: "Coney Island of the Pacific"* (Los Angeles: Donahue Publishing, 2005), 18.

2.   Kevin Starr, *Inventing the Dream: California through the Progressive Era* (New York: Oxford University Press, 1985), 80.

3.   Ibid.

4.   On the loosening of formal conventions in a beachside environment, see John F. Kasson, *Amusing the Million: Coney Island at the Turn of the Century* (New York: Hill and Wang, 1978), 41–50.

5.   Stanton, *Venice California,* 39–40.

6.   Los Angeles City Planning Department, *Technical Report: Oil Production and the Community* (Los Angeles: October 1965), 15.

7.   Federal Writers' Project, American Guide Series, *California: A Guide to the Golden State* (New York: Hastings House, 1939), 417.

8.   Reyner Banham, *Los Angeles: The Architecture of Four Ecologies* (New York: Harper and Row, 1971), 159–60.

9.   Stanton, *Venice California,* 272.

Hanney, Dolores. *Venice, California: A Centennial Commemorative in Postcards, 1905–2005.* Staunton, VA: Center for American Places, 2005.

WALL DRUG

1.   Dana Close Jennings, *The Story of Ted and Bill Hustead's Wall Drug* (Aberdeen, SD: North Plains Press, 1969), 18–39.

2.   Jay Branegan, "In South Dakota: Buffalo Burgers at Wall Drug," *TIME Magazine,* August 31, 1981.

3.   *Chicago Tribune*, July 13, 1947.

4.   Jennings, *Wall Drug,* 40–54.

5.   *New York Times*, March 7, 1971.

6.   *New York Times*, April 4, 1971.

Jennings, Dana Close. *The Story of Ted and Bill Hustead's Wall Drug*. Aberdeen, SD: North Plains Press, 1969.

About the Contributors

Robin F. Bachin is the Charlton W. Tebeau Associate Professor of History at the University of Miami. Her first book was *Building the South Side: Urban Space and Civic Culture in Chicago, 1890-1919* (University of Chicago Press, 2004). Bachin's current book project is *Tropical Urbanism: Modernity, Exoticism, and the Creation of South Florida*. She served as guest curator of an exhibition at the Wolfsonian Museum in Miami Beach entitled "In Pursuit of Pleasure: Schultze and Weaver and the American Hotel." Bachin currently is president of the Society for American City and Regional Planning History. She may be reached at rbachin@miami.edu.

Tom Berson is visiting lecturer in history at Stetson University. A former journalist, he has a BA in American history from Brown University, MA in American Studies from Florida State University, and PhD in history from the University of Florida, where he completed a dissertation entitled "Silver Springs: The Florida Interior in the American Imagination." He may be reached at tberson@ufl.edu.

Art M. Blake teaches U.S. history in the History Department at Ryerson University, Toronto, Canada. His areas of research include urban history and culture (especially New York and Los Angeles), and sound studies. He has published various essays and reviews in this area in addition to his book *How New York Became American, 1890-1924* (Johns Hopkins University Press, 2006). He is working on a new book entitled *Audible City: Sonic Environments and the Politics of Difference in New York and Los Angeles, 1945-Present*. He may be reached at art.blake@ryerson.ca.

Nicholas Dagen Bloom is Associate Professor at the New York Institute of Technology in Old Westbury, New York. He received his PhD from Brandeis University and is the author of *Suburban Alchemy: New Towns and the Transformation of the American Dream* (Ohio State University Press, 2001), *Merchant of Illusion: James Rouse, American Salesman of the Businessman's Utopia* (Ohio State University Press, 2004), *Adventures into Mexico: American Tourism beyond the Border* (Rowman and Littlefield,

317

2006), and *Public Housing That Worked: New York in the Twentieth Century* (University of Pennsylvania Press, 2008). His current project is a book on JFK Airport. He may be reached at nbloom@nyit.edu.

HALLIE E. BOND is curator of the Adirondack Museum. She holds an MA in Museum Studies from the University of Delaware. She has created numerous exhibits, including the NEH-funded "Boats and boating in the Adirondacks, 1840-1940," and is author of *Boats and Boating in the Adirondacks* (Adirondack Museum/Syracuse University Press, 1995). She may be reached at hebond@adkmuseum.org.

LINCOLN BRAMWELL is Chief Historian for the USDA Forest Service. His previous publications include *The Dual Mandate in the Incomparable Valley: The Yosemite National Park Administrative History*, with Andy Kirk (National Park Service, 2009), and he edited *Playing the Odds: Las Vegas and the Modern West*, by Hal Rothman (University of New Mexico Press, 2007). His book *Wilderburbs: An Environmental History of Rural Development in the West*, is forthcoming from the University of Washington Press's Weyerhauser Environmental Books Series, edited by William Cronon. He may be reached at lbramwell@fs.fed.us.

KEN BREISCH is Director of Historic Preservation Programs and Associate Professor of practice in architecture at the University of Southern California. He earned his PhD from the University of Michigan. He is the author of *Henry Hobson Richardson and the Small Public Library in America* (MIT Press, 1997) and coauthor of *Constructing Image, Identity, and Place: Perspectives in Vernacular Architecture, IX* (University of Tennessee Press, 2003) and *Building Place: Perspectives in Vernacular Architecture, X* (University of Tennessee Press, 2005). He may be reached at breisch@usc.edu.

STEVEN BRISSON received a BA in history from Northern Michigan University in 1989 and an MA from the Cooperstown Graduate Program in History Museum Studies in 1992. He served as a curator for the State Historical Society of Wisconsin Sites Division from 1992 through 1995. In 1996, he accepted the position of Curator of Collections for Mackinac State Historic Parks and was appointed Chief Curator in 2004. He is the author of four books on Mackinac history including *Picturesque Macki-*

nac: The Photographs of William H. Gardiner, 1896-1915 (Michigan State University Press, 2007). He may be reached at brissons@michigan.gov.

The late KEVIN BRITZ was the director of the Center of Southwest Studies at Fort Lewis College. Britz earned a BA in history from Knox College, and an MA and PhD in U.S. history from the University of Arizona.

KYLE CIANI is Associate Professor at Illinois State University, where she specializes in the histories of women and gender across the Americas with a focus on social justice issues. Ciani's manuscript, "Childcare in Paradise: The Boundaries of Reform in San Diego, 1850s-1940s," analyzes how the changing culture of work in transborder communities directed familial strategies for surviving and thriving in changing environments. Ciani earned her PhD in the history of women and gender at Michigan State University, and BA and MA degrees from the University of San Diego, during which time she worked for the Zoological Society of San Diego. She may be reached at keciani@ilstu.edu.

AARON COWAN is Assistant Professor of history at Slippery Rock University, where he teaches U.S., urban, and public history. He is also curator of the Old Stone House, a reconstructed 1822 stagecoach tavern museum owned by Slippery Rocky. He received his PhD from the University of Cincinnati in 2007. His dissertation, "A Nice Place to Visit: Tourism, Urban Revitalization, and the Transformation of Postwar American Cities," a study of tourism development in four postindustrial urban centers, received the Ohio Academy of History's Best Dissertation Award in 2008, and is currently under revision for publication. He may be reached at aaron.cowan@sru.edu.

JAMES F. (JEFF) DONNELLY, a public historian, is chair of the City of Miami Beach Historic Preservation Board. He holds a PhD in American Studies from New York University. In New York, he learned to use the built environment in support of his research and teaching at Fordham and New York Universities. Since 1987, he has led tours of the Miami Beach Architectural District (Art Deco District). In 2006, he codirected "Using Buildings to Tell Stories," a National Landmarks workshop for teachers, funded by the National Endowment for the Humanities and is coauthor of *Miami*

Architecture (University Press of Florida, 2010). He may be reached at Jeff-donn@aol.com.

TIMOTHY J. GILFOYLE is Professor of history at Loyola University Chicago, where he teaches American urban and social history. He is the author of *A Pickpocket's Tale: The Underworld of Nineteenth-century New York* (W. W. Norton, 2006); *City of Eros: New York City, Prostitution, and the Commercialization of Sex, 1790-1920* (W. W. Norton, 1992), and *Millennium Park: Creating a Chicago Landmark* (University of Chicago Press and the Chicago Historical Society, 2006). He most recently published *The Flash Press: Sporting Men's Weeklies in the 1840s,* coauthored with Patricia Cline Cohen and Helen Lefkowitz Horowitz (University of Chicago Press, 2008), and is completing an edited version of *The Autobiography of George Appo.* He may be reached at tgilfoy@luc.edu.

ANDERS GREENSPAN hails from the western suburbs of Philadelphia and received his BA in history from Brandeis University and his MA and PhD degrees in history from Indiana University at Bloomington. He is Assistant Professor of History at Texas A&M University–Kingsville. He is the author of *Creating Colonial Williamsburg: The Restoration of Virginia's Eighteenth-Century Capital* (University of North Carolina Press, 2009). He may be reached at historianag@yahoo.com.

J. PHILIP GRUEN is Associate Professor in the School of Architecture and Construction Management at Washington State University, where he teaches architectural history and theory. He has published in the *Journal of the West,* a Routledge anthology, and the *Encyclopedia of American Urban History.* Gruen is revising a manuscript entitled "Manifest Destinations: Tourist Encounters in the Urban American West, 1870-1893"—a work that explores the push-and-pull between urban presentation and the tourist encounter in San Francisco, Salt Lake City, Denver, and Chicago in the late nineteenth century—for the University of Oklahoma Press. He earned his PhD in architecture from the University of California at Berkeley. He may be reached at jpgruen@arch.wsu.edu.

TROY HENDERSON earned his PhD in history at Loyola University Chicago, where he wrote a dissertation on the history of lumberjacks in the Upper Great Lakes. He has also published *Lake Superior Country*, a pictorial history of travel and tourism along the southern shore of Lake Superior. He works at the Michigan Iron Industry Museum. He may be reached at hendersont7@michigan.gov.

STEVEN HOELSCHER, a cultural geographer with research interests in the connections between identity, place, and tourism, is Professor and Chair of American Studies at the University of Texas at Austin. His books include *Picturing Indians: Photographic Encounters and Tourist Fantasies in H. H. Bennett's Wisconsin Dells* (University of Wisconsin Press, 2008), *Heritage on Stage: The Invention of Ethnic Place in America's Little Switzerland* (Wisconsin, 1998), and *Textures of Place: Exploring Humanist Geographies* (coedited, University of Minnesota Press, 2001), and he has published in such journals as *American Quarterly, Annals of the Association of American Geographers, GeoJournal,* and *American Indian Culture and Research Journal.* He may be reached at hoelscher@austin.utexas.edu.

ANDREW HURLEY is Professor of history at the University of Missouri-St. Louis. He earned his PhD from Northwestern University. He is the author of *Beyond Preservation: Using Public History to Revitalize Inner Cities* (Temple University Press, 2010); *Diners, Bowling Alleys, and Trailer Parks: Chasing the American Dream in the Postwar Consumer Culture* (Basic Books, 2001); and *Environmental Inequalities: Class, Race, and Industrial Pollution in Gary, Indiana, 1945-1980* (University of North Carolina Press, 1995); and numerous articles. He may be reached at ahurley@umsl.edu.

MEEGHAN KANE is a PhD candidate in history at the University of South Carolina. She is completing a dissertation entitled "'Varsity Visigoths': Spring Break and the Campus Tradition of Tourism." She may be reached at meeghankane@yahoo.com.

LYNN C. KRONZEK answers to writer, consulting historian, lecturer, public affairs consultant, and editor. An award-winning author of two books and numerous articles about southern California history, her primary interest lies in the contributions of various immigrant/ethnic cultures and communities. She lives and works in Burbank, where her eponymous consulting firm, Lynn C. Kronzek & Associates, celebrated its twentieth anniversary in 2009. She may be reached at LcKronzek@ajula.edu.

C. BRENDEN MARTIN is Professor of history and Director of Public History at Middle Tennessee State University. He holds a PhD from the University of Tennessee and is the author of *Tourism in the Mountain South: A Double-Edged Sword* (University of Tennessee Press, 2007). He may be reached at cbmartin@mtsu.edu.

CHAR MILLER is Director of the Environmental Analysis Program and W. M. Keck Professor of Environmental Analysis at Pomona College. His recent books include *Ground Work: Conservation in American Culture* (Forest History Society, 2007); *Gifford Pinchot and the Making of Modern Environmentalism* (Island Press, 2001); *Deep in the Heart of San Antonio: Land and Life in South Texas* (Trinity University Press, 2004); and *The Greatest Good: 100 Years of Forestry in America*. He is editor of *Water in the 21st Century West* (Oregon State University Press, 2009); *Fluid Arguments: Five Centuries of Western Water Conflict* (University of Arizona Press, 2001); and *On the Border: An Environmental History of San Antonio* (University of Pittsburgh Press, 2001), and he serves as associate editor of *Environmental History* and the *Journal of Forestry*. He may be reached at Char.Miller@pomona.edu.

CHARLENE MIRES is director of the Mid-Atlantic Regional Center for the Humanities and Associate Professor of History at Rutgers University in Camden, New Jersey. She is the author of *Independence Hall in American Memory* (University of Pennsylvania Press, 2002) and the forthcoming *Capitals of the World*, a study of civic boosterism and the search for a United Nations headquarters location. She holds a PhD in history from Temple University and previously worked as a journalist at *The Philadelphia Inquirer* and other newspapers. She serves on the editorial boards of the *Journal of American History, Public Historian,* and *Pennsylvania Magazine of History and Biography*. She may be reached at cmires@camden.rutgers.edu.

EUGENE P. MOEHRING is Professor of history at the University of Nevada–Las Vegas. He received his PhD in 1976 from the City University of New

York. In addition to numerous journal articles and book chapters, he has published five books: *Public Works and the Patterns of Urban Real Estate Growth in Manhattan, 1835-1894* (Arno Press, 1981), *Resort City in the Sunbelt: Las Vegas, 1930-2000* (University of Nevada Press, 2000), *Urbanism and Empire in the Far West, 1840-1890* (University of Nevada Press, 2004), *Las Vegas: A Centennial History* with Michael Green (University of Nevada Press, 2005), and *The University of Nevada, Las Vegas: A History* (University of Nevada Press, 2007). He may be reached at eugene.moehring@unlv.edu.

JUDY MATTIVI MORLEY, founder of the popular Denver History Tours, is an independent consultant who serves as a member of the city's Lower Downtown Design Review Board. She is the author of *Historic Preservation and the Imagined West: Albuquerque, Denver, and Seattle* (University Press of Kansas, 2006). She may be reached at drjudymorley@comcast.net.

JAY M. PRICE is Associate Professor of history at Wichita State University. A native of Santa Fe, New Mexico, he directs the Public History Program at Wichita State. He is the author of *Gateways to the Southwest: The Story of Arizona State Parks, Wichita, 1860-1930* (University of Arizona Press, 2004). Currently, his main project is "Temples for a Modern God," a study of mid-twentieth-century sacred architecture. He may be reached at Jay.Price@wichita.edu.

RAYMOND W. RAST is Assistant Professor of history at California State University, Fullerton. Rast completed his doctoral work at the University of Washington, where he specialized in the history of the American West, urban history, and the history of modern American culture. His most recent publication is an article entitled "The Cultural Politics of Tourism in San Francisco's Chinatown, 1882-1917." He is finishing a book manuscript entitled "Tourist Town: A History of San Francisco, 1869-1919." He may be reached at rrast@fullerton.edu.

E. DUKE RICHEY teaches at McCallie School in Chattanooga, Tennessee. He is finishing a book titled *The Mountains of Youth: Landscapes and Lifestyles of Agelessness in Aspen.* He may be reached at drichey@mccallie.org.

ANDREW C. RIESER (PhD, University of Wisconsin, Madison, 1999) is Associate Professor of history and Chair of the Department of History, Government & Economics at State University of New York, Dutchess Community College. In addition to various articles and reviews on modern U.S. cultural and religious history, Dr. Rieser is coauthor of *The Enduring Vision: A History of the American People, Vol. 2 Concise* (Wadsworth, 2010), author of *The Chautauqua Moment: Protestants, Progressives, and the Culture of Modern Liberalism* (Columbia University Press, 2003), and coeditor of the *Dictionary of American History* (Scribner's, 2002). He lives in Hudson, New York, where he serves on the city's Historic Preservation Commission. He may be reached at rieser@sunydutchess.edu.

ROBERT RUSSELL, an architectural historian, is the Addlestone Professor in the Department of Art History at the College of Charleston, where he teaches classes on modern architecture and the history of cities. Among other topics, he has published on Italian medieval civic architecture, American county courthouses and urban design. He is currently completing a book on the early nineteenth-century American architect William Strickland. He lived in Memphis for three years in the mid-1980s. He may be reached at RussellR@cofc.edu.

BRYANT SIMON is Professor of history and Director of the American Studies Program at Temple University. He is the author of *A Fabric of Defeat: The Politics of South Carolina Textile Workers, 1910-1948* (University of North Carolina Press, 1998), *Boardwalk of Dreams: Atlantic City and the Fate of Urban America* (Oxford University Press, 2004), *Everything But the Coffee: Learning about America from Starbucks* (University of California Press, 2009), and coeditor of *Jumpin' Jim Crow: Southern Politics from Civil War to Civil Rights* (Princeton University Press, 2000). His work on Atlantic City has won awards from the Organization of American Historians, Urban History Association, and New Jersey Historical Commission. He may be reached at brysimon@temple.edu.

J. MARK SOUTHER is Associate Professor of history and Co-Director of the Center for Public History + Digital Humanities at Cleveland State University. He is the author of *New Orleans on Parade: Tourism and the Transformation of the Crescent City* (Louisiana State University Press, 2006), winner of the 2006 Kemper and Leila Williams Prize and the 2007 Gulf South History Award, as well as articles in the *Journal of American History*, *Journal of Urban History*, *Journal of Planning History*, and *Planning Perspectives*. His current book project is "Believing in Cleveland: Managing Decline in a Postwar American City." He may be reached at m.souther@ csuohio.edu.

JAMES TUTEN is Associate Professor of history at Juniata College in Pennsylvania. He is the author of *Time and Tide: The Last Fifty Years of Lowcountry Rice Culture and Its Legacy* (University of South Carolina Press, 2010). Among his recent publications are articles on planters' affinity for Madeira wine. His editorials have appeared in the *Christian Science Monitor*, *Providence Journal* (RI), and *Inside Higher Ed*. Tuten founded the H-Net discussion list on South Carolina, H-SC. He earned his PhD from Emory University, an MA from Wake Forest University, and his BA from the College of Charleston. He may be reached at tutenj@juniata.edu.

WILLIAM S. WALKER is Assistant Professor of history at the Cooperstown Graduate Program (SUNY-Oneonta). He received his PhD in American history from Brandeis University. He is currently working on a book about exhibits of traditional cultures at the Smithsonian Institution after World War II. He may be reached at walkerws@oneonta.edu.

PHOEBE S. K. YOUNG is Assistant Professor of history at the University of Colorado at Boulder. She earned her PhD from the University of California, San Diego. She is the author of *California Vieja: Culture and Memory in a Modern American Place* (University of California Press, 2006, published under her previous name of Phoebe S. Kropp). She is currently working on a book for Oxford University Press on the history of camping and sleeping outside that explores the meanings and politics of nature in American culture. She may be reached at Phoebe.Young@colorado.edu.

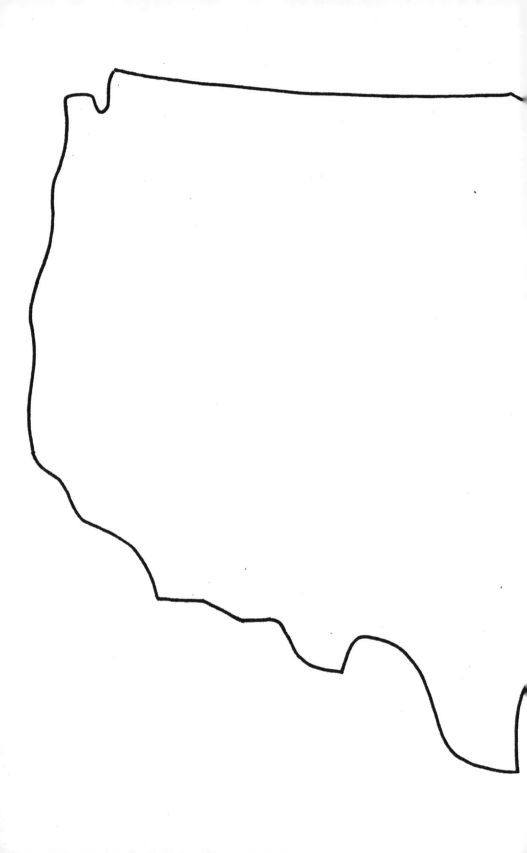